MORAL PREJUDICES

Annette C. Baier

MORAL PREJUDICES

ESSAYS ON ETHICS

HARVARD UNIVERSITY PRESS
Cambridge, Massachusetts, & London, England

To my women students,
past, present, and future

First Harvard University Press paperback edition, 1995

Library of Congress Cataloging-in-Publication Data
Baier, Annette.
   Moral prejudices : essays on ethics / Annette C. Baier.
      p.   cm.
   Includes bibliographical references and index.
   ISBN 0-674-58715-4 (alk. paper) (cloth)
   ISBN 0-674-58716-2 (pbk.)
   1. Ethics.   2. Feminist ethics.   I. Title.
   BJ1031.B254   1994
   170—dc20   93-2442
                                                       CIP

CONTENTS

Preface   vii

1. What Do Women Want in a Moral Theory?   1

2. The Need for More than Justice   18

3. Unsafe Loves   33

4. Hume, the Women's Moral Theorist?   51

5. Hume, the Reflective Women's Epistemologist?   76

6. Trust and Antitrust   95

7. Trust and Its Vulnerabilities   130

8. Sustaining Trust   152

9. Trusting People   183

10. Violent Demonstrations   203

11. Claims, Rights, Responsibilities   224

12. How Can Individualists Share Responsibility?   247

13. Moralism and Cruelty: Reflections on Hume and Kant   268

14. Ethics in Many Different Voices   294

15. A Naturalist View of Persons   313

Notes   327

Credits   359

Index   361

PREFACE

I take the title for this collection from David Hume's early (and later withdrawn) essay "Of Moral Prejudices," which I have long admired and from which I have drawn philosophical sustenance. By dropping Hume's preposition I hope both to lessen the impudence of the borrowing (I was also tempted by his title "Of Impudence and Modesty") and to introduce an intended ambiguity. My essays both concern and display moral prejudices. Because their manner is often not straightforwardly argumentative, they could reasonably be taken as mere rhetorical expressions of my own moral feelings, and of my predilections in moral theory or antitheory. Since my predilections do not always agree with the dominant preferences, many of the essays have as part of their concern to show up the prejudices, in the sense of questionable prejudgments of important issues, that moral theories such as contractarianism rest upon. Like everyone else, I come to moral philosophy with my own prejudgments concerning what is fair and what is unfair, what is cruel and what is humane, what is arrogant, what servile, and what properly self-assertive. I say "I come to moral philosophy" with these already formed judgments, but it is a long time since I first came to it, and the revisions of judgment that have occurred along the way came not only from my philosophical readings, discussions, and reflections but also from my experience as a moral philosopher among moral philosophers and as a female moral philosopher among mostly male moral philosophers.

Most of the essays present views that draw from my reflections on my experience as a woman and as a woman philosopher as well as from my experience as a person capable of sympathy and love. As I say in Essay 2, I see the task of morality to be to improve our lives together, and I do not see separatism as anything but a desperate and temporary measure. However horrifying the record of the past, and it is horrifying, and however persistent into the present the habits engendered in that bad past, the hope that sustains the moral philosopher is the same hope that morality itself is built on, that by taking thought and using our powers of imagination and reflection we can do better, that we can identify the forces that make our lives gentler, more peaceable, and more responsive, and that we can separate out the forces that divide us, that make us angry and violent. Then perhaps we can work out the ways in which the forces that make us gentler might be strengthened, and how they might even inherit the strength of the forces which they have overcome.

As a woman philosopher, I have led a relatively charmed life. I was blessed with parents and sisters who were supportive of my professional ambitions in philosophy, acquired in high school, where an inspiring English teacher, Tracy Gibson, sneaked some Socratic questioning into his literature classes. I was again blessed with encouraging philosophy teachers at the University of Otago and with a splendidly self-confident all-female academic community at Somerville College, Oxford, where my graduate studies took place and where women philosophers such as Philippa Foot and Elizabeth Anscombe made it very clear that the philosophical conversation included women's voices, maybe dulcet but by no means always placatory. That was a good start, and one that made my later experiences of how women academics were regarded in the United States come as a shock. In my first position in the United States, I spent several years as an exploited part-time faculty member at a university which reasonably enough assumed that a woman who took her husband's name and was willing to follow him across the world to his new job would be unlikely to balk at insulting conditions of work. It was one thing to be a woman philosopher in Britain, New Zealand, or Australia. It was another to be a married woman philosopher and to be in the United States. It took me many years to adjust to that, despite my having a gentle, generous, and philosophical husband

and many well-meaning colleagues. The main trouble lay in my own uncertainty as to how care and justice were to coexist. What I learned from my American women students about the obstacles which some of them had had to overcome even to become university students and about the obstacles they continued to face, and what I learned about the difficulties facing younger women colleagues, added to what I was myself experiencing, gave me a belated feminist cause. Earlier I had overoptimistically assumed that women in the Western world had been liberated, that equality of formal rights was enough. (My country, New Zealand, was the first to give women the vote, and I had received more encouragement than discouragement in my professional ambitions.) I discovered that liberation required an ongoing revolution. I also discovered that what Hume calls the "confederacy" that keeps women in servitude gets support from the attitudes of its victims, even when they are discontented victims. It does not take "lordly masters" to oppress women. The customary solicitude of fathers for their daughters' physical safety, the customary initiative and responsibility of husbands as breadwinners and deciders of domicile, the customary domestic duties of women, and their complaisance in accepting all these customs are quite enough to maintain the underprivileged position of women. The vote has not yet led to the other empowerings to which it could and should lead. Nor is legislation all that is needed if we are to dislodge long-entrenched customs and attitudes. Experiments in living also have to go on. (For a while I experimented with renouncing cooking, an activity in which I had once taken almost as much pleasure and pride as I did in my philosophical endeavors. It takes trial and error to find the right balance.)

Hume's "Of Moral Prejudices" concerns prejudices regarding the suitability of dependency and independence in men and in women. He describes two people, a man who is emotionally dependent on wife and daughters and an economically independent young Parisian woman who, while resolving not to risk the "tyranny" of a husband, nevertheless selects a suitable young man to be the biological father of her child. He is then paid off with an annuity and denied any further role in the lives of mother and son. He sues, and the essay leaves the case before the courts. Hume frames these moral tales with a general question about the wisdom of the Stoic philosophers' attempted reforms of what they regarded as "Prejudices and Errors," their attempted reforms of sentiments condoning dependency, especially in women. His essay, on the face of it, repudiates the "grave philosophic Endeavour after Perfection," where perfection is construed as Stoic self-sufficiency or independence, and repudiates it whether this endeavor be made by men or by women. But he does, I think, leave the court of the reader's judgment to give the verdict on just what his own intentions were in drawing these pen portraits of "a Woman of strong Spirit and an uncommon Way of thinking," a woman who avoids marriage so as not to risk becoming the victim of tyranny, in contrast to a marriage-accepting man who becomes virtually enslaved by his marital devotion, who after his wife's death wears a miniature picture of her next to his bosom, and who is not so "affectedly philosophical" as to call his devotion "by the Name of Weakness." Hume is challenging the accepted gender stereotypes under the guise of a recommendation that we not let our philosophic spirit move us to "depart too far from the receiv'd Maxims of Conduct and Behaviour."

Our received maxims for male and female conduct and behavior have changed considerably since Hume wrote, but our gender stereotypes can still do with the sort of challenge that he administers in this essay. Feminists have not exactly embraced Hume as a friendly prophet, and I probably am in a minority in reading him as a protofeminist. Essays 4 and 5 give my reasons for seeing him as an ally in the campaign for a morality that is neither prejudiced against women nor prejudiced about the sorts of contribution which women might make both to moral reform and to the reform of moral philosophy. Essay 5, on Hume's "epistemology," might from its title appear to be out of place in a collection of essays on ethics, but its contents should reassure the reader on that score. Essay 13 presents Hume as a pioneer in the cause of a gentler morality.

The essays collected here do not add up to a theory, let alone a system. A young Canadian philosopher, after I had given a talk in his department, once asked me, "How does someone who does philosophy your way know what the next topic on her agenda is?" (He himself professed to have a logically ordered list of questions that he intended to address, in their proper order, over the course of his philosophical life.) I was a bit stuck for an answer, but said that topics did somehow seem to present themselves, and to have some sort of link with topics I had addressed at some earlier point. I think that this young man was charging me with lack of system, and if so, I stand guilty as charged. There is little system in this collection, but there is a running theme concerning women's roles, and there is some development within the essays on trust. To me, at least, there is a clear emergence of that topic out of the essays written earlier and out of my study of Hume's writings. The topics discussed range from violence to love (if indeed that is such a great range), from cruelty to justice (if that range is any greater). The linking thread is a preoccupation with vulnerability and inequality of vulnerability, with trust and distrust of equals and of unequals, with cooperation and isolation. As far as method goes, my use of anecdote, often of autobiographical snippet, is probably the most noticeable and, some will find, objectionable feature. Some will also object to the acerbic treatment given in several essays to Kant's philosophy. I aim there to provoke the Kantians into explaining just how his ethics can escape the charges I make, but there is an admitted contrast between my constructive use of Hume and my destructive use of Kant. My version of Hume of course also invites rebuttals or return mockery from those who admire his ethics as little as I admire Kant's.

Many of these essays were originally prepared as lectures for particular audiences, often at conferences with themes chosen by the organizers or as essays for anthologies on a particular theme, so whatever unity they have certainly does not come from the sort of logical step-by-step progression that my Canadian questioner wanted. Still, the organizers of these conferences and the editors of these anthologies had some reason to think that I might agree to speak on the topics they gave me. In some cases, other people knew better than I what my next move should be, and I am retrospectively grateful to have been nudged into thinking about topics such as terrorism, which, had I been left to my own philosophical devices, I probably would have avoided. It pleases me to think that such unity in variety as these pieces show is not my own unaided doing, but the outcome of a certain degree of mutual trust between myself and fellow philosophers who were willing to encourage, even to prod, me to go in the directions taken. I followed the thought where I was led.

Even after all this help, I have not yet provided the moral philosophy that I would like to have. Very likely I will never provide it. But I am confident that the next generation of women philosophers, women standing on the shoulders of us older ground-clearing women, will provide it.

I thank the journals and publishers who gave permission for the republication of these essays. I thank the University of Pittsburgh for research time and assistance. I thank Lisa Shapiro for correcting my misquotations and Elizabeth Gretz, of Harvard University Press, for her sensitive editing.

My greatest debt of gratitude is to Collie Henderson, who prepared the manuscript and assembled the pieces that went into making the whole. Without her expert help this book would not have come to be. So involved has she been in the initial production of the individual essays, as well as in their assembly in this book, that I am almost tempted to hold her responsible for the book's shortcomings. Instead we can share the responsibility—the faults are all mine, while any good things in the book should be seen as due to our cooperation in working on it.

Pittsburgh
May 1993

MORAL PREJUDICES

My Commission extends no farther, than to desire a League, offensive and defensive, against our common Enemies, against the Enemies of Reason and Beauty, People of dull Heads and cold Hearts.

David Hume, "Of Essay Writing"

one

WHAT DO
WOMEN WANT
IN A MORAL THEORY?

When I finished reading Carol Gilligan's *In a Different Voice*,[1] I asked myself the obvious question for a philosopher reader: what differences should one expect in the moral philosophy done by women, supposing Gilligan's sample of women to be representative and supposing her analysis of their moral attitudes and moral development to be correct? Should one expect women to want to produce moral theories, and if so, what sort of moral theories? How will any moral theories they produce differ from those produced by men?

Obviously one does not have to make this an entirely a priori and hypothetical question. One can look and see what sort of contributions women have made to moral philosophy. Such a look confirms, I think, Gilligan's findings. What one finds *is* a bit different in tone and approach from the standard sort of moral philosophy as done by men following in the footsteps of the great moral philosophers (all men). Generalizations are extremely rash, but when I think of Philippa Foot's work on the moral virtues, Elizabeth Anscombe's work on intention and on modern moral philosophy, Iris Murdoch's philosophical writings, Ruth Barcan Marcus's work on moral dilemmas, the work of the radical feminist moral philosophers who are not content with orthodox Marxist lines of thought, Jenny Teichman's book on illegitimacy, Susan Wolf's articles, Claudia Card's essay on mercy, Sabina Lovibond's writings, Gabriele Taylor's work on pride, love, and on integrity, Cora Diamond's and

Mary Midgeley's work on our attitude toward animals, Sissela Bok's work on lying and on secrecy, Virginia Held's work, the work of Alison Jaggar, Marilyn Frye, and many others, I seem to hear a different voice from the standard moral philosophers' voice. I hear the voice Gilligan heard, made reflective and philosophical. What women want in moral philosophy is what they are providing. And what they are providing seems to me to confirm Gilligan's theses about women. One has to be careful here, of course, for not all important contributions to moral philosophy by women fall easily into the Gilligan stereotype or its philosophical extension. Nor has it been only women who have been proclaiming discontent with the standard approach in moral philosophy and trying new approaches. Michael Stocker, Alasdair MacIntyre, and Ian Hacking when he assesses the game-theoretic approach to morality,[2] all should be given the status of honorary women, if we accept the hypothesis that there are some moral insights for whatever reason women seem to attain more easily or more reliably than men do. Still, exceptions confirm the rule, so I shall proceed undaunted by these important exceptions to my generalizations.

If Hacking is right, preoccupation with prisoner's and prisoners' dilemmas is a big boys' game, and a pretty silly one too. It is, I think, significant that women have not rushed into the field of game-theoretic moral philosophy, and that those who have dared enter that male locker room have said distinctive things there. Edna Ullmann Margalit's book *The Emergence of Norms* put prisoner's dilemma in its limited moral place. Supposing that at least part of the explanation for the relatively few women in this field is disinclination rather than disability, one might ask if this disinclination also extends to the construction of moral theories. For although we find out what sort of moral philosophy women want by looking to see what they have provided, if we do that for moral theory, the answer we get seems to be "none." None of the contributions to moral philosophy by women really counts as a moral theory, nor is seen as such by its author.

Is it that reflective women, when they become philosophers, want to do without moral theory, want no part in the construction of such theories? To conclude this at this early stage, when we have only a few generations of women moral philosophers to judge from, would be rash indeed. The term "theory" can be used in wider and narrower ways, and in its widest sense a moral theory is simply an internally consistent fairly comprehensive account of what morality is and when and why it merits our acceptance and support. In that wide sense, a moral theory is something it would take a skeptic, or one who believes that our intellectual vision is necessarily blurred or distorted when we let it try to take in too much, to be an antitheorist. Even if there were some truth in the latter claim, one might compatibly with it still hope to build up a coherent total account by a mosaic method, assembling a lot of smaller-scale works until one had built up a complete account—say, taking the virtues or purported virtues one by one until one had a more or less complete account. But would that sort of comprehensiveness in one's moral philosophy entitle one to call the finished work a moral theory? If it would, then many women moral philosophers today can be seen as engaged in moral theory construction. In the weakest sense of "theory," as a coherent near-comprehensive account, there are plenty of incomplete theories to be found in the works of women moral philosophers. And in *that* sense of theory, most of what are recognized as the current moral theories are also incomplete, because they do not yet purport to be really comprehensive. Wrongs to animals and wrongful destruction of our physical environment are put to one side by John Rawls, and in most "liberal" theories there are only hand waves concerning our proper attitude toward our children, toward the ill, toward our relatives, friends, and lovers.

Is comprehensiveness too much to ask of a moral theory? The paradigm examples of moral theories—those that are called by their authors "moral theories"—are distinguished not by the comprehensiveness of their internally coherent account but by the *sort* of coherence which is aimed at over a fairly broad area. Their method is not the mosaic method but the broad brushstroke method. Moral theories, as we know them, are, to change the art form, vaults rather than walls—they are not built by assembling painstakingly made brick after brick. In *this* sense of theory—a fairly tightly systematic account of a large area of morality, with a keystone supporting all the rest—women moral philosophers have not yet, to my knowledge, produced moral theories or claimed that they have.

Leaving to one side the question of what purpose (other than good clean intellectual fun) is served by such moral theories, and supposing for the sake of argument that women can, if they wish, systematize as well as the next man and, if need be, systematize in a mathematical fashion as well as the next mathematically minded moral philosopher, then what key concept or guiding motif might hold together the structure of a moral theory hypothetically produced by a reflective woman, Gilligan-style, who has taken up moral theorizing as a calling? What would be a suitable central question, principle, or concept to structure a moral theory which might accommodate those moral insights which women tend to have more readily than men, and to answer those moral questions which, it seems, worry women more than men? I hypothesized that the women's theory, expressive mainly of women's insights and concerns, would be an ethics of love, and this hypothesis seems to be Gilligan's too, since she has gone on from *In a Different Voice* to write about the limitations of Freud's understanding of love as women know it.[3] But presumably women theorists will be like enough to men to want their moral theory to be acceptable to all, so acceptable both to reflective women and to reflective men. Like any good theory, it will need not to ignore the partial truth of previous theories. It must therefore accommodate both the insights men have more easily than women and those women have more easily than men. It should swallow up its predecessor theories. Women moral theorists, if any, will have this very great advantage over the men whose theories theirs supplant, that they can stand on the shoulders of male moral theorists, as no man has yet been able to stand on the shoulders of any female moral theorist. There can be advantages as well as handicaps in being latecomers. So women theorists will need to connect their ethics of love with what has been the men theorists' preoccupation, namely, obligation.

The great and influential moral theorists have in the modern era taken *obligation* as the key and the problematic concept, and have asked what justifies treating a person as morally bound or obliged to do a particular thing. Since to be bound is to be unfree, by making obligation central one at the same time makes central the question of the justification of coercion, of forcing or trying to force someone to act in a particular way. The concept of obligation as justified limitation of freedom does just what one wants a good theoretical concept to do—to divide up the field (as one looks at different ways one's freedom may be limited, freedom in different spheres, different sorts and versions and levels of justification) and at the same time to hold the subfields together. There must in a theory be some generalization and some speciation or diversification, and a good rich key concept guides one both in recognizing the diversity and in recognizing the unity in it. The concept of obligation has served this function very well for the area of morality it covers, and so we have some fine theories about that area. But as Aristotelians and Christians, as well as women, know, there is a lot of morality *not* covered by that concept, a lot of very great importance even for the area where there are obligations.

This is fairly easy to see if we look at what lies behind the perceived obligation to keep promises. Unless there is some good moral reason why someone should assume the responsibility of rearing a child to be *capable* of taking promises seriously, once she understands what a promise is, the obligation to obey promises will not effectively tie her, and any force applied to punish her when she breaks promises or makes fraudulent ones will be of questionable justice. Is there an *obligation* on someone to make the child into a morally competent promisor? If so, on whom? Who has failed in his or her obligations when, say, war orphans who grew up without parental love or any other love arrive at legal adulthood very willing to be untrue to their word? Who failed in what obligation in all those less extreme cases of attempted but unsuccessful moral education? The parents who didn't produce promise-keeping offspring? Those who failed to educate the parents in how to educate their children (whoever it might be who could plausibly be thought to have the responsibility for training parents to fulfill their obligations)? The liberal version of our basic moral obligations tends to be fairly silent on who has what obligations to new members of the moral community, and it would throw most theories of the justification of obligations into some confusion if the obligation to rear one's children lovingly were added to the list of obligations. Such evidence as we have about the conditions in which children do successfully "learn" the morality of the community of which they are members suggests that we cannot substitute "conscientiously" for "lovingly" in this hypothetical extra needed obligation. But an obligation to love, in the strong sense needed, would be an embarrassment to the theorist, given most accepted versions of "ought implies can."

It is hard to make fair generalizations here, so I shall content myself with indicating how this charge I am making against the cur-

5

rent men's moral theories, that their version of the justified list of obligations does not ensure the proper care of the young and so does nothing to ensure the stability of the morality in question over several generations, can be made against what I regard as the best of the men's recent theories, Rawls's theory of justice. One of the great strengths of Rawls's theory is the careful attention given to the question of how just institutions produce the conditions for their continued support, across generations, and in particular of how the sense of justice will arise in children, once there are minimally just institutions structuring the social world into which they are born. Rawls, more than most moral theorists, has attended to the question of the stability of his just society, given what we know about child development. But Rawls's sensitive account of the conditions for the development of that sense of justice needed for the maintenance of his version of a just society takes it for granted that there will be loving parents rearing the children in whom the sense of justice is to develop. "The parents, we may suppose, love the child, and in time the child comes to love and trust the parents." Why may we suppose this? Not because compliance with Rawls's version of our obligations and duties will ensure it. Rawls's theory, like so many other theories of obligation, in the end must take out a loan not only on the natural duty of parents to care for children (which he will have no trouble including) but on the natural *virtue* of parental love (or even a loan on the maternal instinct?). The virtue of being a *loving* parent must supplement the natural duties and the obligations of justice, if the just society is to last beyond the first generation. And as Nancy Chodorow's work indicates, the loving parents must also accept a certain division of child-care responsibility if their version of the obligations and virtues of men and of women is, along with their version of the division of labor accompanying that allocation of virtues, to be passed on.

Reliance on a recognized obligation to turn oneself into a good parent or else to avoid becoming a parent would be a problematic solution. Good parents tend to be the children of good parents, so this obligation would collapse into the obligation to avoid parenthood unless one expected to be a good parent. That, given available methods of contraception, may itself convert into the obligation, should one expect not to be a good parent, to sexual abstinence, or sterilization, or resolute resort to abortion when contraception fails.

6

The conditional obligation to abort, and in effect also the conditional obligation to sterilization, falls on the women. There may be conditions in which the rational moral choice is between obligatory sexual abstinence and obligatory sterilization, but obligatory abortion, such as women in China now face, seems to me a moral monster. I do not believe that liberal moral theorists will be able to persuade reflective women that a morality that in any conditions makes abortion obligatory, as distinct from permitted or advisable or, on occasion, best, is in their own as well as their male fellows' long-term self-interest. It would be tragic if such moral questions in the end came to the question of whose best interests to sacrifice, men's or women's. I do not believe they *do* come to this, but should they, then justice would require that, given the long history of the subordination of women's to men's interests, men's interests be sacrificed. Justice, of course, never decides these issues unless power reinforces justice, so I am not predicting any victory for women, should it ever come to a fight over obligatory abortion or over who is to face obligatory sterilization.

No liberal moral theorist, as far as I know, is advocating obligatory abortion or obligatory sterilization when necessary to prevent the conception of children whose parents do not expect to love them. My point rather is that they escape this conclusion only by avoiding the issue of what is to ensure that new members of the moral community do get the loving care they need to become morally competent persons. Liberal moral theories assume that women either will provide loving maternal care, or will persuade their mates to provide loving paternal care, or when pregnant will decide for abortion, encouraged by their freedom-loving men. These theories, in other words, exploit the culturally encouraged maternal instinct and/or the culturally encouraged docility of women. The liberal system would receive a nasty spanner in its works should women use their freedom of choice as regards abortion to choose *not* to abort, and then leave their newborn children on their fathers' doorsteps. That would test liberal morality's ability to provide for its own survival.

At this point it may be objected that every moral theory must make some assumptions about the natural psychology of those on whom obligations are imposed. Why shouldn't the liberal theory count on a continuing sufficient supply of good loving mothers, as it counts on continuing self-interest and, perhaps, on a continuing

7

supply of pugnacious men who are able and willing to become good soldiers, without turning any of these into moral *obligations?* Why waste moral resources recognizing as obligatory or as virtuous what one can count on getting without moral pressure? If, in the moral economy, one can get enough good mothers and good warriors "for free," why not gladly exploit what nature and cultural history offer? I cannot answer this question fully here, but my argument does depend upon the assumption that a decent morality will *not* depend for its stability on forces to which it gives no moral recognition. Its account books should be open to scrutiny, and there should be no unpaid debts, no loans with no prospect of repayment. I also assume that once we are clear about these matters and about the interdependencies involved, our principles of justice will not allow us to recognize either a special obligation on every woman to initiate the killing of the fetus she has conceived, should she and her mate be, or think they will be, deficient in parental love, or a special obligation on every young man to kill those his elders have labeled enemies of his country. Both such "obligations" are prima facie suspect, and difficult to make consistent with any of the principles supposedly generating obligations in modern moral theories. I also assume that, on reflection, we will not want to recognize as *virtues* the character traits of women and men which lead them to supply such life and death services "for free." Neither maternal servitude, nor the resoluteness needed to kill off one's children to prevent their growing up unloved, nor the easy willingness to go out and kill when ordered to do so by authorities seems to me to be a character trait a decent morality will encourage by labeling it a virtue. But the liberals' morality must somehow encourage such traits if its stability depends on enough people showing them. There is, then, understandable motive for liberals' avoidance of the question of whether such qualities are or are not morally approved of, and of whether or not there is any obligation to act as one with such character traits would act.

It is symptomatic of the bad faith of liberal morality as understood by many of those who defend it that issues such as whether to fight or not to fight, to have or not to have an abortion, or to be or not to be an unpaid maternal drudge are left to individual conscience. Since there is no coherent guidance liberal morality can give on these issues, which clearly are *not* matters of moral indifference, liberal morality tells each of us, "the choice is yours," hoping that

8

enough will choose to be self-sacrificial life providers and self-sacrificial death dealers to suit the purposes of the rest.

Rawls's theory does explicitly face the question of the moral justification of refusal to bear arms, and of how a just society justly provides for its own defense. The hardships imposed on conscripted soldiers are, he says, a necessary evil, and the most that just institutions can do is to "make sure that the risks of suffering from those misfortunes are more or less evenly shared by all members of society over the course of their life, and that there is no avoidable class bias in selecting those who are called for duty." What of sex/gender bias? Or is that assumed to be unavoidable? Rawls's principles seem to me to imply that women should be conscripted, if anyone is (and I think that is right), but since he avoids the questions of justice between men and women one does not know whether he intended this implication. His suggestion that one argument in favor of a conscripted army is that it is less likely to be an instrument of unjustified foreign adventures will become even stronger, I believe, if half the conscripts are women. Like most male moral theorists, Rawls does not discuss the morality of having children, refusing to have them, refusing to care for them, nor does he discuss how just institutions might equalize the responsibilities involved in ensuring that there be new members of society and that they become morally competent members of it, so one does not know whether he accepts a gender-based division of social service here, leaving it to the men to do the dangerous defensive destruction of life and cities, while the support of new life, and any costs going or contrived to go with that, are left to the women. I hope that is not what he meant.

I do not wish, by having myself spoken of these two traditionally gender-based allocations of responsibility (producing and caring for new human life and the destruction of the lives of those officially labeled enemies) together, to leave the impression that I see any parallel between them except that they have both been treated as gender based and that both present embarrassments for liberal moral theory. Not all allocations of responsibility are allocations of burdens, and parenthood, unlike unchosen military life, need not be seen as essentially burden bearing. Good mothers and good soldiers make contributions of very different sorts and sort of importance to the ongoing life of a moral community, and they should not be seen, as they sometimes are, as fair mutual substitutes, as forms of social

9

service. Good mothers will always be needed by a moral community, in the best conditions as well as the worst; the need for good military men, though foreseeably permanent, is a sign of some failure of our morality, a failure of our effectively acted upon moral laws to be valid theorems for the conservation of men in multitudes. Nor do the burdens of soldiering have any real analogue in the case of motherhood, which today *need* not impose real costs on the mother. If there are significant costs—loss of career opportunity, improperly recompensed drudgery in the home, or health risks—this is due to bad but largely remediable social arrangements, as the failure of parents to experience any especially parental satisfactions may be also due to bad but remediable socially produced attitudes toward parental responsibility. We do not, I think, want our military men to enjoy killing the enemy and destroying their cities, and any changes we made in social customs and institutions to make such pleasures more likely would be deplorable ones. Military life in wartime should always be seen as a sacrifice, while motherhood should never need to be seen as self-sacrificial service. If it is an honor and a privilege to bear arms for one's country, as we understandably tell our military conscripts and volunteers, part of the honor is being trusted with activities that are a necessary evil, being trusted not to enjoy their evil aspects, and being trusted to see the evil as well as the necessity. Only if we contrive to make the bringing into the world of new persons as nasty a business as killing already present persons will there be any just reason to exclude young women from conscripted armies or to exclude men from equal parental responsibility.

Granted that the men's theories of obligation need supplementation, to have much chance of integrity and coherence, and that the women's hypothetical theories will want to cover obligation as well as love, then what concept brings them together? My tentative answer is—the concept of appropriate trust, oddly neglected in moral theory. This concept also nicely mediates between reason and feeling, those tired old candidates for moral authority, since to trust is neither quite to believe something about the trusted nor necessarily to feel any emotion toward them—but to have a belief-informed and action-influencing attitude. To make it plausible that the neglected concept of appropriate trust is a good one for the enlightened moral theorist to make central, I need to show, or begin to show, how it could include obligation, indeed shed light on obligations and their justification, as well as include love, the other moral concerns of Gilligan's women, and many of the topics women moral philosophers have chosen to address, mosaic fashion. I would also need to show that it could connect all of these in a way which holds out promise both of synthesis and of comprehensive moral coverage. A moral theory which looked at the conditions for proper trust of all the various sorts we show, and at what sorts of reasons justify inviting such trust, giving it, and meeting it, would, I believe, not have to avoid turning its gaze on the conditions for the survival of the practices it endorses, so it could avoid that unpleasant choice many current liberal theories seem to have—between incoherence and bad faith. I do not pretend that we will easily agree once we raise the questions I think we should raise, but at least we may have a language adequate to the expression of both men's and women's moral viewpoints.

My trust in the concept of trust is based in part on my own attempts to restate and consider what is right and what wrong with men's theories, especially Hume's, which I consider the best of the lot. I have found myself reconstructing his account of the artifices of justice as an account of the progressive enlargement of a climate of trust, and have found that a helpful way to see it. It has some textual basis, but is nevertheless a reconstruction, and one I have found, immodestly, an improvement. So it is because I have tried the concept and explored its dimensions a bit—the variety of goods we may trust others not to take from us, the sort of security or insurance we have when we do, the sorts of defenses or potential defenses we lay down when we trust, the various conditions for reasonable trust of various types—that I am hopeful about its power as a theoretical, and not just an exegetical, tool. I also found myself needing to use it when I made a brief rash attempt at that women's topic, caring (invited in by a male philosopher,[4] I should say). I am reasonably sure that trust does generalize some central moral features of the recognition of binding obligations and moral virtues and of loving, as well as of other important relations between persons, such as teacher-pupil, confider-confidante, worker to co-worker in the same cause, and professional to client. Indeed it is fairly obvious that love, the main moral phenomenon women want attended to, involves trust, so I anticipate little quarrel when I claim that, if we had a moral theory spelling out the conditions for appropriate trust and distrust, that would include a morality of love in all its variants—parental love, love of children for their parents, love of family members, love of friends, of lovers in the strict sense, of co-workers, of one's country and its figureheads, of exemplary heroines and heroes, of goddesses and gods.

Love and loyalty demand maximal trust of one sort, and maximal trustworthiness, and in investigating the conditions for maximal trust and maximal risk we must think about the ethics of love. More controversial may be my claim that the ethics of obligation will also be covered. I see it as covered because to recognize a set of obligations is to trust some group of persons to instill them, to demand that they be met, possibly to levy sanctions if they are not, and this is to trust persons with very significant coercive power over others. Less coercive but still significant power is possessed by those shaping our conception of the virtues and expecting us to display them, approving when we do, disapproving and perhaps shunning us when we do not. Such coercive and manipulative power over others requires justification, and is justified only if we have reason to trust those who have it to use it properly and to use the discretion which is always given when trust is given in a way which serves the purpose of the whole system of moral control, and not merely self-serving or morally improper purposes. Since the question of the justification of coercion becomes, at least in part, the question of the wisdom of trusting the coercers to do their job properly, the morality of obligation, in as far as it reduces to the morality of coercion, is covered by the morality of proper trust. Other forms of trust may also be involved, but trusting enforcers with the use of force is the most problematic form of trust involved.

The coercers and manipulators are, to some extent, all of us, so to ask what our obligations are and what virtues we should exhibit is to ask what it is reasonable to trust us to demand, expect, and contrive to get from one another. It becomes, in part, a question of what powers we can in reason trust ourselves to exercise properly. But self-trust is a dubious or limit case of trust, so I prefer to postpone the examination of the concept of proper self-trust at least until proper trust of others is more clearly understood. Nor do we distort matters too much if we concentrate on those cases where moral sanctions and moral pressure and moral manipulation is not self-applied but applied to others, particularly by older persons to younger persons. Most moral pressuring that has any effect goes on in childhood and early youth. Moral sanctions may continue to be applied, formally and informally, to adults, but unless the criminal courts apply them it is easy enough for adults to ignore them, to brush them aside. It is not difficult to become a sensible knave, and to harden one's heart so that one is insensible to the moral condemnation of one's victims and those who sympathize with them. Only if the pressures applied in the morally formative stage have given one a heart that rebels against the thought of such ruthless independence of what others think will one see any reason *not* to ignore moral condemnation, not to treat it as mere powerless words and breath. Condemning sensible knaves is as much a waste of breath as arguing with them—all we can sensibly do is to try to protect children against their influence, and ourselves against their knavery. Adding to the criminal law will not be the way to do the latter, since such moves will merely challenge sensible knaves to find new knavish exceptions and loopholes, not protect us from sensible knavery. Sensible knaves are precisely those who exploit us without breaking the law. So the whole question of when moral pressure of various sorts, formative, reformative, and punitive, ought to be brought to bear by whom is subsumed under the question of whom to trust when and with what, and for what good reasons.

In concentrating on obligations, rather than virtues, modern moral theorists have chosen to look at the cases where more trust is placed in enforcers of obligations than is placed in ordinary moral agents, the bearers of the obligations. In taking, as contractarians do, contractual obligations as the model of obligations, they concentrate on a case where the very minimal trust is put in the obligated person, and considerable punitive power entrusted to the one to whom the obligation is owed (I assume here that Hume is right in saying that when we promise or contract, we formally subject ourselves to the penalty, in case of failure, of never being trusted as a promisor again). This is an interesting case of the allocation of trust of various sorts, but it surely distorts our moral vision to suppose that *all* obligations, let alone all morally pressured expectations we impose on others, conform to that abnormally coercive model. It takes very special conditions for it to be safe to trust persons to inflict penalties on other persons, conditions in which either we can trust the penalizers to have the virtues necessary to penalize wisely and fairly, or else we can rely on effective threats to keep unvirtuous penalizers from abusing their power—that is to say, rely on others to coerce the first coercers into proper behavior. But that reliance too will either be trust or will have to rely on threats from coercers of the coercers of coercers, and so on. Morality on this model becomes a nasty, if intellectually intriguing, game of mutual mutually corrective threats. The central question of who should deprive whom of what freedom soon becomes the question of whose anger should be dreaded by whom (the theory of obligation), supplemented perhaps by an afterthought on whose favor should be courted by whom (the theory of the virtues).

Undoubtedly some important part of morality does depend in part on a system of threats and bribes, at least for its survival in difficult conditions when normal goodwill and normally virtuous dispositions may be insufficient to motivate the conduct required for the preservation and justice of the moral network of relationships. But equally undoubtedly life will be nasty, emotionally poor, and worse than brutish (even if longer), if that is all morality is, or even if that coercive structure of morality is regarded as the backbone, rather than as an available crutch, should the main support fail. For the main support has to come from those we entrust with the job of rearing and training persons so that they can be trusted in various ways, some trusted with extraordinary coercive powers, some with public decision-making powers, all trusted as parties to promise, most trusted by some who love them and by one or more willing to become co-parents with them, most trusted by dependent children, dependent elderly relatives, sick friends, and so on. A very complex network of a great variety of sorts of trust structures our moral relationships with our fellows, and if there is a *main* support to this network it is the trust we place in those who respond to the trust of new members of the moral community, namely, children, and prepare them for new forms of trust.

A theory which took as its central question "Who should trust whom with what, and why?" would not have to forgo the intellectual fun and games previous theorists have had with the various paradoxes of morality—curbing freedom to increase freedom, curbing self-interest the better to satisfy self-interest, not aiming at happiness in order to become happier. For it is easy enough to get a paradox of trust to accompany or, if I am right, to generalize the paradoxes of freedom, self-interest, and hedonism. To trust is to make oneself or to let oneself be more vulnerable than one might have been to harm from others—to give them an opportunity to harm one, in the confidence that they will not take it, because they have no good reason to.[5] Why would one take such a risk? For risk it always is, given the partial opaqueness to us of the reasoning and motivation of those we trust and with whom we cooperate. Our confidence may be, and quite often is, misplaced. That is what we risk when we trust. If the best reason to take such a risk is the expected gain in security which comes from a climate of trust, then in trusting we are always giving up security to get greater security, exposing our throats so that others become accustomed to not biting. A moral theory which made proper trust its central concern could have its own categorical imperative, could replace obedience to self-made laws and freely chosen restraint on freedom with security-increasing sacrifice of security, distrust in the promoters of a climate of distrust, and so on.

Such reflexive use of one's central concept, negative or affirmative, is an intellectually satisfying activity which is bound to have appeal to those system lovers who want to construct moral theories, and it may help them design their theory in an intellectually pleasing manner. But we should beware of becoming hypnotized by our slogans or of sacrificing truth to intellectual elegance. Any theory of proper trust should not *prejudge* the question of when distrust is proper. We might find more objects of proper distrust than just the contributors to a climate of reasonable distrust, just as freedom should be restricted not just to increase human freedom but to protect human life from poisoners and other killers. I suspect, however, that all the objects of reasonable distrust are more reasonably seen as falling into the category of ones who contribute to a decrease in the scope of proper trust than can all who are reasonably coerced be seen as themselves guilty of wrongful coercion. Still, even if all proper trust turns out to be for such persons and on such matters as will increase the scope or stability of a climate of reasonable trust, and all proper distrust for such persons and on such matters as increase the scope of reasonable distrust, overreliance on such nice reflexive formulae can distract us from asking all the questions about trust which need to be asked if an adequate moral theory is to be constructed around that concept. These questions should include when to *respond* to trust with *un*trustworthiness, when and when not to invite trust, as well as when to give and refuse trust. We should not assume that promiscuous trustworthiness is any more a virtue than is undiscriminating distrust. It is appropriate trustworthiness, appropriate trustingness, appropriate encouragement to trust which will be virtues, as will be judicious untrustworthiness, selective refusal to trust, discriminating discouragement of trust.

Women are particularly well placed to appreciate these last virtues, since they have sometimes needed them to get into a position even to consider becoming moral theorizers. The long exploitation and domination of women by men depended on men's trust in women and women's trustworthiness to play their allotted role and so to perpetuate their own and their daughters' servitude. However keen women now are to end the lovelessness of modern moral philosophy, they are unlikely to lose sight of the cautious virtue of appropriate distrust or of the tough virtue of principled betrayal of the exploiters' trust.

Gilligan's girls and women saw morality as a matter of preserving valued ties to others, of preserving the conditions for that care and mutual care without which human life becomes bleak, lonely, and after a while, as the mature men in her study found, not self-affirming, however successful in achieving the egoistic goals which had been set. The boys and men saw morality as a matter of finding workable traffic rules for self-assertors, so that they not needlessly frustrate one another and so that they could, should they so choose, cooperate in more positive ways to mutual advantage. Both for the women's sometimes unchosen and valued ties with others and for the men's mutual respect as sovereigns and subjects of the same minimal moral traffic rules (and for their more voluntary and more selective associations of profiteers), trust is important. Both men and women are concerned with cooperation, and the dimensions of trust-distrust structure the different cooperative relations each emphasize. The various considerations which arise when we try to defend an answer to any question about the appropriateness of a particular form of cooperation with its distinctive form of trust or distrust, that is, when we look into the terms of all sorts of cooperation, at the terms of trust in different cases of trust, at what are fair terms and what are trust-enhancing and trust-preserving terms, are suitably many and richly interconnected. A moral theory (or family of theories) that made trust its central problem could do better justice to men's and women's moral intuitions than do the going men's theories. Even if we don't easily agree on the answer to the question of who should trust whom with what, who should accept and who should meet various sorts of trust, and why, these questions might enable us better to reason morally together than we can when the central moral questions are reduced to those of whose favor one must court and whose anger one must dread. But such programmatic claims as I am making will be tested only when women standing on the shoulders of men, or men on the shoulders of women, or some theorizing Tiresias actually works out such a theory. I am no Tiresias, and have not foresuffered all the labor pains of such a theory. I aim here only to fertilize.

POSTSCRIPT

This essay was written before Carol Gilligan had withdrawn the suggestion in *A Different Voice* that there is some intrinsic connection between being female and taking up the care perspective. This essay refers to the early, and not to the revised, Gilligan views, as does Essay 4.

Some clarification may be in order to explain why I conferred on Alasdair MacIntyre the title of honorary woman, when to feminists such as Susan Moller Okin[6] he represents a particularly extreme version of patriarchal thinking. It was MacIntyre's anti-Kantian writings that made me regard him as an ally, and also his nostalgia for a virtues-centered variant of ethics. But I agree with Okin that his increasingly explicit defense of a patriarchal religious tradition does make the honor that I did him look undeserved.

two

THE NEED FOR
MORE THAN
JUSTICE

In recent decades in North American social and moral philosophy, alongside the development and discussion of widely influential theories of justice, taken as John Rawls takes it as the "first virtue of social institutions,"[1] there has been a countermovement gathering strength, one coming from some interesting sources. Some of the most outspoken of the diverse group who have in a variety of ways been challenging the assumed supremacy of justice among the moral and social virtues are members of those sections of society whom one might have expected to be especially aware of the supreme importance of justice: blacks and women. Those who have only recently won recognition of their equal rights, who have only recently seen the correction or partial correction of long-standing racist and sexist injustices to their race and sex, are among the philosophers now suggesting that justice is only one virtue among many, and one that may need the presence of the others in order to deliver its own undenied value. Among these philosophers of the philosophical counterculture, as it were—but an increasingly large counterculture—I include Alasdair MacIntyre,[2] Michael Stocker,[3] Lawrence Blum,[4] Michael Slote,[5] Laurence Thomas,[6] Claudia Card,[7] Alison Jaggar,[8] Susan Wolf,[9] and a whole group of men and women, myself included, who have been influenced by the writings of the Harvard educational psychologist Carol Gilligan, whose book *In a Different Voice* caused a considerable stir both in the popular press and, more slowly, in the philosophical journals.[10]

Let me say quite clearly at this early point that there is little disagreement that justice is *a* social value of very great importance, and injustice an evil. Nor would those who have worked on theories of justice want to deny that other things matter besides justice. Rawls, for example, incorporates the value of freedom into his account of justice, so that denial of basic freedoms counts as injustice. Rawls also leaves room for a wider theory of the right, of which the theory of justice is just a part. Still, he does claim that justice is the "first" virtue of social institutions, and it is only that claim about priority that I think has been challenged. It is easy to exaggerate the differences of view that exist, and I want to avoid that. The differences are as much in emphasis as in substance, or we can say that they are differences in tone of voice. But these differences do tend to make a difference in approaches to a wide range of topics not just in moral theory but in areas such as medical ethics, where the discussion used to be conducted in terms of patients' rights, of informed consent, and so on, but now tends to get conducted in an enlarged moral vocabulary, which draws on what Gilligan calls the ethics of *care* as well as that of *justice*.

"Care" is the new buzzword. It is not, as Shakespeare's Portia demanded, mercy that is to season justice, but a less authoritarian humanitarian supplement, a felt concern for the good of others and for community with them. The "cold jealous virtue of justice" (Hume) is found to be too cold, and it is "warmer," more communitarian virtues and social ideals that are being called in to supplement it. One might say that liberty and equality are being found inadequate without fraternity, except that "fraternity" will be quite the wrong word if, as Gilligan initially suggested, it is *women* who perceive this value most easily. ("Sorority" will do no better, since it is too exclusive, and English has no gender-neutral word for the mutual concern of siblings.) She has since modified this claim, allowing that there are two perspectives on moral and social issues that we all tend to alternate between, and which are not always easy to combine, one of them what she calls the justice perspective, the other the care perspective. It is increasingly obvious that there are many male philosophical spokespersons for the care perspective (Laurence Thomas, Lawrence Blum, Michael Stocker), so it cannot be the prerogative of women. Nevertheless Gilligan still wants to claim that women are most unlikely to take *only* the justice perspective, as some men are claimed to, at least until some mid-life crisis jolts them into "bifocal" moral vision (see *D.V.*, chap. 6).

Gilligan in *In a Different Voice* did not offer any explanatory theory of why there should be any difference between the female and the male moral outlook, but she did tend to link the naturalness to women of the care perspective with their role as primary caretakers of young children, that is, with their parental and specifically maternal role. She avoided the question of whether it is their biological or their social parental role that is relevant, and some of those who dislike her book are worried precisely by this uncertainty. Some find it retrograde to hail as a special sort of moral wisdom an outlook that may be the product of the socially enforced restriction of women to domestic roles (and the reservation of such roles for them alone); that might seem to play into the hands of those who still favor such restriction. (Marxists, presumably, will not find it so surprising that moral truths might depend for their initial clear articulation on the social oppression, and memory of it, of those who voice the truths.) Gilligan did in the first chapter of *In a Different Voice* cite the theory of Nancy Chodorow (as presented in *The Reproduction of Mothering*[11]), which traces what appear as gender differences in personality to early social development, in particular to the effects of the child's primary caretaker being or not being of the same gender as the child. Later, both in "The Conquistador and the Dark Continent: Reflections on the Psychology of Love" and in "The Origins of Morality in Early Childhood Relationships," she develops this explanation.[12] She postulates two evils that any infant may become aware of, the evil of detachment or isolation from others whose love one needs, and the evil of relative powerlessness and weakness. Two dimensions of moral development are thereby set—one aimed at achieving satisfying community with others, the other aiming at autonomy or equality of power. The relative predominance of one development over the other will depend both upon the relative salience of the two evils in early childhood and on early and later reinforcement or discouragement in attempts made to guard against these two evils. This provides the germs of a theory about *why*, given current customs of child rearing, it should be mainly women who are not content with only the moral outlook that Gilligan calls the justice perspective, necessary though that was and is seen by them to have been to their hard-won liberation from sexist oppression. They, like the blacks, once used the language of rights and justice to change their own social position, but nevertheless now see limitations in that language, according to Gilligan's findings as a moral psychologist. She reports their discontent with the individualist, more or less Kantian moral framework which dominates Western moral theory and which influenced moral psychologists such as Lawrence Kohlberg,[13] to whose conception of moral maturity she seeks an alternative. Since the target of Gilligan's criticism is the dominant Kantian tradition, and since that has been the target also of moral philosophers as diverse in their own views as Bernard Williams,[14] Alasdair MacIntyre, Philippa Foot,[15] Susan Wolf, and Claudia Card, *In a Different Voice* is of interest as much for its attempt to articulate an alternative to the Kantian justice perspective as for its implicit raising of the question of male bias in Western moral theory, especially liberal-democratic theory. For whether the supposed blind spots of that outlook are due to male bias, or to nonparental bias, or to early traumas of powerlessness, or to early resignation to "detachment" from others, we need first to be persuaded that they *are* blind spots before we will have any interest in their cause and cure. Is justice blind to important social values, or at least only one-eyed? What is it that comes into view from the "care perspective" that is not seen from the "justice perspective"?

Gilligan's position here is most easily described by contrasting it with that of Kohlberg, against which she developed it. Kohlberg, influenced by Jean Piaget and the Kantian philosophical tradition as developed by John Rawls, developed a theory about typical moral development which saw it to progress from a preconventional level, where what is seen to matter is pleasing or not offending parental authority figures, through a conventional level in which the child tries to fit in with a group, such as a school community, and to conform to its standards and rules, to a postconventional critical level, in which such conventional rules are subjected to tests and where those tests are of a Utilitarian or, eventually, a Kantian sort—ones that require respect for each person's individual rational will, or autonomy, and conformity to any implicit social contract such wills are deemed to have made or to any hypothetical ones they would make if thinking clearly. What was found when Kohlberg's questionnaires (mostly by verbal response to verbally sketched moral dilemmas) were applied to female as well as male subjects, Gilligan reports, is that the girls and women not only scored generally lower than the boys and men but tended to *revert* to the lower stage of the conventional level even after briefly (usually in adolescence) attaining the postconventional level. Piaget's finding that girls were deficient in "the legal sense" was confirmed.

These results led Gilligan to wonder if there might not be a quite different pattern of development to be discerned, at least in female subjects. She therefore conducted interviews designed to elicit not just how far advanced the subjects were toward an appreciation of the nature and importance of Kantian autonomy but also to find out what the subjects themselves saw as progress or lack of it, what conceptions of moral maturity they came to possess by the time they were adults. She found that although the Kohlberg version of moral maturity as respect for fellow persons and for their rights as equals (rights including that of free association) did seem shared by many young men, the women tended to speak in a different voice about morality itself and about moral maturity. To quote Gilligan, "Since the reality of connection is experienced by women as given rather than as freely contracted, they arrive at an understanding of life that reflects the limits of autonomy and control. As a result, women's development delineates the path not only to a less violent life but also to a maturity realized through interdependence and taking care" (*D.V.*, p. 172). She writes that there is evidence that "women perceive and construe social reality differently from men and that these differences center around experiences of attachment and separation . . . because women's sense of integrity appears to be entwined with an ethic of care, so that to see themselves as women is to see themselves in a relationship of connection, the major transitions in women's lives would seem to involve changes in the understanding and activities of care" (*D.V.*, p. 171). She contrasts this progressive understanding of care, from merely pleasing others to helping and nurturing, with the sort of progression that is involved in Kohlberg's stages, a progression in the understanding, not of mutual care, but of mutual *respect*, where this has its Kantian overtones of distance, even of some fear for the respected, and where personal autonomy and *in*dependence, rather than more satisfactory interdependence, are the paramount values.

This contrast, one cannot but feel, is one which Gilligan might have used the Marxist language of alienation to make. For the main complaint about the Kantian version of a society with its first virtue justice, construed as respect for equal rights to formal goods such as having contracts kept, due process, equal opportunity including opportunity to participate in political activities leading to policy- and lawmaking, to basic liberties of speech, free association and assembly, and religious worship, is that none of these goods does much to ensure that the people who have and mutually respect such rights will have any other relationships to one another than the minimal relationship needed to keep such a "civil society" going. They may well be lonely, driven to suicide, apathetic about their work and about participation in political processes, find their lives meaningless, and have no wish to leave offspring to face the same meaningless existence. Their rights, and respect for rights, are quite compatible with very great misery, and misery whose causes are not just individual misfortune and psychic sickness but social and moral impoverishment.

What Gilligan's older male subjects complain of is precisely this sort of alienation from some dimly glimpsed better possibility for human beings, some richer sort of network of relationships. As one of Gilligan's male subjects put it, "People have real emotional needs to be attached to something, and equality doesn't give you attachment. Equality fractures society and places on every person the burden of standing on his own two feet" (*D.V.*, p. 167). It is not just the difficulty of self-reliance which is complained of, but its socially "fracturing" effect. Whereas the younger men, in their college years, had seen morality as a matter of reciprocal noninterference, this older man begins to see it as reciprocal attachment. "Morality is . . . essential . . . for creating the kind of environment, interaction between people, that is prerequisite to the fulfillment of most individual goals. If you want other people not to interfere with your pursuit of whatever you are into, you have to play the game," says a young spokesman for traditional liberalism (*D.V.*, p. 98). But if what one is "into" is interconnection, interdependence rather than an individual autonomy that may involve "detachment," such a version of morality will come to seem inadequate. And Gilligan stresses that the interconnection that her mature women subjects, and some men, wanted to sustain was not merely freely chosen interconnection, nor interconnection between equals, but also the sort of interconnection that can obtain between a child and her unchosen mother and father, or between a child and her unchosen older and younger siblings, or indeed between most workers and their unchosen fellow workers, or between most citizens and their unchosen fellow citizens.

A model of a decent community different from the liberal one is involved in the version of moral maturity that Gilligan voices. It has in many ways more in common with the older religion-linked versions of morality and a good society than with the modern Western liberal ideal. That perhaps is why some find it so dangerous and retrograde. Yet it seems clear that it also has much in common with what we can call Hegelian versions of moral maturity and of social health and malaise, both with Marxist versions and with so-called right-Hegelian views.

Let me try to summarize the main differences, as I see them, between on the one hand Gilligan's version of moral maturity and the sort of social structures that would encourage, express, and protect it and on the other the orthodoxy she sees herself to be challenging. I shall from now on be giving my own interpretation of the significance of her challenges, not merely reporting them.[16] The most obvious point is the challenge to the individualism of the Western tradition, to the fairly entrenched belief in the possibility and desirability of each person pursuing his own good in his own way, constrained only by a minimal formal common good, namely, a working legal apparatus that enforces contracts and protects individuals from undue interference by others. Gilligan reminds us that noninterference can, especially for the relatively powerless, such as the very young, amount to neglect, and even between equals can be isolating and alienating. On her less individualist version of individuality, it becomes defined by responses to dependency and to patterns of interconnection, both chosen and unchosen. It is not something a person *has,* and which she then chooses relationships to suit, but something that develops out of a series of dependencies and interdependencies, and responses to them. This conception of individuality is not flatly at odds with, say, Rawls's Kantian one, but there is at least a difference of tone of voice between speaking as Rawls does of each of us having our own rational life plan, which a just society's moral traffic rules will allow us to follow, and which may or may not include close association with other persons, and speaking as Gilligan does of a satisfactory life as involving the "progress of affiliative relationship" (*D.V.,* p. 170) where "the concept of identity expands to include the experience of interconnection" (*D.V.,* p. 173). Rawls can allow that progress to Gilligan-style moral maturity may be *a* rational life plan, but not a moral constraint on every life pattern. The trouble is that it will not do just to say "let this version of morality be an optional extra. Let us agree on the essential minimum, that is, on justice and rights, and let whoever wants to go further and cultivate this more demanding ideal of responsibility and care." For, first, the ideal of care cannot be satisfactorily cultivated without closer cooperation from others than respect for rights and justice will ensure, and, second, the encouragement of some to cultivate it while others do not could easily lead to exploitation of those who do. It obviously *has* suited some in most societies well enough that others take on the responsibilities of care (for the sick, the helpless, the young), leaving them free to pursue their own less altruistic goods. Volunteer forces of those who accept an ethic of care, operating within a society where the power is exercised and the institutions designed, redesigned, or maintained by those who accept a less communal ethic of minimally constrained self-advancement, will not be the solution. The liberal individualists may be able to "tolerate" the more communally minded, if they keep the liberals' rules, but it is not so clear that the more communally minded can be content with just those rules, nor be content to be tolerated and possibly exploited.

For the moral tradition which developed the concept of rights, autonomy, and justice is the same tradition that provided "justifications" of the oppression of those whom the primary rights-holders depended on to do the sort of work they themselves preferred not to do. The domestic work was left to women and slaves, and the liberal morality for rights-holders was surreptitiously supplemented by a different set of demands made on domestic workers. As long as women could be got to assume responsibility for the care of home and children and to train their children to continue the sexist system, the liberal morality could continue to be the official morality, by turning its eyes away from the contribution made by those it excluded. The long unnoticed moral proletariat were the domestic

25

workers, mostly female. Rights have usually been for the privileged. Talking about laws, and the rights those laws recognize and protect, does not in itself ensure that the group of legislators and rights-holders will not be restricted to some elite. Bills of rights have usually been proclamations of the rights of some in-group, barons, landowners, males, whites, nonforeigners. The "justice perspective" and the legal sense that goes with it are shadowed by their patriarchal past. What did Kant, the great prophet of autonomy, say in his moral theory about women? He said they were incapable of legislation, not fit to vote, that they needed the guidance of more "rational" males.[17] Autonomy was not for them; it was only for first-class, really rational, persons. It is ironic that Gilligan's original findings in a way confirm Kant's views—it seems that autonomy really may not be for women. Many of them reject that ideal (D.V., p. 48), and have been found not as good at making rules as are men. But where Kant concludes "so much the worse for women," we can conclude "so much the worse for the male fixation on the special skill of drafting legislation, for the bureaucratic mentality of rule worship, and for the male exaggeration of the importance of independence over mutual interdependence."

It is however also true that the moral theories that made the concept of a person's rights central were not just the instruments for excluding some persons but also the instruments used by those who demanded that more and more persons be included in the favored group. Abolitionists, reformers, women, used the language of rights to assert their claims to inclusion in the group of full members of a community. The tradition of liberal moral theory has in fact developed to include the women it had for so long excluded, to include the poor as well as rich, blacks as well as whites, and so on. Women such as Mary Wollstonecraft used the male moral theories to good purpose. So we should not be wholly ungrateful for those male moral theories, for all their objectionable earlier content. They were undoubtedly patriarchal, but they also contained the seeds of the challenge, or antidote, to this patriarchal poison.

But when we transcend the values of the Kantians, we should not forget the facts of history—that those values were the values of the oppressors of women. The Christian church, whose version of the moral law Aquinas codified in his very legalistic moral theory, still insists on the maleness of the God it worships, and jealously reserves for males all the most powerful positions in its hierarchy. Its patriarchal prejudice is open and avowed. In the secular moral theories of men, the sexist patriarchal prejudice is today often less open, not as blatant as it is in Aquinas, in the later natural law tradition, and in Kant and Hegel, but is often still there. No moral theorist today would say that women are unfit to vote, to make laws, or to rule a nation without powerful male advisors (as most queens had), but the old doctrines die hard. In one of the best male theories we have, Rawls's theory, a key role is played by the idea of the "head of a household." It is heads of households who are to deliberate behind a "veil of ignorance" of historical details, and of details of their own special situation, to arrive at the "just" constitution for a society. Now of course Rawls does not think or say that these "heads" are fathers rather than mothers. But if we have really given up the age-old myth of women needing, as Grotius put it, to be under the "eye" of a more "rational" male protector and master, then how do families come to have any one "head," except by the death or desertion of one parent? They will either be two-headed, or headless. Traces of the old patriarchal poison still remain in even the best contemporary moral theorizing. Few may actually say that women's place is in the home, but there is much muttering, when unemployment figures rise, about how the relatively recent flood of women into the work force complicates the problem, as if it would be a good thing if women just went back home whenever unemployment rose, to leave the available jobs for the men. We still do not have wide acceptance of the equal right of women to employment outside the home. Nor do we have wide acceptance of the equal duty of men to perform those domestic tasks which in no way depend on special female anatomy, such as cooking, cleaning, and the care of weaned children. All sorts of stories (maybe true stories) about children's need for one "primary" parent, who must be the mother if the mother breast-feeds the child, shore up the unequal division of domestic responsibility between mothers and fathers, wives and husbands. If we are really to transvalue the values of our patriarchal past, we need to rethink all of those assumptions, test those psychological theories. And how will men ever develop an understanding of the "ethics of care" if they continue to be shielded or kept from that experience of caring for a dependent child which complements the experience we all have had of being cared for as dependent children? These experiences form the natural background for the development of moral maturity as Gilligan's women saw it.

Exploitation aside, why would women, once liberated, not be content to have their version of morality merely tolerated? Why should they not see themselves as voluntarily, for their own reasons, taking on *more* than the liberal rules demand, while having no quarrel with the content of those rules themselves, nor with their remaining the only ones that are expected to be generally obeyed? To see why, we need to move on to three more differences between the Kantian liberals (usually contractarians) and their critics. These concern the relative weight put on relationships between equals, on freedom of choice, and on the authority of intellect over emotions. It is a typical feature of the dominant moral theories and traditions since Kant, or perhaps since Hobbes, that relationships between equals or those who are deemed equal in some important sense have been the relations that morality is primarily concerned to regulate. Relationships between those who are clearly unequal in power, such as parents and children, earlier and later generations in relation to one another, states and citizens, doctors and patients, the well and the ill, large states and small states, have had to be shunted to the bottom of the agenda and then dealt with by some sort of "promotion" of the weaker, so that an appearance of virtual equality is achieved. Citizens collectively become equal to states, children are treated as adults-to-be, the ill and dying are treated as continuers of their earlier more potent selves, so that their "rights" can be seen as the rights of equals. This pretense of an equality that is in fact absent may often lead to desirable protection of the weaker, or more dependent. But it somewhat masks the question of what our moral relationships *are* to those who are our superiors or our inferiors in power. A more realistic acceptance that we begin as helpless children, that at almost every point of our lives we deal with both the more and the less helpless, that equality of power and interdependency, between two persons or groups, is rare and hard to recognize when it does occur, might lead us to a more direct approach to questions concerning the design of institutions structuring these relationships between unequals (families, schools, hospitals, armies) and of the morality of our dealings with the more and the less powerful. One reason why those who agree with the Gilligan version of what morality is about will not want to agree that the liberals' rules are a good minimal set, the only ones we need pressure *everyone* to obey, is that these rules do little to protect the young or the dying or the starving or any of the relatively powerless against neglect, or to ensure an education that will form persons to be *capable* of conforming to an ethics of care and responsibility. Put baldly, and in a way Gilligan certainly has not put it, the liberal morality, if unsupplemented, may *unfit* people to be anything other than what its justifying theories suppose them to be, ones who have no interest in each other's interests. Yet some must take an interest in the next generation's interests. Women's traditional work, of caring for the less powerful, especially for the young, is obviously socially vital. One cannot regard any version of morality that does not ensure that caring for children gets well done as an adequate "minimal morality," anymore than we could so regard one that left any concern for more distant future generations an optional extra. A moral theory, it can plausibly be claimed, cannot regard concern for new and future persons as an optional charity left for those with a taste for it. If the morality the theory endorses is to sustain itself, it must provide for its own continuers, not just take out a loan on a carefully encouraged maternal instinct or on the enthusiasm of a self-selected group of environmentalists who make it their business or hobby to be concerned with what we are doing to mother earth.

The recognition of the importance for all parties of relations between those who are and cannot but be unequal, and of their effect on personality formation and so on other relationships, goes along with a recognition of the plain fact that not all morally important relationships can or should be freely chosen. So far I have discussed three reasons women have to be not content to pursue their own values within the framework of the liberal morality. The first was its dubious record. The second was its inattention to relations of inequality or its pretense of equality. The third reason is its exaggeration of the scope of choice, or its inattention to unchosen relations. Showing up the partial myth of equality among actual members of a community, and the undesirability of trying to pretend that we are treating all of them as equals, tends to go along with an exposure of the companion myth that moral obligations arise from freely *chosen* associations between such equals. Vulnerable future generations do not choose their dependence on earlier generations. The unequal infant does not choose its place in a family or nation, nor is it treated as free to do as it likes until some association is freely entered into. Nor do parents always choose their parental role or freely assume their parental responsibilities, anymore than we choose our power to affect the conditions in which later generations will live. Gilligan's attention to the version of morality and moral maturity found in women, many of whom had faced a choice of whether or not to have an abortion, and who had at some point become mothers, is attention to the perceived inadequacy of the language of rights to help in such choices or to guide them in their parental role. It would not be much of an exaggeration to call the Gilligan "different voice" the voice of the potential parents. The emphasis on care goes with a recognition of the often unchosen nature of responsibilities of those who give care, both of children who care for their aged or infirm parents and of parents who care for the children they in fact have. Contract soon ceases to seem the paradigm source of moral obligation once we attend to parental responsibility, and justice as a virtue of social institutions will come to seem at best only first equal with the virtue, whatever its name, that ensures that the members of each new generation are made appropriately welcome and prepared for their adult lives.

This all constitutes a belated reminder to Western moral theorists of a fact they have always known, that, as Adam Ferguson and David Hume before him emphasized, we are born into families, and the first society we belong to, one that fits or misfits us for later ones, is the small society of parents (or some sort of child-attendants) and children, exhibiting as it may relationships both of near equality and of inequality in power. This simple reminder, with the fairly considerable implications it can have for the plausibility of contractarian moral theory, is at the same time a reminder of the role of human emotions as much as human reason and will in moral development as it actually comes about. The fourth feature of the Gilligan challenge to liberal orthodoxy is a challenge to its typical *rationalism*, or intellectualism, to its assumption that we need not worry what passions persons have, as long as their rational wills can control them. This Kantian picture of a controlling reason dictating to possibly unruly passions also tends to seem less useful when we are led to consider what sort of person we need to fill the role of parent or, indeed, want in any close relationship. It might be important for father figures to have rational control over their violent urges to beat to death the children whose screams enrage them, but more than control of such nasty passions seems needed in the mother or primary parent, or parent-substitute, according to most psychological theories. Primary parents need to love their children, not just to control their irritation. So the emphasis in Kantian theories on rational control of emotions, rather than on cultivating desirable forms of emotion, is challenged by Gilligan, along with her challenge to the assumption of the centrality of autonomy, or relations between equals, and of freely chosen relations.

The same set of challenges to "orthodox" liberal moral theory has come not just from Gilligan and other women, who are reminding other moral theorists of the role of the family as a social institution and as an influence on the other relationships people want to sustain or are capable of sustaining, but also, as I noted at the start, from an otherwise fairly diverse group of men, ranging from those influenced by both Hegelian and Christian traditions (MacIntyre) to all varieties of other backgrounds. From this group I want to draw attention to the work of one philosopher in particular, Laurence Thomas, the author of a fairly remarkable article[18] in which he finds sexism to be a more intractable social evil than racism. In a series of articles and a book,[19] Thomas makes a strong case for the importance of supplementing a concern for justice and respect for rights with an emphasis on equally needed virtues, and on virtues seen as appropriate *emotional* as well as rational capacities. Like Gilligan (and unlike MacIntyre) Thomas gives a lot of attention to the childhood beginnings of moral and social capacities, to the role of parental love in making that possible, and to the emotional as well as the cognitive development we have reason to think both possible and desirable in human persons.

It is clear, I think, that the best moral theory has to be a cooperative product of women and men, has to harmonize justice and care. The morality it theorizes about is after all for all persons, for men and for women, and will need their combined insights. As Gilligan said (*D.V.,* p. 174), what we need now is a "marriage" of the old male and the newly articulated female insights. If she is right about the special moral aptitudes of women, then it will most likely be the women who propose the marriage, since they are the ones with the more natural empathy, with the better diplomatic skills, the ones more likely to shoulder responsibility and take moral initiative, and the ones who find it easiest to empathize and care about how the other party feels. Then, once there is this union of male and female moral wisdom, we maybe can teach each other the moral skills each gender currently lacks, so that the gender difference in moral outlook that Gilligan found will slowly become less marked.

three

UNSAFE LOVES

Destroy love and friendship;
what remains in the world worth accepting?

David Hume

What is it to love another person, and is it ever a good idea?[1] The ones who have told us the most or the most insightful things about love are poets and novelists. Philosophers, although they are supposed to be lovers of a sort, tend to be all thumbs when it comes to handling love. But since I am only a philosopher I will look at some of their attempts. According to a recent book-length philosophical analysis of love, "what makes love unusual among the emotions is the human inability to do without it . . ."[2] If this is right, then let us hope that love can be a good thing for us. Otherwise it will have to count as an unfortunate addiction, something we cannot do without but that does not bring us anything positively good either, and that may bring us much sorrow. Robert Brown, the philosopher I quoted, thinks it does usually bring "an immense amount of satisfaction" and yet "often produces as much pain as pleasure. For love is always subject to frustration and rejection, and commonly bound together with such dangerous emotions as jealousy, hate, and fear."[3] We could in a sense "do without" those emotions—that is, we might prefer to be without them, but we would not, Brown believes, choose to be without the love that commonly brings them. Nor is it only emotions dangerous to our fellows, the aggression-feeding emotions of jealousy, hate, and fear of rivals, that love commonly brings with it. There are also those more "dangerous" to the lover than to others: paralyzing grief or reckless despair at the loss or death of loved ones, retreat into a sort of psychic hibernation when cut off from "news" of them, crippling anxiety when they are in danger, helpless anguish when they are in pain, crushing guilt when one has harmed them, deadly shame when one fails them. All of these "dangers" to the lover must be weighed against that immense satisfaction love can bring. And then there are the dangers to the ones who are loved—the danger of overprotection, of suffocation, of loss of independence, toughness, and self-reliance. When love is reciprocal each faces the dangers of lovers combined with those of beloveds. As we catalog the risks of loving, we may begin to sympathize with the conclusion of Jerome Shaffer, who in an article "assessing" the role of emotions in our lives comes down against the lot of them, and in particular against love. He says, "The world might have become a better place when Scrooge found love, but perhaps not in the case of Anna Karenina, and probably not in the case of King Kong . . . love, like the other emotions, has no general claim to value or importance in our lives."[4]

Nor is Shaffer alone among what we might call the philosophical "misamorists," the distrusters of the claims of love. Kant too more or less advises us to keep ourselves to ourselves, *not* to link our fate unnecessarily closely with that of other persons, to remain detached—respecting others, but not getting too mixed up in their lives. Kant does recognize a moral duty of philanthropy, love of our fellows, but he construes this as involving not feeling or emotion but solely goodwill, benevolence, willingness to do things for others, to draw close enough to them to help them. Kant says that in the moral world there is an analogy to the attraction and repulsion that operate in the physical world. "The principle of *mutual love* admonishes men constantly to *come closer* to one another; that of the *respect* they owe one another, to keep themselves *at a distance* from one another."[5] Although he finds room for a duty of love as well as a duty of respect, a duty to draw close and a duty to keep one's distance, his way of harmonizing them is to weaken the "law of love" into a duty to help one's neighbor, with the understanding that one's neighbor does *not* want to be any closer to one—one helps him best by helping him keep his self-respect, keep his sense that he merits respect, is a person one would hesitate to come too close to. So, says Kant, if we express our philanthropy by being generous to a poorer person, "it is our duty to behave as if our help is either merely what is due him, or but a slight service of love, and to spare him humiliation and maintain his respect for himself."[6] This recognizes another danger in love, or rather in being loved—the danger of humiliation, of being seen to need the services of others. Beware lovers bearing gifts—they may be gifts of what you need!

Kant finds another danger closely associated with humiliation lurking in the vicinity of love, especially of emotional and felt love—the danger of self-exposure and vulnerability to harm from others. He speaks in his *Lectures on Ethics* of friendship as "man's refuge in this world from his distrust of his fellows"[7] and advocates caution in taking such refuge. "We must so conduct ourselves towards a friend that there is no harm done if he should turn into an enemy."[8] Kant grants that "we all have a strong impulse to disclose ourselves, and enter wholly into fellowship; and such self-revelation is further a human necessity for the correction of our judgments. To have a friend whom we know to be frank and loving, neither false nor spiteful, is to have one who will help us to correct our judgment when it is mistaken. This is the whole end of man, through which he can enjoy his existence. But even between the closest and most intimate of friends there are still some things that call for reserve."[9] Reserve is called for, Kant says, as much for the other's sake as for one's own, because "we have certain natural frailties which ought to be concealed for the sake of decency, lest humanity be outraged. Even to our best friend we must not reveal ourselves, in our natural state as we know it ourselves. To do so would be loathsome."[10] A great danger in loving friendship, as Kant describes it, is that it will tempt the friends into too great a candor, a candor that is both inconsiderate and imprudent. Polite and prudent reserve, carefully measured "disclosure," is what Kant recommends even toward one's best friends, those toward whom one is frankest and most loving. Kant says that true friendship is merely an Ideal, or an Idea, in Plato's sense. At least twice he quotes the ancient Greek wise saying, "My dear friends, there are no friends" (once attributing it to Socrates, once to Aristotle). In the real world there are false friends and false lovers and false ex-friends and false ex-lovers, ones who either from carelessness or from spite reveal to others what was disclosed to them alone, whose love is likely to turn to loathing if the once loved person fails to keep defects secret or at least out of view. In the real world hot-headed intimates turn confidences into

35

weapons; an intimate can "be capable of sending us to the gallows in a moment of passion, though he would implore our pardon as soon as he had cooled down." Kant clearly thinks that the duty of respect, of keeping due distance, trumps the ideal of loving fellowship. "The whole end of man" is correct judgment, not fellowship. Fellowship is merely a means to this end, and a risky one.

Kant's ambivalence about love, his simultaneous acceptance of a "true" and "very necessary" idea of mutual love and friendship, and his "misamorism" as far as human love goes, his warnings to us not to expect to find any examples of real love in our experience, is the culmination of a long philosophical tradition which we could call the theological tradition. In Plato, in Augustine, in Descartes, we get a similar sort of combination of a very strong definition of what the real thing would be, and a claim that no love between human persons will satisfy this definition. All human loves are doomed to failure. At their worst, they degenerate into mutual loathing, betrayal, and enmity; at their best they are interrupted by death and end in separation and bereavement. The moral, for these "theological" pessimists about human love, is not the very drastic moral that Shaffer draws—that we should try to discover and then to take a medicine that would make us "love-proof"—but rather that we should restrict our love for the "right" object of love, namely, God. Love of God will be a sort of live vaccine that will block any riskier loving. We are to find a person who because omnipresent cannot "forsake" us, who because already all knowing cannot be surprised or shocked at what we reveal of ourselves, who because all powerful has us already in his power, whether or not we give love, so that in loving him we renounce no independence that we ever had or could have.

Not every variant of this theological tradition advising us that love of God is the best love for us says that it will be in any way a reciprocated love. Even the orthodox Christian version of the tradition, which does say that human love of God is to be a response to God's love for man, cannot say that there is much in common between the way we love God and the way God loves us. For our love is love by the ignorant of a fully knowledgeable one, love by the powerless of an all-powerful one. It would be impossible for us even to try to love God in the way God is claimed to love us—powerfully, knowledgeably, generously, as only the highest being condescending to love lesser beings can. If we were to try to imitate that sort of love

36

it would have to be by ourselves loving less powerful and less knowledgeable beings—our infant children, or our domestic pets. So if we are to try to imitate divine love for us, to let it serve as an ideal or an example for us, we will *have* to love someone besides God, we will have to find some even more vulnerable being to love. There is some tension in the Christian story about the sort of reciprocity love at its best involves, and about the relation between human love for God and our love for other mortals. If God's love is the best love, *which* of God's loves is the best—that of the Father for other Persons of the Godhead, or that of God for human souls? Which, if any, should we try to imitate?

Tensions in theology are, if Feuerbach and Freud are right, reflections of tensions in our understanding of our own human situation. Love of an all-powerful God may be seen as a displaced version of love of a more powerful human father. Uncertainties about reciprocity, about whether it is appropriate to expect return divine love, and if it is, if that return love should serve as a model for one's own love, will reflect uncertainties about the human father-child relation. Retreat to love of God after disillusion with human adult loves may be a sort of nostalgia for some recalled or fantasized infant security in the strong arms of a loving parent. So we can learn something about our own ambivalent attitudes toward love by looking at the tensions in the theological tradition, even if we want eventually to demystify it, to bring it back to earth.

Descartes, who can be said to be a heretical adherent of this tradition, gave us a full account of our passion-repertoire and gave love pride of place in his account. He describes love as an emotion that impels us to "join ourselves willingly" to the loved thing or person, and he adds a gloss on this willingness: "I mean . . . the assent by which we consider ourselves henceforth as joined with what we love in such a manner that we imagine a whole, of which we take ourselves to be only one part, and the thing loved to be the other."[11] He later adds that in many sorts of love, such as parental love and deep devotion to a nobler person, the lover may take himself to be not the *better* part of the imagined whole, and so will not be afraid of sacrificing himself to save the loved one, even giving his life. But many male lovers take themselves to be the better parts of the unions they make with women and can be ambivalent about any such union, any treating of oneself as mere "part."

Descartes gives an example of such a love when he portrays for us a grief-stricken husband mourning his dead wife, a husband who while he weeps with sincere distress, also experiences "at the same time a secret joy in his innermost soul" and "would be sorry to see her brought to life again."[12] Descartes seems to be ambivalent about love, or at any rate about love of fellow human persons. He defines it in strong and apparently approving tones ("Love can never be too great," he says), but he also seems to endorse a cautious avoidance of it and shows sympathy with the person who rejoices at escape, at regaining his freedom after experience of the sort of willing union that at least marriage involves. This is not surprising after his sardonic account of adult heterosexual attraction, whose willing endorsement counts as heterosexual love: "For nature . . . bring[s] it about that at a certain age and time we regard ourselves as deficient—as forming only one half of a whole, whose other half must be a person of the other sex . . . nature represents, in a confused manner, the acquisition of this other half as the greatest of all goods imaginable."[13]

Descartes says almost nothing about reciprocity in love. He mentions return love only in passing, and Spinoza, who had read him carefully, spells out explicitly what Descartes had implied both by what he said and by what he did not say: that the one who loves the best object of love, God, cannot hope for return love, but at best for modest participation in divine self-love. Love of God, on this account, is ultimately a form of prudent withdrawal from human loves, especially sexual ones. Even if love of God does not lengthen our earthly life, it is at least safe from any nasty surprises of the sort we sometimes get from human loved ones, when their response or even their return love takes forms that upset, distress, or harm us.

I have labeled Kant's, Descartes', and Spinoza's accounts of love "theological" and called them "misamorists" as far as love between human beings goes. The common feature is a strong sense that human persons are unlovable. We can love, but only our betters, and our fellow persons are rarely much better. So Kant can suppose that respect depends upon averting one's gaze from the possibly "loathsome" full actuality of the respected person. Friendship and love between human persons are dangerous because they risk mutual knowledge. Descartes, although he does not, like Kant, give such free rein to expressions of disgust for normal human persons, does not encourage us, even when lovers, to expect to be loved. Presented in this (admittedly unsympathetic) way, this sounds like pretty sick stuff. What features of the human situation might explain this peculiar theological ideal of love of a superior who must not be expected to love back, and this conviction that we are too defect-filled and inferior to be loved once fully known? Were these great philosophers of our tradition the victims of early childhood traumas of parental rejection, of exposure to scorn and contempt? Did they never experience the great satisfactions of reciprocated love between parent and child, or between human lovers? What soured them? Human persons are of course faulty, but roughly equally faulty, so need not scorn or be disgusted by each other once they know each other. Nor do we have to be perpetually intent on mutual faultfinding and shaming—there can be time also for some mutual admiration and for some mutual teasing. I am not going to try to diagnose the causes of the misamorism of these philosophers, tempting though it is to speculate on the basis of what information we have (Descartes' mother's death in his early infancy and his daughter's early death, Spinoza's rejection by his own community, Kant's puritan upbringing). Instead I am going to turn to some less theological thinkers, ones who conceive of us not primarily as souls in relation to other sinful souls or to a sovereign God but rather as intelligent mammals, at birth literally "attached" to a mother, who then may feed us at her breast. I turn from the *supernatural* theological philosophers of love to the naturalist philosophers of love, those who take umbilical cords, navels, and other basic anatomical reminders of our mammalian condition more seriously than they take our immortal and sinful souls.[14]

David Hume stands out as a philosopher who gives a purely naturalist account of human love. In his *Treatise of Human Nature* he devotes Part II of Book Two (about seventy pages, almost as much space as he gives to causation) to analyzing its forms (and those of hate). What is striking in his account, if we compare it with those of Descartes and Kant, is that he takes the forms of human love to be variants on what he calls "love in animals." (Earlier he had related our reason to "reason in animals," our pride to "pride in animals.") Our biological nature as well as our social organization set the stage for our loving. Hume devotes a section to the "love of relations." He calls the "tie of blood" the "strongest tie the mind is capable of," and he associates our understanding of all "relations," in however abstract a sense, with this one "relation of a different kind," the blood tie. He makes some interesting remarks about a child's love for his mother, his limited toleration of brothers and sisters sharing that love, his intolerance of stepfathers, calling these "pretty curious phenomena." He gives a glowing description of the sort of intimacy that loving friends, loving relatives, loving parents and children may have, and of our need for such intimacy. In the company of a loved and trusted intimate, he says, the mind "awakes, as it were, from a dream: The blood flows with a new tide: The heart is elevated: And the whole man acquires a vigour, which he cannot command in his solitary and calm moments."[15] We rejoice, he says, in the presence of a "Being like ourselves, who communicates to us all the actions of his mind; makes us privy to his inmost sentiments and affections; and lets us see, in the very instant of their production, all the emotions, which are caus'd by any object."[16] Kant might well have been lecturing the ghost of Hume in his warnings about the danger of unguarded intimacy and the likely fate of such unashamed and trusting fools as Hume describes. Hume seems unworried that these candid intimates may find what is revealed "loathsome." Where Kant issues the rule, "don't treat your friends in ways you will regret if and when they cease to be your friends," Hume in fact gives the reverse rule, "don't treat strangers in ways you will regret should they become your friends."[17] Hume's account of love and his apparent recommendation of its delights must seem *reckless* to the Kantian. Risks of betrayal, of looking silly or even loathsome, of getting caught up in others' troubles, of being attacked while our guard is down, are not mentioned at all by Hume. For him these risks of love seem to be outweighed by the evil of solitude. He echoes what Seneca and Boethius said: "A perfect solitude is, perhaps, the greatest punishment we can suffer. Every pleasure languishes when enjoy'd a-part from company . . ."[18] Is it that Hume does not see the dangers that Kant finds in human loves, or is it that he accepts those risks as a fair price to pay for waking from the bad dream of solitude? "Let all the powers and elements conspire to serve and obey one man: Let the sun rise and set at his command . . . He will still be miserable, till you give him some one person at least, with whom he may share his happiness, and whose esteem and friendship he may enjoy."[19]

Hume seems not to share Kant's worries that close friendship, with the mutual candor that it encourages, will destroy mutual esteem. "Love," in Hume's wide sense, has esteem as one of its forms. To love someone, by Hume's definition, is simply to find something attractive or "fine" in that person. He distinguishes different sorts of love both by the *sort* of fine thing found (power, beauty, wit, good nature) and by the perceived social or biological relationship of the lover to the one in whom he finds "fine" qualities. So we "respect" those we consider our superiors, but feel other sorts of love for equals or for "weaker" ones. Parental love is for those who depend upon us in ways we do not depend on them. Hume thinks adults *do* depend on their children, and on other relatives, in many other ways. Children can be "subjects" of their parents' pride, and can sustain their parents' pride, whatever it is taken in, by their sympathy and love. Hume thinks that a person's family's opinion of her matters to her in a special way. "We are most uneasy under the contempt of persons, who are both related to us by blood, and contiguous in place."[20] He tries to give us an account of love that fits in with his account of proper pride. One of the benefits of mutual love is the mutual sustaining of proper pride.

Hume's account of sexual love is relatively straightforward, and brings into prominence a basic biological fact about it that links with his earlier discussion of the "tie of blood." Parental love is the first of love's variants that he discusses, and he ends with "the amorous passion or love betwixt the sexes." What he takes to be distinctive in this form of love, a form which deserves our attention in part "on account of its force and violence," is that it combines three passions—general goodwill arising out of esteem for "the merit or wit" of the loved person, admiration for the loved one's beauty, and what he calls "the appetite for generation," "the bodily appetite," or lust. Whether or not there is a felt desire for "generation" as such, the satisfaction of this appetite is, at least in the forms of the amorous passion tolerated in Hume's culture,[21] likely to have that result. Hume, the biologically realistic philosopher of love, puts "generation" in the center of his account of human love (and of his account of marriage as an institution).[22] This love is not merely, as for Descartes, a matter of a willing uniting with one other person to form "a whole," it is also a matter of willingness to jointly generate a third person, as children's love of parents is a response to those who generated them, to parents and progenitors. There is no "one whole"; there are ongoing families and successive generations. Hume does not of course *restrict* love to love between those linked or about to be linked by some "generative" tie (anymore than he restricts lust to procreative intent), but he is very clear that, to understand love, we must understand our "blood ties" and the mammalian nature of our "descent" and our genealogy. He discusses the way we like to trace descent and boast of the antiquity of our family; he wonders why we care whether we descend from notable ancestors through the maternal or the paternal line, and why we take our father's and not our mother's family name.[23] One might almost say that Hume is *obsessed,* in his account of love, with the circumstances of human generation. But that comes as a relief after the careful avoidance of or disdain for such "unspiritual" matters that we get in Descartes and in Kant.

Charles Darwin read Hume and quoted him with approval, and Darwin's disciple T. H. Huxley wrote a book about Hume's *Treatise,* with particular praise of its naturalism and particular emphasis on the short chapters on reason, pride, and love in animals. Darwin discusses human love not just in *The Descent of Man* but also in *The Expressions of Emotion in Man and Animals.* Naturally his main focus is on the sexual love that is "generative," and on parent-child love, particularly mother-child love, and its expression. Although he does not find love to have the typical "face" that anger, fear, and disgust have, he does suppose that it shows in the eyes and in the voice, and he suggests that the power of music to rouse emotions may lie in its power to evoke dim memories in us, race memories of mating cries, as well as individual memories of the intonations of soothing motherly voices. Darwin postulated, indeed, that before we were a talking species we were a singing species. Our first songs were without words, later came songs with words, and lastly intoned sentences. Our first songs would be love songs, but there would also be marching-off-to-the-hunt rhythmic songs, rousing battle hymns, and so on, which exploited the innately expressive power of tone of voice and of repetition of calls. Here Darwin could have called on Descartes for support, for Descartes had both explored the inner and outer bodily effects of love and other emotions (love "speeds the digestion" and produces a warm steady heat in the chest) and noted how music stirs emotions and how, for this purpose, the human voice is the best musical instrument.

What Darwin says about mother-child love echoes Hume's discussion of it. It is not so much that there is a special face or posture which is the face of mother love, nor even one voice the voice of mother love. It is rather that there is immediate responsiveness to the *range* of faces and voices that the child displays. Love makes us more *aware* of the emotions of the loved one than we would otherwise be, and makes us quicker to make helpful responses. So the face of mother love will be a mobile face—anxiety, relief, pride, contentment will show there, coordinately with the expressed emotions of the child. Similarly, the child will follow the mother's face and voice—love is as much this sort of coordination of emotions between lovers as it is itself a special emotion. Hobbes, Descartes, Hume, Darwin, and many others included love on their lists of human emotions, but, like a mood, it seems as much an activator of other emotions, and of response to the other's emotion, as an emotion itself. Hume treated sympathy as not a special emotion but a disposition or "principle" that communicates emotions from person to person— that "spreads" our distress or our joy to sympathetic companions. Love may be as much like sympathy as it is like the emotions that sympathy can spread. It is a *coordination* or mutual involvement of two (or more) persons' emotions, and it is more than sympathy, more than just the duplication of the emotion of each in a sympathetic echo in the other.

A sympathetic person tends to share the sorrows and joys of all her fellows, as far as she is in a position to recognize them. Sympathy increases joys and sorrows in much the same proportion. Only the person whose own personal ratio of joy over sorrow is exceptionally high or who is surrounded only by those whose misery is exceptionally great will "lose" anything by being a sympathetic person, one whose psyche reverberates, in Hume's phrase, to others' fates. A sympathetic person may in an age of mass communication come to bear the world's sorrows on her shoulders, but also share the world's rejoicings (except that they are less fully reported—weep and the television world weeps with you, laugh and you laugh alone). One's life will be enriched by a capacity for sympathy, and the more enriched the wider the scope of one's sympathy, but the overall balance of joy and sorrow one experiences need not be affected by how prone one is to sympathize in Hume's sense, that is, to empathize, with others. Love is different. It *will* make a difference to the balance, and it is risky and "unsafe" precisely because one does not know, cannot know, just how one's life will be affected by the strong sort of involvement in the life of another that it brings. It is "for better, for worse." It is not just that one takes on an extra set of joys and sorrows to one's own—one does that if one has sympathy for a person over a period of time whether or not one loves her. When one loves, one's occasions for joy, sorrow, and other emotions will become "geared" in a more complex way than just sympathy to those of the loved person, and this may indeed affect the balance of joy over sorrow in one's life. The loved person's indifference will hurt, her boredom will disappoint, her premature withdrawal will grieve one. Her enthusiasms also may shock and disturb one, the intensity of her embrace may maim one, the diseases she carries may kill one, and one may know that they are killing one.

Even in the womb the child may be affected not just by the mother's physical state but by her changing emotional states. The child may then show a certain kind of psycho-physical "sympathy" to the mother's state of mind. Its states may correlate with her states, but not in the complex coordinated way they will correlate when, say, the mother and child *play* together when the child is about one year old. The response then is not just sympathetic sharing of expressed emotions, it is also appropriate *follow-up* responses to what one knows by sympathy that the other is feeling—mischievous delight at the other's temporary bafflement, a frisson of fear at the other's feigned aggression, glory in the other's surrender. There will be a heightened ability to anticipate the next emotional move of the other, to watch for it and to be ready for it.

The coordination of emotions between intimates, in fun and in more serious contexts of repentance and forgiveness, is a much more complex matter than just a duplication of the expressed emotion of one in a sympathetic echo-emotion of the other—and indeed it may not even require sympathy on both parts. Some sort of knowing how the other feels that stops short of sympathetic fellow feeling may be all that is needed for these mutually responsive feelings—just as when the cello replies to the violin in a duo it need not first re-sound the violin's notes. When lovers forgive one another (or one the other) there need not first be felt sympathy with the other's repentance, simply familiarity with that feeling and recognition that this was an occasion for the other to feel it. When lovers laugh at each other's familiar endearing weaknesses—and lovers do laugh at the sorts of weakness that it would be offensive to draw attention to in a stranger—they need not each laugh at *hirself*.[24] Each laughs at the other, but neither need laugh *with* the other, finding lovably ridiculous what the other so finds. Otherwise love would entail self-love and "self, so self-loving, were iniquity."[25] We do not invite others to empathize or sympathize with our loving of our beloved,[26] and we do not expect it of the beloved either. "Love me, love my dog," "Love me, try to love my other loved ones," maybe. But not, or only for metaphysical poets, "Love me, love all my loved ones, and so love yourself." As Hume put it, "when we talk of *self-love*, 'tis not in a proper sense, nor has the sensation it produces any thing in common with that tender emotion, which is excited by a friend or mistress."[27] Hume may be optimistically ignoring narcissists who do feel tenderly about themselves, but surely he is right that love proper is for another, and what we hope for is that the other *reciprocates*, rather than sympathizes with, our love. So we can find tender amusement in our loved ones' harmless faults without wanting them to be tenderly amused at themselves. Lovers clown for each other or are willing to be cast as clowns, but clowns are not expected to be amused at their own antics. The capacity to laugh at oneself which we welcome in each other is not exactly a capacity to find oneself an amusing spectacle. As it is bad form to laugh at one's own jokes, so it is at least dubious form, incurring risk of a charge of narcissism, to laugh with real amusement at oneself, even on those occasions when one welcomes a lover's amusement. If one laughs with one's lover at oneself and one's defects, it should be untenderly, "against that time (if ever that time come) when I shall see thee frown on my defects."[28] To love is to give another the permission to laugh at one, one hopes tenderly, when no one else, not even oneself, has quite that same permission. One of the risks of love, as Kant rightly saw, was that the permitted laughter may lose its tenderness, may take on more of the tough, unamused, almost sardonic character it is supposed to have when we are sometimes urged by character-improvers to see how ridiculously we are acting and reacting, to do a bit of unfriendly jeering at ourselves. Love complicates the occasions for laughter as greatly as it complicates the occasion for anger, for curiosity, for disappointment, for shame at failure, for sorrow. It adds to the varieties of all of these, and so to the degree of delicacy needed for showing the right variety on the right occasion.

Love is not just an emotion people feel toward other people but also a complex tying together of the emotions that two or a few more people have; it is a special form of emotional interdependence.[29] That love involves some sort of tie, relationship, attachment, is a commonplace. Both the theological and the biological accounts relate love the felt emotion to some sort of more-than-emotional tie between persons. For the Christian tradition it is the creator-creature tie which *grounds* love of God, which is a feeling endorsing that ontological attachment. For Descartes felt love is a will to be or to remain attached in a strong ontological way with a more perfect being. For Hume, Darwin, and after them Freud, one form of felt love, the fundamental form, is grounded in the human child's past, literally physical, tie to a maternal parent, and hers to the child, and other forms of felt love create an actual dependency, at least of emotions and occasions for emotions, which goes beyond any that is "willed" by the lover. The fact of the attachment grounds the feeling of attachment and may exceed the desire for attachment. Love the emotion is not the wish for a relationship, it is the acknowledgment and endorsement of one. Love the tie is not produced by our feelings of love, it is what is endorsed and sustained by them. We may have no say in the coming into existence of the tie—children do not choose their mother, nor she them. Adolescent and adult love is something we are said to "fall" into (and out of), something that happens to us. There may always be some choice about sustaining it, but not always about initiating it. As Richard Wollheim says, we choose our friends, make friendships, but "love . . . is a response . . . to a felt relation,"[30] and one we may have had no say at all about initiating.

It may be objected that this may make sense for mother-infant love, but less good sense for mature sexual love. Surely we *do* initiate sexual relationships (these days it had better be the woman who does the proposing, the man the accepting or refusing). Yes, but as Hume pointed out, sexual desire, or "the appetite for generation," is only *one* component of "the amorous passion." The "felt relation" to which sexual love is a response is not just the temporary and voluntarily entered-into "relation" of sexual intercourse. A one-night stand is not the sort of relation whose acknowledgment and endorsement would count as love; otherwise gigolos and other prostitutes would count as lovers. The "relationship" that, when felt and positively responded to, is sexual love, is a mutual involvement that is physical, emotional, cognitive, and conative—it is mutual dependency in pleasures, in hopes, in griefs, in intentions for the future. This is not to say that it must be for a very long future—there are "brief loves" that are from the start known to the lovers as likely to be brief. But they are not mere agreements for mutual erotic services for a limited time. (Kant notoriously took marriage to involve such a mutual agreement, for life.) Where people do "use each other" for erotic pleasure, without any other mutual dependency, there all the current advice about "safe sex" will be appropriate, especially as these pleasure seekers will often welcome the contraceptive "protection" these health-protecting measures will also bring. But will *lovers* want safe sex? Their unsafe sex may be a fitting expression of their in any case unsafe love. Risking their own health is something lovers have always done. Think of all the women who died in childbirth, and who in loving knew quite well the chances that they would so die. Think of the venereal and other diseases that spouses got from one another and passed on to their children. Our loved ones inherit from us, and sometimes inherit our diseases. Of course a lover will, if she lovingly can, avoid "communicating" any disease to her loved one and to her child, but if it takes withdrawal from the love relation to do that, then she will not have opted for "safe loving," however "safe" her sexual and other practices.

It is not very "safe" to love another. If safety is what one values most, the womb or the grave is the best place for one, and, between the two, one will want the best approximations one can get to these places where one is sheltered from or beyond hurt. One will opt for places where one cannot respond emotionally to the emotions and other states of mind of others, cannot be pleased by their pleasure, disappointed at their lack of pleasure, hurt by their indifference, angry at their failure to be angered by insults, saddened by their choice to withdraw rather than forgivably harm, and so on. There is no safe love.

Should we therefore avoid love? We should of course do what we can to "protect third parties," and in love there are always third parties, future lovers, children who may be born to one of the lovers, their lovers and their children. Love tends to be generative and cannot be confined to romantic Romeo and Juliet couplings. The mutual love of couples like Romeo and Juliet is not secure from the generations before them, nor are later generations secure from their love. So of course some sort of "third- (or fourth- or fifth-) party insurance" is incumbent on lovers, and they will want health for the children of their love, but neither venereal nor any other kind of safety is something they can promise each other, their future children, or other persons affected or infected by their love. If all the world (except misamorist philosophers) is to keep loving lovers, it will have to come to accept risk too, and to be willing to share the risk, and to help care for the victims of the worst risks.

Only in the theological tradition has love ever been thought of as life-prolonging for the human lover, as a measure against mortality. On a biological view, mortality and natality go together, setting the framework for human love. Human love sometimes generates new lives, and it has generated some great sonnets. It typically tries to sustain the flourishing life of loved ones, and it makes memorials for dead loved ones, but it does not aim to lengthen the lover's life. Risk of earlier death because of their love is a risk lovers always had to be willing to run, and still must (just as seafarers risk shipwreck, promiscuous seekers of sexual pleasure risk venereal diseases, city dwellers risk air pollution, and citizens risk being involved in their nations' wars). Women were once taught to accept the risk of dying in childbed as a risk that went with their honorable station as loving wives, as prostitutes and their customers accepted the risk of an early death from venereal disease contracted from their less honorable (and contractual) activities, and as all able-bodied men were taught to accept the risk of dying on the battlefield as an occupational risk that went with their honorable station as protective males. There were always of course some civilian deaths in wars, some virtuous wives whose marriage settlement from their husbands included venereal disease, and many children who were bequeathed their parents' diseases. (No men died in childbirth.) Now the risks are less concentrated on special groups. Death in childbed is not so frequent, and the other threats are fairly widely spread. We all, not just male militants, now have to accept the risk of dying in the quarrels our motherlands and fatherlands get into. The main health risk in loving lies now not in childbed but in other painful beds. This risk is not so high for "true lovers" as for mere promiscuous pleasure seekers, but is not negligible. Love is now as risky to the health for all of us as it has always been for women. Now all is fairly fair in love and war, with no more special exemptions.

Most of us believe we should do what we can to reduce the chances of war, especially as we have little reason to hope to be able to confine the risks of unprevented war to a limited population of professional militants. Should we do what we can to reduce the chances of love, given that its risks are also hard to confine? We surely should do what we can to reduce those health risks, but to try to confine them by attempted quarantine would be to restrict love, to outlaw some loving relationships, as some feminists want to morally outlaw love of men, the ones whose forefathers so long oppressed women, infected women, exploited women, and wore them out bearing children to carry on their father's name. Such responses to the risks of love amount to a retreat from generative love, a retreat which, carried to its extreme, would be an attempt to be a monad, to withdraw into safe solitude, into solitary vice. We need neither fear nor expect many to respond this way—as Brown says, love is something some form of which we cannot do without. And as Wollheim says, love is a response to a felt relationship between oneself and another or others, a relationship we find there to be responded to. Both the relations of interdependency and our responses to them, when we will their continuation, are fraught with risks—risks of mutual maiming, of loss and heartbreak, of domination, of betrayal, of boredom, of strange fashions of forsaking, of special forms of disease and of disgrace. But these same relations are also big with the promise of strengths united,[31] of new enthusiasms, of special joys, of easy ungloved intimacy, of generous givings and forgivings, of surprising forms of grace. And as in justice, so in love, it may be impossible to separate the good from the ill.[32]

I said at the start that philosophers have a bad track record when they talk about love, and my own discourse seems to have become a sermon. My sermon secularizes and naturalizes a very old story. My endorsement of the "biological" approach of Hume, Darwin, and some Freudians seems to bring me to a perhaps surprising agreement with the natural law tradition that they had little time for, agreement in putting generative love, and love of progenitors and of progeny, at the center of the cluster of kinds of love. It makes a difference, however, when we drop not just the theology but the patriarchal bias of that version of love. Just how much of a difference this will make we are still finding out. Experiments in loving, in love without domination, are a feature of our time. They may succeed not just in eliminating the special sort of domination that contaminated love in its patriarchal and phallocentric versions but in reducing the danger of any sort of domination in love. Yet even without domination there will still be some power play, for that seems to be essential to the play we all enjoy. Sometimes the play will turn vicious, sometimes the love will go sour. Those are risks we lovers run. Even if some loves are unlucky loves, some loves false loves, still,

> The water is wide, I cannot get o'er,
> And neither have I wings to fly;
> Give me a boat, that can carry two;
> And both will row, my love and I.

four

HUME,
THE WOMEN'S
MORAL THEORIST?

In his brief autobiography, David Hume tells us that "as I took particular pleasure in the company of modest women, I had no reason to be displeased with the reception I met with from them." This double-edged remark is typical of Hume's references to women. Suggesting as it does that what pleased Hume was the women's pleasure in his pleasure in *their* company, it both diminishes the significance of their welcome to him, since "whoever can find the means either by his services, his beauty, or his flattery to render himself useful or agreeable to us, is sure of our affections,"[1] and makes us wonder about the sources of his particular pleasure in their company. Pleasure in the ample returns he got for a little flattery? Yet his flattery of women in his writings is itself double-edged, as much insult as appreciation. Women's "insinuation, charm and address," he tells us, in the section on justice in his *Enquiry Concerning the Principles of Morals,* will enable them to break up any incipient male conspiracy against them. His archness of tone in "Of Love and Marriage" and his patronizing encouragement of the greater intellectual effort of reading history instead of romances in "Of the Study of History" were reason enough for him to suppress those two essays (as he did, but for unclear reasons, and along with the more interesting and more radical "Of Moral Prejudices," in which he describes a man who is totally dependent, emotionally, on his wife and daughter, and a woman who makes herself minimally dependent on the chosen father of her child).[2] It is not surprising that despite his popularity with the women, modest and less modest, who knew him, his writings have not met with a very positive reception from contemporary feminists. They fix on his references to the "fair" and the "weak and pious" sex and on his defense in the essay "The Rise and Progress of the Arts and Sciences" of the claim that male gallantry is as natural a virtue as respect for one's elders, both being ways of generously allaying others' well-founded sense of inferiority or infirmity: "As nature has given *man* the strength above *women,* by endowing him with greater strength both of mind and body, it is his part to alleviate that superiority, as much as possible, by a studied deference and complaisance for all her inclinations and opinions." Hume's "polite" displays of concern for the sex that he saw to be weaker in mind and body are not likely to encourage feminists to turn to him for moral inspiration any more than Kant's exclusion, in the *Metaphysical Elements of Justice,* §46, of all women from the class of those with "civil personality," fit to vote, will encourage them to look to him.

My main concern here is not with feminism, however, but with the implications, for ethics and ethical theory, of Carol Gilligan's findings about differences between males and females both in moral development and in mature versions of morality. Whether those differences reflect women's weakness, their natural inferiority to men in mind and body, or their social inferiority, or their superiority, is not my central concern. I am focusing here on the concept of morality many women have and the sort of experience, growth, and reflection on it that leads them to develop it. My interest in a moral theory like Hume's in this context, then, is primarily with the extent to which the version of morality he works out squares or does not square with women's moral wisdom. Should the main lines of his account prove to be true to morality as women conceive of it, then it will be an ironic historical detail if he showed less respect than we would have liked for those of his fellow persons who were most likely to find his moral theory in line with their own insights. And whatever the root causes of women's moral outlook, of the tendency of the care perspective to dominate over the justice perspective in their moral deliberations, now that we have, more or less, social equality with men, women's moral sense should be made as explicit as men's moral sense and as influential in structuring our practices and institutions.

One way, not of course the only or the best way, to help make it explicit is to measure the influential men's moral theories against it. That is what I propose to do with Hume's theory. This can be seen as a prolegomenon to making wise women's theories influential. Then, once I have examined Hume's theory and its fit or misfit with women's moral wisdom, I shall briefly return to the question of how his own attitude toward women relates to his moral theory.

As every student of the history of philosophy knows, Hume was the philosopher Kant set out to "answer," and both Kant's theory of knowledge and his ethics stand in significant contrast to Hume's. And Kant's views, through their influence on Jean Piaget and John Rawls, are the views which are expressed in Lawrence Kohlberg's version of moral maturity and the development leading to it, the version which Gilligan found not to apply to girls and women as well as it did to boys and men. We may wonder, therefore, whether other non-Kantian strands in Western ethics, as developed in the philosophical tradition, might prove less difficult to get into reflective equilibrium with women's (not specifically philosophical) moral wisdom than the Kantian strand. For there certainly is no agreement that Kant and his followers represent the culmination of all the moral wisdom of our philosophical tradition. Alasdair MacIntyre's attacks on the Kantian tradition and all the controversy caused by attempts to implement in high schools the Kohlberg views about moral education have shown that not all men, let alone all women, are in agreement with the Kantians. Since the philosopher Kant was most notoriously in disagreement with was Hume, it is natural to ask, after Gilligan's work, whether Hume is more of a women's moral theorist than is Kant. We might do the same with Aristotle, Hegel, Marx, Mill, MacIntyre, with all those theorists who have important disagreements with Kant, but a start can be made with Hume.

He is inviting, for this purpose, in part because he did try to attend, for better or worse, to male-female differences and in his life did, it seems, listen to women; and also because he is close enough in time, in culture, and in some presuppositions to Kant for the comparison of their moral theories to hold out the same hope of the reconciliation that Gilligan in *In a Different Voice* wanted to get between men's and women's moral insights. There are important areas of agreement as well as of disagreement or difference of emphasis. I should add two more personal reasons for selecting Hume—I find his moral theory wise and profound, and I once, some years ago, in an introductory ethics course where we had read a little Aristotle, Aquinas, Hume, Kant, Mill, then Rawls and Kohlberg, had my students try to work out what each of our great moral theorists would have said in answer to Kohlberg's test question about whether Heinz should steal the drug which he cannot afford to buy and which might save his dangerously ill wife.[3] By hypothesizing how each philosopher would answer that question, and support his answer, we tried to measure *their* stage of moral development by the Kohlberg method.[4] Hume seemed to check out at as merely second level, stage three, with some stage four features, just as did most of Gilligan's mature women. So I have, since then, thought of Hume as a second "conventional" level challenger of Kohlberg's claims about the superiority of the third postconventional level over the second, or as an exemplar of a fourth level, gathering up and reconciling what was valuable and worth preserving in both the conventional and the postconventional Kohlberg levels—a fourth level which we could call "civilized," a favorite Humean term of approbation. For this reason, when I read Gilligan's findings that mature, apparently intelligent and reflective women "reverted" to Kohlberg's stage three (lower stage of level two, the conventional level), my immediate thought was "perhaps we women tend to be Humeans rather than Kantians."

I shall list some striking differences between Kant's and Hume's moral theories, as I understand them, then relate these to the differences Gilligan found between men's and women's conceptions of morality.

First, Hume's ethics, unlike Kant's, make morality a matter not of obedience to universal law but of cultivating the character traits which give a person "inward peace of mind, consciousness of integrity" (E., p. 283) and at the same time make that person good company to other persons. Hume uses "company" in a variety of senses, ranging from the relatively impersonal and "remote" togetherness of fellow citizens, to the more selective but still fairly remote relations of parties to a contract, to the closer ties among friends, family members, lovers. To become a good fellow-person one doesn't consult some book of rules; one cultivates one's capacity for sympathy, or fellow feeling, and also stands ready to use one's judgment when conflicts arise among the different demands that such sympathy may lead us to feel. Hume's ethics requires us to be able to be rule followers in some contexts, but does not reduce morality to rule following. Corrected (sometimes rule-corrected) sympathy, not law-discerning reason, is the fundamental moral capacity.

Second, Hume differs from Kant regarding the source of the general rules he does recognize as morally binding—the rules of justice. Where Kant sees human reason as the sole author of these moral rules, and sees them as universal, Hume sees them as authored by self-interest, instrumental reason, custom and tradition, and rationally "frivolous" factors such as historical chance and human fancy and what it selects as salient. He sees these rules, such as property rules, not as universal but as varying from community to community and as changeable by human will as conditions, needs, wishes, or human fancies change. His theory of social "artifice," and his account of justice as obedience to the rules of these social artifices, formed by "convention" and subject to historical variation and change, stands in stark opposition to rationalist accounts, such as Aquinas's and Kant's, of justice as obedience to laws of pure practical reason, valid for all people at all times and places. Hume has a historicist and conventionalist account of the moral rules which we find ourselves expected to obey and which, on reflection, we usually see it to be sensible for us to obey, despite their elements of arbitrariness and despite the inequalities their working usually produces. He believes it is sensible for us to conform to those rules of our group which specify obligations and rights, as long as these do redirect the dangerous destructive workings of self-interest into more mutually advantageous channels, thereby giving all the "infinite advantages" of increased force, ability, and security (compared with what we would have in the absence of any such rules), although some may receive *more* benefits of a given sort, say, wealth or authority, than others, under the scheme we find ourselves in. So Hume's ethics seems to lack any appeal to the universal principles of Kohlberg's "higher" stages. The moral and critical stance Hume encourages us to adopt toward, say, the property rules of our society, before seeing the rights which those rules recognize as *moral* rights, comes not from our ability to test them by higher, more general rules but from our capacity for sympathy, from our ability to recognize and share sympathetically the reactions of others to that system of rights, to communicate feelings and understand what our fellows are feeling, and so to realize what resentments and satisfactions the present social scheme generates. Self-interest and the capacity to sympathize with the self-interested reactions of others, plus the rational, imaginative, and inventive ability to think about the likely human consequences of any change in the scheme, rather than an acquaintance with a higher law, are what a Humean appeals to at the postconventional stage.

This difference from Kantian views about the role of general principles in grounding moral obligations goes along in Hume with a downplaying of the role of reason and a playing up of the role of feeling in moral judgment. Agreeing with the rationalists that when we use our reason we all appeal to universal rules (the rules of arithmetic, or of logic, or of causal inference) and failing to find any such universal rules of morality, as well as failing to see how, even if we found them, they should be able, alone, to *motivate* us to act as they tell us to act, he claims that morality rests ultimately on sentiment. This is a special motivating feeling we come to have once we have exercised our capacity for sympathy with others' feelings and also learned to overcome the emotional conflicts which arise in a sympathetic person when the wants of different fellow persons clash, or when one's own wants clash with those of one's fellows. Morality, on Hume's account, is the outcome of a search for ways of eliminating contradictions in the "passions" of sympathetic persons who are aware of both their own and their fellows' desires and needs, including emotional needs. Any moral progress or development a person undergoes will be, for Hume, a matter of "the correction of sentiment," where what corrects it will be contrary sentiments plus the cognitive-cum-passionate drive to minimize conflict both between and within persons. Reason and logic are indispensable "slaves" to the passions in this achievement, because reason enables us to think clearly about consequences or likely consequences of alternative actions, to foresee outcomes and avoid self-defeating policies. But "the ultimate ends of human actions can never, in any case, be accounted for by *reason,* but recommend themselves entirely to the sentiments and affections of mankind, without any dependance upon intellectual faculties" (*E.,* p. 293). A lover of conflict will have no reason, since he will have no motive, to cultivate the moral sentiment, nor will that man of "cold insensibility" who is "unaffected with the images of human happiness or misery" (*E.*, p. 225). A human heart, as well as human reason, is needed for the understanding of morality, and the heart's responses are to particular persons, not to universal principles of abstract justice. Such immediate responses may be corrected by general rules (as they will be when justice demands that the good poor man's debt to the less good miser be paid) and by more reflective feeling responses, such as dismay and foreboding at unwisely given love and trust or disapproval of excessive parental indulgence. But what controls and regulates feeling will be a wider web of feelings, which reason helps us apprehend and understand, not any reason holding authority over all feelings.

The third point to note is that Hume's version of what a typical human heart desires is significantly different from that of both egoists and individualists. The "interested passion," or self-interest, plays an important role, but so do sympathy and concern for others. Even where self-interest is of most importance in his theory, in his account of justice, it is the self-interest of those with fairly fluid ego boundaries, namely, family members, concerned with "acquiring goods and possessions for ourselves and our nearest friends" (*T.*, pp. 491–492). This is the troublesome passion that needs to be redirected by agreed rules, whereby it can control itself so as to avoid socially destructive conflict over scarce goods. Its self-control, in a society-wide cooperative scheme which establishes property rights, is possible because the persons involved in it have already learned, in the family, the advantages that can come both from self-control and from cooperation (*T.*, p. 486). Had the rough corners of "untoward" and uncontrolled passions, selfish or unselfish, not been already rubbed off by growing up under some parental discipline, and were there no minimally sociable human passions such as love between man and woman, love of parents for their children, love of friends, sisters, and brothers, the Humean artifice of justice could not be constructed. Its very possibility as an artificial virtue depends upon human nature's containing the natural passions, which make family life natural for human beings, which make parental solicitude, grateful response to that, and the restricted cooperation thereby resulting, phenomena that do not need to be contrived by artifice. At the very heart of Hume's moral theory lies his celebration of family life and of parental love. Justice, the chief artificial virtue, is the offspring of family cooperativeness and inventive self-interested reason, which sees how such a mutually beneficial cooperative scheme might be extended. And when Hume lists the natural moral virtues, those not consisting in obedience to agreed rules and doing good even if not generally possessed, his favorite example is parental love and solicitude. The good person, the possessor of the natural virtues, is the one who is "a safe companion, an easy friend, a gentle master, an agreeable husband, an indulgent father" (*T.*, p. 606). We may deplore that patriarchal combination of roles—master, husband, father—but we should also note the virtues these men are to display—gentleness, agreeability, indulgence. These were more traditionally expected from mistresses, wives, and mothers than from masters, husbands, and fathers. Of course they are not the only virtues Humean good characters show; there are also due pride, or self-esteem, and the proper ambition and courage that that may involve, as well as generosity, liberality, zeal, gratitude, compassion, patience, industry, perseverance, activity, vigilance, application, integrity, constancy, temperance, frugality, economy, resolution, good temper, charity, clemency, equity, honesty, truthfulness, fidelity, discretion, caution, presence of mind, "and a thousand more of the same kind" (*E.*, p. 243).

In Hume's frequent lists of virtues, two are conspicuous by their absence, or by the qualifications accompanying them, namely, the martial "virtues" and the monastic or puritan "virtues." Martial bravery and military glory can threaten "the sentiment of humanity" and lead to "infinite confusions and disorders . . . the devastation of provinces, the sack of cities" (*T.*, p. 601), so cool reflection leads the Humean moral judge to hesitate to approve of these traditionally masculine traits. The monastic virtues receive more forthright treatment. Celibacy, fasting, penance, mortification, self-denial, humility, silence, solitude "are everywhere rejected by men of sense, but because they serve to no manner of purpose . . . We observe, on the contrary, that they cross all these desirable ends, stupify the understanding and harden the heart, obscure the fancy and sour the temper" (*E.*, p. 270). Here speaks Hume the good companion, the one who enjoyed cooking for supper parties for his Edinburgh friends, the darling, or perhaps the intellectual mascot, of the pleasure-loving Parisian salons. Calvinist upbringing and the brief taste he had in youth of the military life seem to have left him convinced of the undesirability of such styles of life; and his study of history convinced him of the dangers for society both of religious dedication, "sacred zeal and rancor," and of military zeal and rancor. His list of virtues is a remarkably unaggressive, uncompetitive, one might almost say womanly list.

Although many of the virtues on his list are character traits that would show in a great range of contexts, most of those contexts are social contexts, involving relations to others, and many of them involve particular relationships such as parent-child, friend to friend, colleagues to each other, fellow conversationalists. Even when he tries to list virtues that are valued because they are useful and agreeable to their possessor rather than valued primarily for their contribution to the quality of life of the virtuous person's fellows, the qualities he lists are ones involving relations to others—the ability to get and keep the trust of others, sexual self-command and modesty as well as sexual promise, that is, the capacity to derive "so capital a pleasure in life" and to "communicate it" to another (*E.*, p. 245), temperance, patience, and sobriety, are virtues useful (long term) to their possessor; while among those he lists as immediately agreeable to their possessor are contagious serenity and cheerfulness, "a proper sense of what is due to one's self in society and the common intercourse of life" (*E.*, p. 253), friendliness and an avoidance of "perpetual wrangling, and scolding and mutual reproaches" (*E.*, p. 257), amorous adventurousness, at least in the young, liveliness of emotional response and expressive powers—all agreeable traits which presuppose that their possessor is in company with others, reacting to them and the object of their reactions. There may be problems in seeing how a person is to combine the various Humean virtues—to be frugal yet liberal, to be sufficiently chaste yet show amorous enterprise, to have a proper sense of what is due one yet avoid wrangling and reproaches. Hume may, indeed, be depending on a certain sexual division of moral labor, allocating chastity to the women and amorous initiative to the men, more self-assertion to the men and more avoidance of wrangling to the women, but we should not exaggerate the extent to which he did this.

The title page of Book Three of the *Treatise* invokes Lucan's words referring to the lover of difficult virtue, and Humean virtues may be difficult to unify. Only in some social structures, indeed, may they turn out to be a mutually compatible set. Some investigation, not only into what virtue is and what the true virtues are but into the social precondition of their joint exemplification, may be needed in the lover of difficult virtue. Indeed everything Hume says suggests that these are not independent enterprises. What counts as useful and agreeable virtues will depend in part on the social and economic conditions in which their possessors live, just as the acceptability of those social and economic conditions depends on what sort of virtues can flourish there and how they are distributed within the population. Hume points out that the usefulness of a trait such as a good memory will be more important in Cicero's society than in his own, given the lesser importance in the latter of making well-turned speeches without notes, and given the general encouraged reliance there on written records in most spheres of life. The availability, accessibility, and portability of memory substitutes will vary with the customs and the technological development of a society, and Hume is aware that such facts are relevant to the recognition of character traits as functional virtues. The ease of simulation or per-version of such traits will also affect the recognition of virtues—in an age when private ambition is easily masked as public spirit, or tax exemption as benevolence, the credit given to such easily pretended virtues may also understandably sink. The status of a character trait as a virtue need not be a fixed matter, but a matter complexly inter-related with the sort of society in which it appears. This makes good sense, if moral virtues are the qualities that enable one to play an acceptable part in an acceptable network of social roles, to relate to people in the variety of ways that a decent society will require, facili-tate, encourage, or merely permit.

The fourth point I want to stress in Hume's moral theory is that in his attention to various interpersonal relations, in which our Humean virtues or vices show, he does not give any special centrality to relationships between equals, let alone between autonomous equals. Because his analysis of social cooperation starts from cooper-ation within the family, relations between those who are necessarily unequals, parents and children, are at the center of the picture. He starts from a bond which he considers "the strongest and most indis-soluble bond in nature" (E., p. 240), "the strongest tie the mind is capable of" (T., p. 352), the love of parents for children, and in his moral theory he works out, as it were, from there. This relationship, and the obligations and virtues it involves, lacks three central fea-tures of relations between moral agents as understood by Kantians

60

and contractarians—it is intimate, it is unchosen, and it is between unequals. Of course the intimacy need not be "indissoluble," the inequality may be temporary, or later reversed, and the extent to which the initial relationship is unchosen will vary from that of unplanned or contrary-to-plan parenthood to intentional parenthood (although not intentional parenting of a given particular child) to that highest degree of voluntariness present when, faced with an actual newborn child, a decision is taken not to let it be adopted by others or, when a contrary decision is taken by the biological parent or parents, by the decision of adoptive parents to adopt such an already encountered child. Such fully chosen parenthood is rare, and the norm is for parents to *find themselves* with a given child, perhaps with any child at all, and for parental affection to attach itself fairly indiscriminately to its unselected objects. The contractarian model of morality as a matter of living up to self-chosen commitments gets into obvious trouble with the duties both of young children to their unchosen parents, to whom no binding commitments have been made, and of initially involuntary parents to their children. Hume has no problem with such unchosen moral ties, because he takes them as the paradigm moral ties, one's giving rise to moral obligations more self-evident than any obligation to keep contracts.

The last respect in which I wish to contrast Hume's moral philosophy with its more Kantian alternative is in his version of what problem morality is supposed to solve, what its point is. For Kantians and contractarians, the point is freedom; the main problem is how to achieve it, given that other freedom aspirants exist and that conflict between them is likely. The Rousseau-Kant solution is obedience to collectively agreed-to general law, where each freedom seeker can console himself with the thought that the legislative will he must obey is as much his own as it is anyone else's. For Hume, the problem of the coexistence of would-be unrestrained self-assertors is solved by the invention of social artifices and the recognition of the virtue of justice, namely, of conformity to the rules of such mutually advantageous artifices. But the problem morality solves is deeper; it is as much intrapersonal as interpersonal. It is the problem of contradiction, conflict, and instability in any one person's desires, over time, as well as conflict among persons. Morality, in theory, saves us from internally self-defeating drives as well as from self-defeating interpersonal conflict. Nor is it just an added extra to Hume's theory

61

that the moral point of view overcomes contradictions in our individual sentiments over time. ("Our situation, with regard to both persons and things, is in continual fluctuation; and a man, that lies at a distance from us, may, in a little time, become a familiar acquaintance" [*T.*, p. 581].) His whole account of our sentiments has made them intrinsically reactive to other persons' sentiments. Internal conflict in a sympathetic and reassurance-needing person will not be independent of conflicts among the various persons in his or her emotional world. "We can form no wish, which has not a reference to society. A perfect solitude is, perhaps, the greatest punishment we can suffer. Every pleasure languishes when enjoy'd a-part from company, and every pain becomes more cruel and intolerable. Whatever other passions we may be actuated by; pride, ambition, avarice, curiosity, revenge, or lust; the soul or animating principle of them all is sympathy; nor wou'd they have any force were we to abstract entirely from the thoughts and sentiments of others" (*T.*, p. 363).

I have drawn attention to the limited place of conformity to general rules in Hume's version of morality; to the historicist conventionalist account he gives of such rules; to his thesis that morality depends upon self-corrected sentiments, or passions, as much or more than it depends upon the reason that concurs with and serves those passions; to the nonindividualist, nonegoistic version of human passions he advances; to the essentially interpersonal or social nature of those passions which are approved as virtues; to the central role of the family, at least at its best, as an exemplar of the cooperation and interdependency morality preserves and extends; to the fact that moral cooperation, for him, includes cooperation in unchosen schemes, with unchosen partners, with unequal partners, in close intimate relations as well as distanced and more formal ones. And finally, I emphasized that the need for morality arises for Hume from conflicts within each person as well as from interpersonal conflict. It is a fairly straightforward matter to relate these points to at least some of the respects in which Gilligan found girls' and women's versions of morality to differ from men's.[5] Hume turns out to be uncannily womanly in his moral wisdom. "Since the reality of connection is experienced by women as given rather than as freely contracted, they arrive at an understanding of life that reflects the limits of autonomy and control" (*D.V.*, p. 172). Hume lived before autonomy became an obsession with moral and social philosophers, or, rather, he lived while Rousseau was making it their obsession, but his attack on contractarian doctrines of political obligation, his clear perception of the given-ness of interconnection in the family and beyond, his emphasis on our capacity to make others' joys and sorrows our own, on our need for a "seconding" of sentiments, and on the inescapable mutual vulnerability and mutual enrichment that the human psychology and the human condition, when thus understood, entail, make autonomy not even an ideal, for Hume. A certain sort of freedom, freedom of thought and expression, is an ideal, but to "live one's own life in one's own way" is not likely to be among the aims of persons whose every pleasure languishes when not shared and seconded by some other person or persons. "The concept of identity expands to include the experience of interconnection" (D.V., p. 173).

The women Gilligan studied saw morality as primarily a matter of responsibilities arising out of their attachment to others, often stemming from originally given rather than chosen relations. The men spoke more of their rights than of their responsibilities, and saw those rights as arising out of a freely accepted quasi-agreement between self-interested equals. Hume does in his account of justice have a place for quasi-agreement-based rights serving the long-run interests of those respecting them, but he also makes room for a host of responsibilities which presuppose no prior agreement or quasi-agreement to shoulder them. The responsibilities of parents are the paramount case of such duties of care, but he also includes cases of mutual care and duties of gratitude where "I do services to such persons as I love, and am particularly acquainted with, without any prospect of advantage; and they may make me a return in the same manner" (T., p. 521). Here there is no right to a return, merely the reasonable but unsecured trust that it will be forthcoming. (There may even be something of an either/or, duck-rabbit effect between his "artificial virtues," including justice, and his "natural virtues," including mercy and equity, in all those contexts where both seem to come in to play.)

Hume's conventionalism about the general rules we may have to obey to avoid injustice to one another has already been mentioned as dooming his theory of justice to mere "stage four" moral marks, if to get any critical appraisal of customary rules one must have moved on to social contracts or universal principles. Hume is a realist about the historical given-ness and inevitable arbitrariness of most of the general rules that there is any chance of our all observing. Like Gilligan's girls and women, he takes moral problems in concrete historical settings, where the past history as well as the realistic future prospects for a given group are seen as relevant to their moral predicaments and their solutions. Even the fairly abstract and ahistorical social artifices of the *Treatise* are given a quasi-historical setting, and they give way in the *Essays* and *History of England* to detailed looks at actual concrete social and moral predicaments, in full narrative depth.

For Kohlberg, the distrust of abstract ahistorical principles, the girls' need to fill out Kohlberg's puzzle questions with a story before answering them, led to the suspicion that this poor performance on the application of universal principles to sketchily drawn particular cases, shorn of full narrative context, showed that their "reason" was less well developed than the boys' (*D.V.*, p. 28). But the performance might rather have indicated, as it did in Hume's case, a conviction that this was a false model of how moral judgments are made. He endorses the emotional response to a fully realized situation as moral reflection at its best, not as one of its underdeveloped stages, and he mocks those rationalists who think abstract universal rules will ever show why, say, killing a parent is wrong for human beings but not for oak trees (*T.*, pp. 466–467).

At this point it may be asked whether Hume's account allows for any version of stages of moral development, whether it is not one of those "bag of virtues" accounts Kohlberg derides. Can one who thinks morality is a matter of the passions find room for any notion of individual moral progress or development? The answer is yes. Although he does not give us such a theory for the individual, Hume does speak of a "correction of sentiment" and of a "progress of sentiments," especially where "artificial" virtues are concerned. Since morality depends for him on a *reflective* sentiment, and on self-corrected self-interest and corrected sympathy, it is plain that more experience and more reflection could lead an individual through various "levels" of moral response. The interesting questions are those of what the outlines of such an alternative developmental pattern might be. Clearly this is not a matter that can be settled from a philosopher's armchair, and psychological research of the sort Gilligan is doing would be needed to find out how human passions do develop and which developments are seen as moral progress by those in whom they occur, and by others. Some features of women's development, features which would not necessarily show up on the Kohlberg tests, are indicated in the latter chapters of *In a Different Voice*. In the chapter "Concepts of Self and Morality" Gilligan describes transitions from self-centered thinking (which presumably is likely in women reacting to being let down by the fathers of the fetuses the women interviewed were considering aborting, rather than a natural starting point for a girl or woman) to a condemnation of such "selfishness" (or an alternation between "selfish" and "unselfish" impulses) to what is seen as a clearer perception of the "truth" concerning the human relations in which they are involved, leading perhaps to a cool or even ruthless determination to protect themselves from further hurt and exploitation, then later to a revised version of what counts as their own interests, to a realization that those interests require attachment to and concern for others (see especially *D.V.*, p. 74).

If alternatives to Kohlberg's rationalist scenario are to be worked out in detail, probably some guiding moral as well as psychological theory will be needed, as well as empirical tests. There will be a need for something to play a role like that which Rawls's and Kant's moral theory played in getting Kohlberg to look for certain particular moral achievements, and to expect some to presuppose other earlier ones. It might even be that, once we had a nonrationalist yet dynamic moral theory, and an expected developmental pattern accompanying it, empirical tests would show it to be true not merely of women but of men. The gender difference may be not in the actual pattern of development of passions, nor in our reasoning and reflection about the satisfaction of our passions, but merely in our intellectual opinions, as voiced in interviews, as to whether this is or is not *moral* development. For both Gilligan's and Kohlberg's tests have so far looked at verbally offered versions of morality, at intellectual reflection on morality, not at moral development itself, at motivational changes and changed emotional reactions to one's own and others' actions, reactions, and emotions. As I understand it, only in Gilligan's abortion study were people interviewed while actually in the process of making a moral decision—and those women may not have been a representative sample of women decision makers, since they were selected for their apparent indecisiveness, for what was judged their need to think and talk more about their decision. The clear-headed or at least the decisive women simply did not get into this study (*D.V.*, p. 3).

We should not equate a person's moral stance with her intellectual version of it, nor suppose that a person necessarily knows the relative strength of her own motives and emotions. To test people's emotional and motivational growth, we would need emotion and motive experiments, not thought experiments, and they can be tricky to design safely. Hume said, "When I am at a loss to know the effects of one body upon another in any situation, I need only put them in that situation and observe what results from it. But should I endeavour to clear up after the same manner any doubt in moral philosophy, by placing myself in the same case with that which I consider, 'tis evident this reflection and premeditation would so disturb the operation of my natural principles, as must render it impossible to form any just conclusion from the phaenomenon" (*T.*, p. xix). By moral philosophy, here, he means simply the investigation of human nature, in both its unreflective and its more reflective operations. Moral psychology, as he understands it, is indeed a matter of letting reflection and premeditation make a difference to the operation of natural motives and passions, so moral experiments, in the narrow sense of "moral," would not necessarily be contaminated by the reflection or self-consciousness that the self-experimentation would involve. Knowing that when we react in a given situation, what we are doing is being treated as a display of moral character, as a test of moral progress, might merely encourage that progress, not lead to its misrepresentation. But the "experiments" Hume is thinking of are real-life ones, not either our own, after-the-fact versions of them or our responses, intellectual or emotional, to merely imagined situations, in which one knows one is not really involved. Not only are these too thin and sketchy, as Gilligan's girls clearly felt in the story of Heinz and the expensive medicine, but even if a fully worked out fictional narrative were given—a whole novel, let us say—there is still no reason to think that one's response to a fictional situation is a good indicator of what one's own response would be, were one actually in a predicament like that of a novelist's character. Reading good novels and attending or acting in good plays may be the most harmless way to prepare oneself for real-life moral possibilities, but this isn't moral "practice." There is no harmless practicing of moral responses, no trial run or dress rehearsal. Children's play, the theater, novels, knowledge about and sympathy with friends' problems may all play a useful role in alerting us to the complexities of moral situations, but one's performance there is no reliable predictor of what one's response to one's own real-life problems will be. As Aristotle said, the only way to learn to be morally virtuous is to perform virtuous actions—real ones, not fantasy ones. And only from one's moral practice, not from one's fantasy moral practice or rationalized versions of past moral practice, can we learn the stage of moral development a person actually exhibits. As Hume said, it seems that only a cautious observation of human life, of "experiments" gleaned as they occur in the "common course of the world" in people's "behaviour in company, in affairs, and in their pleasures" (ibid.) can found any empirical science of moral development.

Let me repeat that I am not saying that knowledge that one is being observed is what would spoil the results of contrived moral "tests"; what would spoil them, rather, would be the knowledge that the tests are fantasy ones, not real-world ones. I do not want to deny that what one takes to be one's sincere beliefs about what morality demands, as they might be expressed in an interview with a psychologist or in a reaction to a fictional situation, have some connection with one's actual moral choices. But I agree with Gilligan in wondering how close the connection is, especially for reactions to sketched fictional situations. The old question "How can I know what I think until I see what I write?" can be adapted for moral convictions: "How can I know what I judge right until I see what decisions I make and how I then live with them?" But even that may be too optimistic about our ability to size up how we are living with our past decisions—we naturally tend either to avoid recognizing bad conscience or to exaggerate and self-dramatize it in our own follow-up reactions to a moral decision. We tend to interpret our own pasts deceptively, as possibly displaying tragedy or demonic wickedness, but not moral error, stupidity, or ordinary vice. We glaze our own pasts over with the pale cast of self-excusing or, in some cases, self-accusing, self-denigrating, self-dramatizing thought. I see no nonsuspect way, by interviewing people about other people's actual or hypothetical decisions or even about their own past actual ones, to gauge what are or were their *effective* moral beliefs.

I resume my exploration of what sort of pattern of development one might expect as experience of the common course of the world changes our passions as well as the thoughts that guide them when they motivate our actions. Two things that several of the Gilligan women *say* happened to them are that they developed a sense of their own competence to control their lives and affairs and that their attitudes toward selfishness and unselfishness underwent change. Clearly both these dimensions, of general competence at and confidence in responsible decision making and of understanding the relations between self-concerned and other-concerned passions, are ones along which one would expect change and variation, as experience deepens and opportunity widens. A child's opportunity for responsible decision making is small, and yet the child's experience of having to live with others' decisions, to react to inconsiderate decisions, or to be willing to discern, protest, understand, or forgive decisions by superiors which affect her badly is a vital preparation for later responsible decision making. The person who has forgotten what it was like to be the relatively powerless one, the decided-for and not the decision maker, is not going to be able even to anticipate the protests or grievances his or her own decisions produce, let alone be a wise or compassionate decision maker. So development along what we could call the sympathy and memory dimensions—development and enrichment of the ability to understand others' reactions—will be something one hopes will occur in normal development.

Recent studies by Judith A. Hall and Robert Rosenthal and their associates[6] have shown, interestingly enough, that women typically are better readers of other people's *nonverbal* communications of feelings (in facial expression, "body language," and tone of voice) than are men, and that women also are more easily read. It seems to make good evolutionary sense to suppose that there is an innate basis for such superiority, since women have been the ones who had both to communicate with infants and to interpret their communications before the child has learned a natural language. Not only may women's moral voice be different from men's and often unheard by men, but women's *tone* of voice and nonverbal expression may be subtler, more expressive, and understood more easily by other women than by men. Both in the Humean virtue of "ease of expression" and in facility in recognizing expressed feelings, women seem to outperform men.

The second dimension of expected change and development concerns the weight a person gives to the understood preferences of the various others involved in her decision, when she decides. How one sees their interests in relation to one's own will also change as experience grows. Even if infant egoism is where we all start, it seems to be infant egoism combined with infant trust in parents and with faith in the ease of communication of feelings. In parent-child and other intimate relations, Hume says, the other "communicates to us all the actions of his mind; makes us privy to his inmost sentiments and affections; and lets us see, in the very instant of their production, all the emotions, which are caus'd by any object" (*T.*, p. 353). Where we start, in infancy, seems to be in optimism about ease of mutual understanding, even without language, and about harmony in wills. What we may have to learn, by experience, is that conflict of wills is likely, that concealing one's feelings can be prudent, and that misunderstanding is frequent. Hume's own versions of childhood attitudes in, for example, the *Treatise,* Book Two, the section "Of the Love of Relations," show an incredibly strong and dominant memory or fantasy of such parent-child trusting and harmonious intimacy. Parents and children are seen to take pride in one another's achievements and successes, and not to compete with one another for eminence. "Nothing causes greater vanity than any shining quality in our relations" (*T.*, p. 338). But this idyll of shared interests, concerted wills, and shared pride or self-assertion must soon be interrupted by experience of what Hume calls "contrariety," and that "comparison" or competition which interferes with sympathy and cooperation. A most important dimension of the moral development one would look for on a Humean moral theory would be this one, the interplay of what he calls the opposed principles of sympathy and comparison. Although on his account sympathy is what morality chiefly depends upon, the opposed principle of comparison, a due sense of when our interests are or would be in conflict with those of others, and of what is then our due, also plays a not unimportant role in the generation of a sense of the virtue of justice, as he describes it. But the interpersonal problem to which various versions of morality give better or worse solutions, on Hume's account, is the problem of how to *minimize* opposition of interests, how to arrange life so that sympathy, not hostile comparison, will be the principle relating our desires to those of our fellows. Where, on the more contractarian model, morality regulates and arbitrates where interests are opposed, on a Humean view, as on Gilligan's girls', morality's main task is to rearrange situations so that interests are no longer so opposed.

There is, for Hume, an intimate interplay between the operation of sympathy and the sense of what are one's own interests. It may seem that only relative to some already fixed sense of which desires are and are not my own desires could I recognize any reaction of my own as sympathy with another's desires. But in fact, as Hume describes the workings of sympathy, they serve as much to determine, by outward expansion as well as by reinforcement of the inner core, what counts as "my interests." Since he believes that every human desire languishes unless it receives sympathetic reverberation from another (*T.*, p. 363), then unless someone sympathizes with my "selfish" pleasures they will not persist. But that another does so sympathize both makes that pleasure less purely selfish, more "fertile" for others, and also evokes in me a sympathy with the other's sympathy for me—a "double reverberation"—and a grateful willingness to sympathize with that one's pleasures, as long as sympathy is not drowned by comparison of our respective social statuses. Hence Hume can say that "it seems a happiness in the present theory that it enters not into that vulgar dispute concerning the *degrees* of benevolence or self-love, which prevail in human nature" (*E.*, p. 271).

Hume has a famously fluid concept of the self, and the fluid ego boundaries that allows work interestingly in his moral psychology. One could say that, on a Humean version of moral development, the main task is to work to a version of oneself and one's own interests which both maximizes the richness of one's potential satisfactions and minimizes the likely opposition one will encounter between one's own and others' partially overlapping interests. This is both an individual and a social task—a matter of the social "artifices" which divide work so as to increase, not decrease, the real ability of all workers, which conjoin forces so that not just the collective power but each person's power is augmented, and which arrange that "by mutual succour we are less expos'd to fortune and accidents" (*T.*, p. 485). The additional force, ability, and security which acceptable social institutions provide, he later says, must be a "system of actions concurr'd in by the whole society, . . . infinitely advantageous to the whole and to every part" (*T.*, p. 498). This may seem an absurdly high demand to make, one which no set of social institutions has yet met. But if we remember those endless added satisfactions which sympathetic enlargement of self-interest can bring to Humean persons, then we can see that a set of institutions that really did prevent oppositions of interest might indeed bring "infinite" or at least indeterminately great increase of power of enjoyment (such as that he described at *T.*, p. 365). Whether these increased satisfactions in fact come about will depend not just on the nature of the institutions but on the individuals whose lives are structured by them—"a creature absolutely malicious and spiteful" or even a man of "cold insensibility or narrow selfishness" (*E.*, pp. 225–226) will not receive infinite advantages from even the best institutions. Hume, perhaps overoptimistically, thinks that given halfway decent institutions and customs of upbringing, these nasty creatures will be "fancied monsters" (*E.*, p. 235), not real possibilities (he excuses Nero's actions by citing his grounds for fear, Timon's by his "affected spleen").

One dimension of moral development, then, for a Humean version of morality, will be change in the concept of one's own interest. "I esteem the man whose self-love, by whatever means, is so directed as to give him a concern for others, and to render him serviceable to society" (*E.*, p. 297). But equally important, and perhaps slower to develop in women in our society, is a realistic sense of whether or not one's agreeable moral virtues are being exploited by others, whether or not there is any "confederacy" of the more narrowly selfish and of the sensible knaves, free-riding on the apron strings of those whose generous virtues they praise and encourage but do not envy or emulate. Due pride is a Humean virtue, and one cannot be proud of tolerating exploitation. Still, a realistic appraisal of the relative costs and benefits of cooperative schemes to their various participants and an unwillingness to tolerate second-class status require a realistic estimate of just how much real gain the "narrowly selfish" get from their exploitation of others' more generous other-including self-love. By Hume's accounting, the sensible knaves and the narrowly selfish don't do better than their victims—they are "the greatest dupes." The very worst thing the exploited can do to improve their situation is to try to imitate the psychology of their exploiters. The hard art is to monitor the justice of social schemes, to keep an eye on one's rights and one's group's rights, without thereby contracting one's proper self-love into narrow selfishness in its "moralized" version—into insistence on one's rights, even when one gains nothing, and others lose, by one's getting them. A sense of what is due one can easily degenerate into that *amour propre* which is the enemy of the sort of extended sociable and friendly *amour-de-soi* which Hume, like Rousseau, sees as the moral ideal for human beings.

Will there be anything like Kohlberg's level-difference in the moral development of Humean passions, if we see this as a change in concepts of self in relation to others, in our capacity to understand facts about likely and actual conflicts, and in our capacity to sympathize with others' reactions, developed through experience and maturation? For Hume a defining feature of a moral response is that it be a response to a response—that it be a matter of a "reflexion," that it be a sentiment directed on sentiments. One can postulate a fairly clear difference between levels of "reflection," parallel to Kohlberg's jumps in critical ability, if one distinguishes the mere ability to sympathize (and to react negatively to others' feelings) which young children show, a sort of proto-moral response, from that more legitimized version of it which comes when we sympathize with others as right-holders in some conventional scheme and sympathize with their resentments at insult or injury (a level two response), achieving a sort of officially "seconded" sympathy, comparison, sense of self, and recognition of recognized conflicts of interest. One would reserve the title of really moral response to the reflexive turning of these capacities for sympathy, for self-definition, and for conflict recognition onto themselves, to see if they can "bear their own survey." Doing this would involve the sympathetic comparative evaluation of different styles of self-definition, styles of watching for and managing conflicts, of inhibiting or cultivating sympathy. The Humean concept of "reflexion" performs the same sort of job as Kantian reason—it separates the mature and morally critical from the mere conformers. A moral theory which developed Gilligan's women's moral strengths could make good use of Hume's concept of reflection.

I end with a brief return to the question of how this wise moral theory of Hume's could allow its author to make the apparently sexist remarks he did. Now, I think, we are in a position to see how harmless they might be, a display of his social realism, his unwillingness to idealize the actual. Women in his society *were* inferior in bodily strength and in intellectual achievement. Neither of these, however, for someone who believes that reason should be the slave of reflective and moralized passions, is the capacity that matters most. What matters most, for judging moral wisdom, are corrected sentiments, imagination, and cooperative genius. There Hume never judges women inferior. He does call them the "timorous and pious" sex, and that is for him a criticism, but since he ties both of these characteristics with powerlessness, his diagnoses here are of a piece with his more direct discussions of how much power women have. In those discussions he is at pains not just to try to point out the subordination of their interests to those of men in the existing institutions (marriage in particular) but also to show women where their power lies, should they want to change the situation.

As he points out, a concern for "the propagation of our kind" is a normal concern of men and women, but each of us needs the cooperation of a member of the other sex to further this concern, and "a trivial and anatomical observation" (*T.,* p. 571) shows us that no man can know that his kind has been propagated unless he can trust some woman either to be sexually "faithful" to him or to keep track of and tell him the truth about the paternity of any child she bears. This gives women great, perhaps dangerously great, threat advantage in any contest with men, a power very different from any accompanying the "insinuation, address and charms" (*E.,* p. 191) that Hume had invoked as sufficient to break any confederacy against them. The non-self-sufficiency of persons in reproductive respects that he goes on in the next paragraphs to emphasize, and the need of the male for a trustworthy female in order to satisfy his postulated desire for offspring he can recognize as his (a desire Hume had emphasized in the *Treatise* section "Of Chastity and Modesty"), put some needed iron into the gloved hands of the fair and charming sex. Hume gives many descriptions in his *History* and *Essays* of strong independent women, and he dwells on the question of whether the cost of their iron wills and their independence is a loss of the very moral virtues he admires in anyone but finds more often in women than in men—the "soft" nonmartial compassionate virtues. Need women, in ceasing to be timorous and servile, cease also to be experts at care and mutual care? His moral tale of a liberated woman who chooses to be a single mother (in "Of Moral Prejudices") suggests not—that avoidance of servile dependence on men can be combined with the virtues of caring and bearing responsibility, that pride and at least some forms of love can be combined.

POSTSCRIPT

Like Essay 1, this essay was written before Carol Gilligan had clarified and slightly revised her views about women and the care perspective. Indeed this essay was written for the conference at which Gilligan made the clarification.[7]

I now find a slight distortion or oversimplification of Hume's views at one place (p. 58) in this essay. I would not now say that his characterization of the "good" person as "a safe companion, an easy friend, a gentle master, an agreeable husband, an indulgent father" is intended to summarize the person with all or even the most important natural virtues, but merely to characterize the person who has that subset of them which confers moral "goodness," as distinct from moral "greatness" and moral "ability." Hume, as I go on to say here, recognizes a great variety of natural virtues, and he subdivides them in various ways. One way is by varying the narrowness and width of the circle of others with whom the moral judge must sympathize, in order to judge the impact of the character trait on its possessor's fellows. Gentleness typically affects those in the "narrow circle" of family, friends, and workmates. But the general's courage and the diplomat's wisdom may affect very wide circles. These traits therefore have a special moral "importance and weight" (T., p. 613). Hume writes that some natural virtues make their possessor amiable while others make her estimable (T., p. 608). "Goodness" tends to be a term reserved by him for those virtues which make their possessor lovable rather than estimable, qualities which favorably affect the narrow circle around her rather than affecting the "great confederacy of mankind."

This point of Hume's linguistic usage is of interest primarily to Hume interpreters rather than to moral philosophers more generally. It does, however, raise a deeper question concerning just how we can be sure how widely the effects of a given character trait spread their beneficial or baneful influence. The gentle parent may not influence the fate of empires in his lifetime in the way that the great national leader does, but the gentle parent may influence not only his children but also his children's children, just as the violent parent tends to bring about the replication of his own vices in his victims. Hume notes the special degree of shame which attaches to diseases that "affect others," for instance, any venereal disease that "goes to Posterity" (T., p. 303). Most of the natural vices which prevent a person from being "good," in Hume's sense, are ones that may well "go to posterity," and so do have weight and moment. The line between the "great" and the "good," the estimable and the amiable, may be difficult to draw. The "narrow circle," over several generations, can widen out quite dramatically.

My usage of the term "natural vices" may be un-Humean, since Hume requires of a natural virtue that it be the norm, not the exception, in a human population (T., p. 483). All the vices which are opposed to these virtues therefore become in one sense "unnatural." I have discussed elsewhere some of the problems that this makes for Hume.[8]

five

HUME, THE REFLECTIVE WOMEN'S EPISTEMOLOGIST?

We cannot reasonably expect, that a piece of
woollen cloth will be wrought to perfection
in a nation, which is ignorant of astronomy,
or where ethics are neglected.

David Hume, "Of Refinement in the Arts"

Recent feminist work in epistemology has emphasized some themes that I find also in Hume's writings on epistemology, when these are taken to include not just Book One of the *Treatise* and *An Enquiry Concerning Human Understanding* but his claims, in his "ethical" writings, about natural abilities and their relative importance, and the contents of several of his essays as well as passages throughout his *History of England* (especially its Appendices), where his concern is with the difference between relatively "ignorant" and barbaric societies and those more civilized societies in which the arts and sciences have made some progress. I find what might be called a social and cultural epistemology explored there, one which should be of interest to feminists. Of course women can be and are becoming their own epistemologists, and do not need to turn to kindly avuncular figures like Hume for suggestions or for confirmation of their own views. Nor need women agree with one another in their epistemological views. Many will dismiss my fondness for Hume's writings as a sure indicator of my failure to transcend my philosophical upbringing in a patriarchal tradition. Still, the very emphases that some women epistemologists, such as Lorraine Code,[1] place on the cooperative nature of our search for reliable beliefs and on our shared responsibility for successes and for failures should incline us toward a willingness to get helpful support from any well-meaning fellow worker, alive or dead, woman or man. (My Oxford teacher,

J. L. Austin, practiced as well as preached cooperative investigations in philosophy, albeit ones with a strong leader in charge.) To dismiss, as hopelessly contaminated, all recorded thoughts of all dead white males, to commit their works to the flames, could be a self-defeating move. At the very least we should, as Hume advocated, examine each work we are tempted to burn to see if it does contain anything that is more worth saving than patriarchal metaphysics.

Hume is usually labeled an empiricist, and he does talk a lot about what experience alone can teach us. For him this instructive experience consists in the first place in repeated pairings in a succession of lively "impressions," preserved in idea copies. It includes not merely what our senses reveal but also what our passions and their typical *expression* show us. We know from experience what makes us and others angry, and we come to know whose anger we should dread. At the very start of the *Treatise* Hume gives a sort of apology for beginning his work on human nature with an account of the human "understanding," our capacity to retain, retrieve, relate, and use "ideas," those less lively derivative perceptions which would be more naturally attended to, he says, after a prior attention to the experience whose lessons they preserve. His "excuse" for putting ideas first, in his philosophy (and he is surely the first to see any need for any excuse), is that the impressions that philosophers should be most concerned with, and that he will be most concerned with, are human passions, and they usually depend on ideas, so he has to deal with thought and ideas, in at least a preliminary way, before he can do justice to feeling and action. He repeats in the *Abstract* that the reason why relations of ideas, and in particular the "natural" relations that gently select our thought sequences for us, are so important is that "*as it is by means of thought only that any thing operates upon our passions,* and as these are the only ties of our thoughts, they are really *to us* the cement of the universe, and all the operations of the mind must, in a great measure, depend on them" (*T.,* p. 662,[2] first emphasis mine). Theoretical reason (or should we say "imaginative curiosity"?) serves practical reason (or must we say "practical good sense"?). The reason that Hume's treatment of ideas comes before his treatment of passions and actions is precisely what may be termed "the primacy of practical reason."

The vital job of ideas is to remind us what gave pleasure or was useful to whom, at what costs, and to help us to plan for the successful satisfaction of our considered experience-informed preferences. Belief "influences" passion and action, so belief matters. Lively ideas that are not quite beliefs also influence passions (suspicions, misgivings, hopes, fears), so ideas and imagination also matter, even when such ideas are not maximally lively, when they fail to carry total conviction: ". . . images of every thing, especially of goods and evils, are always wandering in the mind" (*T.,* p. 119). Such wanderers have their effects on action as well as on passion and on reasoning. Poets by their eloquence can rouse our passions, even when the vivid conceptions that their tales produce in our minds do not "amount to a perfect assurance" (*T.,* p. 122). The whole of Hume's epistemology, in Book One of the *Treatise,* is in the service of his philosophy of passion and action in Books Two and Three. This is said at the start; it is repeated in places like "Of the Influence of Belief"; it is implied by the conclusion of Book One, whose most despairing moment took the form of a failure to be able to give any answer to the practical questions "Whose favour shall I court, and whose anger must I dread? What beings surround me? and on whom have I any influence, or who have any influence on me?" (*T.,* p. 269); it is reiterated in the Book Three section on natural abilities, and in the *Abstract.* The famous words I have just quoted from Hume's moment of despair, or feigned despair, show that it is not just practical questions but practical social ones that Humean epistemology is to serve. Not just how to get things done but how to win friends and influence people, to placate the right superior powers, to find one's place in a web of social relations, of favor, anger, influence.

The celebrated laments in the conclusion of the *Treatise,* Book One, might be read as the expression of a member of a subject race, the Scots, who had just lost their independence. Hume, speaking English with a despised Scottish accent, writing English with an awareness of his deaf ear for his own lapses into "Scotticisms," hoping for an audience with a readership who did not treat him as really one of them, might also be seen to have been in a position a bit like that of a woman trying to make her way in a profession where she is suspect from the start, a "strange uncouth monster," unlikely to win acceptance from those already securely in possession of whatever "thrones" may exist there. Admittedly, whatever Hume thought he was doing in this celebrated "conclusion of this book," he surely did not think he was merely expressing a literary Scot's frustrations, let alone putting himself into women's shoes or sympathizing with the bluestockings of his day. (Hume's relations with Elizabeth Montague, whose stockings gave us this concept, were cool.) Nevertheless it is not entirely fanciful to see him, in his unsuccessful efforts to "effect a total alteration in philosophy" and in his unsuccessful attempts to breach the academic fortresses of Scotland (the chairs of philosophy he failed to get at Edinburgh and Glasgow), as a suitable male mascot for feminist philosophers in at least the early years of feminism—those during which some feminist philosophers were feeling unappreciated, excluded, ill understood. Hume was, if you like, an unwitting virtual woman. Both his "outsider" position, in relation to the dominant culture whose favor he would have had to court, were he to have succeeded in his academic ambitions, and his radical goals for the transformation of philosophy should make him of some interest to twentieth-century feminists, quite independently of the interesting things he had to say about equality for women and about the means by which they might achieve it.[3]

As far as his understanding of our understanding goes, Hume is famous not merely for his empiricism but for his skepticism, his debunking of rationalist pretensions to intuit causal necessity in individual instances, rationalist pretensions to turn reason on its own supposed workings in such a way as both to articulate and to endorse those workings, and for his challenge to their pretensions to require reason to exert its quasi-divine authority to govern the motivational forces at work in human action and response. This debunking (outside a very limited domain) can be read as an attack on the whole patriarchal theological tradition and on its claims about the relative authority of various human voices: the voice of divine reason; the voice of passion, sometimes of "animal" passion; the voice of plain good sense; the voice of the backward-looking avenger of crimes on account of their odiousness versus the voice of the forward-looking magistrate, inflicting punishment designed to be no more severe than necessary to produce obedience (T., pp. 410–411); the voice of the warlike patriot, condemning the enemy's devilish "perfidy" while calling his own side's treachery "policy" (T., p. 348) versus the voice of the impartial moral evaluator, recognizing perfidy wherever she finds it; the voice of cruel inhumanity versus that of normal human sympathy; the rough masculine voice versus the soft feminine voice; and so on. But it is notoriously much easier to attack a view, and to criticize a culture based on that view, than to indicate persuasively what alternative would, and would sensibly be predicted to be, a better alternative. What is Hume putting in place of the rationalists' sovereign reason, in all the realms where he topples its authority?

As far as validation of matter-of-fact beliefs goes, his official answer, in the *Enquiry Concerning Human Understanding*, is "custom or habit." After pointing out that even experience-informed reason cannot get the premises it would need to argue its way by its own rules of validity to a firm prediction about any future event, and that "there is a step taken by the mind which is not supported by any argument or process of the understanding" (*E.*, p. 41), he goes on, "If the mind be not engaged by argument to make this step, it must be induced by some other principle of equal weight and authority" (ibid.). That principle is said a page later to be custom or habit, and it is important to note that it is said to have authority, not simply to have causal influence. This may seem a disappointing answer. Indeed we might take this to be part of the debunking enterprise, and many do read Hume's "sceptical solution" as a merely ironic solution, as the final turn of his undiminished skeptical doubts about causal inference itself rather than about the rationalists' versions of it. But I do not think that he means "authority" ironically in the passage I have just quoted. He does see the natural association of events which in the past have been experienced as constantly conjoined as carrying epistemic authority. He had argued in the *Treatise* that *all* our thought moves, even the more refined and controlled of them, are "effects" of the gentle and sometimes not so gentle force of natural association working on our minds (*T.*, p. 13), so if anything is to have epistemic authority, if any step taken by the mind is to receive normative endorsement, it cannot fail to be some sort of instance of associative thinking. What gives it its authority will indeed be a special feature not found in any and every associative thought move. The rationalists, Hume believed, had misidentified that special feature. He is offering another way of understanding epistemic authority, one that allows us to give authority to some habits that are not habits of deductive argument and to establish them as rules (*T.*, p. 268).

The "habit" of trying to reduce any thought move that we regard as careful and disciplined to what Hume calls a "demonstration" of reason is a habit that Hume is doing his best to get us (or at any rate his contemporaries) to break. He offers us, as alternatives to demonstration and the habits inculcated by "our scholastic head-pieces and logicians" (*T.*, p. 175), his version of inductive or experienced-based "proofs," complete with eight rules for proving, and a special sort of arithmetic for arriving at experientially based probability estimates, for those cases when our experience has failed to yield constant conjunctions. These are experience-tested and experience-corrected customs. By the end of Part III of Book One, Hume is willing to call them "reason." It is, however, our human variant of "reason in animals," not some quasi-divine faculty, and even the rationalists' preferred thought-move, "demonstration," is there treated as a human (language-mediated?) variant of rigid animal instinct. The deductive logicians' rules and the habits they inculcate are shown to have a narrowly restricted field of application and authority, mainly in pure mathematics, and even that authority is redescribed by Hume as a special case of the more comprehensive epistemic authority that he is suggesting that we should acknowledge. Even in our demonstrative thought moves, he claims, the necessity that we take to license and require the move to the conclusion is like causal necessity in belonging "entirely to the soul" (*T.*, p. 166), a projection onto our subject matter of "the determination of the mind" (ibid.) in inference. So all inference, demonstration as well as causal inference, traces a relation whose necessity is "spread" by the mind from itself onto its subject matter. This is no retraction on Hume's part of his earlier claims that "knowledge" of a priori relations of ideas, arrived at by intuition or demonstration, is different from what we get by experience-tested "proofs." But deductive reason's authority, its ability to *require* us to reach a particular conclusion from given premises, is assimilated to that of experienced-based "proofs" and probabilities.

What is it that Hume believes does give authority to some habits of thought and some social customs; what is it that converts them into normative rules? My answer to this question, elaborated elsewhere,[4] is "surviving the test of reflection," where reflection has its narrower as well as its broader meaning. Not merely must we be able to keep up the custom or habit in question after we have thought long and hard about its nature, its sources, its costs and consequences, but we must be able to turn the habit in question on itself and find that it can "bear its own survey" (*T.*, p. 620). The most authoritative survey is that of the "whole mind," of which the operation being examined will usually be merely one among others. All the operations of "the understanding," namely, memory, demonstration, causal inference, and the use of the "fictions" of the identity of physical and mental continuants (bodies only interruptedly observed; minds, in the first person case, observed to show a more thoroughgoing "variation" than the concept of identity is deemed strictly to tolerate), are eventually tested by Hume by a survey that it takes the passions, including society-dependent passions, to administer. Epistemology in the usual narrow sense (and metaphysics with it) becomes subject to the test of moral and cultural reflection. The questions become "Would we perish and go to ruin if we broke this habit? Do we prefer people to have this habit of mind, and how important do we on reflection judge it that they have it?" What ultimately get delegitimatized are such modes of thought or extensions of some mode of thought beyond some limited domain as are found "neither unavoidable to mankind, nor necessary, or so much as useful in the conduct of life" (*T.*, p. 225). The approved habits are seen to be useful or agreeable, or both, either to their possessors, to their fellows, or to both. They are ones that "bear their own survey," that is, the surveyor of the representative of the "party of humankind," concerned for its well-being.

I said that Hume shifts the source of epistemic authority from deductive reason, where the rationalists had divined it, to reflection. But of course the rationalists, and in particular Leibniz, had themselves given great importance to reflection in its strict sense, so it would be more accurate to say that Hume generalizes the reflective operation so that it becomes an open question whether reason is what is to be paired with reflection, or whether other human psychic capacities have a better claim than deductive reason to being reflective faculties, ones capable of being turned on themselves without incoherence or self-condemnation. Both Locke and Leibniz had spoken in one breath of "reason and reflection" as what gives human persons their self-perceived special status. After Hume, the natural pairing becomes "passion and reflection," or "the moral sentiment and reflection." If Christine Korsgaard is right about Kant,[5] he inherits a Humean pairing of morality with successful reflection, albeit along with a reversion to the rationalists' conviction that reason alone, not informed sentiment, is the source of our moral capacities, both of judgment and of living in accordance with our judgments.

Hume takes passions to be intrinsically reflective, cases of a "return upon the soul" of remembered experience of good and of evil, so that the fuller reflexivity of the moral sentiment is a development of a "return upon the soul" that every ordinary passion involves. Desire for a repetition of a past pleasure, for example, depends upon the revival in memory not merely of the thought, "I enjoyed that," but of the "lively" wish for the pleasure's continuation, a wish often experienced simultaneously with the original pleasure. Desire the passion, as distinct from original instinctive appetite (which in any case soon gets mixed with and altered by the fruits of experience), is a memory-mediated will to repeat a familiar pleasure, a known good. Desires for repetition of pleasures are for minimally reflection-tested pleasures, ones whose goodness returns on the soul, ones not merely good at the time but good in retrospect, desire-generating at a later date. Ordinary experience-informed desire (the "direct" passion) is already an "impression of reflection," and its reflective success is developed and tested more stringently when it becomes the moral wish for the repetition of the special pleasure that one has got from contemplating, say, a good-humored character from a moral point of view. It becomes the wish that the character trait itself be not just an enduring one in this person but repeated in other persons, particularly in young persons where character is still malleable. So "reflection," that hitherto uncontested borrowing by the rationalists from the realm of sense, now gets reappropriated by an "empiricist."

To some extent it is Locke who initiates this return of borrowed goods. Sense is reflective when "inner sense" reflects on sensation and on how we process our ideas of sense. "Ideas of reflection" are cases of sense returned on sense, and on the operation whereby complex ideas of sense are constructed. Locke does not tell us enough about the "reflection" that he thinks is essential to moral responsibility and personhood, but it surely includes the primitive sort of "return upon the soul" that is involved in the Humean informed desire for repetition of familiar pleasures, and involves also some version of moral judgment. Locke officially takes this latter to be the ability to discern and apply a divine law, and there is no overtly reflective ingredient in his account of it.[6] He might have made recognition of divine law a reflexive turn of the human capacity for legislation, a legislation for legislators, a meta-law, but such proto-Kantian thoughts[7] are not, as far as I am aware, to be found in Locke's version of moral judgment. So although there is in Locke a doctrine of reflection that reappropriates the concept for psychic operations which are distinct from "reason," there is not a worked-out application of the concept to moral judgment. That was left for Hume (and even he leaves his readers quite a bit of the working out to do for themselves).

Now why would sensible people, in particular sensible women, have any sympathy for this perennially popular view that authority, epistemic or moral, is ultimately a matter of having survived the challenge of reflective survey? Having become aware that Aristotle favored it ("thought thinking itself"), and that a motley crew of dead and living white males since him have also favored it, should we not just turn our backs, rather than give it another hearing? I myself have raised the question[8] of whether it is not simply a fancy intellectualized version of narcissism, even in its empiricist naturalized version. But although I think this charge may be fair against reflection in its individualist variants (why should whatever I want to want, or love to love, be a "hypergood" rather than a particularly stubborn and self-reinforcing craving?), when we ask, "Why should *we* regard what we collectively, with as much information as we can get, prefer to prefer as our values," a fair answer seems to be "What else could they be?" We have no resources other than our own evaluations, and can do no more, to revise lower-level evaluations, than to repeat our evaluative operations at ever higher, more informed, and more reflective levels. So until a better account of values is offered, we may have no other choice than to discover our values by collective reflection, starting from the base of our several (and collective) less reflective desires, preferences, loves, and loyalties.

A view like Kant's makes a half-hearted gesture toward recognizing the relevance of the question "What do *we* will to will?" Kant's own preferred question is "What can *I* will that we all will?" But unless my meta-willing is responsive to and corrected by what my fellows will to will, we will merely risk proliferating, at the meta-level, the discord and troublesome self-will that drove us in the first place to take a step away from the simple "What do *I* want?" No

coordination is to be expected, except by good luck or preestab-
lished harmony, if each buttoned-up Kantian works out his application of the categorical imperative on his own, in his own private
study. And Kantians do disagree about the content of the moral law.
As is pretty much granted, even by those sympathetic to Kant's
moral philosophy, the Kantian tests underdetermine a moral guide
capable of providing any sort of coordination between actual moral
agents. Kant raises individualism to a higher level. It is high-minded
individualism, but one that should be left with an unchanged guilty
conscience about its failure to facilitate cooperation and coordination. Its ground for guilt remains the recalcitrant self-will that it was
designed to moralize and transform. As long as the contrast between
duties to self and duties to others is kept sharp, so that self-respect
entails the goal of self-perfection while respect for others is paired
with an obligatory regard for their happiness, not their perfection,
then reasoning together can have none except formal common goals.
As long as the difference between autonomy and heteronomy and
that between obeying "self alone" and obeying "others" (the same
others concern with whose happiness is a duty?) is left unmediated
by any recognition that "I" of necessity include my reflective passions and a concern for others' agreement with me, autonomy will
be in danger of deteriorating into pretend-sovereignty over com-
pliant subjects. As long as the realm of ends lacks any procedures for
shared decision making, as long as it is a "Reich," not a cooperative,
then the Kantian gestures toward the need to bring some consideration of "all" into our moral and evaluative reflection and decision
making will remain token and incomplete. Reflection which starts
from guilty self-will seems, in Kant, to get us only as far as a higher
version of self-opinionated moralistic self-will.

But is not this Kantian case one that shows how undiscriminating
the test of reflection is? If the result which Kant endorses really is a
product of genuine reflection,[9] then must we not conclude that we
get as many different reflective "higher" values as we have differing
lower-level psychologies first generating the salient maxims, those
that get tested? Will not the guilt-haunted loner always get, as his
reflective outcome, autonomy and his right to his private space,
along with his vague dreams of an ideal realm of ends, preferably
with himself playing the role of Rousseau's "legislator" while his
fellow ends-in-themselves merely cast their privately arrived-at votes

for or against measures on an agenda that they have had no hand in setting? Will not the sympathetic sociable Humean, naturally influenced by others' views and preferences (but a little worried about the dangers of conformism, and vaguely aware of the need of gadflies), reliably get, as her reflective outcome, not individual autonomy but rule by the "party of humankind," a party with vague plans to safeguard freedom of the press, to protect peaceable dissenters, and to encourage a few cautious experiments in thinking and living? Will not the puritan automatically reaffirm puritan distastes and ambivalences, while the epicurean equally reliably gives normative endorsement to the way of life of *l'homme moyen sensuel*? Must we conclude: *Chacun à son goût réfléchi*?

Whether or not reliance on reflection will eliminate disagreements, it surely does *not* give blanket endorsement to whatever is tested. The Christian's humility, for example, can scarcely be thought to pass the test of reflection, to be something that is a virtue because it can take itself as its object. Incoherence does befall some attempts to turn an attitude of mind on itself, to make itself its own intentional object. The much-discussed problems that beset Kant's attempted demonstrations that some sort of contradiction results when a maxim, such as "if life becomes intolerable, arrange to end it," is tested by his version of reflection (if that is indeed what his tests amount to) concern the selection of the salient maxim as well as the relationship between the universalization move and the reflexive turn. Such problems are real, on any version of "normativity as reflexivity." They are, however, more easily solvable on Hume's version of the authoritative reflection, namely, reflection by "the whole mind," rather than by merely a "sovereign reason" claiming to be its "highest" component.

Humean reflection is by the whole membership of the "party of humankind," listening to and influenced by each other's judgments. It is different from Kantian reflection by isolated individuals, let alone by ones who, in their moral judgments, follow Kant in endorsing a method of public decision making that gives no weight or very reduced weight to the opinions of the "weaker sex" and all the "lower" orders, the servants and the unpropertied. (Hume, of course, is not so *very* much better in his political endorsements. His ideal commonwealth, however, does not explicitly exclude women from voting or standing for office, and has an income qualification for suffrage rather than a straight property qualification.[10]) Asking "am I willing for others to imitate my example?" is a relevant question if the goal is to detect exceptions that one might be tempted to make in one's own favor from some rule that one expects others to follow. It is less relevant for the attempt to find out what rule one *can* actually expect that others will follow, and that they in turn can expect one to follow. To find that out, one must be willing to listen and find out what sort of example others are setting or are prepared to set. As I think is recognized in Hume's account of "convention" and in his characterization of the moral point of view as building on informed sympathy, there is no substitute for listening to others' views.[11] To get from "I will . . ." to "we will . . . ," or even to "I, as one of us, will . . . ," I must first listen to and understand the rest of us. Trying to imagine the other's viewpoint is no substitute for hearing it expressed, and even when all viewpoints are heard, there is still a difficult step to be taken before anyone is in a position to act or speak as "one of us." It is not so easy to act as a member of a realm of ends, especially when there is no agreement about the constitution of that realm. Simply to assume that what I can will others to do to me, they also can and do will me to do to them, without verifying that assumption case by case, is to arrogate to oneself the right to decide for others. It is to assume the pretensions of the patriarch. As, in Kant's version of an ideal commonwealth, women and servants have to rely on propertied men to look after their interests (indeed, to say what those interests are), so all Kantian persons, in their moral decision making, are licensed by Kant's tests to treat all others as virtual women[12] or virtual servants, ones whose happiness is to be aimed at by other moral agents who are confident they know where that happiness lies. Moral decision making, for Kant, is responsible patriarchal decision making, made without any actual consultation even with the other would-be patriarchs.[13]

On the Humean alternative, norms, including norms for knowledge acquisition, are social in their genesis as well as in their intended scope. Mutual influence and mutual criticism as the background to self-critical independence of mind are fostered, not feared as threats to thinking for oneself. In his blueprint for an "ideal commonwealth,"[14] Hume includes elaborate procedures for debate at several levels and for the prolonged consideration of measures which, while failing initially to get a majority vote of elected representatives, had obtained substantial support. There are procedures for appeal, and a special court made up of defeated candidates for senator who received more than a third of the votes who may propose laws, may inspect public accounts, and may bring to the senate accusations against officials. The intricacy of the procedures for giving continued voice even to defeated candidates, the extensive provisions for debate at all levels, the division and balance of powers are all constructive suggestions from Hume concerning how disagreeing individuals with some conflicting interests and some differences of perception of shared interests may still constitute a "realm." A realm must first be constituted, before its citizens can act as members of it. This and other essays[15] give flesh to the rather skeletal account Hume had given, in his moral philosophy proper (if that phrase is not out of place), of the "party of humankind" and how it might organize itself.

Hume's early formal account is, in several respects, more like that of Rousseau's version of the general will than is Kant's (which is more often said to show agreement with Rousseau). From the Humean moral point of view, one must have grounds to expect that other moral judges will concur with one's judgment, one must judge only of matters of general interpersonal concern (repeatable character traits, on Hume's version of this concern), and one must have freed one's mind as best one can of the canker of religious prejudice. It is not clear that Kant really recognizes any of these constraints. (His religious toleration is, like Locke's, limited to other theists, if not just to other Christian sects.) He may think that since reason is supposed to be the same in all, we have a priori reason to expect that we will agree. But this a priori faith comes to grief in the plain facts of the disagreement of equally rational people, especially when each person's reasoning is not submitted to her fellow reasoners for criticism. Hume, unlike Rousseau and Kant, takes the grounds on which we expect others' agreement to be our *knowledge* of their views and our sympathy with their viewpoints. Mutual influence is seen as healthy and normal. "A good-natur'd man finds himself in an instant of the same humour with his company" (*T.,* p. 317), and some degree of good nature is a virtue. It is not only mood or humor but opinion also, which is contagious in our species. There are "men of the greatest judgment and understanding, who find it very difficult to follow their own reason or inclination, in opposition to that of their friends and daily companions" (*T.,* p. 316). This psychological fact about us does not make conformism a virtue or independence of mind an impossibility. Hume himself clearly managed to follow his own reason and inclination in opposition to that of the majority of his Presbyterian friends and companions. Freedom of thought and speech is the value invoked in the quotation from Tacitus on the title page of the *Treatise.* But Hume also believed that every person needs the reaction of fellow persons in order to test and verify privately arrived-at judgments and verdicts. The difficulty of holding on to a view when one meets not merely some dissent but contradiction "on every side" (*T.,* p. 264), even when one has made the case for one's views, is not merely psychological, it is epistemological. The chances that one is right and everyone else wrong are about as great as that the one who testifies to having witnessed a miracle speaks the truth. Hume's epistemology by the end of Book One of the *Treatise* is, like the moral epistemology he goes on to articulate, fallibilist and cooperative.

This social epistemology, launched by the end of the *Treatise,* is only slightly advanced in the *Enquiry Concerning Human Understanding,* despite the promising emphasis in its first section that "man is a sociable, no less than a reasonable being" (*E.,* p. 8) and the hope expressed there that philosophy, "if carefully cultivated by several, must gradually diffuse itself throughout the whole society" (*E.,* p. 10). The tenth section, "Of Miracles," does outline a collective procedure of evidence collection and of verification, both of laws of nature and of particular persons' or groups' reliability as witnesses. This fits with what the long footnote to the ninth section, "Of the Reason of Animals," had recognized to be a source of superiority in reasoning, namely, "enlargement" of experience by information sharing (*E.,* p. 107, note, point 9).

Since the *Enquiry Concerning Human Understanding* ends stuck in the book-burning mood which was merely a passing splenetic moment in the *Treatise* (*T.,* p. 269), its presentation of Hume's "new turn" in philosophy is deliberately limited and partial. If it really is the case that our philosophical science should "be human, and such as may have a direct reference to action and society" (*E.,* p. 9), then any inquiry into the human understanding which is not part of an inquiry into human activity in society will necessarily be too "abstract." It is when Hume turns his hand to writing "essays," intended for a fairly wide reading public, rather than writing "enquiries," intended, perhaps (as M. A. Stewart has suggested is the case with the *Enquiry Concerning Human Understanding*), to get the author a chair of philosophy in Edinburgh (a *very* ill-judged means, as it turned out, to what, with the wisdom of hindsight, we can say was an unwisely chosen end), that his social action-oriented epistemology gets its best expression.

In "The Rise and Progress of the Arts and Sciences," Hume attempts to "display his ingenuity, in assigning these causes," the causes for what by his own account it is very difficult to assign causes for, namely, the flourishing of learning in some societies but not others. His question is not, as in the *Enquiry Concerning Human Understanding*, "what is it for anyone to know anything?" but rather a development of the question of the footnote to the ninth section of that work: "Why do some know more than others?" What is more, the question now becomes not one about differences between one truth seeker and another, but about differences among different human *populations* of truth seekers. The theses which Hume defends, with some but not enough empirical supporting material, are that "the blessings of a free government" are needed if the arts and sciences are to arise; that commerce between neighboring independent states is favorable to the improvement of learning; that the arts and sciences may, once advanced, be "transplanted" from free states into others; that republics are the best as "Nurseries" of the sciences, while civilized monarchies are the best "Nurseries" of the arts; that in states where learning has arisen and flourished, there is an eventual natural decline to be expected, so that, as the centuries pass, such learning tends to migrate from country to country. This "natural history" of learning may strike us as underconfirmed by the historical evidence that Hume cites. His last thesis, that "the arts and sciences, like some plants, require fresh soil," seems overinfluenced by his agricultural or horticultural metaphor of political societies as "nurseries" and "soils" for learning. But what is striking about the whole essay is the very new turn given to epistemology. That any individual's or any group's chance of accumulating a store of truths depends, in the first instance, on the authority structure of the society in which such persons live was a fairly revolutionary bit of epistemology, one which anticipates later moves in this direction by Hegel, Marx, Foucault, Bob Brandom,[16] and Lorraine Code[17] (to name a few probably inadvertent Hume followers). "To expect, therefore, that the arts and sciences should take their first rise in a monarchy, is to expect a contradiction" (*Es.*, p. 117). If a people are treated as slaves of their absolute ruler, "it is impossible they can ever aspire to any refinements of taste or reason" (ibid.). "Here, then are the advantages of free states. Though a republic should be barbarous, it necessarily, by an infallible operation, gives rise to LAW, even before mankind have made any considerable advances in the other sciences. From law arises security: From security curiosity: And from curiosity knowledge" (*Es.*, p. 118).[18] The first important human knowledge is that of jurisprudence, according to Hume's reformed active and social theory of knowledge.[19]

Hume takes the link between the structure of political authority and the prospects for epistemic progress very seriously. "I have sometimes been inclined to think, that interruptions in the periods of learning, were they not attended with such a destruction of ancient books, and the records of history, would be rather favourable to the arts and sciences, by breaking the progress of authority, and dethroning the tyrannical usurpers over human reason. In this particular, they have the same influence, as interruptions in political governments and societies" (*Es.*, p. 123).[20] This spirited defense of freedom of thought, these attacks on "blind deference," put even J. S. Mill's *On Liberty* in the shade. Hume's linking of freedom, authority, and deference in thought with political freedom, authority, and deference is not just a speculative causal thesis but a transformation of the epistemological notions. The norms of thinking are no more clearly separable from the norms of human interaction than the "exchange" and "commerce" of ideas is a totally different sort of commerce from that to which Hume devotes a later essay, "Of Commerce." Mill's "marketplace of ideas" is a more competition-oriented successor to Hume's earlier discussion of intellectual exchange, including such exchange across national boundaries. If Hume gives us an early capitalist social epistemology, Mill gives a high capitalist version. The value of a theory, such as Newton's, is seen to be determined after "the severest scrutiny," a scrutiny coming "not from his own countrymen, but from foreigners" (*Es.*, p. 121). Emulation among scholars of different nations is a bit like international competition in free trade—it settles the value of any one person's or research team's "product." Critical scrutiny, both from competitors and from the "consumer" of the scholar's work, is, Hume argues, an essential accompaniment to freedom of thought in the rise and progress of the sciences.

In "Of Commerce" and "Of Refinement in the Arts," Hume cements the connections he had already made between political, commercial, and industrial life on the one hand and intellectual life on the other. "The same age, which produces great philosophers and politicians, renowned generals and poets, usually abounds with skilful weavers, and ship-carpenters" (*Es.*, p. 270). Hume is not saying that philosophy must guide the weavers' hands—the connection is if anything the opposite one: "Another advantage of industry and of refinement in the mechanical arts, is, that they commonly produce some refinements in the liberal" (ibid.). Progress in these different aspects of a culture is mutually enhancing. Cooperation and coordination, needed in the mechanical arts, are also needed in the liberal arts. Their flourishing makes people *more* sociable, Hume argues. Once people are "enriched with science, and possessed of a fund of conversation," they will not be content to live in rural isolation but will "flock into cities; love to receive and communicate knowledge; to show their wit or their breeding; their taste in conversation or living, in clothes or furniture" (*Es.*, p. 271). Their tempers become refined, and they "must feel an encrease of humanity, from the very habit of conversing together, and contributing to each other's pleasure and entertainment. Thus *industry, knowledge,* and *humanity* are linked together by an indissoluble chain . . ." (ibid.).

I have quoted liberally from these essays, because I think that they develop and give detail to the *Treatise*'s and the *Enquiries*' claim that "man is a sociable, no less than a reasonable being" (*E.*, p. 8). They have been insufficiently appreciated by readers of Hume's first, more "abstruse" works.[21] The *Enquiry Concerning the Principles of Morals* had, in the fourth appendix ("Of Some Verbal Disputes"), followed the *Treatise* in assimilating "wisdom and knowledge" to the virtues. It had also disputed whether there are any virtues that are not *"social* virtues" (*E.*, p. 313). But it took the *Essays* (and the *History of England*) to enrich these social-cum-intellectual virtues into political, cultural, commercial, industrial, and cosmopolitan ones. Later essays such as "Of Money" give us yet more "thick" epistemology. In particular, they advance some interesting theses about the social need and point of representations and

measures of value. Money is found to be "nothing but the representation of labour and commodities, and serves only as a method of
rating and estimating them" (*Es.*, p. 285), but the invention of
money, like the invention of contract (secured exchange of future
goods), can transform a society from an "uncultivated" into a "cultivated" one. Hume's essays on economics are about cultural epistemology as well as economics, and add to what he had already done
in that area in his earlier *Essays: Moral, Political and Literary*.

One last point needs to be added, to complete my sketch of a
case for seeing Hume as a "women's epistemologist." A fairly central part of Hume's characterization of the difference between a cultivated society, where knowledge can advance, and a "barbaric"
society, where no such advance can be expected, concerns the position of women in such societies. Hume, from his experience of the
contributions to culture and to conversation of the Scotswomen and
the Frenchwomen he knew, offers his nonsolemn verdict that "mixt
companies, without the fair-sex, are the most insipid entertainment
in the world, and destitute of gaiety and politeness, as much as of
sense and reason. Nothing can keep them from excessive dulness but
hard drinking . . ." (*Es.*, p. 626).[22] Segregation of the sexes, in social
and work contexts, is seen as a sign of a "rough" and "barbaric"
society, while a social mixing of the sexes is a step toward civilization and the ending of tyranny. Hume sees all tyrannies to be interconnected—the tyranny of husbands over wives, which is discussed
in "Of Polygamy and Divorces," "Of Moral Prejudices," and "Of
Marriage," is likened to the tyranny of absolute monarchs over subjects, discussed in his political essays. Neither of these tyrannies is
independent of the threat of "tyrannical usurpers over human
reason." Some of Hume's more apparently condescending remarks
about woman's special role as a "polisher" and "refiner" of rougher
and more "boisterous" male energies are distasteful to late twentieth-century feminists. But we should not fail to appreciate the radically antipatriarchal stand that inspires them and that Hume takes
throughout his philosophy. He pretty clearly believes that men and
women typically have *different* contributions to make to "industry,
knowledge, and humanity." What he calls "The Judgment of
Females" (*Es.*, p. 537) is valued as a needed corrective to that of the
male, as if the judgment of males is the natural place to start. But
wherever we start, Hume's main message here is that we all need to

work together, to check each other's judgments and scrutinize each other's works, if barbarism is to be held at bay. We reflective women and men need, he argued, "a League, offensive and defensive, against our common Enemies, against the Enemies of Reason and Beauty, People of dull Heads and cold Hearts" (*Es.*, p. 536). Such a league still has plenty of work to do.

One of its main tasks is to continue Hume's attempts to exhibit the links between dullness of head and coldness of heart and between "Reason and Beauty." In this essay I have followed the early Hume in using the word "reason" in a fairly narrow sense, thereby limiting its scope to what can be established by Cartesian (or Kantian) "reason." Hume uses the word "reason" in shifting senses, and by the time he wrote his essays he was not willing to give the term to the rationalists, but used it in a broad sense in which it no longer gets contrasted either with imagination or with passion, and so can be paired with a sense of beauty without any strain. The human version of the "reason of animals," taken in Book One of the *Treatise* to include our deductive and inductive thought moves, gets further animated in Book Two when it becomes the "love of truth," and in Book Three and in later writings it comes to include also our capacity to coordinate our speaking and our actions with the speech and action of our fellows, to coordinate moral and aesthetic judgments as well as factual and mathematical ones. Hume in the end transforms the concept of reason.[23] From being a quasi-divine faculty, something we share with God, reason becomes a natural capacity and one that is essentially shared with those who learn from experience in the way we do, sharing expressive body language, sharing or able to share a language, sharing or able to share our sentiments, sharing or able to share intellectual, moral, and aesthetic standards, and sharing or aspiring to share in the setting of those standards.

TRUST
AND
ANTITRUST

Whatever matters to human beings,
trust is the atmosphere in which it thrives.

Sissela Bok

Whether or not everything which matters to us is the sort of thing that can thrive or languish (I may care most about my stamp collection) or even whether or not all the possibly thriving things we care about need trust in order to thrive (does my rubber tree?), there surely is something basically right about Bok's claim.[1] Given that I cannot myself guard my stamp collection at all times, nor take my rubber tree with me on my travels, the custody of these things that matter to me must often be transferred to others, presumably to others I trust. Without trust, what matters to me would be unsafe, unless like the Stoic I attach myself only to what can thrive or be safe from harm, *however* others act. The starry heavens above and the moral law within had better be about the only things that matter to me, if there is no one I can trust in any way. Even my own Stoic virtue will surely thrive better if it evokes some trust from others, inspires some trustworthiness in them, or is approved and imitated by them.

To Bok's statement, however, we should add another, that not all the things that thrive when there is trust among people, and which matter, are things that should be encouraged to thrive. Exploitation and conspiracy, as much as justice and fellowship, thrive better in an atmosphere of trust. There are immoral as well as moral trust relationships, and trust-busting can be a morally proper goal. If we are to tell when morality requires the preservation of trust and when it requires the destruction of trust, we obviously need to distinguish different forms of trust and look for morally relevant features they may possess. In this essay I make a start on this large task.

It is a start, not a continuation, because there has been a strange silence on the topic in the tradition of moral philosophy with which I am familiar. Psychologists and sociologists have discussed trust, lawyers have worked out the requirements of equity on legal trusts, political philosophers have discussed trust in governments, and there has been some discussion of trust when philosophers address the assurance problem in prisoner's dilemma contexts. But we, or at least I, search in vain for any general account of the morality of trust relationships. The question "Whom should I trust in what way, and why?" has not been the central question in moral philosophy as we know it. Yet if I am right in claiming that morality, as anything more than a law within, itself requires trust in order to thrive, and that immorality too thrives on some forms of trust, it seems obvious that we ought, as moral philosophers, to look into the question of what forms of trust are needed for the thriving of the version of morality we endorse, and into the morality of that and other forms of trust. A minimal condition of adequacy for any version of the true morality, if truth has anything to do with reality, is that it not have to condemn the conditions needed for its own thriving. Yet we will be in no position to apply that test to the trust in which morality thrives until we have worked out, at least in a provisional way, how to judge trust relationships from a moral point of view.

Moral philosophers have always been interested in cooperation among people, and so it is surprising that they have not said more than they have about trust. It seems fairly obvious that any form of cooperative activity, including the division of labor, requires the cooperators to trust one another to do their bit, or at the very least to trust the overseer with his whip to do his bit, when coercion is relied on. One would expect contractarians to investigate the forms of trust and distrust parties to a contract exhibit. Utilitarians too should be concerned with the contribution to the general happiness of various climates of trust, and so be concerned to understand the nature, roots, and varieties of trust. One might also have expected those with a moral theory of the virtues to have looked at trustworthiness or at willingness to give trust. But when we turn to the great moral philosophers in our tradition, what we find can scarcely be said to be even a sketch of a moral theory of trust. At most we get a few hints of directions in which we might go.

Plato in the *Republic* presumably expects the majority of citizens to trust the philosopher kings to rule wisely and expects members of that elite to trust their underlings not to poison their wine or to set fire to their libraries, but neither proper trust nor proper trustworthiness is among the virtues he dwells on as necessary in the cooperating parties in his good society. His version of justice and of the "friendship" supposed to exist between ruler and ruled seems to *imply* such virtues of trust, but he does not himself draw out the implications. In the *Laws* he mentions distrust as an evil produced by association with seafaring traders, but it is only a mention.[2] The same sort of claim can also be made about Aristotle—his virtuous person, like Plato's, must place his trust in that hypothetical wise person who will teach him just how much anger and pride and fear to feel with what reasons, when, and toward which objects. Such a wise man presumably also knows just how much trust in whom, on what matters, and how much trustworthiness should be cultivated, as well as who should show trust toward whom, but such crucial wisdom and such central virtues are not discussed by Aristotle, as far as I am aware. (He does, in the *Politics,* condemn tyrants for sowing seeds of distrust, and his discussion of friendship might be cited as one place where he implicitly recognizes the importance of trust; could someone one distrusted be a second self to one? But that is implicit only, and in any case would cover only trust between friends.) Nor do later moral philosophers do much better on this count.[3]

There are some forms of trust to which the great philosophers *have* given explicit attention. Aquinas and other Christian moralists have extolled the virtue of faith and, more relevantly, of hope, and so have said something about trust in God. And in the modern period some of the great moral and political philosophers, in particular John Locke, have looked at trust in governments and officials, and some have shown what might be called an obsessive trust in contracts and contractors, even if not, after Hobbes's good example, an equal obsession with the grounds for such trust. It is selective attention then, rather than total inattention, which is the philosophical phenomenon on which I wish to remark, tentatively to explain, and try to terminate or at least to interrupt.

Trust, the phenomenon we are so familiar with that we scarcely notice its presence and its variety, is shown by us and responded to by us not only with intimates but with strangers, and even with declared enemies. We trust our enemies not to fire at us when we lay down our arms and put out a white flag. In Britain burglars and police used to trust each other not to carry deadly weapons. We often trust total strangers, such as those from whom we ask directions in foreign cities, to direct rather than misdirect us, or to tell us so if they do not know what we want to know; and we think we should do the same for those who ask for the same help from us. Of course we are often disappointed, rebuffed, let down, or betrayed when we exhibit such trust in others, and we are often exploited when we show the wanted trustworthiness. We do in fact, wisely or stupidly, virtuously or viciously, show trust in a great variety of forms, and we manifest a great variety of versions of trustworthiness, both with intimates and with strangers. We trust those we encounter in lonely library stacks to be searching for books, not victims. We sometimes let ourselves fall asleep on trains or planes, trusting neighboring strangers not to take advantage of our defenselessness. We put our bodily safety into the hands of pilots, drivers, and doctors with scarcely any sense of recklessness. We used not to suspect that the food we buy might be deliberately poisoned, and we used to trust our children to day-care centers.

We may still have no choice but to buy food and to leave our children in day-care centers, but now we do it with suspicion and anxiety. Trust is always an invitation not only to confidence tricksters but also to terrorists, who discern its most easily destroyed and socially vital forms. Criminals, not moral philosophers, have been the experts at discerning different forms of trust. Most of us notice a given form of trust most easily after its sudden demise or severe injury. We inhabit a climate of trust as we inhabit an atmosphere and notice it as we notice air, only when it becomes scarce or polluted.

We may have no choice but to continue to rely on the local shop for food, even after some of the food on its shelves has been found to have been poisoned with intent. We can still rely where we no longer trust. What is the difference between trusting others and merely relying on them? It seems to be reliance on their goodwill toward one, as distinct from their dependable habits, or only on their dependably exhibited fear, anger, or other motives compatible with ill will toward one, or on motives not directed on one at all. Once we have ceased to trust our fellows, we may rely on their fear of the newly appointed security guards in shops to deter them from injecting poison into the food on the shelves. We may rely on the shopkeeper's concern for his profits to motivate him to take effective precautions against poisoners and also trust him to *want* his customers not to be harmed by his products, at least as long as this want can be satisfied without frustrating his wish to increase his profits. Trust is often mixed with other species of reliance on persons. Trust which is reliance on another's goodwill, perhaps minimal goodwill, contrasts with the forms of reliance on others' reactions and attitudes which are shown by the comedian, the advertiser, the blackmailer, the kidnapper-extortioner, and the terrorist, who all depend on particular attitudes and reactions of others for the success of their actions. We all depend on one another's psychology in countless ways, but this is not yet to trust them. The trusting can be betrayed, or at least let down, and not just disappointed. Kant's neighbors who counted on his regular habits as a clock for their own less automatically regular ones might be disappointed with him if he slept in one day, but not let down by him, let alone had their trust betrayed. When I trust another, I depend on her goodwill toward me. I need not either acknowledge this reliance or believe that she has either invited or acknowledged such trust, since there is such a thing as unconscious trust, as unwanted trust, as forced receipt of trust, and as trust which the trusted is unaware of. (Plausible conditions for proper trust will be that it survives consciousness, by both parties, and that the trusted has had some opportunity to signify acceptance or rejection, to warn the trusting if their trust is unacceptable.)

Where one depends on another's goodwill, one is necessarily vulnerable to the limits of that goodwill. One leaves others an opportunity to harm one when one trusts, and also shows one's confidence that they will not take it. Reasonable trust will require good grounds for such confidence in another's goodwill, or at least the absence of good grounds for expecting another's ill will or indifference. Trust, then, on this first approximation, is accepted vulnerability to another's possible but not expected ill will (or lack of goodwill) toward one.

What we now need to do, to get any sense of the variety of forms of trust, is to look both at varieties of vulnerability and at varieties of grounds for not expecting others to take advantage of it. One way to do the former, which I shall take, is to look at the variety of sorts of goods or things one values or cares about, which can be left or put within the striking power of others, and the variety of ways we can let or leave others "close" enough to what we value to be able to harm it. Then we can look at various reasons we might have for wanting or accepting such closeness of those with power to harm us, and for having confidence that they will not use this power. In this way we can hope to explicate the vague terms "goodwill" and "ill will." If it be asked why the initial emphasis is put on the trusting's vulnerability, on the risks rather than the benefits of trust, part of the answer has already been given—namely, that we come to realize what trust involves retrospectively and posthumously, once our vulnerability is brought home to us by actual wounds. The other part of the answer is that even when one does become aware of trust and intentionally continues a particular case of it, one need not intend to achieve any particular benefit from it—one need not trust a person in order to receive some gain, even when in fact one does gain. Trusting, as an intentional mental phenomenon, need not be purposive. But intentional trusting does require awareness of one's confidence that the trusted will not harm one, although they could harm one. It is not a Hobbesian obsession with strike force which dictates the form of analysis I have sketched but, rather, the natural order of consciousness and self-consciousness of trust, which progresses from initially unself-conscious trust to awareness of risk along with confidence that it is a good risk, on to some realization of why we are taking this particular risk, and eventually to some evaluation of what we may generally gain and what we may lose from the willingness to take such risks. The ultimate point of what we are doing when we trust may be the last thing we come to realize.

The next thing to attend to is why we typically do leave things that we value close enough to others for them to harm them. The answer, simply, is that we need their help in creating and then in not merely guarding but looking after the things we most value, so we have no choice but to allow some others to be in a position to harm them. The one in the best position to harm something is its creator or its nurse-cum-caretaker. Since the things we typically do value include things that we cannot singlehandedly either create or sustain (our own life, health, reputation, our offspring and their well-being, as well as intrinsically shared goods such as conversation, its written equivalent, theater and other forms of play, chamber music, market exchange, political life, and so on), we must allow many other people to get into positions where they can, if they choose, injure what we care about, since those are the same positions that they must be in, in order to help us take care of what we care about. The simple Socratic truth that no person is self-sufficient gets elaborated, once we add the equally Socratic truth that the human soul's activity is *caring* for things into the richer truth that no one is able by herself to look after everything she wants to have looked after, nor even alone to look after her own "private" goods, such as health and bodily safety. If we try to distinguish different forms of trust by the different valued goods we confidently allow another to have some control over, we are following Locke in analyzing trusting on the model of *en*trusting. Thus, there will be an answer not just to the question "Whom do you trust?" but to the question "*What* do you trust to them?"—what good is it that they are in a position to take from you, or to injure? Accepting such an analysis, taking trust to be a three-place predicate (A trusts B with valued thing C) will involve some distortion and regimentation of some cases, where we may have to strain to discern any definite candidate for C, but I think it will prove more of a help than a hindrance.

One way in which trusted persons can fail to act as they were trusted to is by taking on the care of more than they were entrusted with—the babysitter who decides that the nursery would be improved if painted purple and sets to work to transform it, will have acted, as a babysitter, in an untrustworthy way, however great his goodwill. When we are trusted, we are relied upon to realize *what* it is for whose care we have some discretionary responsibility, and normal people can pick up the cues that indicate the limits of what is entrusted. For example, if I confide my troubles to a friend, I trust her to listen, more or less sympathetically, and to preserve confidentiality, but usually not, or not without consulting me, to take steps to remove the source of my worry. That could be interfering impertinence, not trustworthiness as a confidante. She will, nevertheless, within the restricted scope of what is trusted to her (knowledge of my affairs, not their management) have some discretion both as to how to receive the confidence and, unless I swear her to absolute secrecy, as to when to share it. The relativization of trust to particular things cared about by the truster goes along with the discretion the trusted usually has in judging just what should be done to "look after" the particular good entrusted to her care. This discretionary power will of course be limited by the limits of what is entrusted and usually by some other constraints.

Is it plausible to construe all cases of being trusted not merely as cases of being trusted by someone with access to what matters to the truster but as some control over that control which is expected to be used to take care of it, and involving some discretionary powers in so doing?[4] Can we further elaborate the analysis of a relationship of trust as one where A has entrusted B with some of the care of C and where B has some discretionary powers in caring for C? Admittedly there are many cases of trust where "caring for C" seems much more than A expects of B even when there is no problem in finding a fairly restricted value for C. Suppose I look quickly around me before proceeding into the dark street or library stacks where my business takes me, judge the few people I discern there to be nondangerous, and so go ahead. We can say that my bodily safety, and perhaps my pocketbook, are the goods I am allowing these people to be in a position to threaten. I trust them, it seems, merely to leave me alone. But this is not quite right, for should a piece of falling masonry or toppling books threaten to fall on my head, and one of these persons leap into action and shove me out of danger, I would regard that as rather more than less than I had trusted these strangers to do—a case for gratitude, not for an assault charge, despite the sudden, unceremonious, possibly painful or even injurious nature of my close encounter with my rescuer. So *what* do I trust strangers in such circumstances to do? Certainly not anything whatever as long as it is done with goodwill, nor even anything whatever for my bodily safety and security of property as long as it is done with goodwill. Suppose someone I have judged nondangerous as I proceed into the stacks should seize me from behind, frightening but not harming me, and claim with apparent sincerity that she did it for my own good, so that I would learn a lesson and be more cautious in the future. I would not respond with gratitude but demand what business my long-term security of life was of hers, that she felt free to subject me to such unpleasant educational measures. In terms of my analysis, what I trusted her with was my peace and safety here and now, with "looking after" that, not with my long-term safety. We need some fairly positive and discretion-allowing term, such as "look after" or "show concern for," to let in the range of behavior which would not disappoint the library user's trust in fellow users. We also need some specification of what good was in question to see why the intrusive, presumptuous, and paternalistic moves disappoint rather than meet the trust one has in such circumstances. "Look after" and "take care of" will have to be given a very weak sense in some cases of trust; it will be better to do this than to try to construe cases where more positive care is expected as cases of trusting someone to leave alone, or merely to safeguard, the entrusted valued thing. Trusting strangers to leave us alone should be construed as trusting them with the "care" of our valued autonomy. When one trusts one's child to one's separated spouse, it is all aspects of the child's good as a developing person which are entrusted to the other parent's care. Trusting him or her with our children can hardly be construed as trusting him or her not to "interfere" with the child's satisfactory development. The most important things we entrust to others are things which take more than noninterference in order to thrive.

The more extensive the discretionary powers of the trusted, the less clear-cut will be the answer to the question of when trust is disappointed. The truster, who always needs good judgment to know whom to trust and how much discretion to give, will also have some scope for discretion in judging what should count as failing to meet trust, either through incompetence, negligence, or ill will. In any case of a questionable exercise of discretion there will be room both for forgiveness of unfortunate outcomes and for tact in treatment of the question of whether there is anything to forgive. One thing that can destroy a trust relationship fairly quickly is the combination of a rigoristic unforgiving attitude on the part of the truster and a touchy sensitivity to any criticism on the part of the trusted. If a trust relationship is to continue, some tact and willingness to forgive on the part of the truster and some willingness on the part of the trusted both to be forgiven and to forgive unfair criticisms seem essential.[5] The need for this will be greater the more discretion the trusted has.

If part of what the truster entrusts to the trusted are discretionary powers, then the truster risks abuse of those and the successful disguise of such abuse. The special vulnerability which trust involves is vulnerability to not yet noticed harm, or to disguised ill will. What one forgives or tactfully averts one's eyes from may be not well-meant but ill-judged or incompetent attempts to care for what is entrusted but, rather, ill-meant and cleverly disguised abuses of discretionary power. To understand the moral risks of trust, it is important to see the special sort of vulnerability it introduces. Yet the discretionary element which introduces this special danger is essential to that which trust at its best makes possible. To elaborate Hume: "'Tis impossible to separate [the chance of] good from the [risk of] ill."[6]

It is fairly easy, once we look, to see how this special vulnerability is involved in many ordinary forms of trust. We trust the mail carrier to deliver and not tamper with the mail, and to some extent we trust his discretion in interpreting what "tampering" covers. Normally we expect him not to read our mail but to deliver it unread, even when the message is open, on a postcard. But on occasion it may be proper, or at least not wrong, for him to read it. I have had friendly mail carriers (in Greek villages and in small Austrian towns) who told me what my mail announces as they handed it over: "Your relatives have recovered and can travel now, and are soon arriving!" Such interest in one's affairs is not part of the normal idea of the role of mail carrier and could provide opportunity for blackmail, but in virtue of that very interest they could give much more knowledgeable and intelligent service—in the above case, by knowing our plans, they knew when and where we had moved and delivered to the new address without instructions. What do we trust our mail carriers to do or not to do? To use their discretion in getting our mail to us, to take enough interest in us and in the nature of our mail (compatibly with their total responsibility) to make intelligent decisions about what to do with it when such decisions have to be made. Similarly with our surgeons and plumbers— *just* what they should do to put right what is wrong is something we must leave to them. Should they act incompetently, negligently, or deliberately against our interests, they may conceal these features of their activities from us by pretense that whatever happened occurred as a result of an honest and well-meaning exercise of the discretion given to them. This way they may retain our trust and so have opportunity to harm us yet further. In trusting them, we trust them to use their discretionary powers competently and nonmaliciously, and the latter includes not misleading us about how they have used them.

Trust, on the analysis I have proposed, is letting other persons (natural or artificial, such as firms, nations, etc.) take care of something the truster cares about, where such "caring for" involves some exercise of discretionary powers. But not all the variables involved in trust are yet in view. One which the entrusting model obscures rather than highlights is the degree of explicitness. To entrust is intentionally and usually formally to hand over the care of something to someone, but trusting is rarely begun by making up one's mind to trust, and often it has no definite initiation of any sort but grows up slowly and imperceptibly. What I have tried to take from the notion of entrusting is not its voluntarist and formalist character but rather the possible specificity and restrictedness of *what* is entrusted, along with the discretion the trustee has in looking after that thing. Trust can come with no beginnings, with gradual as well as sudden beginnings, and with various degrees of self-consciousness, voluntariness, and expressness. My earlier discussion of the delicacy and tact needed by the truster in judging the performance of the trusted applied only to cases where the truster not merely realizes that she trusts but has some conscious control over the continuation of the trust relationship. The discussion of abuses of discretionary power applied only to cases where the trusted realizes that she is trusted and trusted with discretionary powers. But trust relationships need not be so express, and some important forms of them cannot be verbally acknowledged by the persons involved. Trust between infant and parent is such a case, and it is one which also reminds us of another crucial variable in trust relations to which so far I have only indirectly alluded. This is the relative power of the truster and the trusted, and the relative costs to each of a breakdown of their trust relationship. In emphasizing the toleration of vulnerability by the truster I have made attitudes to relative power and powerlessness the essence of trust and distrust; I have not yet looked at the varieties of trust we discern when we vary the power of the truster in relation to the power of the trusted, both while the trust endures and in its absence. Trust alters power positions, and both the position one is in without a given form of trust and the position one has within a relation of trust need to be considered before one can judge whether that form of trust is sensible and morally decent. Infant trust reminds us not just of inarticulate and uncritical or blind trust but of trust by those who are maximally vulnerable, whether or not they give trust.

Trust and Relative Power

I have been apparently preoccupied up till now with dimensions of trust which show up most clearly in trust between articulate adults, in a position to judge one another's performance and having some control over their degree of vulnerability to others. This approach typifies a myopia which, once noticed, explains the "regrettably sparse" attempts to understand trust as a phenomenon of moral importance.[7] The more we ignore dependency relations between those grossly unequal in power and ignore what cannot be spelled out in an explicit acknowledgment, the more readily will we assume that everything that needs to be understood about trust and trustworthiness can be grasped by looking at the morality of contract. For it takes an adult to be able to make a contract, and it takes something like Hegel's civil society of near equals to find a use for contracts. But one has to strain the contractarian model very considerably to see infant-parent relations as essentially contractual, both because of the nonexpressness of the infant's attitude and because of the infant's utter powerlessness. It takes inattention to cooperation between unequals, and between those without a common language, to keep one a contented contractarian. To do more, I must show how both infant trust and other variations along the relative power dimension can be covered and also indicate just where trust in contracts fits into the picture we then get.

Infant trust is like one form of non-contract-based trust to which some attention has been given in our philosophical tradition, namely, trust in God. Trust in God is total, in that whatever one cares about, it will not thrive if God wills that it not thrive. A young child too is totally dependent on the goodwill of the parent, totally incapable of looking after anything he cares about without parental help or against parental will. Such total dependence does not, in itself, necessarily elicit trust—some theists curse God, display futile distrust or despair rather than trust. Infants too can make suspicious, futile, self-protective moves against the powerful adults in their world or retreat into autism. But surviving infants will usually

106

have shown some trust, enough to accept offered nourishment, enough not to attempt to prevent such close approach. The ultra-Hobbist child who fears or rejects the mother's breast, as if fearing poison from that source, can be taken as displaying innate distrust, and such newborns must be the exception in a surviving species. Hobbes tells us that, in the state of nature, "seeing the infant first is in the power of the Mother, so as she may either nourish or expose it, if she nourish it, it oweth its life to the Mother; and is therefore obliged to obey her, rather than any other" (*Leviathan*, chap. 20). Even he, born a twin to fear, is apparently willing to take mother's milk on trust. Some degree of innate, if selective, trust seems a necessary element in any surviving creature whose first nourishment (if it is not exposed) comes from another, and this innate but fragile trust could serve as the explanation both of the possibility of other forms of trust and of their fragility.

That infant trust normally does not need to be won but is there unless and until it is destroyed is important for an understanding of the possibility of trust. Trust is much easier to maintain than it is to get started and is never hard to destroy. Unless some form of it were innate, and unless that form could pave the way for new forms, it would appear a miracle that trust ever occurs. The postponement of the onset of distrust is a lot more explicable than hypothetical Hobbesian conversions from total distrust to limited trust. The persistent human adult tendency to profess trust in a creator-God can also be seen as an infantile residue of this crucial innate readiness of infants to initially impute goodwill to the powerful persons on whom they depend. So we should perhaps welcome, or at least tolerate, religious trust, if we value any form of trust. Nevertheless the theological literature on trust in God is of very limited help to us if we want to understand trust in human persons, even that trust in parents of which it can be seen as a nostalgic fantasy-memory. For the child soon learns that the parent is not, like God, invulnerable, nor even, like some versions of God, subject to offense or insult but not injury. Infant trust, although extreme in the discrepancy of power between the truster and the trusted, is to some extent a matter of mutual trust and mutual if unequal vulnerability. The parents' enormous power to harm the child and disappoint the child's trust is the power of ones also vulnerable to the child's at first insignificant but ever-increasing power, including power as one trusted by the parent. So not very much can be milked from the theological literature on the virtues of trust, faith, and hope in God and returned to the human context, even to the case of infant and parent. Indeed we might cite the theological contamination of the concept of trust as part of the explanation for the general avoidance of the topic in modern moral philosophy. If trust is seen as a variant of the suspect virtue of faith in the competence of the powers that be, then readiness to trust will be seen not just as a virtue of the weak but itself as a moral weakness, better replaced by vigilance and self-assertion, by self-reliance or by cautious, minimal, and carefully monitored trust. The psychology of adolescents, not infants, then gets glorified as the moral ideal. Such a reaction against a religious version of the ethics of trust is as healthy, understandable, and, it is hoped, as passing a phenomenon as is adolescent self-assertive individualism in the life of a normal person.

The goods which a trustworthy parent takes care of for as long as the child is unable to take care of them alone, or continues to welcome the parent's help in caring for them, are such things as nutrition, shelter, clothing, health, education, privacy, and loving attachment to others. Why, once the child becomes at all self-conscious about trusting parents to look after such goods for her, should she have confidence that parents are dependable custodians of such goods? Presumably because many of them are also goods to the parent, through their being goods to the child, especially if the parent loves the child. They will be common goods, so that for the trusted to harm them would be self-harm as well as harm to the child. The best reason for confidence in another's good care of what one cares about is that it is a common good, and the best reason for thinking that one's own good is also a common good is being loved. This may not, usually will not, ensure agreement on what best should be done to take care of that good, but it rules out suspicion of ill will. However, even when a child does not feel as loved by a parent as she would like, or as she thinks her siblings or friends are, she may still have complete confidence that at least many of the goods she cares about can be entrusted to her parents' care. She can have plenty of evidence that, for reasons such as pride, desire to perpetuate their name, or whatever, they do care as she herself does about her health, her success, and her ties with them. She can have good reason to be confident of the continued trustworthiness of her parents in many regards, from what she knows of their own concerns.

As the child approaches adulthood, and as the parents draw nearer to the likely dependency of old age, the trust may approximate much more closely to mutual trust and mutual vulnerability between equals, and they may then make explicit or even formal agreements about what is to be done in return for what. But no such contractual or quasi-contractual agreement can convert the young child's trust and the parent's trustworthiness retrospectively into part of a contractual mutual exchange. At most it can transform what was a continuing relation of mutual trust into a contractual obligation to render some sort of service to one's parents. The previous parental care could become a moral *reason* for making a contract with parents, but not what one received as "consideration" in such a contract. At best that could be a virtual "consideration," perhaps symbolized by the parents' formal canceling of any until then outstanding "debt" of gratitude, in return for the rights the contract gives them. But normally whatever grateful return one makes to another is not made in exchange for a "receipt" which is proof against any outstanding "debt." Only those determined to see every proper moral transaction as an exchange will construe every gift as made in exchange for an IOU, and every return gift as made in exchange for a receipt. Only such trade fetishists will have any reason to try to construe the appropriate adult response to earlier parental care as part of a virtual contract, or as proper content for an actual contract. As Hume says, contract should not replace "the more generous and noble intercourse of friendship and good offices," which he construes as a matter of spontaneous service responded to by "return in the same manner."[8] We can resist this reduction of the more noble responses of gratitude to the fulfilling of contractual obligations if we focus our moral attention on other sorts of trust than trust in contracts. Looking at infant trust helps one do that. Not only has the child no concept of virtual contract when she trusts, but the parent's duty to the child seems in no way dependent on the expectation that the child will make a later return. The child or the parent may die before the reversal of dependency arrives. Furthermore, the parent's knowledge that either the child, or he himself, or both will die within, say, ten years in itself (and disability apart) makes no difference to the parent's responsibility while

contract

he lives, as that is usually understood. Parental and filial responsibility does not rest on deals, actual or virtual, between parent and child.

Trust and Voluntary Abilities

The child trusts as long as she is encouraged to trust and until the trust is unmistakably betrayed. It takes childhood innocence to be able to trust simply because of encouragement to trust. "Trust me!" is for most of us an invitation which we cannot accept at will—either we do already trust the one who says it, in which case it serves at best as reassurance,[9] or it is properly responded to with, "Why should and how can I, until I have cause to?"[10] The child, of course, cannot trust at will any more than experienced adults can—encouragement is a condition of not lapsing into distrust rather than a move from distrust to trust. One constraint on an account of trust which postulates infant trust as its essential seed is that it not make essential to trusting the use of concepts or abilities which a child cannot be reasonably believed to possess. Acts of will of any sort are not plausibly attributed to infants; it would be unreasonable to suppose that they can do at will what adults cannot, namely, obey the instruction to trust, whether it comes from others or is a self-instruction.

To suppose that infants emerge from the womb already equipped with some ur-confidence in what supports them, so that no choice is needed to continue with that attitude until something happens to shake or destroy such confidence, is plausible enough. My account of trust has been designed to allow for unconscious trust, for conscious but unchosen trust, as well as for conscious trust the truster has chosen to endorse and cultivate. Whereas it strains the concept of agreement to speak of unconscious agreements and unchosen agreements, and overstrains the concept of contract to speak of unconscious or unchosen contracts, there is no strain whatever in the concept of automatic and unconscious trust, and of unchosen but mutual trust. Trust between infant and parent, at its best, exhibits such primitive and basic trust. Once it is present, the story of how trust becomes self-conscious, controlled, monitored, critical, pretended, and eventually either cautious and distrustful of itself or discriminatory and reflexive, so that we come to trust ourselves as trusters, is relatively easy to tell. What will need explanation will be the ceasings to trust, the transfers of trust, the restriction or enlargements in the fields of what is trusted, when, and to whom, rather than any abrupt switches from distrust to trust. Even if such occurrences do ever occur (when one suddenly falls in love or lust with a stranger or former enemy, or has a religious conversion), they take more than the mere invitation "Trust me."

In his famous account of what a promise (and a contract) involves, Hume strongly implies that it is an artificially contrived and secured case of mutual trust. The penalty to which a promisor subjects himself in promising, he says, is that of "never being trusted again in case of failure."[11] The problem which the artifice of promise solves is a generally disadvantageous "want of mutual confidence and security."[12] It is plausible to construe the offer whose acceptance counts as acceptance of a contract or a promise as at least implicitly including an invitation to trust. Part of what makes promises the special thing they are, and the philosophically intriguing thing they are, is that we *can* at will accept *this* sort of invitation to trust, whereas in general we cannot trust at will. Promises are puzzling because they seem to have the power, by verbal magic, to initiate real voluntary short-term trusting. They not merely create obligations apparently at the will of the obligated, but they create trust at the will of the truster. They present a very fascinating case of trust and trustworthiness, but one which, because of those very intriguing features, is ill suited to the role of paradigm. Yet in as far as modern moral philosophers have attended at all to the morality of trust, it is trust in parties to an agreement that they have concentrated on, and it is into this very special and artificial mold that they have tried to force other cases of trust, when they notice them at all.

Trust of any particular form is made more likely, in adults, if there is a climate of trust of that sort. Awareness of what is customary, as well as past experience of one's own, affects one's ability to trust. We take it for granted that people will perform their role-related duties and trust any individual worker to look after whatever her job requires her to. The very existence of that job, as a standard occupation, creates a climate of some trust in those with that job. Social artifices such as property, which allocate rights and duties as a standard job does, more generally also create a climate of trust, a presumption of a sort of trustworthiness. On the Humean account of promises and contracts which I find more or less correct,[13] their establishment as a customary procedure also reverses a presumption concerning trustworthiness, but only in limited conditions. Among these is a special voluntary act by the promisor, giving it to be understood that what he offers is a promise, and another voluntary act by the promisee, acceptance of that promise. Promises are "a bond or security,"[14] and "the sanction of the interested commerce of mankind."[15] To understand them is to see what sort of sanction is involved, what sort of security they provide, and the social preconditions of each. Then one understands how the presumption about the trustworthiness of self-interested strangers can be reversed, and how the ability to trust them (for a limited time, on a limited matter) can become a voluntary ability. To adapt Hume's thought, "Hence I learn to count on a service from another, although he bears me no real kindness."[16] Promises are a most ingenious social invention, and trust in those who have given us promises is a complex and sophisticated moral achievement. Once the social conditions are right for it, once the requisite climate of trust in promisors is there, it is easy to take it for a simpler matter than it is and to ignore its background conditions. They include not merely the variable social conventions and punitive customs Hume emphasizes but the prior existence of less artificial and less voluntary forms of trust, such as trust in friends and family, and enough trust in fellows to engage with them in agreed exchanges of a more or less simultaneous nature, exchanges such as barter or handshakes, which do not require one to rely on strangers over a period of time, as exchange of promises typically does.

Those who take advantage of this sophisticated social device will be, mainly, adults who are not intimate with one another, and who see one another more or less as equal in power to secure the enforcement of the rules of the contracting game (to extract damages for broken contracts, to set in motion the accepted penalty for fraudulent promises, and so on). As Nietzsche emphasized, the right to make promises and the power to have one's promises accepted are not possessed by everyone in relation to everyone else. Not only can the right be forfeited, but it is all along an elite right, possessed only by those with a certain social status. Slaves, young children, the ill, and the mentally incompetent do not fully possess it. For those who do possess it, whose offer or acceptance of a promise has moral force, the extent to which use of it regulates their relations with others varies with their other social powers. Women whose property, work, and sexual services became their husbands' on marriage did not have much left to promise, and what was left could usually be taken from them without their consent and without the formality of exchange of promises. Their right to promise anything of significance was contracted into the right to make one vow of fixed and non-negotiable content, the marriage vow, and even that was often made under duress. The important relationships and trust relationships which structured women's lives for most of the known history of our species, relations to spouse, children, fellow workers, were not entered into by free choice or by freely giving or receiving promises. They were, typically, relationships of which the more important were ones of intimacy, relationships to superiors or inferiors in power, relationships not in any strong sense freely chosen nor to chosen others. Like the infant, women found themselves faced with others to trust or distrust, found themselves trusted or not trusted by these given others. Their freely given and seriously taken promises were restricted in their content to trivialities. Contract is a device for traders, entrepreneurs, and capitalists, not for children, servants, indentured wives, and slaves. They were the traded, not the traders, and any participation they had in the promising game was mere play. It is appropriate, then, that Nietzsche, the moral philosopher who glorifies promise more even than contemporary contractarians, was also the one who advised his fellow male exchangers or givers of promises thus, "He must conceive of woman as a possession, as property that can be locked, as something predestined for service and achieving her perfection in that."[17] Nietzsche faces squarely what Hume half faced and what most moral philosophers have avoided facing, that the liberal morality which takes voluntary agreement as the paradigm source of moral obligation must either exclude the women they expect to continue in their traditional role from the class of moral subjects or admit internal contradiction in their moral beliefs. Nor does the contradiction vanish once women have equal legal rights with men, as long as they are still expected to take responsibility for any child they conceive voluntarily or nonvoluntarily, either to abort or to bear and either care for or arrange for others to care for. Since a liberal morality both *must* let this responsibility rest with women, and yet cannot conceive of it as self-assumed, then the centrality of voluntary agreement to the liberal and contractarian morality must be challenged once women are treated as full moral fellows. Voluntary agreement and trust in others to keep their agreements must be moved from the center to the moral periphery, once servants, ex-slaves, and women are taken seriously as moral subjects and agents.

The Male Fixation on Contract

The great moral theorists in our tradition not only are all men, they are mostly men who had minimal adult dealings with (and so were then minimally influenced by) women. With a few significant exceptions (Hume, Hegel, J. S. Mill, Sidgwick, maybe Bradley) they are a collection of clerics, misogynists, and puritan bachelors. It should not surprise us, then, that particularly in the modern period they managed to relegate to the mental background the web of trust tying most moral agents to one another and to focus their philosophical attention so single-mindedly on cool, distanced relations between more or less free and equal adult strangers, say, the members of an all-male club, with membership rules and rules for dealing with rule breakers and where the form of cooperation was restricted to ensuring that each member could read his *Times* in peace and have no one step on his gouty toes. Explicitly assumed or recognized obligations toward others with the same obligations and the same power to see justice done to rule breakers then are seen as the moral norm.

Relations between equals and nonintimates will *be* the moral norm for adult males whose dealings with others are mainly business or restrained social dealings with similarly placed males. But for lovers, husbands, fathers, the ill, the very young, and the elderly, other relationships, with their moral potential and perils, will loom larger. For Hume, who had several strong-willed and manipulative women to cooperate or contend with in his adult life, for Mill, who had Harriet Taylor on his hands, for Hegel, whose domestic life was of normal complication, the rights and duties of equals to equals in a civil society which recognized only a male electorate could only be *part* of the moral story. They could not ignore the virtues and vices of family relationships, male-female relationships, master-slave, and employer-employee relationships as easily as could Hobbes, Butler, Bentham, or Kant. Nor could they as easily adopt the usual compensatory strategies of the moral philosophers who confine their attention to the rights and duties of free and equal adults to one another—the strategy of claiming, if pressed, that these rights are the *core* of all moral relationships and maybe also claiming that any other relationships, engendering additional or different rights and duties, come about only by an exercise of one of the core rights, the right to promise. Philosophers who remember what it was like to be a dependent child or who know what it is like to be a parent or to have a dependent parent, an old or handicapped relative, friend, or neighbor will find it implausible to treat such relations as simply cases of co-membership in a kingdom of ends, in the given temporary conditions of one-sided dependence.

To the extent that these claims are correct (and I am aware that they need more defense than I have given them here),[18] it becomes fairly easy to see one likely explanation of the neglect in Western moral philosophy of the full range of sorts of trust. Both before the rise of a society which needed contract as a commercial device and after it, women were counted on to serve their men, to raise their children to fill the roles they were expected to fill and not to deceive their men about the paternity of these children. What men counted on one another for, in work and war, presupposed this background domestic trust, trust in women not merely not to poison their men (Nietzsche derides them for learning less than they might have in the kitchen) but to turn out sons who could trust and be trusted in traditional men's roles and daughters who would reduplicate their own capacities for trust and trustworthiness. Since the women's role did not include the writing of moral treatises, any thoughts they had about trust, based on their experience of it, did not get into our tradition (or did Diotima teach Socrates something about trust as well as love?). And the more powerful men, including those who did write the moral treatises, were in the morally awkward position of being, collectively, oppressors of women, exploiters of women's capacity for trustworthiness in unequal, nonvoluntary, and non-contract-based relationships. Understandably, they did not focus their attention on forms of trust and demands for trustworthiness which it takes a Nietzsche to recognize without shame. Humankind can bear only so much reality.

The recent research of Carol Gilligan has shown us how intelligent and reflective twentieth-century women see morality, and how different their picture of it is from that of men, particularly the men who eagerly assent to the claims of currently orthodox contractarian-Kantian moral theories.[19] Women cannot now, any more than they could when oppressed, ignore that part of morality and those forms of trust which cannot easily be forced into the liberal and particularly the contractarian mold. Men may but women cannot see morality as essentially a matter of keeping to the minimal moral traffic rules, designed to restrict close encounters between autonomous persons to self-chosen ones. Such a conception presupposes both an equality of power and a natural separateness from others, which are alien to women's experience of life and morality. For those most of whose daily dealings are with the less powerful or the more powerful, a moral code designed for those equal in power will be at best nonfunctional, at worst an offensive pretense of equality as a substitute for its actuality. But equality is not even a desirable ideal in all relationships—children not only are not but should not be equal in power to adults—and we need a morality to guide us in our dealings with those who either cannot or should not achieve equality of power (animals, the ill, the dying, children while still young) with those with whom they have unavoidable and often intimate relationships.

Modern moral philosophy has concentrated on the morality of fairly cool relationships between those who are deemed to be roughly equal in power to determine the rules and to instigate sanctions against rule breakers. It is not surprising, then, that the main forms of trust that any attention has been given to are trust in governments, and trust in parties to voluntary agreements to do what they have agreed to do. As much as possible is absorbed into the latter category, so that we suppose that paying for what one takes from a shop, doing what one is employed to do, returning what one has borrowed, supporting one's spouse are all cases of being faithful to binding voluntary agreements, to contracts of some sort. (For Hume, none of these would count as duties arising from contract or promise.) Yet if I think of the trust I show, say, in the plumber who comes from the municipal drainage authority when I report that my drains are clogged, it is not plausibly seen as trust that he will fulfill his contractual obligations to me or to his employer. When I trust him to do whatever is necessary and safe to clear my drains, I take his expertise and his lack of ill will for granted. Should he plant explosives to satisfy some unsuspected private or social grudge against me, what I might try to sue him for (if I escaped alive) would not be damages for breach of contract. His wrong, if wrong it were, would not be breach of contract, and the trust he would have disappointed would not have been that particular form of trust.

Contract enables us to make explicit just what we count on another person to do, in return for what, and should they not do just that, what damages can be extracted from them. The beauty of promise and contract is its explicitness.[20] But we can only make explicit provisions for such contingencies as we imagine arising. Until I become a victim of a terrorist plumber I am unlikely, even if I should insist on a contract before giving plumbers access to my drains, to extract a solemn agreement that they not blow me up. Nor am I likely to specify the alternative means they *may* use to clear my drains, since if I knew enough to compile such a list I would myself have to be a competent plumber. Any such detailed instructions must come from their plumbing superiors; I know nothing or little about it when I confidently welcome the plumber into the bowels of my basement. I trust him to do a nonsubversive plumbing job, as he counts on me to do a nonsubversive teaching job, should he send his son to my course in the history of ethics. Neither of us relies on a contract with the other, and neither of us need know of any contract (or much about its contents) the other may have with a third coordinating party.

It does not, then, seem at all plausible, once we think about actual moral relations in all their sad or splendid variety, to model all of them on one rather special one, the relation between promisor to promisee. We count on all sorts of people for all sorts of vital things, without any contracts, explicit or implicit, with them or with any third coordinating party. For these cases of trust in people to do their job conscientiously and not to take the opportunity to do us harm once we put things we value into their hands are different from trust in people to keep their promises in part because of the very indefiniteness of what we are counting on them to do or not to do. The subtlety and point of promising is to declare precisely *what* we count on another to do, and as the case of Shylock and Bassanio shows, that very definiteness is a limitation as well as a functional excellence of an explicit agreement.

Another functional excellence of contracts, which is closely connected with the expressness that makes breach easily established and damages or penalty decidable with a show of reasonable justice, is the *security* they offer the trusting party. They make it possible for us not merely to trust at will but to trust with minimal vulnerability. They are a device for trusting others enough for mutually profitable future-involving exchanges, without taking the risks trusters usually do take. They are designed for cooperation between mutually suspicious risk-averse strangers, and the vulnerability they involve is at the other extreme from that incurred by trusting infants. Contracts distribute and redistribute risk so as to minimize it for both parties, but trusting those more powerful persons who purport to love one increases one's risks while increasing the good one can hope to secure. Trust in fellow contractors is a limit case of trust, in which fewer risks are taken, for the sake of lesser goods.

Promises do, nevertheless, involve some real trust in the other party's goodwill and proper use of discretionary powers. Hume said that "to perform promises is requisite to beget mutual trust and confidence in the common offices of life."[21] But performing promises is not the only performance requisite for that. Shylock did not welsh on an agreement, but he was nevertheless not a trustworthy party to an agreement. For to insist on the letter of an agreement, ignoring the vague but generally understood unwritten background conditions and exceptions, is to fail to show that discretion and goodwill which a trustworthy person has. To be someone to be trusted with a promise, one must be able to use discretion not as to when the promise has been kept but, rather, as to when to insist that the promise be kept, or to instigate penalty for breach of promise. To be trusted as a promisor one must use discretion as to when to keep and when not to keep one's promise. I would feel morally let down if someone who had promised to help me move house arrived announcing, "I had to leave my mother, suddenly taken ill, to look after herself in order to be here, but I couldn't break my promise to you." From such persons I would accept no further promises, since they would have shown themselves untrustworthy in the always crucial respect of judgment and willingness to use their discretionary powers. Promises *are* morally interesting, and one's performance as party to a promise is a good indicator of one's moral character, but not for the reasons contractarians suppose.

The domination of contemporary moral philosophy by the so-called prisoner's dilemma problem displays most clearly this obsession with moral relations between minimally trusting, minimally trustworthy adults who are equally powerful. Just as the only trust Hobbist man shows is trust in promises, provided there is assurance of punishment for promise breakers, so is this the only sort of trust nontheological modern moral philosophers have given much attention at all to, as if once we have weaned ourselves from the degenerate form of absolute and unreciprocated trust in God, all our capacity for trust is to be channeled into the equally degenerate form of formal voluntary and reciprocated trust restricted to equals. But we collectively cannot bring off such a limitation of trust to minimal and secured trust, and we can deceive ourselves that we do only if we avert our philosophical gaze from the ordinary forms of trust I have been pointing to. It was not really that, after Hobbes, people *did* barricade their bodies as well as their possessions against all others before daring to sleep. Some continued to doze off on stagecoaches, to go abroad unarmed, to give credit in business deals, to count on others turning up on time for appointments, to trust parents, children, friends, and lovers not to rob or assault them when welcomed into intimacy with them. And the usual array of vicious forms of such trust, trustworthiness, and demands for them continued to flourish. Slaves continued to be trusted to cook for slaveowners; women, with or without marriage vows, continued to be trusted with the property of their men, trusted not to deceive them about the paternity of their children, and trusted to bring up their sons as patriarchs, their daughters as suitable wives or mistresses for patriarchs. Life went on, but the moral philosophers, or at least those we regard as the great ones, chose to attend only to a few of the moral relations normal life exhibited. Once Filmer was disposed of, they concentrated primarily *not* on any of the relations between those of unequal power—parent to child, husband to wife, adult to aged parent, slaveowner to slave, official to citizen, employer to employee—but on relations between roughly equal parties or between people in those respects in which they could be seen as equals.

Such relationships of mutual respect are, of course, of great moral importance. Hobbes, Locke, Rousseau, Hume, Kant, Sidgwick, Rawls, all have helped us to see more clearly how we stand in relation to anonymous others, like ourselves in need, in power, and in capacity. One need not minimize the importance of such work in moral philosophy in order to question its completeness. But a complete moral philosophy would tell us how and why we should act and feel toward others in relationships of shifting and varying power asymmetry and shifting and varying intimacy. It seems to me that we philosophers have left that task largely to priests and revolutionaries, the self-proclaimed experts on the proper attitude of the powerless to the powerful. But these relationships of inequality—some of them, such as parent-child, of unavoidable inequality—make up much of our lives, and they, as much as our relations to our equals, determine the state of moral health or corruption in which we are content to live. I think it is high time we look at the morality and immorality of relations between the powerful and the less powerful, especially at those in which there is trust between them.

A Moral Test for Trust

The few discussions of trust that I have found in the literature of moral philosophy assume that trust is a good and that disappointing known trust is always prima facie wrong, meeting it always prima facie right. But what is a trust-tied community without justice but a group of mutual blackmailers and exploiters? When the trust relationship itself is corrupt and perpetuates brutality, tyranny, or injustice, trusting may be silly self-exposure, and disappointing and betraying trust, including encouraged trust, may be not merely morally permissible but morally praiseworthy. Women, proletarians, and ex-slaves cannot ignore the virtues of watchful distrust and of judicious untrustworthiness. Only if we had reason to believe that most familiar types of trust relationship were morally sound would breaking trust be any more prima facie wrong than breaking silence. I now turn to the question of when a given form of trust is morally decent, so properly preserved by trustfulness and trustworthiness, and when it fails in moral decency. What I say about this will be sketchy and oversimplified. I shall take as the form of trust to test for moral decency the trust which one spouse has in the other, in particular as concerns their children's care.

Earlier in discussing infant trust I said that the child has reason to trust the parents when both child and parents care about the same good—the child's happiness—although the child may not see eye to eye with those trusted parents about how that is best taken care of.

When one parent, say the old-style father, entrusts the main care of his young child's needs to the old-style mother, there, too, there can be agreement on the good they both want cared for but disagreement about how best it is cared for. The lord and master who entrusts such care to his good wife, the mother, and so gives her discretionary power in making moment-by-moment decisions about what is to be done, will have done so sensibly if these disagreements are not major ones, or if he has reason to think that she knows better than he does about such matters. He should defer to her judgment, as the child is encouraged to do to the parents' and as I do to my plumber's. He sensibly trusts if he has reason to think that the discretionary powers given, even when used in ways he does not fully understand or approve of, are still used to care for the goods he wants cared for. He would be foolish to trust if he had evidence that she had other ends in view in her treatment of the child or had a radically different version of what, say, the child's healthy development and proper relation to his father consisted in. Once he suspects that she, the trusted nurse of his sons and daughters, is deliberately rearing the daughters to be patriarch-toppling Amazons, the sons to be subverters of the father's values, he will sensibly withdraw his trust and dispatch his children to suitably chosen female relatives or boarding schools. What would properly undermine his trust would be beliefs he came to hold about the formerly trusted person's motives and purposes in her care of what was entrusted to her. The disturbing and trust-undermining suspicion is not necessarily that she doesn't care about the children's good, or cares only about her own—it is the suspicion that what she cares about conflicts with rather than harmonizes with what he cares about and that she is willing to sacrifice his concerns to what she sees as the children's and her own. Trusting is rational, then, in the absence of any reason to suspect in the trusted strong and operative motives which conflict with the demands of trustworthiness as the truster sees them.

But trusting can continue to be rational, even when there are such unwelcome suspicions, as long as the truster is confident that in the conflict of motives within the trusted the subversive motives will lose to the conformist motives. Should the wife face economic hardship and loss of her children if she fails to meet the husband's trust or incurs too much of his suspicion, then she will sensibly continue as the dutiful wife, until her power position alters—sensibly, that is, given what she cares about. The husband in a position to be sure that the costs to the wife of discovered untrustworthiness are a sufficient deterrent will sensibly continue in trusting her while increasing his vigilance. Nor is he relying only on her fear, since, by hypothesis, her motives are conflicting and so she is not without some goodwill and some sympathy for his goals. Should he conclude that *only* fear of sanctions keeps her at her wifely duties, then the situation will have deteriorated from trust to mere reliance on his threat advantage. In such a case he will, if he has any sense, shrink the scope of her discretionary powers to virtually zero, since it is under cover of those that she cannot merely thwart his purposes for his children but work to change the power relations in her own favor. As long as he gives her any discretion in looking after what is entrusted to her, he must trust her, and not rely solely on her fear of threatened penalties for disappointing his expectations.

The trusted wife (who usually, of course, also trusts her husband with many things that matter to her) is sensible to try to keep his trust, as long as she judges that the goods which would be endangered should she fail to meet his trust matter more to her than those she could best look after only by breaking or abusing his trust. The goods for the sake of whose thriving she sensibly remains trustworthy might include the loving relation between them and their mutual trust for its own sake as well as their agreed version of their children's good; or it might be some vestiges of these plus her own economic support or even physical safety, which are vulnerable to his punitive rage should she be found guilty of breach of trust. She will sensibly continue to meet trust, even when the goods with whose case she is trusted are no longer clearly common goods, as long as she cares a lot about anything his punitive wrath can and is likely to harm.

Sensible trust could persist, then, in conditions where truster and trusted suspect each other of willingness to harm the other if they could get away with it, the one by breach of trust, the other by vengeful response to that. The stability of the relationship will depend on the trusted's skill in cover-up activities, on the truster's evident threat advantage, or on a combination of these. Should the untrustworthy trusted person have not merely skill in concealment of her breaches of trust but skill in directing them toward increasing her own power and increasing her ability to evade or protect herself against the truster's attempted vengeance, then that will destabilize the relation, as also would frequent recourse by the truster to punitive measures against the trusted.

Where the truster relies on his threat advantage to keep the trust relation going or where the trusted relies on concealment, something is morally rotten in the trust relationship. The truster who in part relies on his whip or his control of the purse is sensible but not necessarily within his moral rights in continuing to expect trustworthiness; and the trusted who sensibly relies on concealment to escape the penalty for untrustworthiness may or may not be within her moral rights. I tentatively propose a test for the moral decency of a trust relationship, namely, that its continuation need not rely on successful threats held over the trusted or on her successful cover-up of breaches of trust. We could develop and generalize this test into a version of an expressibility test, if we note that knowledge of what the other party is relying on for the continuance of the trust relationship would, in the above cases of concealment and of threat advantage, itself destabilize the relation. Knowledge of the other's reliance on concealment does so fairly automatically, and knowledge of the other's partial reliance on one's fear of his revenge would tend, in a person of normal pride and self-assertiveness, to prompt her to look for ways of exploiting her discretionary powers so as to minimize her vulnerability to that threat. More generally, to the extent that what the truster relies on for the continuance of the trust relation is something which, once realized by the truster, is likely to lead to (increased) abuse of trust and eventually to destabilization and destruction of that relation, the trust is morally corrupt. Should the wife come to realize that the husband relies on her fear of his revenge, on her stupidity in not realizing her exploitation, or on her servile devotion to him to keep her more or less trustworthy, that knowledge should be enough to begin to cure these weaknesses and to motivate untrustworthiness. Similarly, should the truster come to realize that the trusted relies on her skill at covering up or on her ability to charm him into forgiveness for breaches of trust, that is, relies on *his* blindness or gullibility, that realization will help cure that blindness and gullibility. A trust relationship is morally bad to the extent that either party relies on qualities in the other which would be weakened by the knowledge that the other relies on them. Where each relies on the other's love, concern for some common good, or professional pride in competent discharge of responsibility, knowledge of what the other is relying on in one need not undermine but will more likely strengthen those relied-on features. They survive exposure as what others rely on in one in a way that some forms of stupidity, fear, blindness, ignorance, and gullibility normally do not. There are other mental states whose sensitivity to exposure as relied on by others seems more variable: good nature, detachment, inattention, generosity, forgivingness, and sexual bondage to the other party to the trust may not be weakened by knowledge that others count on their presence in one to sustain some wanted relationship, especially if they are found equally in both parties. But the knowledge that others are counting on one's nonreciprocated generosity or good nature or forgiveness can have the power of the negative, can destroy trust.

I assume that in some forms of trust the healthy and desired state will be mere self-maintenance, while in others it will be change and growth. Alteration of the trust relationship need not take the form of destruction of the old form and its replacement by a new form, but of continuous growth, of slight shifts in scope of discretionary powers, additions or alterations in scope of goods entrusted, and so on. Of course some excitement-addicted persons may cultivate a form of trust in part for the opportunity it provides for dramatic disruption. Trust is the atmosphere necessary for exhilarating disruptions of trust and satisfyingly spectacular transfers of trust, as well as for other goods we value. For persons with such tastes, immoral forms of trust may be preferable to what, according to my test, are moral forms of trust.

It should be noted that my proposed test of the moral decency of trust is quite noncommittal as to what cases of reliance on another's psychology will be acceptable to the other. I have assumed that most people in most trust situations will not be content to have others rely on their fear, their ignorance, and their spinelessness. In some cases, however, such as trusting police to play their role effectively and trusting one's fellows to refrain from open crime, some element of fear must play a role, and it is its absence, not its presence, which would destabilize trust in such contexts. In others, such as trust in national intelligence and security officers to look after national security, some ignorance in the trusting is proper, and awareness that such persons may be relying on one's not knowing what they know will not destabilize any trust one has in them to do what they are entrusted to do. What will be offensive forms of reliance on one's psychological state will vary from context to context, depending on the nature of the goods entrusted and on other relationships between the trusting and the trusted. Variations in individual psychology will also make a difference. Some are much more tolerant than others of having their good nature or preoccupation taken advantage of—not merely in that they take longer to recognize that they are victims of this, but that they are less stirred to anger or resentment by the awareness that they are being deceived, blackmailed, or exploited in a given trust relation. I have used the phrase "tend to destroy" in the test for moral decency in the assumption that there is a normal psychology to be discerned and that it does include a strong enough element of Platonic *thumos*. Should that be false, then all sorts of horrendous forms of trust may pass my test. I do not, in any case, claim that it is the only test, merely that it is an appropriate one. It is a test which amounts to a check on the will and goodwill of the truster and trusted, a look to see how good their will to one another is, knowing what they do about each other's psychology.

It may be objected that the expressibility test I have proposed amounts to a reversion, on my part, to the contractarian attitude which I have deplored.[22] Have I not finally admitted that we must treat trust relationships as hypothetical contracts, with all the terms fully spelled out in order to determine their moral status? The short answer is that contractarians do not have a monopoly on expressibility tests. In any case, I have applied it at a place no contractarian would, and *not* applied it where he does. Where he assumes self-interest as a motive and makes explicit what goods or services each self-interested party is to receive from the other, I have left it open what motives the trusting and trusted have for maintaining the relation, requiring only that these motives, insofar as they rely on responses from the other, survive the other's knowledge of that reliance, and I have not required that relied-on services be made explicit. What the contractarian makes explicit is a voluntary mutual commitment, and what services each is committed to provide. I have claimed that not only is such explicitness rare in trust relationships, but many of them must begin inexplicitly and nonvoluntarily and would not do the moral and social work they do if they covered only what a contract does—services that could be pretty exactly spelled out. My moral test does not require that these nonexplicit elements in trust should be made explicit but, rather, that something else survive being made explicit: one's reliance on facts about others' psychological states relevant to their willingness to continue serving or being served. These states include love, fear, ignorance, sense of powerlessness, good nature, inattention, which one can use for one's secret purposes. It is not part of contracts or social contracts to specify what assumptions each party needs to make about the other in respect of such psychological factors. Perhaps constraints regarding duress and fraud can be linked with the general offensiveness of having others rely on one's ignorance, fear, or sense of powerlessness, especially when these are contrived by the one who relies on them; but contracts themselves do not make express what it is in the state of mind of the other that each party relies on to get what he wants from the deal. What I have proposed as a general moral test of trust is indeed a generalization of one aspect of the contractarian morality, namely, of the assumptions implicit in the restrictions of valid contracts to those not involving fraud or duress. Whereas contracts make explicit the services (or service equivalent) exchanged, trust, when made express, amounts to a sort of exchange of responses to the motives and state of mind of the other. Contractualists and other exchange fetishists can see this as a spiritual exchange, if it pleases them to do so, but it is not voluntary in the way contracts are, nor does it presuppose any equality of need or of power in the parties to this "exchange." The relation of my account of the morality of trust to standard contractarian morality seems to me as close as it should be, and at roughly the right places, if, as I have claimed, trust in fellow contractors is a limit case of trust.

Nevertheless, there are two aspects of my test which worry me, which may indicate that it is not sufficiently liberated from contractarian prejudices. One difficulty is that it ignores the *network* of trust, and treats only two-party trust relationships. This is unrealistic, since any person's attitude to another in a given trust relationship is constrained by all the other trust and distrust relationships in which she is involved. Although I have alluded to such society-wide phenomena as climates of trust affecting the possibilities for individual trust relationships, my test is not well designed for application to the whole network but has to be applied piecemeal. That is a defect, showing the same individualist limitations which I find in contractarianism. The second thing that worries me is that the test seems barely applicable to brief trusting encounters, such as those with fellow library frequenters. As the contractarian takes as his moral paradigm a relationship which has some but not a very complex temporal depth, assimilating simultaneous exchange to the delayed delivery which makes a contract useful, and treats lifelong mutual trust as iterated mutual delayed deliveries, so I have shown a bias toward the medium-length trust relationship, thereby failing to say or imply anything very helpful either about brief encounters or about cross-generational trust. Probably these two faults are connected. If one got a test for the whole network of trust, with all the dependencies between the intimate and the more impersonal forms properly noted, and had the right temporal dimensions in that, then both the morality of brief trusting encounters and the morality of trust between generations who do not encounter each other would fall into place.

Since I have thus oversimplified the problem of morally evaluating trust relationships by confining my attention to relationships one by one, my account of trusting as acceptance of having as it were entrusted and my consequent expansion of trusting from a two-place into a three-place predicate will seem forced and wrong. For there are some people whom one would not trust with anything, and that is not because one has considered each good one might entrust to that one and rejected that possibility. We want then to say that unless we first trust them we will not trust them *with anything*. I think that there is some truth in this, which my account has not captured. For some kinds of enemy (perhaps class enemies?) one will not trust even with one's bodily safety as one raises a white flag, but one will find it "safer" to fight to the death. With some sorts of enemies, a contract may be too intimate a relation. If the network of relationships is systematically unjust or systematically coercive, then it may be that one's status within that network will make it unwise of one to entrust anything to those persons whose interests, given their status, are systematically opposed to one's own. In most such corrupt systems there will be limited opportunity for such beleaguered persons to "rescue" their goods from the power of their enemies— they usually will have no choice but to leave them exposed and so to act as if they trusted, although they feel proper distrust. In such conditions it may take fortitude to display distrust and heroism to disappoint the trust of the powerful. Courageous (if unwise) untrustworthiness and stoic withdrawal of trust may then be morally laudable. But since it usually will take such heroic disruptions of inherited trust relationships for persons to distance themselves from those the system makes their enemies, my test will at least be usable to justify such disruptions. In an earlier version of this essay I said that the ghost of plain trust and plain distrust haunted my account of goods-relativized or "fancy" trust. I think that I now see that ghost for what it is and see why it ought to continue to haunt. Still, such total oppositions of interest are rare, and one satisfactory thing about my account is that it enables us to see how we can salvage some respects in which we may trust even those whose interests are to some extent opposed to our own.

Meanwhile, my account of what it is to trust and my partial account of when it is immoral to expect or meet trust will have to be treated as merely a beginning (or, for some, a resumption, since there doubtless are other attempts at this topic which have escaped my notice). Trust, I have claimed, is reliance on others' competence and willingness to look after, rather than harm, things one cares about which are entrusted to their care. The moral test of such trust relationships which I have proposed is that they be able to survive awareness by each party to the relationship of *what* the other relies on in the first to ensure their continued trustworthiness or trustingness. This test elevates to a special place one form of trust, namely, trusting others with knowledge of what it is about them which enables one to trust them as one does or to expect them to be trustworthy. The test could be restated this way: trust is morally decent only if, in addition to whatever else is entrusted, knowledge of each party's reasons for confident reliance on the other to continue the relationship could in principle also be entrusted—since such mutual knowledge would be itself a good, not a threat to other goods. To the extent that mutual reliance can be accompanied by mutual knowledge of the conditions for that reliance, trust is above suspicion, and trustworthiness a nonsuspect virtue. "Rara temporum felicitas . . . quae sentias dicere licet."[23]

This essay has an antiphonal title, and a final counterpoint may not be out of order. Although I think this test is an appropriate moral test, it is another matter to decide whether and when it should be applied to actual cases of trust. Clearly in some cases, such as infant trust and parental trustworthiness, which could in principle pass it, it cannot actually be applied by both parties to the relationship. That need not unduly worry us. But in other cases it may well be that the attempt to apply it will ensure its failing the test. Trust is a fragile plant, which may not endure inspection of its roots, even when they were, before the inspection, quite healthy. So, although some forms of trust would survive a suddenly achieved mutual awareness of them, they may not survive the gradual and possibly painful process by which such awareness actually comes about. It may then be the better part of wisdom, even when we have an acceptable test for trust, not to use it except where some distrust already exists, the better to take nonsuspect trust on trust. Luhmann says that "it is a characteristic mark of civilizing trust that it incorporates an element of reflexivity."[24] But to trust one's trust and one's distrust enough to refrain from applying moral tests until prompted by some distrust is to take a very risky bet on the justice, if not the "civilization," of the system of trust one inhabits. We may have to trade off civilization for justice, unless we can trust not only our trust but, even more vitally, our distrust.

seven

TRUST AND ITS VULNERABILITIES

They fle from me that sometyme did me seek
With naked fote stalking in my chambre,
I have sene theim gentill tame and meke
That nowe are wyld and do not remembre
That sometyme they put theimself in daunger
To take bred at my hand . . .

Sir Thomas Wyatt

Most of us are tame enough to take bread at someone's hand.[1] And we do thereby put ourselves in danger. So why do we do it? What bread is good enough to tempt us into the hands of possibly dangerous people-tamers? Or do we simply prefer being gentle, tame, and meek? Trust in trustworthy people to do their more or less willing and more or less competent bit in some worthwhile cooperative enterprise whose benefits are fairly shared among all the cooperators is to most of us an obviously good thing, and not just because we get better bread that way. The only ones who might dissent from the value of trust are those "wild" loners who value their independence more than anything else, who prefer to get their bread baked by solo efforts rather than to join with others in any sort of joint scheme. To such extreme individualists this essay and Essays 8 and 9 will have nothing persuasive to say. Most of us are fairly tame, and what John Locke said is true of us: "Men live upon trust."[2] But we do not always live well, upon trust. Sometimes, like Elizabeth I of England, we have to report that we "in trust have found treason,"[3] or, less regally, betrayal, or, even less pompously, plain let-down. Trust is a notoriously vulnerable good, easily wounded and not at all easily healed.

Trust is not always a good, to be preserved. There must be some worthwhile enterprise in which the trusting and trusted parties are involved, some good bread being kneaded, for trust to be a good thing. If the enterprise is evil, a producer of poisons, then the trust that improves its workings will also be evil, and decent people will want to destroy, not protect, that form of trust. A death squad may consist of wholly trustworthy and, for a while at least, sensibly trusting co-workers. So the first thing to be checked, if our trust is to become self-conscious, is the nature of the enterprise whose workings are smoothed by merited trust.

Even when the enterprise is a benign one, it is frequently one that does not fairly distribute the jobs and benefits that are at its disposal. A reminder of the sorry sexist history of marriage as an institution aiming at providing children with proper parental care should be enough to convince us that mutual trust and mutual trustworthiness in a good cause can coexist with the oppression and exploitation of at least half the trusting and trusted partners. Business firms whose exploitation of workers is sugar-coated by a paternalistic show of concern for them and the maintenance of a cozy familial atmosphere of mutual trust, are an equally good example. Trust can coexist, and has long coexisted, with contrived and perpetuated inequality. This may well explain and to some extent justify the distrust that many decent vigilant people display toward any attempt to reinstate a climate of trust as a social and moral good. Like most goods, a climate of trust is a risky thing to set one's sights on.[4] What we risk are not just mutually lethal betrayals and breakdowns of trust but exploitation that may be unnoticed for long periods because it is bland and friendly. The friendly atmosphere—the *feeling* of trust—is of course a pleasant thing, and itself a good, as long as it is not masking an evil.

Trust and distrust are feelings, but like many feelings they are what Hume called "impressions of reflexion," feeling responses to how we take our situation to be. The relevant "situation" is our position as regards what matters to us, how well or badly things are going for us. The pleasant feeling that others are with us in our endeavors, that they will help and not hinder us, and the unpleasantly anxious feeling that others may be plotting our downfall or simply that their intentions are inscrutable, so that we do not know what to expect, are the surface phenomena of trust and distrust, and this surface is part of the real good of genuine trust, the real evil of suspicion and distrust. But beneath the surface is what that surface purports to show us, namely, others' attitudes and intentions toward us, their good (or their ill) will. The belief that their will is good is itself a good, not merely instrumentally but in itself, and the pleasure we take in that belief is no *mere* pleasure, but part of an important good. Trust is one of those mental phenomena attention to which shows us the inadequacy of attempting to classify mental phenomena into the "cognitive," the "affective," and the "conative." Trust, if it is any of these, is all three. It has its special "feel," most easily acknowledged when it is missed, say, when one moves from a friendly "safe" neighborhood to a tense insecure one. It has its (usually implicit) belief component, belief in the trusted's goodwill and competence, which then grounds the willingness to be or remain within the trusted's power in a way the distrustful are not, and to give the trusted discretionary powers in matters of concern to us. When we trust we accept vulnerability to others.[5]

A third obvious way in which trust can go wrong is when the belief-cum-feeling-cum-intention of trust is faked—when a person is only apparently trusting. False pretenses can infect a trust relationship, and it may continue, apparently healthy, for long periods, while all the time harboring such low-grade infection. A wife may not really trust her husband further than she can see him, but she might pretend she does, perhaps pretend to herself that she does, and close her ears to any unwelcome messengers. Alternatively, she may indeed really count on his marital fidelity, but not because she trusts him. She may rely instead on her unuttered threat advantage (when, say, she controls the money, and is known to have her reliable spies, so that the husband does not dare stray). Real trustworthiness, like real trust, involves feelings, beliefs, and intentions, which sometimes can be faked. The trustworthy person will feel some concern for the trusting, and this feeling will be especially noticeable if things go wrong. She will believe that she is responsible for what she is trusted for, and intend to discharge that responsibility competently and with a good grace. A "good grace" excludes not merely resentment of the responsibility but also a too calculative weighing of the costs of untrustworthiness and the benefits of trustworthiness. Should one do what one is trusted to do only because one fears that the response to discovered untrustworthiness would be very costly to one, then that very attitude, if known, would be a good enough reason for those who had trusted one to cease trusting. They might not cease relying on one, but their reliance would no longer be on one's goodwill.

Trust is an alternative to vigilance and reliance on the threat of sanctions, trustworthiness is an alternative to constant watching to see what one can and cannot get away with, to recurrent recalculations of costs and benefits. Trust is accepted vulnerability to another's power to harm one, a power inseparable from the power to look after some aspect of one's good.

Trusting the untrustworthy who parade as trustworthy ("You know you can trust me!") and living up to what another presents as her trust in one, when that is not really trust but reliance on her evident power to punish those who fail her ("I am trusting you and don't you forget it!"), are among the most common sorts of disease in a trust relationship. Healthy trust rarely needs to declare itself, and the mere occurrence of the injunction "Trust me!" or of the reminder "I am trusting you" is a danger signal. Even when such pronouncements are not insincere, they may still be false, and will be, if trust has been confused with reliance on threats.

A "Trust me!" speech act (I suppose that J. L. Austin would have called it a "commissive" illocutionary act) or its gestural equivalent will be false in a more straightforward way when the implied prediction that the truster will not be "let down" proves false, not because of any deceit but because of the trusted's false estimate of his competence to "hold up" the truster. If, during one of those exercises which I believe some psychotherapists get their patients to play, I am encouraged to let myself fall back into the arms of the fellow patient behind me, whose job is to say "Trust me!" and then to catch me, I do my bit, go limp and fall, but my weight proves too much for the appointed catcher, so that I am literally let down, then I will naturally feel sore both toward the false supporter and toward the psychotherapist who choreographed my downfall. Some of those we trust let us down through their false estimate of their willingness to support us. If my upbringing has encouraged me to rely on male escorts for defense against attack, but, when we are attacked by angry Australian magpies, my gentleman escort instinctively ducks behind me, using me as a "living shield," then I will blame both my escort and, more, my own silly acceptance of the myth of male protectiveness.

Thomas Scanlon[6] has helpfully separated out the different but related moral principles that he believes should govern the conduct of anyone who says "Trust me!" to others or who somehow communicates encouragement to trust. The first principle (Principle M) forbids manipulation of others by deliberately raising false expectations in them about how one will respond to something one wants them to do. The second (Principle D) requires one to take due care not to lead others to form reasonable but false expectations about what one will do, where they would face significant loss if they relied on such false expectations. The third (Principle L) requires one to take steps to prevent any loss that others would face through reliance on expectations about one's future behavior, expectations that one has either intentionally or negligently (that is, by infringing Principle M or D) led them to form. Principle L could demand a very great deal of us, if we really tried to live by it—it would require us to *notice* what others are coming to rely on in us, and to protect them against loss from such reliance by whatever steps were needed. The fourth principle, the fidelity principle (F), does not require us to do more than we have assured another we will do; it requires us to do precisely what we assured them we would do. (I have given Scanlon's principles in a somewhat oversimplified form. His main aim is to show that the fidelity principle is what makes a promise binding, whether or not there is a "social practice" of promising or a special recognized force to the words "I promise," and his careful wording of the fidelity principle[7] has that end in view.)

The psychotherapist who instructs me to "Trust him!"—that is, tells me to trust the weakling behind me to catch me—is manipulative, negligent, and fails to prevent the loss I incur through his manipulation, but since he himself need not have said "Trust *me*!" he need not have offended against the fidelity principle. The one who offends against that is the fellow patient who, as per instructions, says "Trust me!" even if he rightly fears that he cannot catch and support me. He offends against Scanlon's principles D, L, and F but not against M, since he really has no wish that I should fall into his arms—we are both merely following instructions. But do most of us on reflection accept Scanlon's principles? Do we not regularly and without guilt try to manipulate each other (in advertising, for example), take little care what expectations we may be arousing (in the wild birds and squirrels that we feed, and in the charities we give to), impose losses upon one another by giving misleading indicators of our intentions (in poker, in clever bargaining, and in our military strategies), let others down and often be forgiven for so doing, and sometimes even be invited to repeat the performance?

John Updike has a marvelous variant of the common tragi-comedy of the let-down and its typical effects. In his story "Trust Me" a three-year-old boy, Harold, is lovingly bullied by his father into leaping into the deep end of a public swimming pool, where the father waits to catch him. "It'll be all right, jump right into my hands," encourages the father. The child trustingly jumps, the father misses the catch, the child goes briefly under, the father fishes him out and lands him, coughing and spluttering, on the pool side. He picks the child up, to comfort him, and is quickly joined by his alarmed wife, Harold's mother. Updike goes on: "His mother swiftly came up to the two of them and, with a deftness remarkable in one so angry, slapped his father on the face, loudly, next to Harold's ear ... His mother's anger seemed directed at him as much as at his father ... Standing wrapped in a towel near his mother's knees while the last burning fragments of water were coughed from his lungs, Harold felt eternally disgraced. He never knew what had happened; by the time he asked, so many years had passed that his father had forgotten. 'Wasn't that a crying shame,' the old man said, with his mild mixture of mournfulness and comedy. 'Sink or swim, and you sank.' Perhaps Harold had leaped a moment before it was expected, or had proved unexpectedly heavy, and thus slipped through his father's grasp. Unaccountably, all through his growing up he continued to trust his father; it was his mother he distrusted, her swift sure-handed anger."[8]

It is not really so unaccountable that distrust should be directed not so much at those who once or twice let one down in the most obvious way, who manipulated one or gave one what turned out to be false assurances, but rather at those who prove angrily unfor-giving of the letters-down, who do not forgive those who forgive others, who show themselves to be completely reliable punishers of the ones who violate the fidelity principle and even of their forgiving victims. Harold could continue to trust his father (who, after all, did competently save him after first endangering him), for he had shown the child affection, and manipulated him out of a will to share the fun, flawed only by a faulty estimate of what frolicsome feats were feasible for the pair of them. Incompetence is more easily remedied than ill will, and Harold doubtless learned a little from his sorry experience. (He learned what and what not to expect from his father. Harold keeps on trusting and, if need be, forgiving those loved ones who let him down in the well-meaning way his father did.) Harold's mother showed concern for her child and anger at her husband who had endangered him, along with impressive slapping competence. Was she not a faithful mother and guardian? If trust were simply belief in the dependability of a person to do some range of things, on cue, then we would have to say yes. Harold could count on his mother to attack anyone who harmed or endangered her child. Like a mother cat or a well-programmed robot, she could be counted on to leap into action to protect her young. But trustworthiness is not just mechanical dependability, and trust is not merely confidence in a range of particular actions in a range of particular circumstances. The trustworthy can show their trustworthiness in surprising ways, and to trust is to be willing to give the trusted the benefit of the doubt when the surprise is, initially at least, unpleasant. For to trust is to give discretionary powers to the trusted, to let the trusted decide how, on a given matter, one's welfare is best advanced, to delay the accounting for a while, to be willing to wait to see how the trusted has advanced one's welfare.

As we sometimes but not always wisely delay gratification, so we sometimes can delay knowing or understanding just what others are doing with what matters to us. The pathologies of trust therefore have to include both the truster's bad timing of the demand for an account and also the trusted's misuse of discretionary powers, both by too adventurous uses of them (as perhaps Harold's father was guilty of) and by a refusal to relax some inflexible rule, that is, by a refusal to use discretion at all, by simply falling back on reliance on some stimulus-response mechanism, on some automatic pilot, be it instinctive anger or rigid principle. To say, "I can trust him to remember my birthday: he has given his bank a standing order to send the same flowers each year on that date. Short of bank collapse, I can count on it," would be to speak at least ironically, if not sourly. One frequent thing that goes wrong with a personal trust relationship is that it degenerates into one of mutual predictability. Not merely does this make it boring (as in marriages that freeze into unimaginative, repetitive, and numbingly dependable mutual service), but it also lessens the likelihood that anyone's good is really being furthered by the dependable behavior. For, as Aristotle emphasized, judgment is continually having to be used when we really aim at anyone's well-being. Turning over to automatic pilot is not often a serious possibility for those whose goal is the good of another—or even when their goal is their own good. The assurance typically given (implicitly or explicitly) by the person who invites our trust, unlike that typically given in that peculiar case of assurance, a promise or contract, is not assurance of some very specific action or set of actions, but assurance simply that the trusting's welfare is, and will one day be seen to have been, in good hands.

An institutional example may, at this stage, be a good thing, since I do not want to suggest that it is only in the context of personal relationships that trust is a good and its diseased variants an evil. There are interesting differences between the trust of intimates and what is good about it and the nature and value of more impersonal trust, and each is prey to some sicknesses peculiar to that type,[9] but the main dimensions of fragility are the same, and there are interdependencies between a healthy climate of impersonal trust and the likelihood of a strong trust relationship of a more personal sort. For good marriages, and for marriages whose ending is not too disastrous for the spouses themselves and for their children, there must be well-functioning background institutions such as divorce courts, for when marriages break up, and, in more normal times, schools, legislatures, supreme courts, and regulatory agencies whose decisions affect such matters as family planning and the planning of both spouses' careers, not to mention banks, insurance agencies, and others whose policies affect the security each spouse can have.

But let us leave the domestic scene and turn to the academic arena. Universities have boards of trustees, to whom the welfare of the institution is entrusted. And an elaborate chain of trust relationships usually goes from these trustees to president, provost, dean, chairpersons, and their appointees within departments. At each of these levels the one in whom trust is placed is not merely a rule applier but a decision maker. Rules there certainly will be, and applying them will not always be such an easy and automatic matter, but no set of university regulations will decide for university administrators everything that they have to settle, in their day-to-day activities. When times are tough and cuts have to be made, no rule will tell them what to do. They have discretionary powers—their job is to think about the mission of the university, to listen to all sorts of advisors and affected parties, and then to work out priorities as best they can. If they do their job competently and with an appropriately firm will to the good of the institution (seen always in light of its mission), their decisions need not be predictable; they may surprise many, disappoint some, relieve others. Some timid or tired administrators do become predictable in their decision making, and to that very extent, show themselves unwilling to use discretionary powers, and so show themselves as unsuitable recipients of our trust. For example, when a cut in spending is judged necessary, a mechanical spreading of it across all administrative units is usually a sure indicator of dereliction of the duty to think about what should be done, rather than a sign of a deep thoughtful commitment to equality (especially given the sort of units which are being accorded equal treatment). In some institutions such mindless "equal sharing" of burdens becomes the rule, a predictable administration response to any fiscal crisis. But I do not think that anyone would be tempted to give those administrators awards either for superior wisdom or for dogged integrity, let alone for boldness of vision. It is understandable that those who do not wish any longer to have to think about the good of their university might fall back on already-made decisions, such as those structuring an institution into various schools or faculties, and then simply say, "Let them share the cuts equally," regardless of their unequal needs, unequal opportunities, or unequal history of previous shares of burdens and benefits and of use made of the benefits. Such a ruling would be a use of discretionary powers that amounts to a refusal to use them. It would be like the policy of the relative whose birthday gift of flowers came with mindless regularity on the right day. In these cases it is not that there is no attention to the good of the person or body at which the person is theoretically aiming. But it is not the sort of attention that would be given by a trustworthy so thoughtful well-wisher. To trust is to let another think about and take action to protect and advance something the truster cares about, to let the trusted *care for* what one cares about. Thoughtless care verges on "careless care," on plain failure to give care.

It might be thought that where we have answerable officials, who may be removed from office for poor performance of what it is their responsibility to do, no question of trust will arise. University presidents, provosts, and deans, it might be said, are not "trustees." But it would be too swift to suppose that because we do not call them trustees, no trust and entrusting has gone on. We cannot and do not rely simply on the conditional threat of removal from office to motivate officials to discharge their responsibilities properly. We do hold them "accountable," but the accountant's audits, so to speak, will be infrequent. We have no choice but to entrust them with some matters, where constant checking on performance is either impractical or undesirable. Nor does the fact that there is some reliance on the threat of sanctions mean that there will be no room for trust. In our attitude toward other people whom we are counting on, we typically combine trust on some matters with careful checks on others.

In dealings with those we know a little and are willing on that basis to have business dealings with, we typically do partition the matters we have them see to into those where we check up on them and those where we do not. Some failures of such normal business dealings occur because of the fuzziness of the understanding of just where the division falls. If one stands over one's builder, watching and querying every move she makes, she may well refuse to finish the job, since what self-respecting builder would put up with such apparent lack of *any* trust in her professional skill and standards of care? Is she, the builder, not supposed to be the one with the know-how? If the client thinks he knows so much more, why did he hire the builder in the first place—why not hire unskilled workers to obey the client's commands? One pathological case is the shrinking of the trust dimension to near zero, along with a commensurate expansion of the area where constant checking and testing is going on. Contract is the useful contrivance we have for such cases where trust has shrunk to near zero, where as much as possible is spelled out, where checks and tests are always in order. Another unhealthy condition is where there is such an exaggerated fear of insulting the other that *any* checking, even on matters where honest mistake or miscounting is both easy and easily detected without offense, or any request for an account of the trusted's activities regarding what was entrusted, is seen as tactless, dangerous to the cooperative relationship.

Rules to guide us on where to trust, where not to, where to insist on precise specification in a contract, where not, are notoriously lacking. We seem to have no choice but to trust our own trust or suspicion on these matters, to check when we harbor suspicions that checks may reveal some bad performance, to trust when we have no such suspicions; to spell matters out in an enforceable contract when we judge that the other bears us "no real kindness," as Hume put it, and to leave things more casual when we judge that the mutuality and "good offices" are a little "more generous and noble."[10] Some suspicions will be unbased and costly, some contracts regrettable and destructive of fellowship; while some trustings will turn out to have been naive and unwise—that is only to be expected. But if the alternative to sometimes giving trust is the policy of trying to check everything out, to protect all one's dealings with others by formal contracts, or the empowerment of Leviathans to stand guard over all of us, then the costs of that policy, especially its opportunity costs, may sensibly persuade us to become like the child Harold in the Updike story, and to take a few letdowns in our stride.

If to trust on a given matter is to leave that matter to the trusted, to see no need, for a while, to check up on how she is doing, to assume that she is doing just fine, that her memory, competence, and goodwill (Hume's "kindness") are all as one expected when one entrusted the matter to her, then, some might say, only fools ever trust. For are not locks and checks always sensible or, at the very worst, a slight waste of time and resources? Might trust itself be pathological? I resist that thought, but I can accommodate the cynics who ask it by allowing that it would usually be foolish, in one's attitude toward a given person on a given matter, not to mix trust on some matters with doubts and prudent checkups on others. It would be offensive to make a surprise visit to check up on the babysitter, but only sensible, with a new untried one, to arrange to phone during the evening and to stick to that arrangement. If one is asked to trust an ally to defend one from missile attacks, and is trusted not to retaliate oneself, what checks should one want and accept? Some evidence not just of good past performance, but that each party is now managing to do what it is trusted to do and not to do? (Now meaning at this minute? Now meaning today? The really hard questions are these, of the details, of the timing of the audits.)

It takes trusters and *their* functional virtues as well as trusted ones and *their* functional virtues to keep a trust relationship healthy. And most participants will need both sets of virtues, since stable trust is usually mutual trust. Scanlon's principles forbidding manipulation by the deliberate arousing of false expectations, requiring us to take due care not to raise false expectations, to prevent loss to those who rely on our doing what we have encouraged or allowed them to rely on our doing, and to do precisely what we have assured them we will do, are all principles for those who *invite* our trust. They need perhaps to be supplemented by a few principles for the potential trusters or, at least, since trusting is rarely something we *decide* to do, by an analysis of some virtues that are displayed in our dispositions to trust or to distrust. To the extent that the will is involved, that it makes sense to speak of considering whether or not to trust, what principles could be offered for those considering trusting (or acting as if they trusted), considering whether to continue or resume trusting considering how much insurance they need to take out against loss contrived or negligently caused by others, or by reliance on their false assurances. How much vigilance and checking is worth the cost? And which locksmiths, guards, accountants, and insurers are trustworthy? (The best cover for a burglar is the police force or the security and insurance professions.)

But what principles can we offer? How many times should we forgive? How much tact must we show? And what principles are there for those who find themselves trusted although they never invited the trust, whose only assurances to the trusting have been their continuing to behave as expected, whose only "Trust me!" has been the failure to issue the warning "Don't trust me!" Or for those once trusted ones who find themselves inexplicably mistrusted? Francis Bacon tells us that "base natures, if they find themselves once suspected, will never be true,"[11] and we may presume that nobler natures will rise above suspicion, will not live down to the distrust they may encounter. But what is our advice for those who are instinctively distrusted and for those who, like Saul Bellow's self-deprecating protagonist in *More Die of Heartbreak,* suspect that "there's something about the slenderness of my face and my glance suggesting slyness. Some people don't feel at ease with me and sense that I am watching them. They suspect me of suspicion."[12] Such meta-suspicions can be as self-confirming as trust in trust or the will to believe. Their costs are opportunity costs, while the costs of unlucky trust and meta-trust can be more dramatic and less easily overlooked. What is the magic formula for the right mix of trust and suspicion, meta-trust and meta-suspicion?

I am myself skeptical of the chances of success of the Scanlon Kantian enterprise of trying to formulate "valid" moral principles intended to sum up what we expect of participants in a trust relationship. Is it likely that we will come up with rules on how many times betrayal should be forgiven, or how distrust is properly focused after "enough" betrayals, or how long insulting distrust should be ignored? (How many rapes should a woman take, before turning against all men? After one rape, how should she focus her future distrust? How should her male acquaintances react if they all become "unfairly" distrusted by her?) I am skeptical both of the insistence that there must be such general moral rules that codify our moral beliefs and of the assumption that we can establish their validity in a non-question-begging manner, without taking some form of trust on trust. I shall return to this point in Essay 8. So that we can appreciate the full complexity of trust situations that any principles that we endorse would have to cover, I shall give two more anecdotes, illustrating the vulnerabilities incurred by trust and also showing, I think, the difficulty of formulating any useful rules about how not to misplace our trust or to misuse our capacities for being trustworthy. They are both stories of trust leading to unpleasant surprises.

First Anecdote. A student accepts her tutor's offer of a rental cottage in the west of Ireland during the summer to get on with her dissertation (since steady rain can be expected). The cottage is delightfully situated, delightfully primitive, delightfully isolated; the weather unexpectedly fine. Her farmer landlord comes on foot each evening to bring her milk and buttermilk, the latter so that she can make soda bread on her peat fire. (His wife has instructed her in the finer points of how to do this, since there is no local store, and the staple diet is whole wheat bread, milk, a few locally grown vegetables and when one is lucky, some locally caught fish.) He brings one or two of his several young children with him on his evening visits, and often stays for a cup of tea and a piece of bread. He is not a great talker, and the children are shy, so there is more companionable silence than conversation on these business-cum-social occasions. A month passes and the time for departure approaches. On the evening of the last milk delivery, the landlord arrives without any accompanying children. As usual, he is offered a cup of tea; as usual he accepts. He lingers longer than usual and makes some conversational moves, offering stories about adventurous young academic women tenants of former years. Has she found the coast and countryside worth exploring? Has she found the cottage acceptable? Yes, she replies, it has all been fine. Was the bed comfortable? Surprised and slightly alarmed at the length and direction of the conversation, she gives a curt affirmative and remarks that it is getting dark, and that he still has a long walk home. At that he rises and grabs her by the arms, purporting to admire their fine muscles (developed after an unexpectedly athletic and unintellectual summer). She shrugs him off and asks him to leave. He informs her that he cannot possibly, at this hour, walk home by the road, alone—both his and her reputation would be ruined. There are in fact only two houses to be passed on the road to his home farm, and she finds it difficult to believe that watchers will be waiting there, behind the lace curtains. Nor is her future reputation in the area of very great concern to her. But she humors him, agreeing that he might, as he proposes, take the uninhabited hill track home. Shrewdly sizing up her weak points, he tells her that the trouble with that plan is that with his stiff leg (an old badly healed fracture), it will be difficult, perhaps dangerous, for him to clamber up the hillside behind the cottage to where he can join the track across the peat bogs on the ridge. Would she take pity, and accompany him up the hill, to the track? Impelled by visions of him lying on the hill behind the cottage, injured and needing first aid, she reluctantly goes with him up the hill toward the ridge track. Pretending to lurch for needed support, he trips her up with his stiff leg, brings her down on the steep hillside, and attempts rape. Her newly developed muscles come into action fairly effectively, and he is eventually dispatched, to stumble ignominiously home. Even at the time, she cannot help finding the situation slightly comic, and she suspects that the charge "she asked for it" may in this case have some justice. Next day she herself walks to the farm (along the road) to pay the rent and the milk bill to his wife, who keeps the household accounts, and to make her goodbyes to the two of them. They ask her to give their kind regards to her tutor, their regular tenant. She assures them she will.

This, I suppose, is a story of one forgiving too many, as well as of misjudgment of the extent of "real kindness," of the undefined limits of normal friendliness, especially of cross-cultural friendliness. The costs were minor, but that was unforeseeable, plain good luck.

Second Anecdote. A young faculty member (the first woman to be appointed in her department) soon after her appointment finds herself the object of amorous attention from two married colleagues, both of them old and close friends of her chairman. He, a charming bully, eventually informs her that he had known all along that it was a mistake to appoint a young unmarried woman, that only trouble would follow. "They" had, he tells her, passed around the photo that she had been required to submit with her job application from abroad, and had discussed how high the risk of such trouble was, and whether it was worth taking. Outraged, but also resigned to the inevitability of a few "pioneer" dangers facing women entering professions where the professionals were unaccustomed to having women colleagues and had not yet worked out civilized conventions of coexistence, she does her best to put up with the tense and unhappy working conditions. One of her two married "admirers" considers moving away to a new position, to escape the difficult situation. This provokes his friend, her chairman, to explosions of rage. Accosting the "troublemaker" in a public hall of the university, where faculty are standing around chatting and students are passing on their way to and from classes, he gives her the news of his old friend's possible departure, then shouts, "See what you have done! Why don't you get yourself married and out of circulation!" Shocked, she gathers her dignity around her as best she can, and immediately writes and submits to the vice chancellor a letter of instant resignation, complaining of her chairman's behavior. She is called in by the vice chancellor, who implores her to withdraw her letter. After giving thought to the slim chances of finding another university job in mid-year, she reluctantly agrees, but immediately sets about applying for positions elsewhere for the following year. Her chairman, unapologetic and as far as she is informed unreprimanded, continues on his charming macho way. When at the end of the year she leaves for a new job, he makes her an embarrassingly fine farewell present of a first edition of her favorite author, as if to make it difficult for her to keep her grievance alive and well.

In this sorry story, the young woman felt let down, but by whom exactly? Not the two admirers, who doubtless let their wives down, and made life difficult for their new colleague, but in the latter case not by breaking any of Scanlon's principles. Nor did the chairman betray any personal trust his new appointee had in him, since he was so obvious (if likable) a scoundrel that she had distrusted him from first meeting and had tried to be on her guard in dealings with him. Nor did the university break any contracts or explicit assurances that it had given. Still, it was the chairman, as an officer of the university, and the university community more generally who were at fault, and the fault was untrustworthiness of a kind that I think Scanlon's principles fail to capture. The victim in this story had trusted her welcome into the university community, taking it to be acceptance as a full colleague. The acceptance had, perhaps, been ambiguous in its quality, and she may be seen to have had "fair warning" of the sexism that was eventually shown so blatantly. But as we all know by now, it is exceedingly difficult to formulate and implement regulations to prevent all such "betrayals" of women. Was this victim deceitfully manipulated? Not exactly. Had she been negligently misled into expecting a nonsexist working environment? By whose negligence? Was there failure to prevent losses she faced because of false reliance on her colleagues' decency? One might construe the efforts to get her to withdraw her proud but imprudent resignation as in accord with, not against, the loss prevention principle. And since no specific assurances on sexism were ever given, or asked for, the fidelity principle was not infringed. But still, surely, she was let down.

In these two anecdotes, the disappointed trust may have been a bit silly, but not necessarily pathological. For what in each case was the realistic alternative to the trust that was shown? For the tenant to have maintained preemptive distrust of the Irish landlord, from start to finish, was of course a possibility. It would have been possible for the woman faculty member, from the moment of appointment, to have cynically expected the worst of the no-more-than-normally-sexist university, or to have refused a job in such a place, or to have rebuffed all friendly approaches from the men there. But living either unemployed or with sustained watchful distrust of those one sees daily and depends upon in normal daily activities is a high price to pay for avoidance of ugly let-downs. It is not clear that giving people and administrations the benefit of the doubt, as long as it still is *doubt,* not certainty (while at the same time developing one's muscles), is not the better policy, even given the serious costs of this policy. There are few fates worse than sustained self-protective self-paralyzing generalized distrust of one's human environment. The worst pathology of trust is a life-poisoning reaction to any betrayal of trust. Trust makes life "commodious," in Hobbes's sense, and without it we really are in conditions where our lives will be solitary,

145

poor, and nasty, even if not short or "brutish" (the brutes are in some ways better at trust than we are).

Both these stories focused on trust by a woman, in one case of an individual man, in the other of an institution run by men. Do such tales have any general significance, or is their moral one for women only? Male-female relations can, I believe, serve fairly well to model a wider class of relationships of trust and distrust, where the power of the different parties is unequal, or is shifting and uncertain. The common use of the metaphor of "rape" for any sort of shafting of the weaker, insufficiently vigilant, or inadequately armed itself suggests that rape serves as a paradigm for us of a wider class of moral violations. Of course real rape need not involve any abuse of trust. Distrust is no protection against it. But in cases such as date rape and incestuous seduction, the unsuspecting trust of the victim is part of the sorry story. The trust-increased vulnerability of the victim and the peculiar trust-dependence of the fragile good entrusted (intimacy with another, closeness that always holds a faint possibility of future mutually sought sexual intimacy) means that what the victim can suffer is not just a grave harm, but the poisoning of a once-possible future or an erstwhile good. It can result in at least a temporary allergy to any such goods. These dangers make this case symbolic of other important cases of the abuse of trust. Not everyone can, like Harold and the tough protagonist of my first anecdote, bounce back from being let down, ready for more of the same, for further adventures in trusting. Bad enough betrayals of trust lead not just to loss of a particular entrusted good but to a lasting inability to partake of that sort of trust-dependent good. And if the trust-dependent goods are the most precious, then this is a severe disability.

In my second anecdote there was no question of rape or rape equivalent, but merely of insult, exploitation of inferior bargaining power, and possibly of conspiracy to maintain this inferiority. The shift in the status of women from a position of exclusion from most professions to reluctant permission to enter, the uncertainties as to whether in being allowed this entry they were also being accorded equality in other historically related matters, such as sexual freedom and sexual initiative—all these provide good models of the pathologies of trust and distrust in conditions where power is shifting, where old monopolies are being challenged, double standards slowly eroded. Problems at the international level, say, between "great" powers possessing nuclear weapons and upstart lesser powers like Iraq who "dare" arm themselves with equally lethal weapons and dare act as ruthlessly in pursuing their own perceived interests (in particular by invading neighboring territory) as great powers are known to have done (the USSR into Afghanistan, the United States in Panama), present us with a spectacle that, were it not so dangerous in its ramifications, could cause a sour smile or two. The pseudo-moral indignation of the powerful when their "inferiors," especially their recent allies, act as if they too were powerful, as if there were no double standard, is a phenomenon that we should be very familiar with from many contexts besides the international one, in particular, from the frequent male reaction to female ambition or "uppityness." When small insignificant or medium-sized less significant allies or former allies, such as New Zealand or Iraq, oppose the will of great powers by banning arms in unacceptable ways or arming in unacceptable ways, great powers feel outraged and even betrayed, as if some understanding about who bows the knee to whom has been broken. And when, as in the case of Iraq, there was fear of really destructive power, of more lethal equality than was expected, the powerful were at first nonplussed. The "balance of power," if it leaves a great power less relatively great, will reliably look dangerously upset to such a power.

Relations between those of unequal power are, one would think, what we are most practiced in, since real equality is so rare. So one might have thought that trust and trustworthiness in such relations would be the standard kind. In a way it is—the trust of a child in a loving parent is a standard example of trust. But the distrust of the adolescent is equally paradigmatic, and often attended by equal distrust of the adolescent by the parent. Hume noted[13] how upset we can get when inferiors advance upon us, and we are particularly upset when what they advance in is power to make their resentment felt. Growing teenage children are obvious cases of inferiors in formidable advance. Pathologies of trust occur where there is the will to monopolize and hang on to power, to keep the underdogs under, to prevent inferiors from advancing.

Families usually work out ways of giving increasingly equal voice in decision making to growing children, and have coming-of-age ceremonies. Bodies such as the United Nations and every federal union have worked out devices for facilitating cooperation and trust between bodies of unequal and shifting relative power. The idea of the right of each state to one vote, regardless of the relative size and power of that state, is a device for empowering the less powerful and for approximating to conditions of equality, and so of mutual vulnerability and stable interdependence. Conventions concerning embassies and the treatment of diplomats serve a similar function, to give a voice to every nation however small, even in the capitals of its temporary enemies. As Hume noted,[14] rules of good manners and "mutual deference" serve a purpose similar to the rules of justice and give rise to informal rights or dues. All bills and lists of rights empower the less powerful, so that they are less vulnerable to the more powerful, so that they can avoid begging for favors.[15] But it takes cooperation, in particular the cooperation of the powerful, to get rights and civilities respected. When great nations give themselves "airs of superiority" and "eagerness for victory,"[16] then even if they do not offend against the laws of nations concerning the sacredness of the persons of ambassadors, they insult and offend lesser powers, and may in extreme cases provoke in the insulted nation that anger which Grotius likened to the bite of a desperate ferocious dying beast.[17] It is difficult for nations which are not treated with due respect as nations[18] to feel bound by the laws of nations (such as the law to refrain from the use of poisoned arms). If the more powerful members of the United Nations veto or disregard its censure when *they* are censured, yet organize military coalitions to give teeth to the censure that they initiate, then the substitution of might by right (or their coalescence), will be only pretense. Until the smaller nations can trust the larger nations to respect the judgment of an international body when it goes against them as much as when it supports them, no real empowering of the weaker, and no real disempowering of the dangerously strong, will have been effected by any international "one nation one vote" rule. It is not then surprising if smaller nations try to empower themselves by other, more destructive, means. Until there is, on the part of the stronger, exemplary obedience to the rule of international law, respect for United Nations censure, and respect for the authority of the World Court, there will be no good reason for weaker nations to trust stronger nations. Once the stronger have abused the trust of the weaker, then the burden of proof is on them to patiently demonstrate their goodwill, to attempt to show new trustworthiness, should they thereafter want to recover anyone's trust.

The dangers of trust I have so far sketched range from the most obvious, trusting the untrustworthy, to the less obvious, bad judgment as to what matters to check up on and when, what matters to entrust and what to keep under one's own control, bad judgment as to when to give those who have once proved untrustworthy a second or a third or an nth chance. Willingness to use discretionary powers is part of what one trusts the trusted to do, and discretion is also a vital part of what the truster needs, discretion in judging when trust is worth its risks, and whether, after some of the risks have eventuated, the best response is indignant complaint and unforgiving withdrawal of trust, or whether apologies and new starts are acceptable. Once the betrayed have opted for sustained distrust and are about to up and leave, discretionary judgment, say, as to whether farewell ceremonies are or are not tolerable, is also called for. There is a presumption in favor of such ceremonies. As Niklas Luhmann has emphasized, the arts both of tactful invitation and of tactful withdrawal are among the civilizing arts. It is not just that, for all the injured party knows, she might one day want to return and so had better not burn too many bridges in her self-righteous storming off. (Or burn too many oil wells in her vindictive retreat.) It is also that there are always innocent parties who are endangered by the expression of (possibly justified) resentment. For example, the Irish landlord's wife of my first anecdote, that patient, long-suffering, and neighborly woman who had instructed her husband's "victim" in bread making, was surely owed a normal farewell, whatever the misdemeanors of her husband. And the college tutor was owed the continued goodwill of her Irish landlord and lady. Had the insulted young faculty member of the second anecdote actually walked out mid-year, her students would have been abandoned mid-course. *They* would have been let down. Trust comes in webs, not in single strands, and disrupting one strand often rips apart whole webs. Sometimes we judge that this has to be done, despite the cost to "innocent" victims. And all of us, as ones caught up in such webs of trust, know that sometimes the abrupt cessations of friendly and mutually trusting relationships mysteriously inflicted upon us by some people can be responses to the offenses of others in the same web. We come to learn to share each other's penal burdens and burdens of suspicion. There are times, for all of us, when "they fle from me that sometyme did me seek . . ."

Discretion is needed here, too, in judging how long we should put up nonresentfully with unexplained withdrawals of trust or with sudden failures to meet our trust, even when we believe that the ones whose behavior changed probably had good reason to change, given the letdowns they themselves suffered from third parties. If my faithful mail carrier,[19] who has always delivered my letters to my door rather than leaving them in the mailbox at the end of the long drive I share with two neighbors whose houses are nearer to the road, stops this service without warning, this may be because one of my neighbors let her wolfhound run free, and the mailman, who comes on foot, was badly bitten while returning down the drive. If I suspect this possibility, I will of course "forgive" the mailman. But if it turns out that not merely the mailman, on foot, but every other delivery person, bitten or unbitten, knowing about the dog or not, after as well as before the dog's owners move away, takes to leaving deliveries for me at the end of the drive, although for a while they still deliver to the other houses who share the drive, then it will look as if it is my undemandingness, rather than any other factor, that explains the deterioration of service. It will probably be only a matter of time until the service deteriorates for my neighbors too. "He that injures one, threatens an hundred," as Bacon reminds us, so we must take care that our individual willingness to forgive does not put others in danger.[20] Over-willingness to excuse untrustworthiness, like undue distrust, may not merely deprive me of a good but destroy a mini-system, a little network of mutually beneficial expectations. Uncomplaining or automatically forgiving long-suffering invites its own continuation. Demanding one's rights belligerently is certainly one way to destroy trust, but never standing up for them or not bothering to find out if they are being ignored is an equally effective destroyer of a network of trust.

Unforgiving rigidity and, at the other extreme, easygoing willingness to keep on forgiving are both dysfunctional weaknesses, if our goal is to maintain and repair a network of beneficial trust, one composed of normally faulty human persons. Both unwillingness to be part of such a web, given the real risks of being let down, and naive optimism in entering it are usually threats to its continued good health. But reliable guidelines on how to judge the risks of trust, how wisely to decide whom to take bread from and whom to offer it to, are very difficult to find. We may be betrayed not only by those whom we trust but also by overreliance on any of the mixed bag of precepts that our moral tradition offers us or, indeed, by any refinements of them that we might concoct. To forgive seventy times seven the same wrong from the same person or even from persons of some one group (if only we could be confident how to group people in trust-relevant ways) would be treachery to one's fellows, who could also become victims. To look too hard before one leaps into any cooperative scheme can ensnare one into lonely paralysis and sometimes spoil the game for others. "Nothing venture, nothing win." To trust any such moral maxim, it seems, would be to be deceived. Quintus Cicero writes: "All things are full of deceit, snares and treachery. As Epicharmus said, 'The bone and sinew of wisdom is "Never trust rashly."'"[21] But how are we to tell rash trust from wise trust, sensible ventures from silly adventures? There are, as far as I have yet discovered, no useful rules to tell us when to trust or even when we should have trusted. ("Never trust rashly" is an utterly useless rule, if the ghost of Epicharmus will forgive my saying so.) If our Kantian rational capacity to be law-abiders, to apply guiding rules, cannot give us much help here (in the absence of suitably trustworthy rules), and if even our spontaneous mistrust can prove fairly unreliable, then what capacity of ours can we trust to distinguish rash from appropriate trust? I have already appealed at many points to our powers of judgment, those very powers that we expect those whom we trust to exercise. The truster too must possess them, in order to recognize their presence in others, those to whom she entrusts the care of what matters to her. How can we recognize and develop such skills of judgment? In what conditions are they likely to be shown?

eight

SUSTAINING
TRUST

> Thus, two men pull the oars of a boat by
> common convention for common interest,
> without any promise or contract: thus gold
> and silver are made the measures of
> exchange; thus speech and words and
> language are fixed by human convention
> and agreement.
>
> *David Hume,* Enquiry Concerning the Principles of Morals, app. 3

Essay 7 concentrated on the perils of trusting and the difficulty of finding any rules to help us navigate our way through life so as to avoid the perils of leaky boats and unreliable rowers without thereby sacrificing the goods that trust promises, and sometimes delivers. We have to rely on our own judgment and on our ability to improve our judgment, if we are to enter and sustain mutually beneficial relationships of trust-involving cooperation. Trust is acceptance of vulnerability to harm that others could inflict, but which we judge that they will not in fact inflict. Must we develop great psychological insight into the motives of our fellow persons, in order to judge whom to trust? In particular, must we become adept at discerning when our fellow persons' motives are egoistic, when altruistic?

This seems to be the assumption that is made by Bernard Williams, in his lead essay in the helpful and informative volume *Trust: Making and Breaking Cooperative Relations,* the product of a Cambridge symposium and edited by Diego Gambetta.[1] Williams asks what could motivate people to cooperate, where to "cooperate" is taken to involve some of the cooperators letting some other cooperator(s) have the immediate control of some of the actions necessary for the intended cooperative outcome—in my terms, letting someone "take care" of something that matters, leaving it to them. (Israel's leaving its defense against Iraq to the United States, for a while, is a perfect example.) Why on earth, Williams asks, would rational persons (or nations) make themselves thus vulnerably dependent on others, or take on the burdens of proving dependable themselves when others' good is left in their control? His answer, in short, is that they have no good reason to do this, or at least none we can count on. "Vertrauen ist gut, Sicherheit noch besser" (Trust is good, security even better).[2] The would-be trusted will dependably sacrifice the good of the trusters to their own perceived good, if it comes to a choice. Neither any "macro-motivation," egoistic or altruistic, nor either type of "micro-motivation" can be relied on to make people into trustworthy cooperators. Egoistic macro-motivation would be shown if, for example, because of fear of some Hobbesian sovereign, or as members of a chain gang, we felt we must cooperate with whatever partners we had been allocated. Altruistic macro-motivation would be shown, Williams believes, if we felt we must keep all our promises. It would be "micro" if, say, we took only promises by and to selected persons, say Nietzsche's sovereign free spirits, to be really binding. (As Nietzsche said, such promise-worthy ones are ones whom we fear to let down.) Then, when anyone was given a promise, she would have to judge if the promisor saw her as a free spirit, so respect-worthy enough to have it kept. Micro-motivation is sensitive to particular context, to our knowledge of the particular person whom we would have to trust in order to cooperate on a given matter, whereas macro-motivation is general, directed at people of a given easily recognizable sort, in some recurrent recognizable type of social context. All possible motivations to cooperate are taken, plausibly enough, to be sensitive to perceived costs, but the micro-motivations are, in addition, sensitive to any special information or special hunches we may have about the given individual who wants us to trust him and to particular feelings, such as love or fear, that we may have toward him. If we let ourselves become "dependent," in Williams's sense, on loved ones or selected loved ones, by trusting some things that matter to us to their control, that will usually be micro-motivation. If we distrust the second-hand car salesman just because that is what he is, that will be macro-motivation; whereas if we distrust him on the basis of his especially shifty eyes, that will be micro-motivation. Williams grants that the distinction may not be a sharp one. (We may distrust anyone with eyes like that.)

But in any case it turns out to matter little for Williams which sort of motivation is macro and which micro, which egoistic, which altruistic, since he concludes that, outside intimate friendship, no one sort can be depended on to do the trick of giving rational persons a motive to become "dependent" in the way a trusting cooperator must or to become "trustworthy" in the way a trusted cooperator should. If anything is to be a "solution" to the "problem" of how society-wide trust-involving cooperation is to be motivated, it will, he concludes, be some judicious mixture of motivations. The most promising mixture, he judges, will be a combination of "egoistic micro- and non-egoistic macro-motivations," in "the combination of egoism and a few moral principles," such as "keep promises" (or, presumably, "live up to any assurances you have given"). Williams hints that there may be richer nonegoistic macro-motivation than that found in such attempts at minimally principled action; there might be what he says "might, very recklessly, be called Durkheim's solution,"[3] but he warns that there are well-known and grave problems about how to prevent encouragement of such nonegoistic macro-motivation from degenerating into "ineffective humbug," especially when people are "constantly and professedly expressing egoistic micro-motivations in much of their life."[4]

After this gloomy opening consideration of the "structural" problems that face any reliance on trust to oil the wheels of our society-wide joint ventures, it is not surprising that many later contributors to the *Trust* volume are pessimistic about our chances of creating and maintaining socially extensive trust. Geoffrey Hawthorn, in his fine essay "Three Ironies of Trust," seems equally pessimistic about less extensive trust, more or less limiting its altruistically motivated variants to perfect and perfectly asexual friendship—"the one wholly no-fault relation there is."[5] This verdict of Hawthorn's is given after he approvingly quotes Shakespeare's verdict in his Sonnet 138, that love's best habit is in seeming trust, and

> Therefore I lie with her, and she with me,
> And in our faults by lies we flattered be.

Friendship, provided it can avoid or forgive (or even selectively welcome?) lies,[6] can be no-fault in its acceptance of the risks of trust. But lies are not so very easily completely avoided in friendship, and the unwelcome ones are not at all easily forgiven. "Just as there can be treachery in a kiss, so too there can be betrayal in an honourable mien."[7] The trust of members of an "aristocracy," originally linked by ties of friendship and by a shared code of honor, may enjoy a brief flourishing, but will not last long. (Hawthorn's first two "ironies" of trust are that socially extensive trust cannot be created except in some sort of "aristocracy"; and that having been so created, it will dependably be eventually undermined by the aristocrats who for a while sustained it.)

I think that the distinguished Cambridge group who studied trust together accepted Bernard Williams's philosophical analysis of it too trustingly, and one of the questionable aspects of it, highlighted by Hawthorn's use of it in application to the illuminating case studies he presents (of the breakdown of agricultural workers' trust in the Indian Congress party in Northern India, and of the "devious" creation in post–World War II Korea of a successful economic system out of extensive mistrust, which was itself employed to police the system), is its sharp contrast between egoistic and nonegoistic motivation. It does seem a little extreme, does it not, to find parental solicitude and perfect friendship between honorable males the only cases of human nonegoistic micro-motivation? And more than a little odd to see commitment to moral principles to be typically motivated by wholly nonegoistic considerations? Any woman who has painstakingly (and sometimes painfully) overhauled her morality to eliminate all appearance of condoning exploitation knows better than to think that reflective moral commitments lack some element of enlightened egoism.[8] Nor is "keep promises" a very suitable example of a moral rule that would have to be adhered to out of nonegoistic motivation, if the force of promises lies either, as Hume thought, in the accepted threat of the penalty of loss of reputation in the event of one's nonperformance[9] (or, as Atiyah[10] thinks, in such participation as promises have in the general force of mutually advantageous exchange). Williams is looking for some moral rule that, if observed, would inhibit the more powerful and less dependent parties to a cooperative venture from defecting and so defrauding the more dependent members—a moral constraint, that if effective would prevent, say, bank officials from doing what Charles Keating and his collaborators did when they defrauded their depositors. (As well as some constraint to stop frightened depositors from withdrawing their savings from other banks, after such a scandal.) But wily would-be defrauders can fairly easily avoid giving promises, should they be burdened by compunctions about breaking them. They may simply point to the promises that others, who insure them, are giving. There are very many more-or-less trusted powerful persons who have given no formal promises to those dependent on them. It is the *inept* politician who makes rash and unnecessary promises, rather than herding his sheep by other less dangerous means. A promise can boomerang[11] on the promisor—that is the whole point of what Hume called these "artificial contrivances for the convenience and advantage of society,"[12] and it takes the extensive mutual trust of the members of a society to keep this contrivance well serviced, with its coercive teeth in good shape. If its implicit threats are not credible, if we reinstate defaulting promisors after a brief and profitable formal penance in the bankruptcy courts, then we have ourselves to blame if promises lose their public force, and if politicians and bank managers do not even bother to avoid giving lying promises. "Read my lips" has come to mean "Truster, beware."

Our actual motivation, in situations where trust comes into play, is not very helpfully seen as a mixture of egoistic and nonegoistic, unless we can be fairly sure which strands are egoistic, which altruistic. But many of our motives resist easy classification in these terms. Is parental concern egoistic or nonegoistic? It is treated by Hawthorn as a rare exceptional instance of nonegoistic motivation,[13] but others, such as Richard Epstein,[14] take concern for the continuers of one's own selfish genes, plausibly enough, to exhibit a variant of egoism. Is our pleasure in each other's company, and our preference for a life that gives us opportunities to get some such pleasure, egoistic or nonegoistic? Is it egoistic to wish to have the respect of others? Is our will to sustain friendships to be decreed egoistic to the extent that our concern for our friends is for ones who are "second selves" to us? Is the desire for revenge, even when we must bring the temple down on ourselves as well as on our enemies, egoistic? Is patriotism a clear case of extended egoism, or is "selfless patriotism" a possibility? The ego's boundaries are less clearly marked than are most nations' boundaries, but in the absence of clear boundaries we cannot be sure when our concern is for ourselves alone, when for others. Where does a person stop? Is the skin the ego's barbed-wire boundary? Is the hair a no man's land?[15] The clothes mere protection of the border? The reputation an everyman's land? Even in the area where motivations do seem to be fairly easily classified as "egoistic," such as personal ambition or vanity about one's appearance, the "ego" that is thereby tended is a fairly fluidly bounded thing, and apt, like Absalom's hair, to get entangled with others and caught in the outer fringes of other living things. To trace the "line or hyperplane" that Robert Nozick takes to bound a person's space[16] is no easy matter, and we need to be clear about when and for what purposes we think that effort worth making. Some important variants of trust do take the form of alliances and other forms of willingness to let others close enough to us to be able easily enough to invade our "space," to "violate" us, in the trusting confidence that they will not in fact do this. But what counts as "intrusive," as coming too close in, varies enormously both from context to context and from culture to culture. One allows one's physician forms of intrusiveness that one might deny even to a lover. One expects conversational partners not to get so close that we get their spit along with their spiel, but as Allan Gibbard notes,[17] this varies considerably from culture to culture. (It seems to depend on how far from the equator the conversation takes place. While one might have expected those in colder climates, like emperor penguins, to huddle for warmth and so to tolerate closeness to nonintimates, in fact it is the warmer climes that have developed human customs allowing the greatest conversational moving in.)

Important though it is for everyone's sake that we have standards, even if shifting ones, of what counts as invasion of ourselves, and that we be able more or less to count on one another to observe those standards, there are equally important variants of trust that take the form of toleration of absence and distance. To let others on whom one depends be far from one can be as risky as letting them get very close. Roughly speaking, intimates are trusted away from us, strangers are trusted close up.[18] But that *is* very rough, since it takes trust to let the strange surgeon go off, taking one's loved one with him, out of one's sight and into the operating theater for emergency surgery (and surgeons, I have found, are on the whole reluctant to let the patient's relatives go with them in there), and there are occasions when it takes more trust to let an intimate up close than to let a stranger. If one has a splinter down one's fingernail, or something in one's eye, one's ham-handed beloved may be the last person one wants to allow to try to remove it. This example suggests that the special risk of close quarters is vulnerability to some particularly painful and easily inflicted forms of harm. Knifing, strangling, and smothering are primitive and "easy" ways of killing selected victims, provided one has entry to the victim's presence. Torturing is equally easy if one is close. The forms of harm that can be inflicted from afar are of course equally serious, and can be equally painful, but we do seem to have a special horror of those typically inflicted at close quarters, especially if inflicted by those who not only have been let past our guards but who themselves were supposed to be our guards. (Think, for example, of child abuse by priests, or of Indira Gandhi's assassination.) When we trust another to come close, we let down our guard against these primitive terrors and evils. If betrayed in such a way by such a trusted one, we typically know exactly what is happening, but are powerless to stop it. Those we trust away from us have powers to harm us in other ways, and what we then renounce is our ability to keep track of, let alone to control, what they are doing with what matters to us. Up-to-date knowledge is not always control, but it is needed for most forms of control. Those we trust utterly (if any) can come as close as they please behind our defenses and go as far as they please out of our vigilant gaze, without our becoming anxious. The two apparent dimensions of trust, renunciation of guard or defense and renunciation of intelligence, do really seem to be two, neither reducible to the other.[19] And our motivation for either type of renunciation seems better characterized as concern for some more or less shared good than as either egoistic or altruistic.

I have been talking of our acceptance of vulnerability to intimates and strangers, but of course a large part of our lives is spent with people who are in neither of those relationships to us—colleagues, business acquaintances, neighbors, fellow committee members, who to some degree do get behind our guards and whom we certainly do not keep a very close track of. Earlier I said that micro-motivation would be the sort usually involved when intimates are trusted on all the matters, distant and close, where we do trust them. But the contrasting terms "micro-/macro-motivation" do not serve to sort our motives any better than "egoistic/nonegoistic," and Williams himself indicates that he has some qualms about this classificatory contrast. He allows that an adequate account "would involve a good deal of elaboration and qualification."[20] As he sketches it, macro-motivation is shown whenever an agent "regularly" performs acts of cooperation of a certain labeled sort, such as fidelity to his promises or, presumably, obedience to the laws of his country or to the orders of armed police. These are all cooperative acts, and ones that may be regularly displayed, generating patterns of conduct. Micro-motivation, by contrast, will, he writes, be shown in "friendly relations towards a given person" or, I suppose, in special fear of a particularly brutal-looking police officer. But in our friendliest relations with those closest to us we fall into habits of trusting cooperation as regular as those we show with officials and strangers. Up to a certain age, sometimes all too young an age, we trust relatives such as uncles not to make what we later learn to call sexual advances. (Then one may switch to micro-motivation, sizing up one's uncles one by one.) One gets into bed as usual with one's spouse, trusting that he has not suddenly succumbed to any brain disease that would turn him into a mad aggressor (as in fact happened with a couple I knew) just as mindlessly as one sits down in the empty seat on the bus, trusting that the person beside whom one seats oneself does not have a switchblade at the ready. (In some cities one does learn to look before one sits, to try to employ "micro-motivation.") Our attitudes and actions in our dealings with persons standing in all degrees of closeness and distance from us fall into pretty regular patterns of habitual behavior and so to some degree show what Williams and others call macro-motivation. We trustingly surrender our passport to whatever person occupies the appropriate-looking booth when we cross a country's borders—it does not occur to us to try to check to make sure that this is not some terrorist masquerading as an immigration official, and no more does it occur to us to check to make sure that the dark sleeping shape in the marriage bed is our spouse, rather than, say, some possessor of the ring of Gyges or some devil in sudden possession of our spouse's body. We take many appearances on trust, and we would go mad if we did not and could not. We trust uniforms, badges, and framed certificates on professionals' walls, all of them fairly easily faked.

It is toward normal appearances, familiar uniforms, and badges of office as much as to the individual people who are playing their allotted parts in the normal scene that we should perhaps utter Cicero's solemn incantation "uti ne propter fidemve tuam captus fraudatusve sim!" (That I not be deceived and defrauded through you or my trust in you).[21] So what do the wise person and the wise society do to guard against false pretenders, without giving up on trust? If there are none except unhelpful rules to guide the would-be wise, what help is there? Fortunately our intelligence is not artificial, and so we do not have to depend on algorithms or even on our own skill in coming up with them. We have powers of judgment, and we can use them not merely in case-by-case decisions whether to trust a "Trust me!" invitation (which in any case is rarely a matter of voluntary decision), but in the design and overhaul of institutions, schemes of cooperation, procedures of certification, and procedures for inspecting and repairing all such procedures and schemes. We can invent institutions and procedures as well as algorithms, and we have powers of observation that can tell us how well or badly a given institution or a set of interlocked ones is working, whether the institutions are encouraging or discouraging the trust they need for their own best workings. It takes very little observational acumen to realize that a savings bank system is not working when its elderly clients cut their wrists in their baths on losing the modest savings that they had looked forward to donating to a home for abused children.[22] A system that punishes trust in bank officials as brutally as that declares itself an obscene failure. Where judgment is tested and given scope is not in the recognition of failures, but in the redesign of the system.

Cicero, quoting Ennius, says "Nulla sancta societas nec fides regni est" (No society is sacred, no trust is safe, where rulership is concerned).[23] It is power, the opportunity to acquire power after power and to sustain monopoly of power, that is a proven corrupter of trustworthiness and so of networks of trust. (I am assuming, of course, that money is one form of power.) What we easily can come to see to be a twin truth to that is that the meekness, servility, and undemandingness of the relatively powerless are equally responsible for this corruption. Domination and obedience, self-promotion and self-abasement, whatever the motives that prompt them, work together to corrupt schemes of cooperation. The practical judgment we have to hope some of us sometimes display is that needed to find a way to empower and embolden the relatively powerless and to disempower and humble the dangerously powerful.

Alliances of the relatively powerless alter power distribution in an obvious manner, which blocks monopoly of power. The invention of the concept of a universal right was a piece of practical genius that empowered the less powerful, and there are other such advances to encourage us. Unions of different peoples to recognize and to try to enforce rights—in, for example, the World Court and the United Nations—obviously benefit the weaker, but to see what they offer the stronger takes some breadth of vision, some attention to the fact that eminent power in nations has never lasted more than a few centuries, so that roles can be expected eventually to be reversed. The present relative powerlessness of once mighty Britain and Austria is instructive in this important lesson. Not just the breakup of empires but the outcome of wars can effect the disempowerment of the once mighty, but this is a dangerous method. Hugo Grotius, discussing that most unequal of situations, the making of a peace treaty and the redrawing of boundaries after a war in which one nation has forced another to surrender, wisely writes: "As in making peace, it scarcely ever happens that either party will acknowledge the injustice of his cause, or of his claims, such a construction must be given, as will equalize the pretensions of each side, which may be accomplished, either by restoring the disputed possessions to their former situation, or by leaving them in that state, to which the war has reduced them."[24] The victor may by this rule get some territorial spoils of war, but the main aim is to "equalize the pretensions of each side," so that both victor and vanquished can take their place again as functioning members of a community of nations, respecting each other's rights. Humiliating the vanquished is not among the arts of peace. (And disarming them usually is humiliating them.)

On the home front, the makers of the U.S. Constitution did a fairly good job of designing a system to replace colonial domination and misrule. The new system was intended to distribute power in such a way that its abuses would be minimized. It obviously is not a perfect system, but at least it shows what can be done in the way of collective creative design (which in this case was minimally helped by guiding rules, since what old rules for constitution framing that existed were deemed to have been discredited by the bad record of the nations whose constitutions they supposedly blessed). And we can, if it pleases us to do so, try to extract from this last example of relative success a sort of reusable "recipe" for designing lasting schemes of cooperation not just in governing nations but in other spheres. "Ingredients" such as empowerment of the more vulnerable, equal respect, balance of power, provision for amendment, a place for the hearing of grievances, all give us ideas that we could try incorporating into rules for the design of other stable schemes of trust-involving cooperation, so that all trust comes closer to being mutual trust, and so also to mutual vulnerability.

It is not always exactly *stability* that we want, however. *Was* the United States constitutional scheme in fact stable? Did it survive its own Thirteenth Amendment, abolishing slavery, or its Fifteenth Amendment, ruling out denial of the right to vote on grounds of "race, color, or previous condition of servitude"? Was the Constitution reconstructed along with the South, rather than simply "amended" by these changes in the basic structures of the social scheme of cooperation? Did the Nineteenth Amendment, which more than doubled the number of participants in the political scheme of government by extending suffrage to women, merely swell the electoral rolls, but not alter the basic scheme? Fortunately we do not need to develop hard and fast criteria for the identity of a constitution over time. This one changed fairly radically in some of its basic provisions, and it took one civil war and quite a bit of civil disorder from the fighters for women's suffrage to effect these changes, and further civil disorder to make the Fifteenth Amendment really take effect. "Stability" seems not quite the right word for this intermittently tempestuous progress. But Article V of the Constitution, the procedure for amendment, did its work, and the First Amendment continues to do its intended job of testing the ground for further amendments. Hence I think we can say that this is a splendid example of the creative design of a self-transforming but not altogether self-repudiating scheme of government, of making the notoriously untrustworthy, the governors, relatively trustworthy. We could amend Nietzsche's pronouncement, and say that some good things provide for their own continuous selective self-overcoming.

It might be queried whether this fairly successful scheme is in fact a scheme of cooperation that requires mutual *trust* for its smooth working. Need the judicial arm trust the executive arm, or either of them trust the legislature? Do the voters trust their representatives, and do they need to? Are they, the voters, trusted with anything significant by anyone or any agency? It is true that the scheme's proven strength lies to a significant degree not merely in the balance of judicial, executive, and legislative power but in the checks it provides for, so that trusting, in the sense of handing over to the discretion of the trusted, is strictly limited. Amendments such as the Twenty-second, limiting presidential terms to two, show proper fear of the abuses that prolonged power would make tempting to a president. Vesting one's interests in governing has been effectively blocked, for presidents but not for senators and judges. Particularly with the judicial branch, whose highest officials do not have the check of the prospect of standing for reelection or reappointment to keep them honest, "trust" seems the proper word for what is given. We entrust the interpretation of our laws and our constitution to these people, for their lifetime, subject only to their "good behavior" (Article III), which for all the constitution specifies is to be taken to mean no more than "noncriminal behavior." We surely do have special standards of behavior for Supreme Court judges, but there is no police force to detect putative failures to live up to these standards, no special court to decide on guilt or innocence. There are of course the normal procedures for indictment, but in general we trust our judges to monitor their own trustworthiness. This is a tremendously important case of public meta-trust.

Although the Supreme Court is perhaps the most obvious place where, to get the expected cooperative behavior from those on whom others are dependent, we rely not on procedures of investigation and threat of sanctions but simply on these officeholders' trustworthiness, their sense of our sense of the central importance of that particular bit of our total network of social and public trust. And this is not the only case where the Constitution entrusts vital matters, rather than arranging for regular vigilant checks on performance, along with penalty for bad performance. (And even then, we have to trust the checkers and the penalizers.) Legislators are vulnerable to defeat at the next election for performance that appears unacceptable, but this check does not prevent, and has not prevented, the existence of ongoing schemes of bribery by special interest groups, who can successfully offer their bribes to one after another corrupt members of Congress. The vulnerability of the bribe acceptors to exposure and defeat at the polls does not entail any vulnerability for the bribers—they need not care if their tame congressman is the same one as before or an equally bribable replacement for him, as long as he is in their control. Is it foolish to entrust our interests to legislators who, as a group, we know from experience to be all too ready to be more "influenced" by powerful special interest groups than by those whose interests they are elected to represent? If the threat of exposure and defeat at the polls does not effectively monitor the good behavior of our lawmakers, and pretty obviously it does not, should we invent some more effective invigilation and penalizing devices? Not necessarily, since then we might have to invigilate the invigilators, and hold penalties over their heads. We trust our lawmakers to develop their own mutual monitoring devices, as we trust other professions (lawyers, physicians) to develop and administer codes of professional ethics. Of course we can and often do exercise our First Amendment rights to protest, to cry "Shame!" and to demand some action to end abuses. But the action that is then best is not necessarily a new device of detection, judgment, and punishment. An adjustment to the network of trust, rather than the withdrawal of trust and its replacement by closer inspection and threats of penalties, might be the more efficient, as well as the "nicer," solution. Difficult although it may be to invent the right such adjustment, it is no more difficult than inventing a punitive system that avoids inviting abuses of the trust that is inevitably placed at some point in the penalizers, or the policers of the police.

The point of my brief amateur excursion into constitutional law is to illustrate that even in the case where faith is most likely not to be kept, that is, in government, there are some success stories of the construction and preservation of networks of trust or, rather, of judicious mixtures of trust and vigilance. So even if we have no recipe for how to show good judgment as to where to trust, where to invigilate, and even if our understanding of human motives and their typology is not very great, we have some instructive precedents, cases where fairly good judgment has been shown. From such precedents we can hazard some informed guesses about the conditions in which trust will be warranted. The pronouncement of Ennius, that rulers and those hoping to be rulers are signally untrustworthy, is itself such an informed rule of thumb. It is the *position* of ruler that is seen to create the danger, not just the personal character of the one who occupies that position or the motives behind her conduct. The American success story is a story about the design of positions of power that are not of too much, too long, and so too corrupting power, and the orderly transfer of power to some whom the earlier powerful ones may have helped rather than hindered in their rise to power. Those who occupy such positions can still be reasonably expected to hold some social bonds sacred, and to keep some faiths. The design of a position is itself the design of pressures and influences on any occupier of it. Any president has the watchful press as constant companion and has Congress with its powers (such as war-making powers) to work with—to pressure and be pressured by. The National Archives and its historians are there to remind of past and future verdicts. So even if we lack any useful rules for individuals on when to give and when to withhold trust, we are not entirely without guidelines on how to design roles for individuals that will help them avoid the worst forms of untrustworthiness, or of oppressively burdensome trust, or of overly vulnerable trusting. But it will be the historians, the constitutional lawyers, the international lawyers, the administrative scientists, the economists, the sociologists, the anthropologists, the ethologists, and the psychologists who will have the information that will inform any trustworthy rules of thumb of this sort. Philosophers in their armchairs need plenty of not-purely-philosophical books on their desks and colleagues in other disciplines correcting their thoughts, if they are to get very far in formulating such indirect guidelines for trusting, guidelines, that is, on the design of social roles that provide the circumstances of appropriate trust.

In the Gambetta volume there is a splendid and reassuringly upbeat essay entitled "The Biological Evolution of Trust and Cooperation," by Patrick Bateson. What is cheering about it, after Bernard Williams's gloomy estimates of our slim chances of achieving or maintaining extensive social trust, is not merely Bateson's brisk dismissal of the usefulness of the concept of altruism, and its implied contrast with egoism,[25] but his bypassing altogether of the question of what *motives* might produce trusting and trustworthy behavior.[26] By inspiring stories of the way lichens, sticklebacks, and dunnocks propagate their kind by fairly successful schemes of cooperation, he directs our attention away from the ill-formed question, "What egoistic or altruistic motives might lead agents to behave in cooperative and trust-preserving ways?" to the better question, "In what conditions has cooperative behavior, and in particular trusting cooperative behavior, been known to occur and to have been sustained or replicated?" Now of course in a species like ours whose members, unlike the algae and fungi that compose lichens, do have motives and, unlike the stickleback and dunnock, do reflect upon those motives and consciously adopt and try to stick by general policies of action, motives will of course be among the actual conditions that will determine what degree and type of cooperative behavior will occur. But they may not be easy for us to discern and analyze. Other ways of characterizing the conditions for cooperation may be more reliably accessible to us than motive specifications.

Bernard Williams's first "reality condition" is what he calls "Hume's Axiom," that only motivations motivate.[27] (This is about as helpful as our current insight into determining motives is likely to become.) Now Hume famously described how some of our motives can be shaped or reshaped by the institutions of our society. The "interested passion," he believed, is given what he called "an oblique direction" by conventions establishing property rights, contractual rights, and rights to govern as well as by accompanying customs such as record keeping and reputation spreading. By now it is merely an intellectual exercise or game (one that social philosophers seem addicted to) to try to figure out what might have been the "right angle" of self-interest, from which it has, under the pressure of millennia of social evolution, shifted to its present "oblique angle." What we now have is a form of "interest" that is permeated by social and cultural factors—by language, by the inherited network of social roles, by the family as a social unit (with all its advantages and problems, as far as trust is concerned), by our ever faster and more extensive means of communication of information (about people, about their transactions, about climates of trust), by all our varied devices for assuring and reassuring each other, for insuring against various sorts of loss, and for protecting our varied investments. And our less interested affections, such as benevolence, are equally twisted by cultural forces, such as tax exemptions and religions that teach that by benevolent acts we pile up for ourselves treasures in heaven.

"Hume's Axiom," when understood with due Humean modesty about our limited insight into human motives, does little to limit and nothing to classify the range of our actual motivation. Take for example our wish to have others "second," or agree with us on, our decisions, policies, and attitudes. Whatever its origins, this drive is now shaped by our conversational conventions, our inherited cultural values, perhaps even by fashionable contractualist moral theories. Hume writes[28] of his own moral theory that "it seems a happiness in the present theory, that it enters not into that vulgar dispute concerning the *degrees* of benevolence or self-love, which prevail in human nature; a dispute which is never likely to have any issue." To understand trust, we too will do well to avoid that vulgar unsettleable dispute. To understand it in a way that can help us give and withhold it more wisely, we will need to hazard a well-informed guess about what, in given conditions, we need and do not need to know as well as what we do and do not need to guard, or, rather, about the *relative* importance of certain sorts of knowledge and certain sorts of guards.

I have argued that we do not need to wait until we have expert insight into human motivation and can recognize "altruistic" motivation should we encounter it, before we can design schemes of cooperation that will encourage both trustworthiness and trust, and then judge the comparative success of different schemes. What motivation does the U.S. Constitution assume in politicians and citizens? Not anything much more detailed than a concern for life, liberty, and the pursuit of happiness, along with a due estimate of the dangers of the form of happiness of those hungry for political power. Must we suppose that any participant in a reasonably well functioning scheme, some human analogue to the way parent birds cooperate to care for their young, will have given some implicit assurances to the other participants who are trusting her to do her bit, and so will be subject to the moral principles that Scanlon[29] articulates, and in particular subject to his "fidelity" principle? Fidelity is certainly the virtue of those who do not let down others when they have encouraged them to trust them, as most holders of political office have. Is fidelity adequately analyzed as doing precisely what one assured another one would do, if and when the other wanted that assurance, and is relying on it? That understanding of it would account very well for the popularity that the term "fidelity" enjoys in the insurance business, where explicit assurances are sought, given, and relied on. Scanlon's principle is intended to articulate a moral principle that does not presuppose the existence of any particular social practice, such as that which Hume believed gave the words "I promise" their special force, or, presumably, the practice of having Presidents take oaths of office, and of dividing our social labor in such a way that some people and some companies have the job of selling others insurance. Hume spoke of "fidelity to promises" as if that were just one special case of fidelity, and he speaks also of "fidelity to the marriage bed" as another such special case. (The marriage ceremony, as he understood it, was unlike typical promises in that it was fixed in content, not flexible to varying individual wills and wishes.) In both these cases explicit assurances are wanted and given, and fidelity consists in living up to them. Both these cases, Hume believed, require the background presence of a social convention giving the words "I promise...," "I take this man..." their binding force, what J. L. Austin called their illocutionary force. Scanlon believes that there is some virtue appropriately called "fidelity" which does not depend on any social custom, but which could be and should be displayed by Crusoe and Friday, by any two people who can somehow communicate their intentions to one another.

I agree with him, and I think with Hume too,[30] that there must be some sort of trustworthiness or fidelity that is possible and desirable independently of the existence of what Hume called "social artifices," such as those instituting private property, or contract, or insurance policies. Hume took sustained friendship to require such a virtue. He is also committed to the virtue of "truth," which I take to be not merely veracity but a more general trustworthiness. (The words "truth" and "troth" share common etymological roots.) No social custom, such as that giving the words "I promise" their special force, could ever be established on the Humean story unless those hypothetical parties to a Humean convention, who see the need for and the possibility of binding promises, are "true to their word," that is, to their acceptance of the cooperative scheme inventing contracts.[31] So *some* general moral virtue, which one might try to spell out in a moral principle, is certainly presupposed both by Hume's "fidelity to promises" and by "fidelity to the marriage bed." Has Scanlon captured that virtue in his Principle F? Or in that, along with his other principles requiring nonmanipulation, due care, and loss prevention? Do the circumstances of sustainable and so appropriate trust include our willingness to conform our conduct to Scanlon's principles?

In Essay 7 I expressed doubts about whether we do sincerely accept moral principles as demanding as Scanlon's first three, and doubts also about whether Principle F captures the most basic sort of trustworthiness and fidelity that we hope for from one another.

Indeed I expressed doubts that *any* principle we can spell out would capture the full complexity of this core virtue. I suggested that any attempt we might make to show the validity of a principle like Scanlon's Principle F would turn out to be question begging, since we would find ourselves having to take some form of trust on trust, in order to "validate" principles like Scanlon's fidelity principle, or Hobbes's fifteenth "law of nature" (to give mediators of peace safe conduct), or Hugo Grotius's version of that law. I shall now defend that claim.

Scanlon's version of moral justification, invoked to apply to his fidelity principle, is spelled out in his essay "Contractualism and Utilitarianism."[32] It is the disarmingly simple procedural requirement that we be able to justify to our fellows the rule or policy on which we are acting, where to justify a rule is to show that "no one could reasonably reject [it] as a basis for informed, unforced general agreement."[33] (Scanlon seems not to mean anything very limiting by "*basis* for . . . agreement," but simply to be requiring that the principles not be reasonably rejected, however "basic" or less than basic they be, relative to other principles. A "basis for agreement" is simply something to agree on.) So what we have is a variant both of what we could call "Hume's Motive," the wish or need to have our fellows second our practical proposals, and of the contractarian thought experiment where basic moral principles are selected by their being agreed on by reasonable people or, rather, for Scanlon, by their not being rejected by reasonable people who are aware of the relevant costs, opportunity costs, and benefits and opportunity benefits of what they are accepting or rejecting.

Let us imagine Scanlon proposing his fidelity principle as a basis of agreement to all those who have this Humean motivation, and who are such that the concept of their accepting or rejecting it, and purporting to do so with reason, gets application. Suppose there are some holdouts, call them "Friends,"[34] who object to a principle that would deprive people of the freedom to do what they judged best when the time came to act, a principle that would require them to do what they had given others to believe that they would do. The only assurance it is proper to give, these dissidents suggest, is the assurance that we will on every occasion do what we then deem best. Scanlon, let us suppose, tries to reassure them that, even given their convictions, they can in reason accept his principle, which does not require that more particular and more limiting assurances ever *be* given, but simply that, *should* they have been given, they be honored. Our Friends, unconvinced, reply that it is not so easy to avoid giving some sort of often inadvertent assurance to others on specific matters (or to be sure when the second, third, fourth, fifth, and sixth clauses of Principle F do and do not hold good in the real world),[35] so that they would in fact find themselves having, on moral grounds, to seem to break this principle—say, when someone has said to them, "You are, I hope, going to Meeting tonight?" and they have replied, "Yes, of course," but then find that some urgent call on their charitable instincts arises to prevent their going. At this point the difficulty of knowing what does and does not count as an assurance arises, since, by hypothesis, we are not relying on the use of a special form of words, "I assure you," as the criterion. Suppose it is agreed that an assurance has in this instance been given. Scanlon can reply that his principle imposes only a prima facie duty, not an all things considered one, and that it explicitly allows the assurer to get off the hook if the assured gives consent to his change of plan, a consent very likely to be given to the charitably straying, non-meeting-going Friend, at least by an equally charitable person.

But suppose that our objector, unpacified, patiently replies that the point is that no Friend should want or ask for specific assurances from a Friend, that the freedom to change one's mind for good reason is of such high moral value that it should not be tampered with; that Friends *trust each other, without special assurance,* to do on each occasion what anyone should always do, namely, what she then judges best. Principle F, from the Friends' standpoint, offers a standing temptation to take too much thought for tomorrow, to crave a form of security that ought not to be sought and that is the very antithesis of trust. Such cravings for security, they might reasonably say, destroy a climate of trust, endanger true Friendship, and are unacceptable curbs on our freedom of morally goodwill. ("Security is good, trust even better?") Scanlon may reasonably be skeptical that Friend really means what she says: "Come now," he might say, "you can't disapprove of *all* specific assurances and commitments, you must allow *some* covenants. And if it is the Bible you are appealing to, is not the commandment not to take thought for the morrow accompanied and explained by the assurance that a heavenly father is taking thought for one?" Our Friend may reply,

"Yes, indeed, but assurances are a divine creator's prerogative, not for use by mere fallible and incompletely informed creatures, for whom the liberty to change their mind in the light of new information is a *vital* liberty."

Scanlon has another reply[36] for the Friend who is skeptical about the wisdom of promulgating his proposed principle of fidelity. He can point out that any who have the sort of conscientious objections to assurance-giving that the Friend purports to have can always explicitly disown assurance-giving on their own part. They can simply add "but don't take that as an assurance" to any expression of intention they give to another, just as we do often say "I'll try to be there, but I can't promise" to deter our fellows from unfortunate reliance on our expressed intentions. Could not Friend, if she accepts the due care principle, accept the duty to add "don't take that as an assurance" to any expression of intention that she utters, and so keep her prized freedom to change her mind without letting her exercises of it unduly endanger others? Yes, the Friend might generously accept the onus of disclaiming, if Friend must live in a society where there is disagreement on the value of assurance-giving, and where the demanding due care and loss prevention principles are generally accepted. Constantly making disclaimers will be a nuisance, but not a very great one. She will, however, find herself presented with frequent occasions of temptation when others try to give *her* assurances. Of course she need not accept and rely on them, but it will ask great strength of will of her to ignore other people's insistent "You can count on me to do X." Scanlon's Principle F is restricted to assurances given to those who want to receive them. If Friend does *not* want the assurances she receives, then by Scanlon's principle, the assurer will not be bound to live up to the assurances, and so Friend should not expect that these unwanted assurances will have any binding force. But how does Friend know whether the assurer was aware whether or not his assurances were wanted? By hypothesis assuring is not a *social* practice, so we cannot assume that it requires either formal acceptance by the assured, after it has been offered, or a formal request for it, before it is given. Uncertainty is bound to occur frequently. If it is to be avoided, then we will have to impose another verbal inconvenience on our Friends—that of explicit rejection of any assurances offered them. Some gesture meaning "I do not want and do not accept your assurance" will have to become

171

accepted currency. But now we seem to be driven to social practices after all. The question now becomes: given that there is disagreement about the value of assurance-giving, should we make it into a fairly formal social practice, or should we institute a social practice (say, wearing "F" on one's clothing if one is a Friend) for indicating that one neither gives nor receives assurances? It seems to me that life goes better if we assume that the onus to bother with formal indicators is on the would-be assurer and the would-be assured, not on others. Scanlon's own wish to free us from unnecessary institutional clutter, to keep the rule-governed social practices to the needed minimum, seems to me to argue for rather than against restricting binding assurances to fairly formally given ones, that is, to argue in favor of treating assuring as a social practice.

But Scanlon may not believe that Friend really sees no value in assurance-giving or really will be seriously inconvenienced by the need to ward off unwanted assurances and to prevent others from thinking that she is giving them wanted assurances. He then will have to decide whether to believe that Friend speaks sincerely, and really *does* believe that even if we should accept divine assurances, we should give none but very general and fairly empty ones ourselves (and the divine assurance in question is itself about as nonspecific as it could be). Perhaps Friend deceives herself, or, worse, deceives him—she may be merely using her apparently pious and moralistic talk as a mask for a ruthless reformist will to topple a capitalist economy by undermining faith in the value of its sacred moral currency, the assurance or quasi-contract. (For if too many Friends are around, assurances may indeed come to lose their force.) Might Friend be a Communist agent, who not only does not believe what she has said about divine assurances but does not take any such moral discourse seriously in the first place? Should Scanlon trust her? Unless one trusts one's fellow discussant to be engaged, as she purports to be, in the same enterprise as oneself, in this case that of seeking agreement on morally acceptable principles that can serve as a basis for action and interaction, then the whole justificatory discourse becomes a farce, or a contest of wits.

We know that the exchange of moral slogans at the international level can be such a contest, can be mere attempted manipulation and intimidation. Between mutually distrustful parties to a parley, claims about moral acceptability or unacceptability are rightly discounted, not even dignified with the label hypocrisy, so little expectation is there that anyone would take them seriously. Until we can trust those with whom we are talking to be doing with words what the form of their words suggests (proposing, counterproposing, raising serious objections, seriously considering the merits of a proposal), no justificatory discourse can be sustained, no principles get ratified or vetoed. But if we can trust each other to mean what we seem to say in such a context, then the attempt at validating a basic fidelity principle by inquiring if anyone rejects it will be superfluous, at least in that context. Some more basic sort of fidelity must already be implicitly recognized and exhibited in our speech behavior, if our putative acceptances and rejections of principles are to carry any force. If they do not, then nothing that we say about our acceptance or rejection of proposed principles will be worth the wind it is written on. (Similar points I think hold good for the validation, and the application, of other candidate "basic" trust-facilitating principles, such as Hobbes's or Grotius's laws. The "reason" that shows us the force of such theorems of peace must itself use words, and use them sincerely, nonarrogantly, and nonmanipulatively.)

At this juncture the persistent seeker after validated (universally acceptable) articulated moral principles might respond that Scanlon's principle of fidelity and any other trust-protecting moral laws that we can spell out do indeed apply to speech itself, not merely to speech acts using the words "I promise," "I solemnly swear," "I assure you," "I guarantee." Some assurances will be taken to be *tacit*. Kant claimed in his lectures on ethics that any breach of the duty of veracity, the duty to say only what one believes, was also a breaking of a "pact," and so a breach of the duty to keep promises, since any act of speaking itself constitutes an implicit assurance or promise of one's sincerity, made to one's hearers.[37] So the principle of fidelity would then indeed apply to any verbal act of acceptance of the principle of fidelity. This, one might say, is desirable reflexivity in a norm, not undesirable question-begging in its validation. This response would be, I think, a fair one, but it offers little comfort to Friends or to those who are perplexed about whether there might not be some truth in Friend's position, as I have given it, let alone to those trying to decide whom to trust to be what they claim to be, mediators of peace, and when to meet apparent trust and when to disregard or betray it in the name of "higher" values or more important trusts. "Trust those who sincerely assure you that they accept the fidelity principle" and "Meet the trust of the trustworthy" can be added to "Don't trust rashly" and the rest of the useless rules for giving trust. As an intellectual exercise, it may be satisfying to find principles that apply to their own endorsement, but that scarcely gives those principles a basic role, let alone selects for us which principles, if any, we have reason to endorse, and whose endorsement to take seriously. My hypothetical Friend might endorse "Don't give assurances," and be perplexed at first when asked, "Are you assuring me that you believe you should not give assurances?" but able, after a minute's thought, to explain patiently, "No, you should not *need* assurances that I am speaking sincerely, and I am not offering you any. If you distrust me, we should stop the conversation, or talk through some intermediary whom we both trust." The Friends' rule can satisfy the reflexivity test[38] as easily as the fidelity principle and, like it, can also be used by manipulative speakers as a snare for the unwary.

Would there be any point in trying to spell out a more basic principle than Principle F, what we might call Principle T, that hypothetically regulates all our talk when it is trustworthy? What J. L. Austin called the "sincerity condition" of any illocutionary act[39] seems as good as we can hope to get here—the deceptively simple requirement that one actually be doing what one purports to be doing in speech—to be joking if that is what one seems to be doing, really expressing one's regrets if that is what one's words in their context make it seem one is doing, affirming (possibly by double negatives) if one's words suggest that, really giving an assurance if that is what one leads others to think, endorsing if one purports to be endorsing, translating others' remarks accurately if that is what one purports to be doing, and so on. Austin's is a quite general non-deceit rule, one I think that Kant would have been happy with. But its helpfulness as a guide, or even as a standard of criticism, is limited. It insists that we keep the verbal appearances in line with the reality of the speaker's actual intentions. But neither appearances nor reality is here so evident, even to those in the best position to get the evidence. Do rhetorical questions, such as this one, *appear* as questions despite their not being sincere askings, and so have to count as insincere? Does an ironic "Yeah, yeah" count as insincere, or does it *appear* as what it is, irony? When Sydney Morgenbesser famously uttered this with an interrogative intonation from the back of the lecture hall in which Austin, the inventor of sincerity conditions, had just put forward the thesis that, while we could affirm with double negatives, we cannot deny with a double affirmative, was Morgenbesser affirming, denying, querying, joking, or all of these? "Let your yea be yea; and your nay, nay" is *not* what sincerity conditions amount to, given the complex speech acts that we sometimes sincerely want to perform. (Equivocation is a form of speech, and has its role to play.) Recent philosophers such as Austin, Paul Grice, and Stanley Cavell[40] have, in Hume's phrase, "exerted their genius" in the philosophical enterprise of trying to make our implicit norms of speech more explicit, and their work helps us to appreciate the complexity of speech norms. In my view, John Locke got as close as anyone to summing up the essence of our norms for speech when he wrote of the importance of teaching children to show, in their speaking, what he termed "civility": "that decency and gracefulness of Looks, Voice, Words, Motions, Gestures and of all the whole outward Demeanour, which takes in Company, and makes those with whom we converse, easie and well pleased."[41] Locke discusses the norm of looking into the face of the one to whom we are speaking; he takes it to be a basic rule of speech, more important to impart to learners, he thinks, than all the rules of grammar.[42] (Shifty eyes are a primitive warning of untrustworthiness, in speech as in other matters.) Speech is our cooperative and trust-facilitated activity *par excellence,* and speech acts are successful only if they "take in Company," if they get across to our conversational partners. Austin's concept of illocutionary "uptake" and Grice's concept of the complex intentions involved in meaningful talk may be seen to have Lockean roots. We *do* cooperate in speaking, even in our uses of speech to wound and insult. We do trust each other to more or less play according to our unformulated and not fully unformulatable (and perhaps shifting) norms of "decency" in speech. And trustworthy speech, like a more or less trustworthy mail service, is one of the tough pervasive webs of trust that we can, if we are clever, use to strengthen and proliferate other life-enhancing webs of trust.

I have spent some time discussing Scanlon's principles, not because I disagree with his claim that there is a more primitive sort of fidelity and trustworthiness than that involved in conformity to the rules of any social practice, but because of my doubts whether this important virtue is adequately captured in his principle or principles. But had they not come very close to analyzing the content of what we take trustworthiness to be, they would not have absorbed my interest so much. My disagreement is in part with his principles themselves, in part with his belief that principles will capture the sort of trustworthiness we look for in one another, and in part a disagreement about the places where our speech practices do come in to enable us to trust each other in specific matters. Rules must be not just supplemented by good judgment but also based upon it, if they are to serve us well, and our existent social practices of giving verbal assurances yet disclaiming that this is what we are doing, endorsing principles but refusing to endorse them, and of accepting and rejecting social practices all build on our primitive cooperative practices, such as the nonverbal expression, mating, and child rearing, that at a general level we share with the stickleback and the dunnocks; on special versions of nonverbal expression, such as the resigned shoulder shrug, the acquiescent bowing of the head, the supplicatory begging gesture, that we share with apes; and on special human gestures, such as encouraging smiles, questioning eyebrow raisings, various forms of eye contact and avoidance of it, and voluntary mutual disablements, such as the handshake. We do put trust in most of these gestures, and both the languages we learn and teach and the social practices we learn and teach rest upon our trust in them. They are so natural and habitual to us that it takes a Darwin to get us to notice them and the extent of our reliance on them.[43] Our more explicit and self-conscious trustings rest on these more primitive ones.

We do not, typically, worry about our fellows' motives for smiles, shrugs, greetings, glances, and handshakes, and we do not need to know their motives in order to trust such gestures to be what they seem to be. Their currency is strong and established. Trust as a good[44] is, as Albert Hirschman has pointed out, one of those goods that, like language and like all habits, increases its strength, wears thick not thin, by constant use.[45] In conditions where there is little or no mutual trust, such as in my thought experiment involving an assurance-craving and later a suspicious Scanlon in relation to an assurance-refusing Friend (who might be an impostor), it is hard to see how trust could get started except with the help of a third party, trusted by both the others. Only if trust is already there in some form can we increase it by using what is there to contrive conditions in which it can spread to new areas. Good parents do this, when they use the trust that the child already has in them, and in their eyes and gestures, to teach trusting and trustworthy habits of speech, which then become involved in so many other cooperative practices where trust is present.

This is also what we typically do with that trusted nonverbal seal of trust, the handshake. Only because we feel safe in the hand-grip of the other can we use this sealer of the bargain, this sacred secular symbol of reciprocal trust in reciprocal services. And why do we trust it? The Romans, I am told, had an arm shake rather than a handshake—they grasped each other by the elbow, thereby immobilizing each other's strong right arm. So the handshake is a remnant of a mutually disempowering gesture—and still does disempower the hand. The secular oath implicitly expressed by it is something along the lines of this: "Should I prove faithless, then may my right hand lose its cunning, as it has at this moment in your hand's grip!" But of course the real cunning of the hand, and of the brain behind it, is to use itself thus to limit its own freedom to strike a mean blow, to see when it serves our own long-term goals to make ourselves vulnerable, to disempower ourselves, and to empower others. Arm wrestling continues to be a flourishing barroom sport, and we know that some have stronger arms, wrists, and hands than others. What then can be our motives for ever being willing to shake hands, let alone to use this gesture, this remnant of a contest, to solemnize our mutual assurances, on those occasions when it is not friends or Friends that we are dealing with, and therefore assurance-giving is in order?[46] Should we shake hands only with altruists? The one whose hand is offered has indeed, by extending it, shown me that he has no spiked mitt concealed in his palm, but how do I know that his hand will not crush mine, as a prelude to my more total disempowerment? And how do I know that my outstretched hand will be accepted, not treated with suspicion? I do not know, I take it on trust, without any hypotheses about the egoism or altruism of the person to whom I extend my hand. On occasion I may indeed distrust, refuse an offered hand, and try to retreat out of range rather than advancing toward the would-be handshaker, but not because I suspect him of self-interest. On occasion a formal mutual bow is a safer mutual assurance than a handshake—especially when one of the parties obviously has more power than the other. The handshake is offered between more or less equals ignorant of the details of each other's motivation, the bow or the curtsy (which also momentarily disempowers the potentially aggressive torso or the striking knee) between unequals who are equally ignorant on this score. The handshake (and to a lesser degree these other deferential self-disempowering gestures) is a mini-case, but a significant one, of our exercise of an ability to *change* conditions in ways that make limited trust a bit less limited, and to do so without great insight into motives. It is also a case of the use of trust to let trust grow, the use of a natural social practice to build up more contrived social practices.

The forms of trust that through their use strengthen and extend trust are usually those, like the handshake and the reliance on more detached third parties as intermediaries, which are reciprocal and occur between those who have arranged, if need be contrived, some sort of rough equality of power and of vulnerability (or at least some movement in that direction), so as to avoid the force of Ennius's dictum. (When a third party is called in as intermediary or mediator, the original parties are equally vulnerable to the danger that the "middle term," the third party, is a wolf in sheep's clothing, furthering her own interests or serving as an agent for a fourth interested party.) In relationships where some governing of the weaker by the stronger is unavoidable, particularly in the care of children, there are devices whereby the strong can selectively disempower themselves, to be free of the corruptions of power. Solemn vows, the institution of godparenting as contrived supervision of parents by "trustees" of the family (a variant on reliance on a third less "interested" party), and similar arrangements for schools and other places where innocent trust is very easily betrayed unless such measures are taken to disempower the persons in the position of immediate parental authority are all cases, like contract, where by words we fetter ourselves, in this case against the siren voice of manipulative power. As in the handshake we let our hands lose their cunning for a moment, in order that their cunning not be used in ultimately regrettable trust-destroying ways, so in vows and in the entrusting of guardians, trustees, arbitrators, and commissions with some power over us, we use our wily tongues to arrange that they themselves will cleave, as it were, to the roofs of our mouths, whenever they are seen to be used over those in our charge in bullying or overly manipulative ways. Our effort here is to try to see to it that we not be deceived, nor let others be let down, by our unmerited self-trust in our own powers of well-meaning agency. We all know that we should not trust ourselves in positions of predominant power—our corruptibility there is proven, and amply documented. So, clever species that we are, we have evolved ways of giving our proven untrustworthy conduct in such conditions oblique and better directions. We have the handshake and larger versions of it, such as the American Constitution, we have vows of renunciation of various sorts of obviously dangerous power, we have various sorts of acts for empowering more trustworthy or less temptation-prone others sufficiently for them to supervise us and halt our heedless use of dangerous degrees of power. (Perhaps we need an international version of godparenting, nations advising other nations on their conduct toward weaker nations.) In such conditions we paralyze ourselves a little, the better to move toward trust-enhancing and trust-increasing forms of cooperation.

But there are other conditions in which our trustworthiness is equally well proven, and where cautious self-trust is appropriate. We do, after all, pass on to new generations the enabling, empowering, and eventually equalizing arts of speech. We give what Hume called "the new brood" the power to say no to us, to disprove our theories, to mock our pretensions, to question our values, to disempower the father figures, to write our obituaries. We encourage *these* "inferiors" to advance on us, even to out-do us. As Bateson pointed to the facts of successful cooperation between parent birds in the propagation of their kind (whatever speculations we might entertain about bird motives or proto-motives), so we can point to the fact that we propagate our powers of speech. We produce new speakers, ready to claim and redefine their rights. Wittgenstein's question "Why do we bring up our children?"—itself enough to bring to a full stop the philosopher who had been intent on sorting our motives into egoistic and nonegoistic—can be adapted to "Why do we empower them with speech?" We *do* this, and we can trust ourselves to continue doing it. So we have at least some clues about the conditions in which mutual trust is appropriate, and in which even the more powerful can prove trustworthy. When the more powerful welcome and facilitate the growth of power of the less powerful, and delay and deplore the decline of others' nonthreatening power (say, of the aged), then they usually can trust and be trusted by those less powerful ones.

The modest interim conclusions I draw from my exploration of the circumstances of sustainable and appropriate trust are that the more appropriate questions are: Whom should I trust on a given matter, myself or someone else? If another, who better than whom, and on the basis of what sort of credentials? If I cannot or do not need to know the details of the other's motives for working with me, in order to judge her trustworthiness, what *would* it be good to know, that I have a reasonable chance of being able to find out without unreasonable effort? Given that I am in shifting power relations with those on whom I depend, what sorts of power must I get, or relinquish, in order to work with them to ensure that the positions that some occupy (and that I may someday occupy) are not positions of trust-threatening powerlessness or powerfulness? What changes are needed in our social practices to create better conditions for mutual trust? Granted that we are going to let some others past our guard (or, in bad conditions, let them help form our guard), which others, and for the sake of what goods? Granted that we are not going to keep track of the current doings of everyone whose actions matter to us (let alone to control them), what matters do and do not call for our personal surveillance? What up-to-the-minute knowledge can we do better without? What guards can we do better without? When is baring the throat our best defensive strategy? Given that we will grant some discretionary powers, on what matters should we do so, and to whom in preference to whom? When, if ever, should we ask for an accounting from those we have trusted—when and for how long should we have faith that all will be well?

Philosophers are typically better at questions than at answers, and in any case all these questions have to be asked and answered in concrete circumstances, case by case. Their best answers there may turn out to confirm some general thesis, such as that trust is appropriately placed in those who, for whatever motives, welcome the equalization of power, who assist the less powerful and renounce eminence of power, who, when they ask us to delay the accounting of their use of discretionary power, do so for reasons that we will eventually see to have been good (as good parents correctly tell their young children "one day you will understand, but not yet. And it is so that you will one day understand, and be my equal, that I ask you now to trust me"). But even if such a thesis is correct, the difficult judgment is not the plausibility of such a general thesis, given a range of particular cases of sustained and broken trust, but the acceptance or rejection of the judgments made about the individual cases themselves. The appropriateness of trust, of sustaining trust, and of supporting institutions that call for trust is judged case by individual case, not just when trust is given or withheld, but retrospectively, when all the accounts, or enough accounts, are in. If to trust is to be willing to delay the accounting, then, when trust is successfully sustained, some accounts are bound to be outstanding. And as for sustainable accounts of trust, we may have to wait equally indefinitely before we get them.

POSTSCRIPT

I have eliminated the first quotation which prefaced this essay in its original publication in the *Tanner Lectures,* since it is the same one with which I concluded Essay 3—a verse from what is obviously one of my favorite songs. But it would be perfectly appropriate to substitute two later stanzas of the same Elizabethan song:

> I leant my back up against some oak,
> Thinking that he was a trusty tree;
> But first he bended and then he broke,
> And so did my false love to me.
>
> Oh love is handsome and love is fine
> And love is a jewel when it is new;
> But when it is old, it groweth cold
> And fades away like morning dew.

My discussion of Scanlon's fidelity principle, in the latter part of this essay, takes a principle which he formulated in order to explain how promises can morally bind us independently of any social institution of promising and raises questions about that principle's acceptability in contexts where no social practices are present to limit or assist its application. Scanlon was concerned only to locate a moral principle which explained the binding power of promises. He did not purport to define "the most basic sort of trustworthiness," so it may be that I have criticized his account for failing to do something that he did not claim it could do. Defenders of Scanlon could reasonably argue that even if his principle does not exhaust the content of the most basic virtue of fidelity, it might still succeed in capturing that part of it which makes promises morally binding.

My story about the Friends was intended to show that some conventional indicator either of intent to give a binding assurance or of the absence of this intent (and also of willingness or unwillingness to accept such an assurance) must be present for Scanlon's fidelity principle not to be reasonably rejected. So I was trying to argue that he had failed to do what he did set out to do, to show how promises bind independently of the acceptance of any social practices. But since I was also concerned to challenge what I took to be his Kantian contractualism and Kantian assumption that all of morality could be encoded in general principles, my argument against his account of promises is interwoven with an attempt to criticize the contractualism and to show that neither his fidelity principle nor any higher derivative of it captures the most basic sort of trustworthiness that we expect of one another. It might have been better if I had separated out my case against his analysis of a binding promise from my disagreements with the more general aspects of his version of Kantian contractualism. As I say on page 176,[47] my disagreement is both about the general acceptability of the principles which he formulates, when left unmodified by institutional escape clauses, and also about the role played by our speech practices in the particular case of promising. I have discussed promises at greater length elsewhere.[48]

nine

TRUSTING PEOPLE

In the Sciences, every one has so much,
as he really knows and comprehends:
What he believes only, and takes upon trust,
are all but shreds; which however well in
the whole piece, make no considerable
addition to his stock who gathers them.
Such borrowed Wealth, like Fairy-money,
though it were Gold in the hand from which
he received it, will be but Leaves and Dust
when it comes to use.

John Locke, Essay, I, 4, 23

John Locke, casting off the dead hand of Scholastic learning and arguing for critical examination of received opinions, for freedom of thought, for the need for each person to inquire for herself and to question old orthodoxies, warns us against "blindly embrac[ing] and confidently vent[ing] the Opinions of another." Such borrowed gold will turn to dust and leaves in our hands, he warns. And most of us have no quarrel with his social program here. We are heirs and beneficiaries of his campaign against the tyranny of master doctrines: "And it was of no small advantage to those who affected to be Masters and Teachers, to make this the Principle of *Principles*, That Principles must not be questioned: For having once established this Tenet ... it put their Followers upon a necessity of receiving some Doctrines as such; which was to take them off from the use of their own Reason and Judgment, and put them upon believing and taking them upon trust, without farther examination: In which posture of blind Credulity, they might be more easily governed by and made useful to some sort of Men, who had the skill and office to principle and guide them."[1]

Yet it was also Locke who noted that we live upon trust, and who saw governmental authority as a power sensibly entrusted by the people to their government (as long as some conditions are met). Do we live on fairy money? Need conformity to authoritative decrees of duly appointed authorities be a posture of blind credulity? Locke himself did much to show us how to combine trust with some vision and some security against the "Sort of Men" who would like to dominate and manipulate others. Trusting people, governments, teachers, or private persons can indeed be dangerous, and some people therefore try to economize on trust.

My title, "Trusting People," is deliberately ambiguous. Some of us in certain contexts are trusting people, while others in the same contexts are suspicious people. That is one sense of my title. The other sense of my title and part of my topic concerns trusting *people,* as distinct from trusting human institutions and the roles we and our ancestors have designed for them, for a succession of persons to fill—trusting presidents and vice presidents, trusting fathers and clergymen. For it may well be that some roles tend to pressure a not-so-trustworthy person into being more trustworthy or tempt a formerly trustworthy person into treachery or corruption. My assumption will be that we would, other things equal, prefer to be able both to trust individual persons and to rely on the institutions that structure their conduct, and so prefer to be able to regard it a good thing if people are trusting people. But of course we cannot afford to encourage our children or one another to be more trusting until we have reasonable assurance that those whom we are encouraging them to trust by and large will not let them down. We cannot simply label trustingness a virtue, anymore than we can simply call loyalty and trustworthiness virtues. Those who are worthy of the trust of their co-workers in, say, the drug business or as loyal gang members are not necessarily the better for their trustworthiness, and those who put their trust in those who perpetuate exploitation or domination are not to be admired for their willingness to trust. Still, despite these clear cases of deplorable forms of trusting and meeting trust, I think that an adaptation of Royce's[2] claim about loyalty can be made for the pair trust and trustworthiness, namely, that the bad forms tend to be temporary since self-undermining, while the forms that are self-strengthening and that tend to produce meta-trust, trust in trust-involving relationships and forms of cooperation, are the ones that we have good reason to welcome from a moral point of view. Not loyalty to loyalty, but trust in sustained trust, trust in it in full knowledge of its risks as well as its benefits, and trustworthiness to sustain trust may well be the supreme virtues for ones like us, in our condition.

Diego Gambetta, in his concluding essay to the collection of essays on trust which he edited,[3] raises the question of whether we can trust trust, or whether our well-documented experience of betrayals does not rather suggest that we should be suspicious of it and minimize the contexts in which we expect it of others or offer it to others. He quotes Jon Elster and Karl Moene, "We may hope that trust will come about as the by-product of a good economic system ... one would be putting the cart before the horse were one to bank on trust, solidarity and altruism as the preconditions for reform."[4] Elster and Moene allow that "some amount of trust must be present in any complex economic system."[5] Even the most competition-encouraging systems do rely on some trust in contracts, the most controlled economies on some trust in those administering the controls. But whatever may be the case for economic systems, what are we to say about moral networks? Can we trust trust, at least outside our business deals? Gambetta's answer to this question is a fairly pessimistic affirmative. After noting how distrust tends to spread and to disable, he writes, "Trust, even if *always* misplaced, can never do worse than that, and the expectation that it might do at least marginally better is therefore plausible." His guarded conclusion that "it may be rational to trust trust, and distrust distrust"[6] really endorses the rationality not so much of trusting trust as of relying on it, since if our choice is between doing very badly by encouraging distrust and doing marginally better by encouraging trust, then it is dubious that choosing the latter option really counts as *trusting* trust, by Gambetta's own definition. Trust, he writes (here drawing on the analyses given by the others who contributed to the volume), "is a particular level of the subjective probability with which an agent assesses that another agent or group of agents will perform a particular action, both *before* he can monitor such action (or independently of his capacity ever to be able to monitor it) *and* in a context in which it affects *his own* action ... [a probability] high enough for us to consider engaging in some form of cooperation with him."[7] But Gambetta's own estimate of the disastrous costs of mistrust is based on a fairly careful monitoring of its record, for example, in the Mafia, and of the better record of trust-involving social structures.

His is a dubious case of meta-trust precisely because his knowledge-based case for the "rationality" of encouraging trust is so strong. "The condition of ignorance or uncertainty about other people's behaviour [that] is central to the notion of trust"[8] is not met in his version of meta-trust. We might, fairly implausibly, suppose that Gambetta's considerable knowledge of the comparative record of trust-relying and mistrust-relying social strategies might be merely historical, and without projective predictive value. The excessively risk-averse will, I suppose, find the philosophical "problem of induction" a *practical* problem, so that any attempt to learn from experience will involve risk taking, but it still will not yet amount to trusting, if that is risk-taking reliance on others' hoped-for behavior. In any case Gambetta does not appear to be suspicious of all reliance on probability estimates, and in particular on past monitorings of people's performance as a guide to their future behavior, so this way of importing some ignorance into his guarded preference for trust over distrust, enough for it to count as trust in trust, is purely hypothetical.

Is there then any such phenomenon as trust in trust? That depends on our definition of trust. For the individual, as distinct from the social scientist and the would-be reformer of human habits, there frequently are cases in which our previous experience of where trust has more or less worked and where it has invited disaster gives us very little basis for any probability estimate about the other's reliability in the case before us. A Peruvian artist selling his paintings at a fair in a U.S. city was recently faced with two strangers and possible clients, a couple who would buy a certain large painting only if the artist could arrange its transport to their home. The artist, unable to close his stall right then and unwilling to miss or postpone the sale, proposed that one of the couple watch his stall while he transported the painting, guided by the other buyer. Perhaps he had done this on previous occasions without mishap, but there must have been a first occasion when twenty or thirty paintings were left in the custody of a stranger, just because she had shown herself willing to purchase one such painting. Social scientists may know the frequency with which con artists in this country lure merchants away by promising to complete a sale elsewhere, while leaving their accomplices minding the store, but the foreign artist was innocent of such statistics. He just trusted the couple who wanted to buy, and such fairly ordinary trust, shown by an adult in a novel situation, might well be seen to involve meta-trust, a snap judgment that on this occasion trust is more sensible than losing a sale through suspiciousness. If trust is taken to be always trust in people,[9] then this meta-trust is best construed as trust in one's own judgment concerning the other's trustworthiness. Then there will be trust in trust, and it may be displayed quite often by ordinary people. It may be harder for social scientists to find room for it. The more one knows about people (oneself included), the less one has occasion strictly to trust them, or to trust trusting them. An omniscient and otherwise omnipotent God will of necessity lack one ability that his human and animal creatures have—to give or withhold trust. The traditional religious commandment has been that we should trust God, not that we should live up to any divine trust in us. It is an important fact about trust that it cannot be given except by those who have only limited knowledge, and usually even less control, over those to whom it is given.

It was not trust in trust which I tentatively promoted to supreme virtue for ones like us, with finite mutual knowledge and mutual control, but trust in sustained trust, along with trustworthiness to sustain trust. And the temporal stretch is important. Gambetta defined trust as willingness to cooperate with another *before* monitoring her performance, perhaps even without any capacity ever to monitor it. I have made a similar point in suggesting[10] that trust is willingness to give discretionary powers, to postpone checking and accounting. But except in rare cases, there will eventually be some contrived or fairly automatic accounting, and with it some discovery of how well or badly the trusted person performed. One-shot brief trustings do occur, but except when fatal, they will usually be followed by retrospective "monitoring" of their outcomes by the trusters. It is the cases where we repeat a previously ventured type of trusting or sustain an old trust that present the most interesting dimensions of trust, and these are also those most important for our lives together. (What we *see* as a repetition of a familiar form of trusting, or see as a mere continuation of an old trust, will of course affect our willingness to trust.) Because sustained trust is experienced trust, is a willingness to postpone any further accounting because past accounts have been satisfactory, its conditions are both some relevant knowledge and some relevant ignorance about the trusted. Should any form of meta-trust be put forward as candidate for the position of moral centrality that Royce believed "loyalty to loyalty" to have, it had better not be one of the blinder variants of trust or of meta-trust.

But I am not really concerned to elevate any virtue to supremacy. Even if we could effect some sort of unification of the virtues by relating them all to due trust and due trustworthiness (and some often-neglected virtues, from gentle ones like tact, discretion, patience, and the avoidance of bitterness to feistier ones such as resilience, alertness to the oppression of those who are too oppressed to protest on their own behalf, and inventiveness in the redesign of roles, do come to the fore once we look at trust relationships), we will still need a whole host of virtues, more or less democratically ruling in our souls, balancing each other's likely excesses. The theoretical exercise of seeing how we could illuminatingly map the interrelationships of the virtues is of course one that appeals to philosophers, but it is not part of my present aim to show that due trust and due trustworthiness can lord it over other virtues. My aim here is less imperial, more modest—to imitate Hume, it is to bring the topic of trust and distrust a little more into philosophical fashion (its fashion in films, novels, and short stories is already established, and it is catching on in applied ethics) to increase our understanding of our own selective trust in selective trust, to increase our self-consciousness of our own capacities for creating the conditions for sensible trusting.

Parents of small children these days surely face a very difficult problem. On the one hand they want to surround the child with an atmosphere of mutual trust, to help the growing child to trust them, trust herself, and trust their will to help, not hinder, her in her attempts to explore, enjoy, and also control the world around her, to learn to walk, talk, and generally participate in human activities. On the other hand the child has to be put on guard against dangers, deterred not just from too adventurous experiments with the non-human environment but also from unselective trust in older persons, since some do not wish her well. How to strike the right balance in the child between undue trust in others and in her own ability to do things safely with others, on the one hand, and undue timidity, fear, and suspicion, on the other, seems a task that requires the wisdom of a Solomon or a Queen of Sheba. But somehow many parents bring it off. We do seem to have some innate capacities, not merely for trusting and meeting trust, but also for trustworthy transmission of discriminating trusting, despite our inability to analyze, let alone to reduce to any kind of rule, the dispositions that we manage to encourage. Of course not all do manage to pass on their own more or less functional mix of trust and vigilance, and not all have it to pass on. Still, praise be, some have it, and do pass it on.

After I gave a lecture on trust in which I retold John Updike's story "Trust Me" about a child who forgives his father for failing to catch him when he jumps trustingly into a swimming pool in response to his father's assurance that he will catch him,[11] a friend told me the following bit of family legend. His father had reported his childhood experience (trauma?) of having been encouraged by his father to climb up onto a fairly high and slippery place, under which the father stood with outstretched arms, as if to catch the child, or at least to break his likely fall. The child duly climbed, and duly fell. His father stepped aside, simply watching while his child fell and injured himself, and then helped him up, and tended his wounds. The hurt and bewildered child demanded of his father, "Why did you do that?" and got the reply, "So that, from now on, you will know that *no one* is to be trusted." Having heard this grim tale, I marveled a bit that my friend trusted me with it—indeed that he and his father had anything but extreme suspicion of apparent friendship. Those whose willingness to trust has been so dramatically punished will have to make very special efforts if they are to transmit anything but watchful suspicion to those who follow them. Still, the wish to do better for the next generation than the previous generation did for us is a force not to be underestimated, even if the wish is only occasionally father to the successful deed.

And how would we recognize success in this transmission of attitudes? What mixture of caution and enterprise, trust and wariness, does the benevolent godmother wish the child's parents to somehow encourage in the child, either by providing models to be imitated or, at worst, by providing object lessons of what to avoid? Can anything except unhelpful platitudes be said about the mixture that we reasonably welcome in young people or in one another? Do we welcome different degrees and kinds of trust and mistrust at different ages? Is it healthier for the four-year-old than for the fourteen-year-old to trust the stranger who is offering some sort of treat? Is it any better or worse for the forty-year-old or, for that matter, for the eighty-year-old?

We do seem to expect that with increase of age there will come increased acceptance of the truth of the maxim that there is no free lunch, so that the question "what does this person want from me and would it be dangerous for me to give it?" will reliably arise for, say, the fourteen-year-old who is invited to accept favors from strangers. But for the four-year-old it is usually just false that there is no free lunch—her lunch does not normally come poisoned or with strings attached, so there is no very good reason why she should be suspicious of what seem to be free gifts. And even for forty- and sixty-year-olds there can be free gifts, which it would be graceless to refuse because of our suspicion that Hume may be right, that even "the more generous and noble intercourse of friendship" involves some expectation of return service, of some "recompense."[12] A. S. Byatt puts it nicely in her story "Art Work," a story about an artist, his wife, Debbie, and their cleaning woman, Mrs. Brown. "Mrs. Brown has always had an awkward habit of presuming to give the family gifts..." (A description follows of the "awful" and "flamboyant" sweaters she has knitted for the children.) "The real sufferer is Debbie, whose imagination is torn all ways. She knows from her own childhood exactly how it feels to wear clothes one doesn't like, isn't comfortable and invisible in, is embarrassed by. She also believes very strongly that there is more true kindness and courtesy in accepting gifts gratefully and enthusiastically than in offering them. And, more selfishly, she simply cannot do without Mrs. Brown, she needs Mrs. Brown, . . ."[13] Receipt of gifts can alter a relationship, creating expectations of some return, and the exchange of gifts can cement relationships more than we sometimes welcome.

As Hume noted, we come to like those whom we have benefited (or whom we think we have benefited), and as Kant noted, for some people, himself clearly included, graceful acceptance of gifts, and so of indebtedness, does not come easily. Kant in his lectures on ethics said, "A friend who bears my losses becomes my benefactor and puts me in his debt. I feel shy in his presence and cannot look him boldly in the face. The true relationship is cancelled and friendship ceases."[14] Gratitude is for Kant a duty, and against the grain of the autonomy-loving man. In *The Metaphysics of Morals: Metaphysical*

First Principles of the Doctrine of Virtue, he writes that "one cannot, by any repayment of a kindness received, *rid* oneself of the obligation for it, since the recipient can never win away from the benefactor his *priority* of merit, namely having been the first in benevolence."[15] But true benevolence, for Kant, will not risk humiliating its beneficiary. It will disguise itself, and the virtuous benefactor will "show that he is himself put under obligation by the other's acceptance or honored by it . . ."[16] This Kantian game of debt-avoidance and fake debt-acknowledgment by proud, mutually respectful persons is clearly an adolescent or an adult game—children are innocent of its ploys and counterplays. They do not naturally fear those bearing gifts, nor are they hesitant to appear to be making gifts. Belief in the possibility of making and taking free gifts is one of the blessings of childhood, and it seems a terrible condemnation of our society that this innocent blessing has to be withdrawn or circumscribed. It is one thing to encourage reciprocity and the expectation of the expectation of reciprocity, quite another to warn against all bearers of gifts.

It is not in all cultural settings that young children have to be instructed to beware strangers offering sweets. There are varying climates of trust. Indeed the move from one, my native New Zealand, which was fairly kind to innocent trusters and where houses were regularly left unlocked, to more menacing social climates, in Great Britain (where I was warned against gypsies and where unlocked doors were certainly discouraged), in the United States (where one must give only store-wrapped candy to children coming to the door at Halloween, since unwrapped or home-wrapped sweets might be poisoned), and in Austrian towns (where not just doors but front gates are often kept locked and even not-so-young women are warned that unaccompanied women in the city streets or cafés at night may be taken as "fair game" by men on the prowl), was what first led me to think about trust and about the historical and cultural factors affecting its presence and types. A city like Vienna, as long as its memories of its Nazi period and its occupation by foreign armies are still vivid, will be understandably uncertain of the safety of its streets at night. (On my arrival there by train shortly before the Allied occupation ended, in 1955, a concerned gentleman who had shared a train compartment with my woman friend and me insisted on taking us to some religious society for the protection of women, who had an office at the station and who duly found us "safe" lodging in a nunnery. Even on my return ten years later to a much more relaxed city, going to evening concerts alone was still regarded as risky for a woman.) To some extent what climate of trust a city or a nation enjoys is an accident of military history, and of whether one was victor or vanquished. But it is also a matter of the culture that continues through and between wars, and the sort of upbringing a country gives to its young. A friend of mine who attended a parochial Catholic school for girls in the United States told me how puzzled she was by the religion classes she had to attend at school, until she was informed by more clued-in schoolmates that what this mysterious stuff amounted to was simply coded instructions on how to remain a virgin. Sex education is all very well, but one hopes that it need not come in the guise of theology, or in a way that gives a girl to understand that the world she is part of divides into wise and cautious virgins on the one hand, and, on the other, predatory males along with their "fallen" victims, along with two dubious categories—those who have chosen to marry rather than burn, and those who have been called to be priests, administering the moral rules for others and making interesting rules for themselves.[17]

Religious traditions are places where we find it preached that trust in God and trust in religious superiors who speak on God's behalf are virtues. It is not surprising that philosophers have tended to shy away from talking much about trust, given its guilt by association with such suspect monkish virtues as obedience. The current mini-revival of philosophical interest in trust in applied ethics brings some dangers of a return to that unholy alliance of moral commands to "trust and obey." Wherever the roles of an institution have given some people authority to give orders to other people, as in the church, in hospitals, in the military, and in most political systems, there will be a tendency to construe trust in a more powerful person as involving willingness to obey orders rather than to take instruction or counsel, to take advice, to be patient and defer satisfying one's reasonable desire to understand what is going on, to learn some valuable discipline, or to conform to authoritative laws which others have made. Even in the military, where a case can be made for the need for some to give commands and for others to obey them, we now encourage moral checks by the commanded on the content of at least some of the orders. By and large, trust is a virtue only when it is not trust in authoritative commanders. Where such positions of command are deemed unavoidable, then vigilance and nonparalyzing distrust will displace judicious trust as the functional virtues of that sort of highly asymmetrical cooperative scheme. Even when we agree that we need them, we should maintain some continuing distrust of those institutions that create commanders; if we have learned anything from our individual and collective lessons in regrettable trusting, it is surely that power corrupts. Trustworthy institutions will be those that distribute power in such a way that this corruption is less likely. In a medical context, for example, we should not expect physicians who are dictators within their realm to exhibit trustworthy behavior anymore than we should expect it of any other would-be almighty ones, or their favored spokesmen, in religious or in nonreligious organizations. Trustworthy people, we could say, are to be expected only to the extent that the roles we have given them to play are trustworthy roles. Of course there will be occasional saints who do not succumb to the temptations a badly designed role puts in their way and some especially vicious people who function badly even in the best designed of social roles. The most we can hope for is that the places we encourage or allow people to occupy and the procedures we have that select who does occupy a given role will both control the damage done by the very vicious and, while placing no reliance on the likelihood of saints, give any who turn up the chance to show their special gifts, not in resisting temptation, but in wonders of a more positive kind.

Granted the need for trustworthy institutions and institutional roles, it will still be rightly said that not all relationships of trust are between role players or structured by institutions and the power that they distribute. Do we not sometimes just trust a *person,* as a person, rather than as a priest, a military commander, a chief surgeon, a customer, or whatever? Yes, we surely do, and sometimes we trust animals, put ourselves in their power. In extreme cases, someone looks us in the eye and says "follow me," and we drop everything and do so. But it may on the whole be better to give such instant devotion to friendly cats than to those with pretensions to be kings. A remarkable fact about us is that we do form quick judgments about the trustworthiness of strangers, on the basis of some combination of eye contact, tone of voice, and other cues given by bodily expression and, perhaps, by our unconscious sense of smell. Such judgments serve to launch us into personal relations of trust on matters great and small. I stagger under a load of heavy suitcases in a foreign airport and a stranger says, "Let me help you with those." I glance at him, and do, although I have no assurance that he is not a thief in bourgeois clothing. I offer my assistance in an airport to a stranger, a man trying to carry both his suitcase and a one-year-old child. I expect that he will be glad to have me take his case, since I am walking unladen in the same direction. He glances at me and says, "Thank you. Could you take her?" I marvel that the child is willing to cling to a stranger, and wonder as I carry her if she should be so willing. And so I ponder trust, wise and foolish trust, and ponder the mysterious bases of our trustings and distrustings.

This may be the appropriate point to apologize, if that is what I am now doing, for the excessively anecdotal nature of my remarks about trust. I do have some distrust of abstract theorizing in moral philosophy,[18] so I am in general more tolerant than are many of my colleagues of other approaches, of case studies (from fictional or real cases), of "natural histories" such as those of Hume or Rousseau, of perusal of autobiographies and biographies, of consultation with anthropologists, sociologists, historians. But on this topic in particular it would seem that a bit of self-revelation is only proper—to borrow all my examples of rash or wise trusting from other people's lives would be to misrepresent the basis for whatever considered views I have about trust. I do not take my own case to be atypical, or at least not atypical for women,[19] but of course I may have been luckier or unluckier than most in some sorts of trustings and distrustings, so that some bias may be present in my approach. We have to trust others to discern such bias, since we are very bad at doing it for ourselves, and therefore a little bit of relevant life history along with our more general reflections on trust seems only right and proper. I know, however, that I will not convince many of my fellow moral philosophers on this matter.[20] The impersonal style has become nearly a sacred tradition in moral philosophy, and examples of departure from it, such as Rousseau's *Confessions* (or Augustine's) are not altogether encouraging examples. The selective anecdote is very far from purportedly full confessional flow, but certainly has its own dangers, including those of bias. Nevertheless it seems to me time to experiment a bit with styles of moral philosophy, especially for those of us who, like Hume, hope that moral philosophy can be accurate without being "abstruse" and might even "reconcile truth with novelty."

We all do make snap judgments about people as a basis for our decision to put or not to put ourselves in their hands on some matter, and even "profound inquiry" and the most "abstract speculations" into our moral capacities will have to accommodate not just that we do this, but that bad judgment here is the exception, not the rule.[21] Is it that the really bad judges on this matter do not survive to get into our epistemological records? Unfortunately infants depend more on their parents' willingness to encourage trust and a developing judgment of whom to trust than they do on their own initial capacities. Those who die in infancy do not often die from their own bad judgment. Any who are burdened from the start with distrust of those who offer food or care will be severely handicapped, and trustworthiness toward them will call for special skills and virtues, but it will not be judgment that such special caretakers will first be trying to impart as much as prejudgment attitudes, the very capacity to trust. Unless we have that, there will be no scope for judgments about whom to trust or about what matters to trust to a particular person.

Some innate or soon acquired willingness to show some trust in those who stand in a parental capacity to the child is the primitive basis of other, more judgment-mediated, trustings. But this does not give us exactly a case of trusting persons *qua* persons, as distinct from trusting those in a given role. For parenthood is a social role, even if we also want to call it a natural role. Even our most spontaneous trustings may be trustings (or distrustings) of those in a given role, where the role-filler cannot be entirely separated from the role filled. We do engage fairly instinctively in natural "rituals," such as hugging, exchanging smiles, taking and shaking hands, and these can be seen to define simple roles, with some primitive role differentiation. Those for whom trustworthiness or treachery are possibilities, we might say, are ones who can have eye contact with one another or answer each other's calls. Calling and answering are primitive cooperative practices, involving a role for caller that is distinct from that of answerer. Infants delight in learning variations of these responsive activities and playing games involving them. They may risk little by a smile in return for a smile, but more perhaps by taking another's offered hand. The handshake is learned in almost all societies as the symbol of some mutual trusting, and it grows out

195

of more asymmetrical trustings of small hands into larger ones, offered to support or to guide.

The supporting hand can turn into the abducting or the abusive hand, and the guiding hand can lead into traps and dangers. The trusting one always puts herself in the trusted's power, and by her trusting increases the power of the one who is trusted. In the case of the very young, the trusted older person whose hand is taken will be one who already has more power than she does, more physical strength and more knowledge of how to get what is wanted. By cooperative trusting behavior the truster renounces some of her own small power to control matters, and as long as the more powerful trusted one wants what the truster wants, this voluntary renunciation of control will advance the truster's goals, will get her where she wants to be, and will often help her to increase her own strength and ability. When matters work out well, her voluntary giving up of power will be an investment whose returns will be an ultimate increase for her. But if things go badly, she will be harmed, not helped, by her trusting. Risk is of the very essence of trust.[22]

When the trust is mutual, the risks are on both sides, and most trust is to some degree mutual. Even the youngest child has some power to hurt and harm—when I take the stranger's little girl into my arms in the airport, I *might* be rewarded by having my ear bitten or my hair pulled. Normally we do not even think of such possibilities, nor do we expect the very small child to think of the bad possibilities of being in the stronger arms of another. If one actually reviewed all the possible bad outcomes of some avoidable dealing with another before embarking on it, the calculated risk which one then would take, if one went ahead, would scarcely warrant the label "trust." Trusting is taking not-so-calculated risks,[23] which are not the same as ill-judged ones. Part of what it is to trust is not to have too many thoughts about possible betrayals. They would turn the trust into mistrust.[24] There can be mistrustful reliance on another, reliance accompanied by predictions that the relied-upon will prove unreliable. The alternative to trusting another is not always avoidance of being in their power—that is sometimes unavoidable, and sometimes when it is avoidable it is nevertheless chosen, but mistrustfully, and with some misgivings. It takes a fairly generous person not to respond to such mistrust with mistrust of her own. Francis Bacon wrote that "base natures, if they find themselves once suspected, will never be true,"[25] and not-so-base natures, who remain true, may still develop mistrust of their own. There can be mistrustful fidelity. Mistrust can bring out the worst in the mistrusted, as trust can bring out the best. Albert Hirschman has pointed out that trust, like other of our moral resources, increases with use, decays with disuse.[26] Both trust and mistrust tend to be self-fulfilling and tend to be contagious.[27]

The handshake, that sacred sealer of deals, is a nice example of a gesture that combines trust and caution. It is the remnant of a mutually disempowering gesture, a mutual putting out of full action of the strong manipulative right hand. The mutuality of its disempowering effect protects each party, so that little is risked by the gesture itself. Yet there is still a sense in which one must trust the partner to a handshake—not merely trust him to honor whatever deal the handshake seals, but trust him to be what he purports to be, a partner in a reciprocal and nonharmful gestural exchange. Even when the handshake seals no bargain but is merely a greeting, it does make some pretenses, and these, like all pretenses, can be false. The pretense is of equality, reciprocity, goodwill. Should the hand I shake have a concealed spiked mitt in its palm, I will be a victim. Should the hand have an open wound and the shaker some deadly disease communicated by body fluids, I may become the victim of an ill-judged handshake. Normally we do not think at all of such possibilities—as Locke said, we live on trust. Sometimes we are surprised in less unpleasant, but nevertheless disturbing, ways. I recall my first introduction in Austria, when I trustingly held out my hand to shake that of the man to whom I was being introduced, and was astounded to find it lightly taken and raised to the man's lips. Why should this have upset me? Is this not a charming Old World gesture? It is a gesture intended not merely for use between gentlemen and ladies who spend time on the care of their hands (as distinct from women with hands rough and earthy from gardening, or inky from writing) but also between those unequal in perceived power to take the initiative. The man is active, the woman passive. Her hand is taken and subjected to a kiss. There is a mutual vulnerability of a sort—the man does risk a dirty or germy hand at his lips. But the symbol is quite other than that of the handshake; to kiss a woman's hand is a symbol of fake devotion to a more delicate and more passive person. To submit to this custom is, for a woman, indeed to submit. For one reared in the more egalitarian cultural climate of New Zealand, where handshakes or mutual nose rubbings are the rule (and bowings and curtseyings are hastily improvised for the occasional royal visit), Austrian polite greetings came at first as a genteel shock, a matter for wonder and later for amusement. "Handkusse an die Frau Gemahlin" (Handkisses to your lady-wife), a bit of telephone pleasantry which an Austrian real estate agent used in a business conversation with my husband, surely cries out for ridicule.

Our everyday gestures do put us into short-lived roles vis-à-vis one another, ones that involve some mutual trusting and that may be symbolic of the longer-lasting roles that we fill or are expected to fill. I have dwelt on variations of the greeting and of hand-takings because they are simple cases of putting ourselves in the power of others, and they show both how natural it is for us to do this (the embrace is common to all cultures, the handshake between equals to very many) and how cultural variation can come in to shift the power relations, to vary the degree of reciprocity. Earlier I claimed that trustworthy people are to be expected only to the extent that the roles we give them to play are trustworthy roles. I modified this claim by allowing that spontaneous trust, cued by some hard to analyze feature of the trusted person's face, stance, voice, and general aura, certainly happens, as does spontaneous distrust, and is minimally role-affected, but our lasting relationships with others are rarely based only on such instant recognitions. We may, on the basis of eye contact or other sorts of instant attraction, be willing to have more intimate contact with another for a night or so, but few of us would take marriage vows just because we had looked into another's eyes and liked what we saw. (Liked the version of ourselves we saw there?) Some do marry and marry happily, on the basis of very selective premarriage mutual knowledge of one another, so we do seem able to make fairly sound judgments of trustworthiness on the basis of fairly restricted data, and that is clearly a vital human cognitive skill. But we also make bad errors here, and how disastrous their consequences are will often depend on just how the roles that we enter are structured. The design of the roles of husband and wife has changed and is still changing, and obviously such changes both pressure the spouse into certain sorts of trustworthiness, while perhaps also creating temptations for other sorts of infidelity, and limit the severity of the harm that

comes from disappointed trust. That people married when divorce
was not yet a possibility is a fact to marvel at. It shows either their
amazing confidence in their powers of mutual assessment for trustworthiness or the compelling force of those drives that, in traditional societies, were channeled into matrimony—the need for a
sexual mate and the wish to have children socially recognized as
one's own.[28] If it was better to marry for life than to burn, the fires
had to be very fierce indeed.

Women, when faced not merely, like men, with a no-exit form of
marriage but also with the loss of their property rights at marriage
and with the obligation to obey their husbands, took extraordinary
risks, and often bad risks, by choosing to marry. But of course their
options were limited. Choosing to be an unmarried governess or a
housekeeper was also choosing to be in the power of some master,
and so for all its horrors, Victorian marriage may well have seemed,
to women who had any choice, to be the safer bet. The changes in
the design of marital roles in the last hundred years in Western societies have radically altered the climate of trust and distrust between
marriage-inclined men and women, and show us just how "manners
makyth men." Novels such as those of Ivy Compton Burnett,
describing terrible family tyrants and the protective ploys and coun-
terploys of those forced to live under one roof in intimacy and
mutual distrust, document for us not so much the nastiness of our
own nature as the horror that was the Victorian family. The raw
material, male and female, is doubtless much as it always was, but
husbands are less likely to be ruthless bullies, wives and daughters
less likely to be wily schemers, sons less likely to be plotting
takeovers from their fathers once we have the changes we now have
in the rights of wives, in women's opportunity to have careers outside the home, and in young men's freedom to move away from
paternal control and to have ambitions finer than becoming patriarchs in their turn. Facing us now are real problems that are the
results of greater sexual freedom and the breakdown of a patriarchal
tyranny, and that create their own climate of insecurity and distrust.
But whatever the problems, they are a great advance over those
faced by people living in the straitjacket of the sort of family
described for us by Compton Burnett or Ibsen. The specter of deadly
venereal disease haunting human sexual intimacy, in and out of marriage, is no new phenomenon. When the marriages it entered were

"till death do us part," there was no protection. When a double standard operated, making divorce easier for husbands than for wives to initiate, women were at special risk, risk over and above that which childbirth then involved. Tragic as our present sexual scene may be (given the AIDS epidemic), what woman in today's society would choose to change places with her 1890s counterpart?

Changes in marital and other family roles (for example, in children's rights) affect the expectations it is reasonable for us to have of one another, affect what we can trust each other with, and for. Other changes in institutional design are equally effective controllers of our climate of trust. Universities who have appointed an ombudsperson, to whom complaints can be made without alerting complained-of superiors, thereby alter all the other roles in their hierarchy. Chairpersons and deans become more trustworthy by the sheer background presence of well-designed procedures for complaint. This is not because these officers will fear exposure of any abuses of power they may be tempted to; it is because they will be less likely to feel the temptation. Just as the procedures for judicial appeal affect the powers and role of judges in lower courts, so the creation of the job of ombudsperson alters the powers and role of other university officers, and so alters the opportunities and temptations they have for abuse of their power. These are obvious ways by which we can mold people to make them more trustworthy, and so be able to afford to encourage people to be more trusting.

Niklas Luhmann[29] distinguishes between our "familiarity" with and "confidence" in our customs and institutions and our "trust" in one another, as we encounter each other in the society that is structured by our customs and institutions. He pairs confidence with danger, trust with risk. Both involve our willingness to act in ways that we cannot be sure will not lead to disappointment or disaster. If we are confident, we ignore the danger, which is quite different from saying that we are ignorant of its existence. If we have confidence in, say, our court procedures, then if we are accused of a crime of which we are innocent, we will expect acquittal, even though we know of cases where the system failed. Risk is unlike danger, Luhmann thinks, in that we *take* risks, whereas we can have no choice but to face dangers. To trust is to venture, to assess and accept risks; to distrust is to be averse to, and to avoid, such risk taking. I have not drawn a sharp distinction between danger and risk, or between our confidence or lack of confidence in our institutions and our trust or distrust of those who fill roles in them, and whose lives are lived in the structure they impose. This is because I think that there is a continuum between our most and our least "chosen" vulnerabilities to others, so that Luhmann's "danger" and "risk" will merge. Nor do I think that all our trusting and risk taking is toward individuals, in or out of institutional roles. We take risks when we redesign roles; we place our trust, in Luhmann's sense of the term, in procedures as well as in people. Luhmann emphasizes the interdependence of confidence in our social systems and trust, understood as risk taking by individuals. When there is unhappiness with and lack of confidence in structures that we take ourselves to be powerless to change, we have no choice but to keep on living within them, but if we are also so risk-averse that most of us will not invest, say, in government bonds or in industries vital to that system, then the system may change. "Thus lack of confidence and the need for trust may form a vicious circle. A system—economic, legal, or political—requires trust as an input condition. Without trust it cannot stimulate supportive activities in situations of uncertainty or risk. At the same time, the structural and operational properties of such a system may erode confidence and thereby undermine one of the essential conditions of trust."[30] By parity of reasoning, where the societal and institutional conditions of trust are met, there will be willingness to take risks to support the structure and also to venture to try to improve it. Because I have refused to separate the human role-filler very sharply from the variety of natural and humanly designed roles that she finds herself filling, sometimes by necessity and sometimes by choice, I have not drawn Luhmann's distinction between confidence in structures, despite their structural flaws and dangers, and willingness to give trust. For those we give our trust to, or withhold it from, are themselves molded by these structures, and the position from which we trust or distrust will be one of natural or social power or powerlessness. We begin as natural beggars, trusting that our begging hands will get bread, not a stone, and having no natural inclination to bite the hand that feeds us. From the start we engage in some more or less equal exchanges (of smiles) and venture into some mutual trustings, slowly progressing to less restricted equalities and more equal reciprocities. And we learn soon enough whom and what to distrust:

those brandishing whips, guns, or other means of attempting to get us in their power and those attempting to hold a monopoly of power, to prevent rather than to assist the less powerful from advancing toward equality, and so toward the optimal conditions for mutual trust.[31]

ten

VIOLENT DEMONSTRATIONS

When is life-endangering violence to be morally excused, or at least forgiven? Does the fact that what endangers human life is someone's violent or coercive action (hijacking a plane, shooting a hostage, planting a bomb in a store) rather than a more insidious death dealing (laying down slow-acting poisonous wastes, using life-endangering chemicals in marketed meat and wine, selling human blood that one knows is infected with a fatal disease) make the death dealing more unforgivable? Does the fact that the killing is done openly, with an eye to publicity, make it better or worse than killings done quietly and with attempted secrecy? Does the fact that the terrorist typically identifies, to her victim and the world, the group on whose behalf she claims to act make her better or worse than the intelligence agent who tries to kill anonymously or pseudonymously? The person we call a terrorist typically does her violence in the public eye, and lets the public know whose cause she believes to justify her violence. She is a violent demonstrator.

Like most demonstrators, she need not expect the demonstration itself to bring about the changes she demands. A successful demonstration gets attention. In one way or another this attention, she hopes, will prepare the ground for other methods, either violent ones like the assassination of leaders and armed uprisings or nonviolent ones like negotiation, legislation, and elections. Even when the hope of eventual success is faint, when the demonstrator acts more in despair than in hope, that attention be given to the cause seems important. That it may be a losing cause, even that the demonstration itself may reasonably be thought to hasten its defeat, need not affect the perceived need to get attention, to proclaim one's cause. The terrorist's heroes can be not just Israel's Stern gang, whose members graduated into national leaders, leading "just wars," but also Samson, who brought down the Temple on himself as well as on some of his enemies and on some innocent victims. The terrorist puts on a spectacular show of self-righteous violence that may or may not be believed to be helping her toward her group's victory. It is no new phenomenon that people grow more reckless of the lives of others as their own lives become more wretched, insecure, and intolerable. People who have been dispossessed, degraded, and humiliated but whose spirit has not been broken understandably want to proclaim their grievances, whether or not they expect the proclamation to advance their cause. They expect the demonstration to get their cause noticed, to put it in the limelight. The ones we call terrorists are ones who have succeeded in that goal, and used violence to succeed in it.

Not all of those who resort to the self-righteous violence we call terrorism have been driven to it by the extreme mistreatment of the group for whom they claim to act. Some simply choose terrorism to advance a political goal such as the collapse of capitalism, although they have suffered no significant maltreatment by capitalists. Some are driven to terrorism by extreme mistreatment in the home rather than in the polis. Terrorists typically are angry or resentful about something, but it is very easy to deceive oneself about what it is that angers one. Some self-appointed demonstrators for groups with real public grievances are avocational terrorists, who are looking for dramatic and violent outlets for what are essentially private angers. We could call them terrorists for emotional hire. Doris Lessing, in *The Good Terrorist*, gives a convincing portrayal of such angry, pathetic, and dangerous people, flailing about for a social cause to which to attach their variously caused private rage. "We Are All . . . Angry," proclaim her characters, both men and women, as they court violent confrontation with authorities, "Angry About . . . Ireland, About Sexism, About . . . Trident."[1] As long as the display of outrage is thrilling, attention getting, and fulfilling, their "cause" will have served its purpose for them. But other terrorists, Palestinians, for example, do have in the cause they proclaim the genuine cause of their anger. (This is not to say that they may not also have private angers that find expression in their terrorist activities.) We need to distinguish, then, between what we could call the self-deceived and the honest terrorist. In what follows I shall be speaking of the honest terrorist.

We do, and we should, give the terrorist our attention. To attempt to frustrate the terrorist's "demonstration" by denying it media coverage, as once proposed by John O'Sullivan of the London *Times,* would be to censor information that surely the public has a right to get. We should get all the information we can about the incidence of violence, wherever it occurs (in the home, in the school, in airports), so that we can know what we are risking in all these places. We have a right to available information about the incidence of deaths from drunken driving and other causes of highway fatalities, about the safety record of different airlines, about the likelihood of disease in different parts of the world we might travel to or settle in, and so on. As we should make public what information there is about AIDS, so should we make public the available information about the incidence, in different parts of the world, of any political violence that affects civilians, including terrorism, whether self-deceived or honest. The terrorist wants our attention and, in fairness to us, should get it.

It is not plausible to suppose that the terrorist aims to deter people from congregating in or traveling to the parts of the world where she has acted or from traveling on the airlines whose planes have been hijacked. We do not aid and abet her if, like the University of Maryland Center for Philosophy and Public Policy, we publish[2] figures about where terrorist attacks have occurred and about the occupations of the main victims. The terrorist, at least if the politically motivated hijacker is a typical terrorist, may be ill named. She need not want to terrorize us from traveling or from crossing paths with her. For what good would that do her? Nor surely does the politically motivated hijacker expect to produce such generalized gibbering terror in the hearts of either her audience or her target population[3] that their normal activities grind to a halt. The terrorist wants the shocked attention of her audience population, but scarcely expects by occasional bombings to bring about the internal collapse of even the target population's economy or morale. Those who, like the Red Army Faction in Germany, did aim at such an internal collapse were as much assassins and guerrilla fighters as they were terrorists. Internal terrorism, terrorism by nationals against the regime of their own nation, is often indistinguishable from guerrilla war, and often involves carefully targeted rather than randomly chosen victims. I am distinguishing terrorism from assassination, taking terrorism to involve the random murder of members of the target population. Such randomness, however, is compatible with some selectivity—the IRA will try to give its own supporters some assurance that they will not be among its victims. Random selection of victims within a group taken to exclude the terrorist's own supporters is the terrorist's chosen method. Terrorism can be state terrorism or revolutionary terrorism. The forms it takes when it is state terrorism are particularly evil, because then the murder of randomly chosen victims can be on a grand scale. This can serve its purpose of stilling active opposition to the regime even when the policy is secret and unannounced, but widely known, as in the disappearances in Argentina. I shall not address the special features and special evils of state terrorism,[4] but restrict myself to protest or revolutionary terrorism.

Assassins, by their carefully targeted killing, may expect to discourage persons from assuming public leadership of certain parties, corporations, and regimes, or diplomatic status for certain countries, but the terrorist can scarcely expect to deter tourism or even membership in the military forces of the target or audience populations. The average tourist's or military person's chances of being a victim of terrorism are not high enough for that. In Essay 6 I suggested[5] that the terrorist is an expert at discerning trust relationships that the rest of us so take for granted that we can in good times ignore them and trust in fellow passengers, in fellow shoppers, and so on. Michael Walzer says of terrorism that "its purpose is to destroy the morale of a nation or a class, or undercut its solidarity; its method is the random murder of innocent people."[6] As already indicated, I am following Walzer's usage in using the label "terrorist" for those whose method is the random murder of people in some sense "innocent." But if the terrorist's purpose really were to destroy the morale of a nation or class by terror, then the efficient terrorist would increase her killings as much as is compatible with randomness. She would shoot all except a random one or two of the passengers on the hijacked plane or ship. If terrorists do have both the purpose and the method Walzer ascribes to them, then there have been pathetically few efficient (nonstate) terrorists. Our usual principle of charity requires that we look for purposes that allow us to see actual politically motivated random killings as a little more "rational" than most would be on Walzer's construal of them, even if we agree with Thomas Schelling that, given the limits of what a rational terrorist can expect to achieve, the actual dangers posed or likely to be posed to human life by nonstate terrorism are relatively insignificant.[7] The terrorist, unlike the assassin, kills fairly randomly. Unlike the subversive or the revolutionary guerrilla fighter, she does not kill in the expectation of thereby destroying the enemy or its regime. If the terrorist, like the subversive, aimed at the total collapse of the target community, then the more "enemy" deaths the better, even at a cost in their randomness. Such killing could be done anonymously, without proclamations. The subversive can destroy efficiently and anonymously, postponing self-identification and bids for recognition until she takes over in the graveyard and ruins she has wrought. But the one we label the terrorist typically does make proclamations as she kills—indeed she often seems to include her target population within her audience population. She typically does identify her group to her victims, and to the rest of us. Like the soldier she has standard-bearers, at least in the rear. She herself is a sort of standard-bearer, using her victims as a sort of living flare.

The terrorist who is a violent demonstrator risks her own life to raise her standard in the chosen place. Like standard-bearers in old-fashioned armies, she risks her life as well as that of others to make her symbolic and declaratory point. The military standard-bearer wears a uniform, and hopes, if he kills at all, to kill only those wearing enemy uniforms, whereas the terrorist's victims can be in mufti. Nor does the terrorist's own clothing, like the soldier's, proclaim a bloody profession. She may don some identificatory scarf once she has taken over the plane, and she may pick as her first victim any who *are* wearing the military uniform of the target community, but even her military victims will be used as scapegoats, as sacrificial victims. Their death will not, by their killers, be seen as an intended increase in "enemy dead," a boost to the "body count." The killing is not incipient genocide, nor is it done to diminish the number of the opposing forces, to remove living obstacles to the ter-

rorist's cause. Hijackers have been very sparing in their use of lethal force. Terrorist bomb throwers are restrained, not saturation,
bombers.

What perceived point is there to the killing that violent demonstrators do? I have already given the answer: it is a sure way to get
attention. As a child may kick or bite whoever is handy, when its
more civil demands go unheeded or ignored, so desperate peoples
may seize and sometimes kill the easiest suitable "others," when they
see no hope of recognition by less lethal means. Their action is not
irrational, or rather it is irrational only if they have reason to believe
that they will get our serious attention more readily by other means.
They may also be regarded as irrational if there is reason for them to
be aware that their cause is not necessarily doomed, but that terrorist activity will doom it. Have they reason to think that terrorist
activity can defeat an otherwise live cause?

"No deals with terrorists" is not a policy that has been, or is
likely to be, consistently carried out. History gives us evidence of
many deals made with those regarded as guilty of terrorism. In Pales-
tine and in Ireland, the British made deals. The Home Rule eventually granted to the Irish was admittedly not a deal with the leaders of
the unsuccessful 1916 Easter Rebellion, all of whom had been executed as criminals, but it was made with the new leaders who took
over as their successors, working in the same way for the same cause.
Shows of bloody force in which there were nonparticipant victims
and determination to get, bear, and use arms without the permission
of the ruling power did not disqualify the Irish from eventual recognition and success, anymore than it disqualified those earlier rebels
against British rule, the American colonies. The prospects for the
success of a cause do not seem in the past to have been reduced by
resort to unauthorized force, by violent demonstrations that cost
some innocents their lives. Or are we to reserve the term "terrorism"
for the violent tactics of only the ultimately unsuccessful defiers of
powers that claim authority over them?

The terrorist who is a violent demonstrator need not be acting
irrationally. Is she acting immorally? Do we, and should we, condemn all violent demonstrations? Should we excuse violence when it
is a last resort to draw attention to a claimed serious wrong? Should
we require that the excusable violent demonstrator have some sort
of mandate from the aggrieved group for whom she claims to act,

some sort of license to kill on their behalf? How like must that be to the sort of license that soldiers and other state-licensed killers have for their lethal activities? Do states ever license violent demonstrations, as distinct from more "utilitarian" killings?

Our attitudes to killing and to violent assault seem, in their baroque complexities, more amenable to historical and psychological explanation than to rational systematization and justification. Like the criminal law on assault and murder, our moral attitudes to violence and killing are bearers of the vestiges of attitudes acquired during our long history as a species which has lived by its lethal skills, and sometimes propagated by rape and sexual violence. As meat eaters we had to be able to take life, and some of us had to be very good at killing. As patriarchs, half of us became very good at throwing our weight around, violently if we felt like it, to get our way. The important moral questions have always been "Whom or what may I assault and kill and when and how may I kill it?" not "May I assault and kill?" Boundaries between human and non-human, between fetus and infant, between one's own domestic and someone else's, between ingroup and outgroup, ally and enemy, military and civilian, attacker and defender, guilty and innocent, authority and protester against authority or aspirant to authority have to be learned, and learning them, rather than just learning "Thou shalt not kill," constitutes our education in the morality of violence.

Most of us here had the luxury of learning these lessons as members of fairly well recognized groups with recognized territories and authority structures, groups whose rights to defend their official values from perceived attack or to express their expansionist colonial values were taken for granted. As a New Zealander I, for example, learned early that it had been allowable for the British troops protecting my colonialist ancestors to kill Maoris who resisted British rule, that their killing was in a different moral category from the "barbaric" assaults of Maori tribesmen on white settlements, let alone the Maori's occasional ritual eating of an uninvited missionary or intruding British official. I later learned that it was allowable for my uncles and older schoolfellows to set sail around the world to Europe in order to kill Germans and Italians or, closer to home, to kill our Japanese Pacific neighbors, since we were at war with these peoples and God was on our side. Still later, once peace was made, I learned that it was retrospectively allowable for at least some of those German, Italian, and Japanese to have killed my fellow countrymen, since they were soldiers whose job was to kill, and they may have been nonculpably ignorant that God was not on their side. As I went on to study history, it became clear that the answer to the question of who or what it is that makes someone a soldier or other member of a military force, rather than a mere murderer or barbaric warrior, the question of who gives out the licenses to kill, could not simply be "authorities of a nation-state." For I learned that the nation-state was a relatively recent and for a long time a largely European phenomenon. Many who with some sort of blessing took up arms against fellow persons got their licenses and their blessings from different authorities, such as popes and Holy Roman Emperors for the crusaders, or even their own visions, as for Joan of Arc. (A Viennese production of Schiller's *The Virgin of Orleans* portrayed her as a saintly terrorist.) And once there *were* nation-states, there were Cromwells who conscientiously rejected their anointed sovereigns and tried armed takeovers and Washingtons who raised armies against the colonial powers that were. Both the wars before the emergence of the nation-state and all the civil and religious wars within and across such states show the moral learner that the authority to raise an army, to issue licenses to kill, is highly contested and fiercely fought for. Indeed much of the organized and deliberate killing of human persons by human persons has occurred in contests for the monopoly of the right to raise armies and to authorize that and other uses of deadly force.

Wars of religion, whether between Jews and Egyptians, Jews and Babylonians, Jews and Romans, Christians and Muslims, Catholics and Protestants, or Hindus and Muslims, also remind the moral learner that we are not merely a contentious and violence-prone species but a religion-prone one, and that in the center of several of our religions we have enshrined the idea of sacrificial killing. Not only are we willing to kill heretics and heathen to defend the true religion, but the god we worship is a god who requires sacrificial killing. The idea of scapegoats and of spotless human sacrifices is all too familiar. We have been taught that higher beings require that innocent life be taken. We learned about sacrificial violence when we learned that the god in whose image we are made would attend better to us and to our prayers if living things were sacrificed on his altars, that he could demand the sacrifice of Isaac by his father, and would later sacrifice his own son. We in these traditions cannot pretend to be unfamiliar with expressive and demonstrative killing. We and our gods deliberately kill not just our competitors and our threatening enemies but selected innocents. As long as our gods are bloodthirsty gods, the sacrifice of selected innocents in bloody spectaculars can be counted on to get our respectful attention.

As Christianity limits the sacrificial killing to one actual death, safely in the past, and merely symbolically or sacramentally rebreaks (and eats) that one body all down the *annos domini* and thereby civilizes the human sacrifice, simultaneously restricting and ramifying it, so to a lesser degree does the terrorist violent demonstrator both ration and broadcast her violence. Like the Christian god, the terrorist is willing to include self-sacrifice along with the sacrifice of suitable others (the crucified has to be both a person of the god to whom the sacrifice is made and a human being, one of those needing redemption). This offensive parallel should not be pushed too far. (Like the terrorist, I intend to offend.) I use it to remind us that, while learning about domestic expressive violence in the patriarchal home, many of us also simultaneously learned of solemn ritual violence in our various patriarchal Sabbath and Sunday schools. We should not claim it incomprehensible that the terrorist can do what he or she does (and now is the time to switch from "she" to "he").

The violent demonstrator's tactic is to command the attention of the more powerful, to display the seriousness of his purpose and the ruthlessness of his will to those whom he has good reason to think respect strength of will and are therefore unlikely to ignore the particular violent show he is putting on, his sacrifice of the more-or-less innocent. He counts on his show of deadly force to command our fearful respect, if also our revulsion. He wants not love but recognition for his will, for his right and his group's right to join the other violent assertors of will in the world.

Demonstrations of force that at least risk death to nondemonstrators are something that established powers are addicted to. In 1988 I happened to witness on July 14 over the Seine in Paris (its banks and bridges crowded) a flyby by antiquated bombers and fighters as well as by the latest of death machines. And I watched on television the deaths of the spectators in Germany at the U.S. airshow over

Ramstein air base, an inadvertently fiery demonstration of killing power did not prevent the Farnborough airshow in Great Britain shortly after Ramstein. Violent demonstrations of lethal force are an accepted part of normal life. That so many attend these shows itself bears witness to the truth of the assumption that a show of deadly force commands awed attention.

The pilots at Ramstein did not deliberately kill themselves or their innocent victims (guilty only of wanting to gawk at the death machines doing their stuff, so only averagely guilty). The terrorist deliberately pulls the trigger or throws his bomb. He not only risks killing innocent people but, like the performer of a ritual human sacrifice, aims at exactly that. This puts his category of violent demonstration into a special class, different from the Ramstein killings. His is, we might say, high-minded demonstrative murder rather than high-minded demonstration-caused manslaughter. The morality of violence we have learned puts great weight on the distinction between intended and merely foreseen killing—or, rather, puts great weight on it outside of battlefields. (Are military airfields battlefields?) For the gunner on the battlefield, let alone the bayonet wielder, is not just foreseeing the enemy's death as a side effect of the main intended effect (victory); he is intending to kill. The doctrine of double effect, even by its devotees, gets a supplement for use on battlefields in the doctrine of the just war. Only as long as we can draw clear lines round some fields, marked "fields for battles between duly licensed and uniformed intentional killers," and other areas marked "enemy cities, suitable for strategic but not saturation bombing, for foreseen but not intended killing of civilians," or "hospitals, suitable for knowing but unintended lettings die, or acts of choosing whom to save," or "our own cities, suitable for knowing pollution," or "seas, great for dumping wastes, since who knows where that poisoned bread on the waters will turn, or when it will return," can we continue to polish and treasure the distinction between deliberate targeted killing and knowing but deplored (and sometimes less focused) killing. The bomber and the dumper are usually spared the sight of their victims, the knowledge of whom exactly they have killed and how they died. The reproaches of such faceless victims will be easier to ignore than those of face-to-face killings, especially when the killers are themselves not barefaced, but mere masks for higher authorities who gave the orders.

These fine moral distinctions learned off the battlefield will not and should not make much sense to those who can discern no lines between battle- and other fields, whose right to raise armies is contested, whose license to authorize violence is not recognized by the club of licensors, whose flags do not get treated as national flags or get given the respect granted to papal banners, Red Cross, or United Nations banners. The terrorist's group is an outlaw group, since it is refused in-law status, and for outlaws all fields are battlefields.

Does that mean that the doctrine of the just war should extend beyond the fields where recognized armies clash, should be generalized into a doctrine of just violence? As most armies have claimed their war to be a just war, so assassins and terrorists will reliably see their violence as just or righteous violence. The rules of fair violent play will not be much use if they and their interpretation are as highly contested as the prizes for which the violent fights go on. We need, I suppose, a new Grotius, or a new Hobbes, or both to work out the rights of violence and nonviolence for all groups at odds with other groups, for groups who are not yet nations and ones who are recognized nations, for the dispossessed and wretched of the earth as well as its successful proprietors, for minorities as well as majorities, for the refugees, the desperate, and homeless as well as the conspicuous consumers of tourism and pleasure cruises. The first step toward getting articles of peace for our condition is to eschew righteous indignation, to put ourselves in the shoes of those driven to terrorism, to entertain the thought that there but for the lottery of history (and perhaps but for saving cowardice) go we.

There indeed, or very close, went our revered rebel ancestors and many of our heroes and heroines. Do we on reflection prefer that people meekly tolerate oppression, dispossession, nonrecognition, indignity? That they sit quietly in the shadows watching others flaunt their status, exercise their privileges, put on their shows of lethal force, give each other medals for their violent killing? Do we sincerely admire the gentleness that the less powerful have in the past shown the more violent powerful? Do we, for example, admire the docility with which women for so long put up not just with domination but with male violence in and out of the home? Or do we agree with Nietzsche that only stupidity or smallness of soul can explain why women did not use their allowed rule of the kitchen to poison more of the masters? Do we admire good, faithful, obedient slaves

213

more than rebellious slaves? Do we encourage protest of perceived wrong?

Protest, demonstration, and rebellion always involve some danger to human life, and these endangering protests regularly seem unjustified to many of those who have not suffered the injustices or inhumanities that are protested, and to those with limited imaginations or limited sympathy. The real risks entailed by demonstrations against perceived wrongs must be tolerated, if we think self-respect a primary good, and if we respect each other's sense of justice and injustice, right and wrong. Nonviolent demonstration is not easily prevented from escalating into violent demonstration, and that can lead to rebellion. In accepting nonviolent protest, we accept at least the risk of violent protest.

We will of course deplore violent demonstrations, prefer nonviolent to violent protest, hope for nonbloody revolutions. We will try to teach our children that strength and violence are not the same. We will hope that their protests, when they must strongly protest, will not involve human sacrifice. But if we fail, we should not be very surprised. Nonviolence is not easy, and our own practice has not been exemplary. (Nor does violent self-denunciation necessarily reduce the amount of violence.)

The terrorist presents us with a distorted mirror of ourselves, which makes us exceedingly uncomfortable. He provokes extreme reactions in us—shrill outrage even from the descendants and heirs of successfully violent rebels, or vicarious thrills at such dramatic self-assertion, or self-punitive guilt, a masochistic welcoming of the small shiver of apprehension that the terrorist's next victim could be oneself.

Were one actually to become such a victim, should moral indignation then mix with the terror one would undoubtedly feel? That, surely, depends entirely on the particular terrorists, the predicament of the group for which they claim to act, and the basis of that claim. It seems to me in principle no harder, no less appropriate, to forgive the terrorist who sincerely believes that he has no other effective way to make his seriously aggrieved group's case than to forgive the glory-seeking or super-security-seeking national leader in whose war one dies as a conscript or as a civilian victim. And it should be easier to forgive one's terrorist killer, with his high-minded motives, his drive to right wrongs, than to forgive the profit seeker from whose poisonous wastes one dies. When what the terrorist strikes for is basic recognition rather than glory, for redress of perceived injustice rather than for profit or special privileges, his motives at least will not be unforgivable.

Can and should one forgive him his methods? He "uses" his victim to draw attention to his cause. Is this deplorable method harder to forgive than the methods of generals who use human cannon fodder to ensure that they win their battles and get their medals or memorial statues, or scientists who withhold their discoveries of AIDS blood tests or remedies until they secure their best chances of a Nobel Prize? All these people sacrifice the life ("use" the death) of those who die because of their decisions. The terrorist is just more open than most about his willingness to use his fellows, when he judges that his goal justifies it. None of these methods is humane, all of them are ruthless. The terrorist's methods (if he is, say, a Palestinian) are not clearly more inhumane than the treatment he and his people have suffered. We can and should deplore the inhumanity of his methods, but until our own humanity is a bit more exemplary, and our intolerance of inhumanity closer to home a bit more active, we will not be in a very good position to feel a special righteous indignation at the terrorist's methods.

That the terrorist and his people have suffered inhumane treatment does not justify, but might excuse, his inhumanity. If he, a representative of the victims of exclusion, wrong, or inhumanity, acts inhumanely toward members of groups who he thinks could have prevented or ended or lessened the wrongs his people suffered, then he acts as a sort of blunt instrument of retributive justice, a blind avenger meting out the kind of inhumane and violent punishment that punitive authorities regularly administer.[8] Parents who strike children who are disrespectful, church authorities who burned witches (disrespect indeed, to set up as rival magicians), schoolmasters who beat insolent pupils, all respond to perceived wrongs with violence. For them to plausibly claim to be punishing, they must have made some effort to separate the innocent from the guilty, but the effort need not have been very successful. We are quite familiar with the custom of penalizing a whole school class for the misdemeanors of unidentified individuals within it, punishing all one's children for the mess or noise or other nuisance made by some of them, one knows not whom. Nor do all punishers have official licenses to punish. Parents' licenses to use violence seem to be as self-issued as the terrorists'—official authorities may step in to limit parents' rights to treat their offending children with violence, and so officially concede some limited punitive rights, but the prima facie right of parents to punish, to be prosecutor, judge, jury, and executioner, is often taken as a natural one. Should we grant each other the right to anger-blinded vigilante justice against our own relatively powerless children or pupils, but not against strangers who are citizens of offending alien powers? And if so, why?

The terrorist's violence is not a straightforward case of punitive reactive violence (albeit inaccurately aimed) anymore than it is ritual human sacrifice (of the not quite spotless), or a small ruthless war, or a case of a dangerous display of deadly force that ends in accidental death. I have likened aspects of the terrorist's violence to these violent acts closer to home (and more amenable to our control) to help us understand it, not to classify and judge it. The categories of the "innocent," of "deserved punishment," "soldier," "declared war," "permitted display" all presuppose a mutually accepted authority structure, and that is precisely what the terrorist and his victims and critics lack. Michael Walzer accuses those who produce apologies for terrorism, and in so doing point to parallels with tolerated violence, of "erasing all moral distinctions along with the men and women who painfully worked them out."[9] He accuses them (us) of a "malign forgetfulness" of the historical past. I do not think that we need be guilty of those dreadful impieties to question whether our hard-won deontological moral categories help us much in trying to understand terrorism and respond appropriately to it. We can stick to our old authoritarian moral notions, which work well enough within an established authority structure of the sort within which they were forged, but when we extend them into the no man's land beyond it, they will not get agreed application; they will at best half-fit. I have tried to place the terrorist's violence in our familiar violent landscape without fully assimilating it to the forms to which I have likened it. I have done this multiple likening as a preventive against too hasty or too self-righteous judgment, but I have not done much to guide any judgment or to describe helpful and appropriate reaction. It is fairly easy to say that the clearer it is that the terrorist's group's case is *not* being listened to in decision making affecting it and that less violent ways to get attention have been tried in vain, the more excuse the terrorist has; that his case is the better the more plausible his claim to represent his group's sense of injustice or wrong, not just his own; that the more limited, the less indiscriminate, his violence, the less outrage will we feel for his inhumanity. Those are not daring conclusions.

If we are to respond to terrorism not just with trite moral comparisons of what is better, what worse, but in a way that we could reasonably believe might eventually end terrorism, then we have to hope for a new Grotius-cum-Hobbes, who will codify neither the old honor code of the generals, soldiers, and diplomats of established powers nor the maxims of enlightened self-interest for single persons but, rather, the arts of successful peacemaking, of forming workable plans for lasting peace, ways of removing the group grievances that threaten peace. Such a theorist would need to have a benign memory for any small periods of peace and incidents of successful peacemaking or satisfactory settling of grievances that our historical past and recent past contain. From these we might get some useful potions against continued violence, some recipes for stable and contagious nonviolence. Impressive efforts at peacemaking, and success at truce making, went on in the summer of 1988 when the General Secretary of the United Nations, Javier Perez de Cuellar, showed exemplary willingness to talk with aggrieved troublemakers and to do so with exemplary patience, indefatigability, and a gentle non-moralizing dignity. Grotius wrote: "The person, who has authority to begin a war, is the only one to whom the right of making peace can properly belong, according to the general maxim, that everyone is the best judge in the management of his own affairs."[10] This general maxim needs to be balanced with the equally plausible "no man is a fit arbitrator in his own cause," Hobbes's seventeenth law of nature. Grotius thought that it followed from his maxim that only kings and sovereign powers can make war and peace. But when wars or at least fighting and violence are conducted because of disagreement or contest over sovereignty and authority, then less definite conclusions follow even from the dubious maxim that everyone is the best judge in her own affairs. When there no longer are restricted battlefields, when violence spreads to and threatens all of us, then the "making of peace" (in both senses) becomes our affair, and we will do best to treat as war any organized violence that it becomes our affair to try to end. We should not be too picky about which vio-

217

lence is "war," and who had a right to start or end it. Successful peacemakers will not reserve their ear solely for the duly appointed representatives of recognized nation-states, with previously agreed-on rights to declare war and make peace. The first thing we must do to deter terrorism is to provide aggrieved groups a better way than violence to get our serious attention. Successful peacemakers will realize that the contentious and touchy groups for whom a civilized plan of coexistence needs to be found have not merely different degrees of power but different degrees of past recognition, shifting boundaries, and varying customs of appointing representatives, giving and transferring authority, raising armies, conducting wars, selecting scapegoats.

The evil of terrorism is the more general evil of violence, when this is resorted to by representatives of disaffected groups and used on randomly selected representatives of resented other groups. To mitigate this evil we need to provide a less deadly equally effective or more effective way for resentful groups to express their grievances, and we also need to find a way to reduce the general human tendency to choose violent methods over less violent ones, even when violence does not increase effectiveness. Only when we have nonviolent people, and people who have effective nonviolent ways open to them to express their grievances, can we expect to be rid of terrorists. Denouncing terrorism is not only pointless but can be counted on to increase the anger and resentment that terrorism expresses.

When, to get guidance on the morality of killing, of violence and nonviolence, we turn to the great moral philosophers, we find some striking silences. Aristotle fails to integrate his passing ruling out of murder[11] into his more general account of virtuous and vicious conduct. Does the wrong of murder lie in the fact that the murderer breaks the law, that he takes more than his fair share of liberty, so fails to display justice in the narrow sense? Which sorts of assault and killing will a wise lawmaker forbid? Aristotle is silent on these questions. Perhaps they admit of no general answer, or perhaps prohibition is not the best way to go about limiting violence or reducing the extent of killing.

Hobbes, whose laws of nature have as their point the ending of the general war which shortens human lives, does not include "Do not kill" among his moral commandments. Hobbes realized the pointlessness of trying to lessen violence by commandments forbidding it and the difficulty of formulating any rule concerning it that rational persons could accept. His rules, his theorems of peace, enjoin us to seek peace when there is hope of it, to lay down our "right of nature" when others do, to keep covenants, to show gratitude, to cultivate a number of peaceable dispositions, to give peacemakers safe conduct, to submit to arbitration, and so on, but there are no rules forbidding either lying or violent assault with whatever powers we have left once we have laid down our right to all. Hobbes sees the point of *all* of his "true moral philosophy" to be to lessen violence, and he sees also that this must be done indirectly, not by laws telling us how violent we can be when and to whom.

Hume, who follows Hobbes in thinking that only a successful cooperative scheme can avoid the threats presented by the opposition of human passions, is virtually silent on the wrongs of assault and murder. His artifices redirect avidity, which he takes to be the only motive to violence that calls for (or perhaps that admits of) social redirection. Envy and revenge, he writes, may lead us to ravish goods from each other, but they operate only at intervals and against particular superiors or enemies.[12] Envy and revenge do not therefore pose the general threat to society that avidity does, and Hume offers no remedies for the threats they do pose. Of course magistrates, once invented, will presumably make criminal many forms of assault besides assault in the course of robbery, but in doing that they will not be enforcing any of those basic moral constraints that Hume calls the "laws of nature." We no more find a Humean equivalent of the Sixth Commandment, "thou shalt not kill," than we find a Hobbesian equivalent.

Did Hume think we must just tolerate the violence against persons that envy and revenge can motivate, that we must content ourselves with redirecting avidity, so avoiding avidity-motivated violence against persons? He regards envy as "an irregular appetite for evil,"[13] dependent on the workings of the principle of comparison that blocks the normal human sympathy which would lead us to rejoice in, rather than envy, another's joy. Envy is in principle avoidable, on Hume's version of our psychology, and even where it is not avoided, it can surely be got to take a nonviolent form, once social artifices direct natural ambition into nonviolent and socially constructive competition. But revenge is harder to avoid, contain, or transform, if Hume is right about our nature. He lists resentment and the desire to punish our enemies as primitive human appetites, as inevitable (in appropriate conditions) as lust. Resentment and vengefulness are passions we have and ones we sympathize with in others; they are regular rather than irregular human appetites for evil.

Resentment of "enemies" leads naturally to violence, and Hume's version of morality seems to contain no remedy for it. Gentleness is a "natural" virtue, but we will not expect it to be shown toward those whom we resent as enemies, as ones who have harmed us or humiliated us. The best remedy for resentment will be removal of its grounds, not control of its expression. I think Hume saw that justice, and other "artificial" virtues dependent on rational cooperation, are powerless against deeply resentment-rooted violence, and this is the terrorist's sort.

Hume distinguishes the sort of calm deterrent punishment for lawbreaking that good magistrates will administer from angry avenging.[14] Those who see themselves to have been injured will want to avenge themselves, and will be prone to violence. Humean magistrates take over the punishment for injustice that victims might otherwise violently inflict; indeed, that is one of the magistrates' main functions. But since, as we have seen, to inflict bodily injury (unless that is incident to violent seizure) does not count as a Humean "injustice" and since any revenge violence seems also ungoverned by any "laws of nature," then whatever magistrates do to try to retain their claimed monopoly of violent methods will count as something other than just "the execution of *justice*," if justice is restricted to what Hume calls the "three fundamental laws of nature, *that of the stability of possession, of its transference by consent, and of the performance of promises.*"[15] The magisterial function that will be exercised when laws forbidding civilian violence are enforced will be either (if what I have just argued is disputed) the *decision* as well as the execution of justice, or that cooperation beyond what justice requires that Hume thinks magistrates rightly enforce when they arrange for public works, such as building harbors, and for the disciplining of armies. Hume does not, like Locke, include one's person as part of one's property, and his laws of justice protect property rather than persons. If wrongs against the person are to be recognized by the magistrate, it will be by those optional extra cooperative schemes that Humean magistrates have discretionary powers to institute. Civilian violence against civilians will take on the same sort of status as tax fraud or draft evasion—a matter of breaching a local magistrate's requirement, not breaking of a law of nature.

Magistrates will find terrorists guilty of criminal violence, if they succeed in arresting them, and if their violence occurs in the territory the magistrates govern. But since the terrorists in question rarely recognize the authority of these magistrates, they will have no cause to feel moral guilt for their violence on the grounds of its disobedience. It *is,* from the magistrate's point of view, uncivil disobedience, but terrorists will understandably not care about that.

The protest which stems from resentment of injury and indignity has a vital positive role to play in Hume's moral theory, a role which can perhaps guide us in our response to terrorist violence. This is the role of drawing the attention of cooperators and mutual recognizers of rights to those who are dangerously excluded from their schemes of right-recognition and right-protection. In the *Enquiry Concerning the Principles of Morals* Hume adds a significant new circumstance of justice, namely, that all those with power to make their resentment felt be included in the cooperative scheme. If, say, women are excluded, despite their power to make their resentment felt, the scheme will be unstable, and so not serve its purpose of increasing security. If women or the members of some race, class, or language group are excluded, then they must be expected to demonstrate their power to make resentment felt, in order to force entry to vital cooperative schemes from which they are excluded.

Exclusion is not itself an "injustice" to those excluded, as Hume construes justice and injustice. It may be not just inhumanity but also "inequity," and it certainly will be *folly* if the excluded do feel resentment and have power to make it felt. We should understand terrorist violence as a demonstration of this power to make resentment at exclusion felt. The proper response to it is not counterviolence or moral condemnation but inclusion, at least in cooperative schemes we set up in order to listen to one another's grievances. The best response is removal of the grounds for the deepest resentment. That is no easy task, of course, but we make the task unduly hard for ourselves if we fetter ourselves with moral indignation. Hume, like Hobbes, realizes the pointlessness of moral injunctions to avoid violence against human beings, especially when these injunctions are directed by those with security of life and with recognized rights

221

against desperate insecure persons, resentful at exclusion from our various clubs that, "under shelter of our governors," allow us but not them to "taste at ease the sweets of society and mutual assistance."[16] The Humean "natural" moral virtues of humanity, equity, and plain prudence should prompt us to try to respond, by appropriately conciliatory moves, to the terrorism that demonstrates the resentment of exclusion felt.

One of the toughest challenges to the peacemaker is to find a mutually face-saving way whereby a group of former terrorists can, when it suits their former opponents, be accepted into the community of states and candidate-states. Because this community includes some states reasonably seen as just as guilty of state terrorism as the group is of group terrorism, to demand a unilateral renunciation (and so admission) of terrorism by those hoping to make the transition from group to state seems unrealistic. We need to find the right tactful incantations for the ceremony of graduation into legitimacy. History surely can give us useful suggestions for tried and true face-saving diplomatic phrases.

A new Grotius might be content to postpone, perhaps indefinitely, the list of fixed rights of violence and nonviolence (for individuals and for more-or-less organized groups), to turn from the deontological moral language of patriarchs to a gentler moral language. She might try to codify the methods and discover the characteristics of successful peacemakers, of ones who might have a hope of bringing about at least long truces in our wars and incipient wars within and across national boundaries—class wars, battles of the sexes, and confrontations between militant religions, between hostile ethnic groups, between capitalists and socialists, between pacifists and armed defenders, between group terrorists and state terrorists, between terrorists and "legitimate" forces. A list of the functional virtues of peacemakers would be a start, to be supplemented by a list of the functional virtues of the parents of peaceable but spirited children, the functional virtues of the successful teachers of nonviolent self-assertion to adolescents, the functional virtues of adult electors who choose strong gentle leaders and reject macho bullies.

Lists of productive virtues, alas, do not tell us how to bring those virtues into being, any more than lists of rights tell us how to ensure respect for them. Lists of gentleness-producing and gentleness-preserving virtues would, however, at least purport to embody some empirical history-tested knowledge about what does and does not produce violence and gentleness. We would then be committed to trying to find out not just what produces gentleness in individuals but what produces the parental ability to preserve and replicate gentleness, what produces the ability of some teachers and some leaders to strengthen and inspire it, and so on. For this empirical knowledge to come about, or increase, we will need benign remembering of historical examples, as well as social science and psychology, to ground our moral philosophy. We will need information about what institutional structures and chains of authority have relatively good or bad records, records of nurturing gentle or violent people. We will need to study variants of the family and modes of family governance, schools and governance in them, different political parties and what sort of people flourish within their differing structures. We will be aiming at discovering the roots and soil of violence and gentleness, and at pooling what knowledge we have.

I have presented mainly proclamations and protests, not worked-out plans or programs. I may also have employed a little more verbal violence, and more moralizing or meta-moralizing, than one might hope for from a believer in a nonjudgmental morality, in a morality of nonviolence, in the ideal of a moral philosophy which would contain tested recipes for producing and sustaining gentleness and other tested antidotes to violence. I have perhaps shown myself more hypothetically willing to forgive the terrorist than to forgive many of those who wax morally indignant about the terrorist. A completed moral philosophy of the kind I would hope we might eventually get would contain recipes against the urge to moralize and to meta-moralize as well as against other forms of anger and violence. But I do not yet know those recipes. In the absence of moral knowledge, we all, like the terrorist, tend sometimes to fall back on homeopathic cures, and so on mere violence as a response to violence.

eleven

CLAIMS, RIGHTS, RESPONSIBILITIES

> God having designed Man for a sociable
> Creature, made him not only with an
> inclination, and under a necessity to have
> fellowship with those of his own kind; but
> furnished him also with Language, which
> was to be the great Instrument and common
> Tye of society.
>
> *John Locke,* Essay, III, 1, 1

Our sociability is a matter not just of our tastes but of our capacities. Language not only helps us cater to our sociable tastes but is itself a social capacity, one that we enjoy exercising. We may learn it largely by spontaneous imitation, but others teach us its finer points, and we both need and welcome initiation into the various roles that speech involves—teacher and learner, speaker and hearer, asker and answerer, proposer and seconder, challenger and defender, proclaimer and dissident. Speech, once we are fully initiated into it, introduces us to the plurality of social roles that are briefly taken on by speakers and to the social expectations as to who is to play which role when. We learn when it is our turn to speak, and what sort of speech we may make. In learning this we learn our rights as language users. Because our language is shared in common with those from whom we learn it, and because we all learn the full range of speech acts, there is a built-in tendency for us to see our rights as speakers not as special rights but as shared rights and to see our due "turn" at speaking to be to an equal share of the speaking time. Our nature as speakers is such that we can be counted on to use speech to claim universal rights to speech, and also to contest some of these claims. Our nature, more generally, is such that we can be counted on both to voice claims to a variety of universal human rights and to contest such claims. We are a right-claiming and right-recognizing species, and these claims have a built-in potential for contested universalization.

Disputes about Rights

Every group of human beings with any sort of social organization, that is to say every group of human beings, recognizes something very like rights, as well as responsibilities, attaching to other roles besides speech roles within that organization. The rights or proto-rights of parents with respect to children, chiefs over their warriors, or other such role-related rights will be recognized. Because we are social animals, one of whose socially learned activities is talking, we have words naming the fairly long-lasting roles that some play, and forms of words in which role players can claim their rights, and in which others can at times contest the content and the scope of these rights. We are a challenging and defensive species—there is always someone around to ask, "Why should the chief not only get first pick of the captives after a battle but be able to take as many as he wishes as his slaves?" and there will usually be someone around to answer such a challenge, to tell us in detail about precedent, time-honored custom, stability, constitutional prerogatives. The very nature of speech virtually ensures this. Because we are talking animals, and because we do divide social labor into a variety of roles with a variety of powers and responsibilities, and because we do not all take turns in assuming all roles, there will regularly be challenges to role-related rights, and defenses of them, and there will be claims to the extension of some rights, and disputes about the legitimacy of such claims.

Other animal species with any analogue of status in human communities, say, apes who recognize some degrees of dominance in a troop, often have habits that mitigate the inequality that dominance introduces. The social device of dominance itself avoids mutually disadvantageous infighting, but its cost is high for the dominated. The various rituals of deference, and of begging and response to begging, lessen this cost. We are a species whose members recognize status (to avoid the war of all against all), and who have a strictly limited willingness both to beg and to give to those who beg. The conditions of the form of human justice that recognizes universal human rights include not just moderate scarcity, vulnerability to the resentment of one's fellows, and limited generosity, all of which Hume recognized, but also a limited willingness to beg, a considerable unwillingness to ask, even when, if we did ask the powerful for a handout, it would perhaps be given us. What we regard as ours by right is what we are unwilling to beg for and only limitedly willing to say thank you for. We seem to be getting less and less willing both to beg and to give to beggars. The increasing tendency to talk of universal rights and the extension of their content correlates with this decreasing ability to beg or to respond generously to beggars.

When we go back beyond this century, we find that the famous proclamations of rights were not of universal human rights. Charters and bills of rights have typically been assertions or reassertions of the rights of some limited group. The Magna Carta asserted the traditional feudal rights of barons against the king and, in Hume's words, "introduced no new distribution of the powers of the commonwealth, and no innovation in the political or public law of the kingdom." He says that although it introduced "some mixture of Democracy" into the constitution, it also "exalted still higher the Aristocracy," who then became "disorderly and licentious tyrants," what he calls "a kind of Polish Aristocracy."[1] The U.S. Bill of Rights spoke of, and meant, the rights of men, not of women, and not even of all men, since slaves were excluded. This is typical of proclamations of rights. They voice the grievances or the remembered grievances of some group against some present or past oppressor. They may demand an extension of what hitherto was a right of a more circumscribed group, but there will always be some who are affected by the right-holders' exercise of their rights who are implicitly or explicitly excluded from those on behalf of whom the rights are claimed. Slaves, nonlandowners, the poor, women, criminals, children, nonhuman animals have all been out-groups in relation to those in-groups who have claimed their rights in famous proclamations and manifestos. There is a perceptible drive to generalization, a questioning of monopoly rights, but even famous clarion cries such as "The poorest he that is in England has a life to live as has the richest he" spoke of he, not she, seeing the woman's life as merely an adjunct to the man's. A century passed after this famous protest by one of Cromwell's soldiers before Mary Wollstonecraft, Ann Lee,[2] and other women doubled the pool of rights-claimants by putting

226

women in. Ann Lee, a true radical, had the insight to identify one root of women's exclusion: patriarchal religion. The four-personed God she worshiped was two-fourths female, so that equality of the sexes, as well as of the races, was assured in her Shaker version of Christianity.

Human nature displays its contradiction-engendering variety both in such bold universalizing moves as Ann Lee's and also in her refusal to her faithful of what had been a near-universal implicit right, the right to reproduce one's kind. She perhaps saw that the other root of the oppression of women was marriage itself, that the inherent dynamics of sexual reproduction, along with the different asymmetric natural powers men and women possess in reproduction (men to force sexual intercourse; women to blur or conceal the track, that men want kept and revealed, of the paternity of their children), regularly produce some variant of a trade in women, and their consequent oppression. Her radical remedy was a renunciation of the old assumed general right to sexual intercourse and to parenthood or, perhaps more accurately, a granting of a monopoly of that right to those outside the Shaker community. The damned were to provide the blessed with the continuers of their faith. This new mix of universal and special rights—a universal gender-blind, race-blind right to participate in the running of the community as well as in all its forms of skilled work (tradition has it that the circular saw was invented by a Shaker woman), along with the denial of a general right to parenthood—lasted amazingly long. The mutual parasitism between the damned and the saved worked fairly well for a century and a half.

Fascinating and instructive as this bit of cultural history is, I cite it only as an example of a dramatically great universalizing impetus, an extension of rights, being accompanied by an equally dramatic reduction of other rights. For my thesis is not just that we are a species which claims and contests rights, and that the contest is especially great when claims are made about universal rights, but that we are a species which trades rights, which relinquishes old ones for new ones, which circumscribes some in order to extend others. Rights by their very nature tend to clash. Ann Lee's husband's time-honored marital rights clashed with the radical rights which she claimed in founding a new ascetic woman-led religion, and he did not last long as one of its adherents. Rights are constantly having to

227

be balanced and adjusted—that is part of their nature, and it expresses the nature of us their creators. Human beings are not merely claimants and contestants, we are plea bargainers, compromisers, fixers, and adjusters. To get any list of rights that we can take seriously and live with without infringing, we must deny or severely limit other worthy candidate-rights, ones some others can be counted on to be proclaiming. Different groups make different tradeoffs among the candidates for universal rights. We in the late twentieth century give more weight to the universal right to free expression than to what might well seem the equally vital universal right to an unmolested childhood. We in effect allow child pornography, and we even tolerate, in the name of freedom, the market in sexual excitants in the form of so-called snuff movies, which the purchasers believe, sometimes correctly, to have involved the actual abuse, torture, and death of the involuntary child (and other) "actors." Our current tradeoff of universal rights is as bizarre as was the Shakers', and seems almost to vindicate their belief that sex is the devil.

Lists of universal rights, if they are both to cohere and to get anything like general assent, must be so vague as to be virtually empty. Usually they combine vagueness with an implicit limitation of the class of right-holders, and a consequent limitation of those whose assent is deemed of any consequence. Life, liberty, and the pursuit of happiness did not mean to include the life of Indians and slaves, the liberty of women, or the Mormons' original version of the pursuit of happiness. This declaration was a protest by white, male, largely landowning (or at least land-possessing) colonists against a colonial power, just as the Magna Carta was a protest by Norman barons who in the previous century had, along with their royal leader, seized and conquered English soil. They were protesting against that leader's successor who, they thought, was encroaching on what they had expected to be their own powers over the conquered land and people. In both cases a set of expropriating conquerors quarreled among themselves over the division of the fairly recent spoils. The rights asserted were those of an upper class against a previously acknowledged sovereign, with only token concern for the dispossessed, indigenous population and with no intention whatever to extend the claimed rights to those who had traditionally been relegated to an inferior status, namely, slaves and women.

There was nothing radical in the demands of the American "revolutionaries." The extent of the British royal power to tax had been disputed ever since its inception (as a substitute for feudal military service). The American "revolution" was cheered on by many European conservatives, who rightly saw that no radical social experiment was afoot here, merely a redrawing of national boundaries so that a new sovereign state emerged. Unlike the French Revolution, which struck terror into the hearts of privileged classes everywhere, the American "revolution," for all its prohibition of titles, reaffirmed most of the traditional European class prejudices and its traditional sexist and racist attitudes. Tocqueville noted (and shared) the racism and was impressed at the freedom of young unmarried white American women, compared with their French counterparts, and at the willing bondage of the married women. As far as classes went, he saw only one class, a merchant class, intent on gaining wealth. (That is to say, he saw only one class *among the white males.*) While noting and discussing slavery and variations in wealth, he apparently did not see the difference between free men and slaves, landowners and landless, capitalists and wage earners, employers and employed as class differences. Viewed from his aristocratic vantage point, the absence of the top two European classes, royalty and nobility, amounted to a total abolition of classes. But that was surely a distorted view, from the top down. Like many claims about rights, the Americans' claims were mainly protective and conservative, not innovative or radical. The radical proclamations came later, from the reformers, abolitionists, and feminists.

Claims to rights, even ones cast in universal or pseudo-universal form beginning "All men" or even "All persons"[3] can be used to shore up and protect traditional privileges (by which I mean not anything technical but merely rights or powers that not all have, although most would like to have them) as well as to attempt to claim powers or liberties not yet possessed. Bills of rights can serve either a conservative or a radical reforming purpose. Just what they do depends on the relation of their content and their understood scope to the political and social system within which the claims are made. In the social context of the United States today, to affirm the universal adult right to a vote by secret ballot is simply to reaffirm the present system. To claim the right of every able-bodied citizen to meaningful work for a living wage would be revolutionary. But in

Singapore or, until recently, the Soviet Union the latter claim would be merely to reassert the going system. Different societies have made different tradeoffs between the perennial candidates for universal rights. We in the United States today have traded in so-called welfare rights for individual liberties. Although the preamble to the Declaration of Independence speaks of a right to life and to the pursuit of happiness, we interpret this in the most minimal and negative way, so that we do not consider adult gun owners to have violated a child's right to life when the child dies, shot by another child who has taken his parents' legally possessed and loaded gun, to enhance his game of cops and robbers. Smokers and steel-mill owners, similarly, are not charged when a person dies of lung cancer after years of sitting in committees with pipe-smoking colleagues, or after years of residence in a city where the profits of the local rich come from air-polluting steel mills. No rights to the pursuit of happiness are thought to have been infringed when Vietnam veterans have to "pursue their happiness" in hospitals and mental hospitals, or when the unemployed and homeless pursue it on city ventilator shafts in winter. The emphasis has been on the free pursuit, not on the chances of achievement. It does not seem to worry most of us that the way our free enterprise and formal equality of opportunity works out, the United States has one of the worst male-female differentials in earnings among the so-called developed nations,[4] that starting salaries in the academic profession are on average $2,000 lower for women than for men, and that the difference increases the higher the rank.

In the United States we seem effectively to fear bureaucratic intervention and its abuses far more than we fear inequity and unfair inequality. This may be the lasting heritage of that rebellion against a central authority which gave this nation birth. But, as I have emphasized, that was a rebellion of the haves, not of the have-nots, and one traditional role of central authorities has been to act as defender of "the people," in its old sense, that is to say the underprivileged, against the greed and domination of the barons, landowners, and capitalists. "We the people" need to organize ourselves and to have agents and spokespersons, if we are effectively to assert our claims against those claiming to be superior to the people, be they kings, barons, oil barons, state governments, officials, exploiting profiteers, or profiteering arms dealers and warmongers.

The O.E.D. gives as very early senses of the English word "people" (a transliteration of the Latin *populus*) the sense "persons in relation to a superior," as in "peers and people" *(populus senatusque);* the sense "the commonality, the mass of the community as distinguished from the nobility and ruling class"; and, interestingly, "those to whom one belongs, the members of one's tribe, family, association, church, etc." Other senses include laypersons as distinct from clergy and a very old sense in which all animals are people, many of them, however, "feeble people." The family resemblance in all these senses is the exclusion of governors, superior authorities, and overlords, and "government by the people" becomes a splendid paradox.

The language of rights can be used to defend and to challenge entrenched powers and privileges. It can be used by both sides in any contested issue, by kings and subjects, employers and employees, capitalists and the unemployed, monopolists and free marketeers. There is no agreement on what anyone's rights are. Even as far as positive legally recognized rights go, it takes lawyers' wrangling and court procedures to get a decision on what a given person's rights are. And when we go beyond legal rights to moral rights and human rights, the wrangling spreads from lawyers to all of us. Is the language of rights then morally empty or neutral? Does it give no guidance to our lives as moral beings?

Rights as Rights of Disputants

It is often claimed that, although the concept of a right had a secure if limited place in Roman law, the conduct of our moral and social debate primarily by assertions of rights is a modern phenomenon. Since Grotius and Hobbes, the main question—outside the Kantian tradition, which keeps the Thomistic primacy of law-imposed obligations—has become not what responsibilities or duties we have but what rights we have. Duties in the rights tradition are seen to be founded on others' rights to their performance rather than, as in the Thomistic and Kantian tradition, any case of a recognized right being seen merely as a case where some specific obligation binds one to act in a specific way to another. Laws come to be seen to protect and recognize prior rights, not to found them. If there really is this difference between, say, Grotius and Aquinas, and between moral debate conducted in the language of basic rights and that conducted in the earlier language of basic laws and obligations (a language Kant preserves), it would be somewhat surprising if it made no substantive difference, if it were a merely verbal change. It is more likely that some of the reasons for the supposed change would be changed perceptions of what needed emphasis, of where the burden of proof lay, of what procedures of discourse would best express the range of moral convictions that were competing to be heard, and that the language of rights did assist some such shifting of agenda and of emphases. Changes in other social structures, such as the courts and the legislatures, changes in the relation of church power to secular power, contests of jurisdiction between canon law and civil law, disputes between Catholics and Protestants, might be cited as explanatory causes for why the language of rights became the *lingua franca* of moral discussion. I am not a historian, nor an anthropologist nor a lawyer, so I shall merely wave a deferential hand in the direction of such explanations and claim the philosopher's traditional arrogant prerogative of transcending the nitty-gritty of historical change and of attempting to give a "transcendental deduction" of the very possibility of the development in question or, to put it less pretentiously, to suggest that a special feature of the concept of a right encouraged such development.

My thesis, not a new one,[5] is that the language of rights is the language of language users who are becoming conscious of themselves as individuals. As a first step in that process they, we, are prone to fetishism. Especially when we have not merely language but also the institution of private property, we like to make, out of our own powers, spiritual fetishes in the form of rights, things we have and can trade. The powers thus externalized and objectivized are our individual powers to participate in and benefit from cooperative practices, and most fundamentally in speech. If there is any basic right, it is the right to be heard, to participate in normative discussion. One's first claim is the claim to a voice, to one's turn to speak and be listened to. It is to speech itself, and the cooperation necessary for a language to be learned and used, that we can turn to see both where rights or proto-rights can always be found and also to see why disagreement about rights is normal, once we get not merely to exercise or to attempt to exercise our speakers' rights but to speak about rights, to turn our discussion to them. For disagreement is one of the distinctive cultural products that speech makes possible. Without speech, there can be (and usually is) conflict, but not disagreement. My grandmother used to say to her quarreling grandchildren: "Little birds in their nest agree ..." She was a wise woman, but there is reason to disagree doubly with this bit of folk wisdom. Some little birds peck weaker little birds to death in the nest, and even those that peaceably coexist cannot, properly speaking, be said to agree. What is there for them to agree about? Lacking language, and so lacking any way of making proposals, they cannot second or agree with any, nor dispute and disagree. Language gives us the "moral equivalent" both of conflict and of harmony, of fighting and of accord and mutual aid. And, just as important, it diversifies the forms both of accord and of discord.

Locke, whose views I invoked at the start, was well aware of the vital importance of speech as not just an expression of but a foundation for our moral natures. In his splendid writings on education, he discusses first the needs of the prespeech child: fresh air, loose clothing and freedom of movement, regular cold foot-baths, a plain diet replete with fresh fruit, as much sleep as is wanted, a variety of homemade and eventually self-made playthings, patient and confident but unrelenting toilet training, gradual training in hardiness, self-denial, and respect for parental authority (all of the last three are to be done without reliance on either the rod, except as a "last Remedy,"[6] or counterproductive bribing by "sugar plums." The punishment of clear disapproval, and consequent shame, the reward of esteem, and consequent pride, are to suffice). He then goes on to consider the child's initiation into the arts of speech as well as into other civilizing arts like dancing (which he says gives both "graceful motions" and "becoming confidence"[7] to children). In his long discussion of the arts of language, Locke downplays the importance of teaching rules of language. As in ethics, so in language, one learns "more by Practice than Rules."[8] Most of his discussion is devoted to what we would call the pragmatics, not the semantics or syntax, of language, to initiation into speech act competence, not vocabulary, grammar, or composition, which he thinks children will soon pick up for themselves. His concern is that children learn to play an appropriate role in the conversation going on around them: learning not to interrupt, continually contradict what others are saying, or engage in "loud *wrangling*,"[9] but also learning to take

233

some active part in the conversation. Locke thinks the last lesson is easy to teach, unless the children's spirit is already broken by misuse of the rod. He devotes a lot of space to the need for young people to learn to avoid such rudeness of speech as disrespectful interruption, "self-conceited" contradiction, and "positive asserting, and the Magisterial Air."[10] He finds these faults not only in beginners in the arts of conversation but also among "grown People, even of Rank amongst us." "The *Indians*," he goes on, "whom we call Barbarous, observe much more Decency and Civility in their Discourses and Conversation, giving one another a fair silent Hearing, till they have quite done; and then answering them calmly, and without Noise or Passion."[11] I think therefore that I can claim the support of Locke for the thesis that the right to a fair hearing, to one's turn to speak, is a fundamental right.

I turn also to Hobbes, one of the other thinkers usually credited with bringing the language of rights from the moral background into the moral foreground, for an account of what the power of speech introduces into human life. Speech, Hobbes says, is "the most noble and profitable invention of all other ... without which, there had been amongst men, neither Common-wealth, nor Society, nor Contract, nor Peace, no more than amongst Lyons, Bears, and Wolves."[12] The uses of speech, Hobbes says, are first to use words as "Markes or Notes" to register noticed important facts or to register long trains of thought, as a possibly private aide-memoire. The second use, more interesting for my purposes, is as "Signes," to "signify ..., one to another, what they conceive, or think of each matter; and also what they desire, feare, or have any other passion for." Not merely does language enable us to "register" our findings concerning causes and effects, but to "Counsell, and Teach one another" and to "make known to others our wills, and purposes, that we may have the mutuall help of one another."[13] He goes on to show how a vitally important product of speech is the capacity to count and number things, and to reckon or reason, where reasoning is essentially reckoning in interpersonally settled "signs," not merely in private marks, and where the reckoning process itself is more than that desire-regulated train of thoughts or imaginings which can spy out the likely future for us or reconstruct some past train of events, a capacity Hobbes thinks is "common to Man and Beast."[14] Reason and "right reason" require a common currency of words and a shared standard of correct reckoning. "But no one mans Reason, nor the Reason of any one number of men, makes the certaintie . . . the parties must by their own accord, set up for right Reason, the Reason of some Arbitrator, or Judge, to whose sentence they will both stand . . ."[15] Hobbesian reason is a human cultural invention co-temporal with the invention of authority, and several of the uses of speech which Hobbes had earlier analyzed must go into the creation of reason and the setting up of a court, or arbitration panel, of right reason. He had already[16] claimed that "*True* and *False* are attributes of Speech, not of Things. And where Speech is not, there is neither *Truth* nor *Falsehood*." Reason is a way of reckoning that preserves truth, and right reason settles disputes about truth and about reckoning, where the disputes themselves are made possible by speech, by "affirmation" and the use of "negative names" in refusal and denial. Hobbes carefully lists the moods into which speech users will need to go from time to time, the "interrogative, optative, infinitive" as well as the (for him soon to be crucial) imperative mood. But along with "Commandement" he also lists "Narration, Syllogisme, Sermon, Oration" among the sorts of speeches we will produce, and also[17] forms of speech to praise, magnify, and that form of speech which "is by the Greeks called Makarismós, for which wee have no name in our tongue."

Hobbes does not support me in my claim that speech gives us the moral equivalent of both accord and mutual help, and also conflict and mutual attack. For he joins Locke in deploring the use of speech in raillery and ridicule, and says it is an "abuse" of speech to use words "to grieve one another: for seeing nature hath armed living creatures, some with teeth, and some with horns, and some with hands, to grieve an enemy, it is but an abuse of Speech, to grieve him with the tongue."[18] Hobbes takes these "abuses" of speech in insults and dishonorings (including such withdrawals from the conversation as falling asleep while another is speaking to one) to be among the important causes of that "war of all against all" for which he invokes the verbal antidote of right reason and of contract. In as far as such verbal "abuses" flourish in "the natural condition of mankind," they are taken by Hobbes to be just as "natural" to speech users as are the more constructive "uses" of speech, that get us out of that condition. My claim that where there is speech there will be disagreement, wrangling, and dispute, that where there is diction there will be contradiction, can then be made Hobbesian, as long as it is true that where there is use there will also be abuse. In any case verbal disagreement and contradiction need not degenerate into dispute, let alone into grievous insult. Both disagreement and the need to find ways of settling the disagreements that tend to degenerate into dispute and impassioned conflict can be taken to be consequences of the "most noble and profitable invention of speech."

This noble invention makes everyone who becomes a language user a claimant, one who advances verbal claims, listens to how they are received, defends them, and sometimes corrects, amends, or retracts them. As participants in conversation we acquire the proto-rights of such participants to have our say, to affirm or deny what others say, to be heard. Sometimes those rights are anything but equal. Children in bygone epochs were restricted to a minimal conversational role in the presence of their elders, and Plato gives Socrates' co-conversationalists the role only of providing Socrates with material for correction, and of yea-saying his moves. Most human conversations, especially about the norms to govern human communities, have been elitist, not democratic, conversations, in which the majority of the people were to play the role merely of reciting "amen" to whatever their "betters" had concluded. Still, the fact of speech itself empowers each speaker. The minimal and basic power to say no, to protest, is there from the start, as is the power to interrupt, to clamor for a say, when others monopolize the conversation. These powers, sometimes very costly to exercise, are, I suggest, the foundations of human rights.

These powers do not themselves dictate the specific content of any right which may reasonably be claimed, but they do direct attention to individual participants. Rights belong to individual persons, and are rights to what individuals can have and do. They may belong to individuals as occupants of thrones or White Houses, and they may come to be recognized as belonging also to artificial persons, to corporations and states. Any right is someone's right, in a sense in which it need not be true that any law is someone's law, or even that any responsibility is someone's. Our generation may collectively have a responsibility to clean up rivers, lakes, and the atmosphere, but until we appoint officers with special powers and responsibilities to see to this, the responsibility is not yet any single person's and belongs to us collectively, not yet distributively. By contrast if we, our generation, have a right to, say, Social Security benefits because of what we have paid in, we have that distributively. Each of us has it. The language of rights is the language of speakers becoming conscious of themselves as individual participants in the cooperative practice of speech and other cooperative practices. Rights claimants are cooperators conscious of themselves as individuals, claiming what they see as their due share of the fruits of cooperation.

The Peculiarity and the Parasitism of Rights

I do not think it is very controversial to claim that the use of the language of rights is one which draws attention to the presence and claims of individuals. Most of those who have recently written on the origins of our concept of right and on the distinctive features of rights-based moral theories are agreed on this (Richard Tuck,[19] Ronald Dworkin,[20] J. L. Mackie,[21] Joseph Raz,[22] Joel Feinberg[23]), and most critics of rights-based theories object precisely to this "individualism," to what is seen as an overattention to individual demands and claims at the expense of attention to needs of the collectivity, needs which no single person may be voicing. If this "possessive individualism" is to be distinctive of the language of rights, and not a universal unvarying feature of all moral discourse, then one would expect that rights attach to single individual persons more basically than do obligations (which in their original sense are ties between two or more parties) or responsibilities and duties. The latter may be jointly possessed and jointly performed. Laws typically are laws of groups, not of individuals, and respect for law is also something that a community can show collectively as well as individually. The language of rights directs attention to individual persons, and to them not as duty-bearers or contributors to the human task but as beneficiaries or claimants to a share of what is produced by the performance of that task. Nor is this all. The language of rights pushes us, more insistently than does the language of duties, responsibilities, obligations, legislation and respect for law, to see the participants in the moral practice as single clamorous living human beings, not as families, clans, tribes, groups, classes, churches, congregations, nations, or peoples.

Given the complicated and repeated inversions which Richard Tuck has traced in the medieval history of the concepts of *ius* and *dominium* in relation to *lex,* it takes a rash philosopher to suggest that there is any one thread linking the changing uses and giving us a basis for a contrast with the concept of obligation *(obligatio)* and of responsibility. I shall make a rash suggestion covering the earliest use of *ius* in Roman law, where it was what a successful contestant in a dispute won,[24] through the later *iura praediorum,* which entitled home builders to conduct their drains through neighboring home owners' property and to block their daylight to some degree, on through the medieval interpretation of Justinian (after the rediscovery of the *Digest* in the twelfth century), for whom justice is the continuing determination to give everyone his or her *ius* (and for whom *dominium* is a kind of *ius*), through the Renaissance lawyers such as François de Connan to Grotius and beyond. Connan says that the *ius,* say, of a settler on vacant land differs from the consequent and correlative obligation of others not to dispossess him, and from his having legal case to enforce discharge of that obligation in "reason, role and scope," not in "the cause, the matter and the end."[25] The "scope" of the right is a single settler, who is to have *dominium* over the settled land. The scope of the obligation is other individuals and also collectives, such as municipalities or religious orders. My suggestion concerns just this difference in scope, role, and order of reasons which Connan perspicuously presents. Rights, I suggest, differ from obligations in that they primarily attach to individual persons, whereas parties to a tie of obligation, and responsibility holders, can as easily be collectives as individual persons. Rights differ also in their individuation, since what rights we recognize is affected by this key fact, that we see them as essentially the possessions of single persons, whereas our obligations can be to do things that no single individual could possibly do, things such as repaying a national debt or cleaning up our rivers. Obligations and responsibilities are what we have collectively or individually, and are to do what can be done either cooperatively or singly. Rights primarily have individual living persons in their scope, and are to actions that single individuals can perform or to goods that individuals can possess.

This is not, of course, to deny that Connan's point, about how the rights of a settler give rise to obligations of later-comers, could be applied as readily to a group of Benedictine monks, obedient to some religious superior, or applied to a family, as to a single settler.

The right may belong to some group, who can therefore claim, "*We* have a right to this land." But when they, say, the monks, claim this, the claim is different from their recognition of their obligations when they say, for example, "We have an obligation to organize soup kitchens for the local paupers and to offer up masses for the souls of our departed brethren." Some of their obligations are to the sort of things it requires some organization into a collective to do, whereas none of their rights is to what it takes organization into a collective either to voice a claim to or to exercise. When rights are possessed, as of course they can be, by some "us" rather than some "me," that is accidentally, not necessarily, the case. But some obligations and responsibilities, including very important ones such as obligations to future generations, must be ours, not mine, and any that are mine must, like individual monks' duties to officiate in certain ways at certain places and times, grow out of the arrangements made to discharge the collectively owned obligation, by dividing that moral task into individually dischargeable derivative duties.

The suggestion, then, is that throughout the twists and turns of the history of the concepts of *ius, dominium, droit, recht,* and right, the concept remains more closely tied to single persons and the sort of goods they can have (to liberty, to control of material goods, to power to command others) than is the wider-ranging and, in my view, more fundamental concept of responsibility.

If we look at Grotius's use of the term *ius,* which is often taken to inaugurate our modern tradition of rights-based moral and social theories, we find him appropriately starting by considering what sort of good a single living person can possess and which of these goods are transferable to others. Inalienable goods are life, honor, and freedom, and so rights to them are to be inalienable. Other goods possessible by single human beings, such as land and labor power, are alienable, or *wandelbaer.* (Tuck in his discussion makes the interesting claim that the recognition of a right to liberty, treated as *dominium,* or total control, and so including the right to renounce, was convenient to slave traders, who could persuade themselves that the Africans whom they traded had already renounced liberty for life. Molina's and Suarez's recognition of a right or *dominium* to individual liberty, was, ironically enough, part of the justification of slavery, while Grotius's limitation on that right, his doctrine that liberty was an inalienable good, was a step in the direction of de-legitimizing slavery and the slave trade.[26]) Thus Grotius can give his famous definition of a right as "a moral quality annexed to the person justly enabling him to possess some particular privilege or to perform some particular act."[27] Rights are the sort of thing most naturally annexed to individual persons, since they are *to* such goods or powers as can be enjoyed or exercised by a single person, occasion by occasion. This is not to deny that, for the very existence of the goods that rights secure (life, or free speech), there must earlier have been some cooperative activity (between parents, and between parent and child, between language transmitters and those to whom it is transmitted), but rather to make the simple claim that "I live and I speak, and so exercise my rights to life and speech" makes very easy sense to us, whereas "I made a law" or "I made reparations to the Native Americans for their past mistreatment" make little sense. Laws must be collectively made, many obligations must be collectively discharged, but rights attach essentially to individual persons, and only derivatively to collectives.

Obligations and responsibilities can be to the sorts of action which must be done collectively, so that for the discharge of the obligation a group must organize itself and divide the moral labor. If we, as a generation, are to fulfill our obligation to future generations, we need to appoint officials with specific duties. Moral labor, the moral task, in this case, as in many others, has to be divided up by social agreement. It does not come naturally predivided, as does labor in childbirth. I have in the past challenged the view that because we have a responsibility or an obligation to clean up our messes for the sake of the future generations who could be poisoned by those messes, future generations therefore must be said to have rights against us, rights to unpoisoned air and water.[28] But if we did want to say that they had such rights, they would not be rights collectively possessed, by each successive generation, to the air around at that time, which they then would have to divvy up, rationing to each person his fair quota. Air divides itself into the lungs breathing it, river water cools or quenches the thirst of those bathing in or drinking it, without need for any allocative agency. (Where it is scarce, as it may be, allocation will be necessary, but then the case for cross-generational obligations and rights immediately becomes more questionable. How much coal should we leave our great-grandchildren's generation? An unanswerable question, unlike the easily answered, "Should we leave lakes and rivers polluted or unpolluted?"[29]) Even where, although the water is not scarce, it will take organization to give each her turn at access to it or to conduct it into homes, the job of such organizers will be not to "divide" the collective entitlement but to facilitate receipt of a self-apportioning and self-renewing good. My thesis, then, is that while collective responsibilities and obligations are not or are not always self-apportioning, collective rights are. If someone fails to get access to, say, our collective inheritance of the West European literary tradition, that will be because someone or some community denied him an education or access to public libraries, or because he did not avail himself of the opportunity of access. It is not that the rest of the library users greedily consumed his portion as well as their own. By contrast, our collective obligation to pass on this tradition to the next generation is not self-apportioning. We do need to organize ourselves and allocate special responsibilities to some, in order to discharge this collective obligation.

This feature of rights, that they are rights to dues that, once recognized, do not have to be allocated but come as it were pre-allocated, may explain why many want to say that respect for basic rights requires us not to do anything, merely to refrain from interfering with each other's exercise of these basic rights. For I can get my air, continue my life, enjoy my liberty and public libraries, and have my right of reply to charges against me without having to wait to discover which air is my air, which life my life, which liberty mine, which books the ones I am allocated, which say is my say; whereas to discharge my responsibilities, I must first find out what my responsibilities are, I must consult my fellows. I think this popular doctrine, that rights define a sort of core morality that demands of mutual right respecters an essential minimum of cooperation and coordination, is half right. Rights do define a sort of individualist tip of the iceberg of morality, one that takes no extra organization to stay afloat, but that is because it is supported by the submerged floating mass of cooperatively discharged responsibilities and socially divided labor. Basic rights, I am claiming, are rights of access to self-allocating public goods.

The right to one's say shows very well this parasitism of rights on other less individualist moral concepts. If the "say" in question is a reply to criticisms levied against one, then indeed it is easily seen who has it, and in a sense what it is that she has. But for how long can I speak in my own defense and expect my accusers to listen? The rules that fix the substance of what counts as the say I have a right to must be socially agreed ones, agreements that it may take courts or other organizations to bring off. Similarly with my right to life. In a sense it is correct that, in order for it to be respected, all that must be done by others is that they not kill me. But although what that means may seem clear enough when I am a reasonably tough adult, it was less clear when I was a helpless newborn, and will be less clear when I am a helpless incapacitated old person. Cooperation is needed to specify the precise content of such a right as well as to preserve the supply of the good that gives this right its name and its individuality. Cooperation between parents, or perhaps between a state that issues a license of parenthood and individual potential parents, is needed for the reproduction of human life in a form that can still be seen as a good: cooperation is needed both to preserve the liberty we have a right to and to specify its limits and scope. We need cooperation to keep our various wells self-supplying and unpoisoned as well as to regulate access to the wells.

So my claim is that although basic rights are indeed to what individuals can have, exercise, and enjoy, it is not just as single individuals, separate centers of value, sovereign selves but, rather, as individual participants in a cooperative practice that we have basic rights, individual as they intrinsically are. Rights can be claimed, and when any attempt is to be made to claim or to "vindicate" any of these individual rights, the claim and the vindication themselves have to employ the socially coordinated practice of speech. The claimants and vindicators must exercise some social powers as participants in discourse. Such declarers, proclaimers, and vindicators may often shout to the empty air, not to any respectful audience, or may be heard but laughed out of court, or contradicted or heckled or shouted down, but the very attempt to claim rights itself exercises basic hard-to-suppress rights to speak up for oneself and one's people, rights that the public good of speech itself gives us. We the people, once adult, have, not only with one another but with any contrasting overlords, some actual equality of the essential powers of speech. We may not all be equally eloquent or get equally wide audiences, and some may speak in accents or dialects which reveal origins more "lowly" than others, but that need not impair communicative force, especially the force of protest. "People" in the singular is a collective noun for an aggregation of ones who can follow each other's speech and gesture, and so who can make claims and counterclaims both on one another and on any would-be overlords. But for this sort of community, that constituted by a common language or mutually comprehensible collection of languages, to be there, the individual human beings making up "the people" must be seen not as each "autonomous," each making her own laws, but as members of a "republic of letters," obeying common conventions of speech and accepting shared responsibilities to protect the common wealth that speech brings. Ends in ourselves we may be, each of us a separate valuable source of voice, of suggestion and demand, but we have this status only as members of a republic of such ends in themselves. It is only as participants in a cooperative practice that we can have any rights. The concept of responsibility, of being properly responsive to our fellow cooperators, is the more fundamental one, and its linguistic origins are obvious. Rights are the tip of the iceberg that collective and individual responsibilities support.

Such a conceptual foundation for the concept of a right, one basing it on our human nature as individual speakers and as speakers who transmit our powers and standards of speech to new arrivals, leaves it open, a matter of unending debate, what universal rights, besides the equal right to have one's say, can plausibly be claimed. Still, it might seem to prejudice the question of the content of such rights toward the rights of freedom of speech and worship, toward procedural rights and away from so-called welfare rights. Consent will seem to become as basic as the framers of the United States Constitution made it, and the concerns of those who were unhappy until the Constitution was amended with explicit recognition of rights to speak, and to put speech to religious uses, to assemble to talk and to petition, appear eminently appropriate. If the language of rights is to be used, to what more appropriate end than to claim the rights intrinsic to language participants? Lest it be thought, however, that I am retracting my earlier claim that speech is the moral equivalent of discord as well as accord, rights themselves the moral human equivalent of talons, saber teeth, horns, and antlers, instruments of self-defense and of attack as well as of mutual aid, let me add a remark about the Second Amendment, the claimed right to keep and bear arms at all times. If rights are spiritual weapons, the right to speak the great equalizer, should they be used to secure what they can replace? If the First Amendment seems a natural starter for a bill of rights, the second seems a most unnatural follow-up. The language of rights does not itself rule out any particular content, but it does make some proposed contents to universal rights look a little dangerous for the very survival of the formal structure of right-recognition itself. The right to rebel against tyrants is one of the oldest and most venerable claimed rights, and it is indeed a last-resort right, a right to fall back on violent self-defense when its moral equivalent (debate, petition, protest, wrangling, and litigation) fails. Such appeals to God-or-Nature must remain as an ultimate last resort, a dangerous safeguard, but are a limit case of exercise of a right, if rights are essentially to one's role-related powers in a cooperative enterprise, and one among whose achievements is to be a better way than fighting to settle perceived conflicts of interests. Such a limit case right must, I think, just as much as the quintessential right to speech, be recognized, if we recognize any rights. But to recognize the right to rebel against tyrannical governments is one thing, to recognize a right to keep arms at all times quite another. It seems almost contradictory to the very idea of recognizing any rights, an invitation to a reversal to raw force and violence, rather than its civilized and cooked variants, contradiction, protest, disputation. It is a bit like using one's powers of speech to take a vow of silence, as Trappists do. It is indeed a possible thing to do with the forged cultural instrument of a social practice of rights recognition and protection, but it is an anomalous and self-endangering thing to have done. It is the right to cease to rely on appeal to one's rights. And because rights, like a monetary currency, depend for their very existence on trust in them, then the right to distrust them, and to promote that distrust, is a strange and right-undermining right.

Rights, Interests, Responsibilities

The language of individual rights naturally leads to the concept of an individual human interest. Individual interests come to be seen as what rights protect, and the individuation of interests piggybacks upon that of the rights that protect them. Often we claim rights before we are very clear about what is valuable about what we are claiming, so that consciousness of our vital interests demands more of us than awareness of our rights. Indeed I would say that the language of vital interests is the proper complement, perhaps even successor, to the language of rights. Perceived vital interests are rights which have transcended or transvalued themselves, and once we talk the language of interests, we are bound to recognize public as well as private interests as vital. Meanwhile, we have both concepts, rights and interests. The language of rights, once we have it, and while we still use it, will and should be used to protect what we see to be vital and protectable individual human interests. I see no reason why we should not include the so-called welfare rights among the universal rights we recognize. If the role of rights is to mitigate the effects of dominance without requiring begging, then there should be rights to whatever vital goods we the people can otherwise only get by violence or by begging, that is, food, shelter, and help when we are not yet capable or are incapacitated. But our perception of what we want to fight or beg for, if we cannot claim them as ours by recognized right, that is to say our perception of which of our interests are vital interests, varies greatly from culture to culture and from epoch to epoch, as does our collective ability to cooperate so as to protect these interests. Even in one culture at one time there will probably be considerable disagreement about which interests are most vital.

If we do allow that there is a right to self-defense, if need be by violence, it, like the right to some share of the earth's common stock of food or the right to one's turn at useful paid work in the community into which one is born, will be based on an interest different from any specifically speech-related interests. Rights to self-defense, and to work, and to join the "banquet of life" are all as much "welfare rights" as they are "procedural rights." None of them has anything intrinsically to do with speech or with the roles we play as speech participants. But it would surely be absurdly narcissistic of us to use our powers of speech to talk only about talk, or to use our capacities to claim and to recognize claims, to propose and second, to declare and vindicate only to protect that very practice. The language of rights is worth protecting only if it finds something as well as itself to talk about, and if it is used to assert some rights as well as the right to speak. It must indeed protect itself, if it is to protect any human interest, but unless it is protecting, as best the current conditions allow, some vital human interests in addition to our vital interest as participants in speech, it will become merely a branch of contemporary literature, of talk about talk, and the U.S. Constitution with its past and future amendments will be merely texts about texts. We do have a fundamental and vital interest in our cooperative practice of speech, and in the rights it gives birth to, but we surely have an equally vital interest in other cooperative practices (now thoroughly permeated by speech), such as the production of food and shelter for us the people and the care of the very young, the sick, and the very old. As Locke's account of a good education emphasizes, no one becomes a participant in that most noble and civilizing practice of speech unless first fed, sheltered, and treated as one of us, the people. It is only decent filial piety for participants in the language of rights, in speech becoming conscious of itself, for us to use that language to recognize rights to the greatest equal protection that we are collectively in a position to afford for those basics of human life which our exercise of our rightly treasured power of speech itself presupposes. The most primitive of these basic prerequisites is protection against torture, against the infliction of pain that substitutes screams and groans for voice. That is indeed so basic that it seems too weak to say that the victims of torture are victims of the violation of a right. They are victims of violation itself, of violence at its most evil. If we have any responsibilities, the responsibility to prevent torture, to respond to the cries or stifled cries of the tortured, is surely the most self-evident. Unless we recognize that, we renounce morality itself.

Speakers, conscious of themselves, recognize the rights that speech essentially entails. Rights-recognizers, conscious of their dependence on and debts to those who sustain human life, protect as best they can the interests that must be protected if human lives are to be sustained. Rights to speak, to one's turn (in speech, and in all those civilizing procedures which define turns), sustain the very possibility of any rights and so of any alternative to begging as a way of softening the effects of dominance. The so-called welfare rights sustain rights-claimants. We have a vital interest in the goods protected by both sorts of rights. But as I said earlier, rights are the tip of the moral iceberg, supported by the responsibilities that we cooperatively discharge and by the individual responsibilities that we recognize, including responsibilities to cooperate, in order to maintain common goods, such as civilized speech, and civilized ways of settling disputes. For it takes more than rights to settle disputes about rights.

HOW CAN INDIVIDUALISTS SHARE RESPONSIBILITY?

Those of us who find methodological individualism a limiting and ultimately stultifying assumption in social philosophy, yet who are grateful for the freedom of thought and speech that encourages us to voice our discontents with this and other orthodoxies of the liberal tradition, have no difficulty in making room in our more communitarian social philosophy for the value of independence of thought, the virtue of sturdy individualism. Any intelligent society will provide for its own vigorous but peaceable criticism, for a supply of unorthodox views to keep its own orthodoxies honest. So the liberal communitarian will see there to be a collective responsibility to nurture independence of thought in the members of society, a collective responsibility to nurture in individuals a sense of their individual duty to avoid mindless conformism. Just as the methodological individualist can and usually does recognize some duty to associate, so the social constructionist in ethics and political philosophy can recognize a shared public duty to encourage individuals to think their own thoughts, have their own reactions. Anyone who treasures her own freedom of thought and speech will want to protect it, and to encourage in others those independent thoughts whose expression requires its presence.

Kant, writing about the social virtues, says, "It is a duty to oneself as well as to others not to *isolate* oneself . . . but to use one's moral perfections in social intercourse . . . While making oneself a fixed center of one's principles, one ought to regard this circle drawn around one as also forming an all-inclusive circle of those who, in their disposition, are citizens of the world."[1] Good citizenship, at least for propertied males, will be part of moral virtue for the principled Kantian with virtuous cosmopolitan sentiments. Clearly Kant did not mean "cosmopolitan" to exclude "patriotic." Just as each principled person will not isolate himself from his fellow citizens, in a state where the rule of law, administered by just magistrates, harmonizes with the rule of the self-legislated moral law, so each principled nation will not isolate itself, but will have not merely respect for but social ties to other nations living under their own rule of law. It is to be a sort of Leibnizian harmony of moral monads, organizing themselves into associations that enhance and preserve rather than threaten the individual sphere and freedom of each. The tightest possible association between persons will be by life-long contract within marriage (a form that Kant avoided) or friendship tied by vows of friendship,[2] the next will be the quasi-contractual tie of fellow citizens under a common magistrate and a common law, and the loosest but not unimportant tie that of cosmopolitan sentiment linking all mutually respectful autonomous persons in practices of "affability, sociability, courtesy, hospitality, and gentleness (in disagreeing without quarreling)."[3] (Presumably these cosmopolitan sentiments are to be largely reserved for those who are citizens of nations with whom our own nation is not currently at war, since Kant takes perpetual peace to be more an idea or ideal of practical reason than a realistic expectation.)

This is one picture, a very individualist one, of the relationship of an individual person and her moral responsibility to more encompassing spheres of action and responsibility, in particular, to the nation-state and the so-called family of nation-states. The individual person is to be a "fixed center" of her principles, but is to take it as an individual duty to avoid isolation. At one revealing place early on in the *Metaphysics of Morals*, Kant endorses Ulpian's three principles of right, *Honeste vive, neminem laede,* and *sui cuique tribue* ("Live honestly, harm no one, to each his own") and his gloss on the latter two runs this way: "*Do not wrong anyone* . . . even if, to avoid doing so, you should have to stop associating with others and shun all society . . . (If you cannot help associating with others), *enter* into a society with them in which each can keep what is his."[4] Citizenship, indeed any interaction with others, is to be entered into only if one need not break one's version of the moral law to do so, only if one can do so without wronging oneself or others. Just how one possibly could "shun all society" is unclear, and it may be that Kant took it to be only a theoretical option. What is of interest for my purposes is his taking of social cooperation and group membership as not of primary moral importance, as something that we can indeed make morally tolerable, but which involves some moral risks that would be avoided in solitude.

This is only one strain in Kant's thought, and it is in some tension with the version of the categorical imperative that tells us to act as members of a realm of ends. A one-member realm would be a limit case of a realm, and if one exiled oneself to some small island and lived alone, then, however one acted, it would be a bit strained to call that acting as a member of a realm, from whose other members one had rightly exiled oneself for fear of wronging them or oneself. It would be a very loose social union, if it united the solitary occupants of some such archipelago only by the mutual agreement to leave each other alone. Kant's "realm of ends" is usually construed, both by him and by his commentators, as some sort of republic in which the *res publicae* are more extensive than a collective willingness to leave each other undisturbed. At the very least there will be the "public goods" of courts of justice and penal institutions. Yet problems remain about how each person's sphere or circle is to fit into any larger all-inclusive circle, how the autonomy of each is to be reconciled with the lack of any right of resistance against tyranny, and with the status of passive citizenship with which all women, servants, and unpropertied persons are supposed to content themselves.[5] The metaphor of circles or spheres combining to make larger circles or spheres requires either a Nozickian notion of a "space" around each individual sphere or the Cartesian and Spinozist concept of a "twisted circle," if the individual small circles are to fit snugly into a super-circle. But Kant's demotion of more than half of humanity into second-class personhood is actually more like the remedy that Descartes took when hypothesizing the shape of the particles or the separately moving parts of his plenum universe. Some particles are now spherical, he supposed, while others have had to keep less regular shapes in order to fit into the interstices between the heavenly spherical bodies.[6] This Cartesian physics, where the movement of the more perfect spherical bodies required the adjustive movement of smaller, more flexible, and less heavenly bodies, seems to have been taken over by Kant into his moral metaphysics, where the moral place and allotted space of servants and women is adapted to allow free movement for the autonomous male circles or spheres.

This republic of republics, the United States of America, whose "more perfect union" its constitution seeks to further, was found by one early observer, Alexis de Tocqueville, to have a national characteristic for which he coined the word "individualism." He took that peculiarly American trait to exhibit not some admirable combination of sturdy self-reliance, determination to think for oneself, and resistance to blind social conformity but, rather, a complex of tendencies that originate "as much in the deficiencies of the mind as in the perversity of the heart."[7] What exactly did he mean? And do those contemporary theorists of American democracy (such as John Rawls) who look to Kant for help in articulating the basic moral principles underlying our public norms look to a theorist whose own thought displays the sort of elitist or at least selective individualism that Tocqueville found to derive from "erroneous judgment, more than from depraved feelings"? (I say elitist, for the individualism that Tocqueville found in America was found in its white males, not in its blacks or its married women.)

The noun "individual" is a relative latecomer to the English language, not occurring until the seventeenth century. The earlier adjectival form has the sense of "indivisible." Individualism, as Tocqueville defines it (and as its coiner, he cannot be defining it wrongly), is not so much a determination to be one unified self, not to divide oneself up into plural *personae,* as a disposition of "each member of the community to sever himself from the mass of his fellow-creatures; and to draw apart with his family and friends."[8] The O.E.D. gives as its first sense of "individualism" the sense that Tocqueville gives it, then moves to more recent senses: "self-centred feeling or conduct as a principle, a mode of life in which the individual pursues his own ends or follows his own ideas, free and independent individual action or thought, egoism." Here we have included both the near egoism that Tocqueville intends the word to convey plus the independence of thought and action that gives us our concept of sturdy individualism as a virtue.

Egotism, Tocqueville thinks, originates in blind instinct, but he finds individualism to be more reflective, a product of judgment, even if erroneous judgment. "Egotism blights the germ of all virtue: individualism, at first, only saps the virtues of public life; but, in the long run, it attacks and destroys all others, and is at length absorbed in downright egotism. Egotism is a vice as old as the world, which does not belong to one form of society more than to another: individualism is of democratic origin ..."[9] He contrasts the close but limited ties binding people together in aristocracies with democracies, where "the bond of human affection is extended, but it is relaxed." American ties are theoretically to all fellow Americans, but in fact "the interest of man is confined to those in close propinquity to himself." And even that interest has narrow bounds: "not only does democracy make every man forget his ancestors, but it hides his descendants, and separates his contemporaries from him; it throws him back forever upon himself alone, and threatens in the end to confine him entirely within the solitude of his own heart."

What prevents this threatened solipsism, on Tocqueville's analysis, is voluntary association of individualists, with the press as communicative vehicle. White male Americans struck this aristocratic French observer as constantly ready to form a new association, be it to provide entertainment, to enforce temperance, or to send missionaries to the antipodes. He writes, "The first time I heard in the United States that a hundred thousand men had bound themselves publicly to abstain from spirituous liquors, it appeared to me more like a joke than a serious engagement,"[10] but then he saw it was no joke, but a manifestation of a special need in democracies, an "artificial" creation of mutual ties, through voluntary association of like-minded people. "In democratic countries the science of association is the mother of science; the progress of all the rest depends on the progress it has made."[11] So voluntary association compensates for individualism, and the press facilitates communication between far-flung individuals united in various common causes, including political causes.

So where is the deficiency of the mind and the perversity of the heart? Why should this "individualism," when combined with an eagerness for voluntary association and the cultivation of a free press, lead to egotism and to the sapping of the virtues of public life? Why should it lead to a forgetting of ancestors and an ignoring of the

251

interests of our descendants? Among the voluntary associations eventually formed will be the Daughters of the American Revolution and various organizations to protect parks, wilderness areas, and other goods for our descendants. What public virtues are threatened by replacing inherited ties with voluntary loyalties, by replacing fixed rank with equality of opportunity for advancement, deferential with independent thinking, especially once slavery is abolished, and once women get the vote? Public life will surely be different in a democratic republic, peopled by geographically and socially mobile individualists, than in a republic where the domiciles and ranks of persons are more fixed, where association is less voluntary and more hierarchical, but why should it not have its own virtues? And in particular, why should democratic individualists lose the memory of what they owe their ancestors who forged the democracy, or be less concerned than others to preserve what they value for their descendants?

If recent historians of this nation such as Gordon S. Wood[12] are right, some of the framers of the U.S. Constitution were themselves appalled at what it seemed, by the end of their lives, that they had wrought. They had intended to institute a republic which would foster the traditional republican virtues of public service in the gentry and appreciative docility in the lower classes, leaving traditional hierarchical ties between master and slave or servant (not to mention man and woman) largely untouched. Wood, in *The Radicalism of the American Revolution,* quotes Thomas Jefferson's lament in 1825, "All, all dead, and ourselves left alone amid a new generation whom we know not, and who knows not us." Instead of the classical republican virtues, the new republic was spawning the new commercial and capitalist virtues of individual market enterprise, conspicuous consumption in the working class as well as among their "betters," a radical egalitarianism that threatened traditional class structure, with all too little public spiritedness. So within one generation there was that "forgetting of ancestors," or at least of their aspirations, that Tocqueville found striking.

Rather than look only at Tocqueville's own answers to these questions, which plausibly enough point to the risks of leaving the protection of public values to voluntary support for them, to support which may wax and wane, to the dangers of majority despotism and the fickleness of the mass of voters, I shall return to Kant, and to the

version of republicanism that he erected on his individualist foundations. I do this in part because of the recent appeal to Kant by one of
the ablest and most influential defenders of this republic's liberal tradition, John Rawls, and in part because of the general enthusiasm
among moral philosophers for Kant's views, or at least for those of
them that are most familiar, through the regular teaching of Kant's
Groundwork of the Metaphysics of Morals.[13] If Rawls sees Kant,
rather than Mill, Locke, Hume, or Burke, as giving us a moral and
social philosophy which best articulates the basic principles of this
nation's scheme of cooperation, then we more detached observers (I
speak as a U.S. resident who is not a U.S. but a New Zealand citizen,
and who did not imbibe the ideology of American democracy with
my mother's milk, nor with my school lessons in history and social
studies) presumably may without irrelevance turn there, to understand what relationship there is, and is believed to be, between individual autonomous persons and the life that they live together under
one constitution and one set of laws, and between individual and
collective responsibility. I shall ignore the complication brought in
by the fact that this nation is a federal union of states, so that we all
live under both state and federal law, since this by no means unimportant aspect of American political life is not one that Rawls has
emphasized nor one whose relationship to individualism Tocqueville
had views about.[14] Kant's remarks about federations of republics, in
Perpetual Peace,[15] while they build on his earlier views about cooperation between fellow citizens within a republic, do not have much
to say about the way that such federation affects or is affected by the
sort of autonomy that belongs to individual citizens, nor about the
way the individual responsibility of persons for their own choices
somehow sums, in a democratic republic, to the states' and the
nation's responsibility for its choices—say, the choice to fight the
Gulf War and to inflict the massive casualties that the Iraqi people
suffered in that war, or to return the Haitian refugees to Haiti, or to
cut down Oregon's forests to supply timber, or to fail to get aid to
the starving in East Africa, or to have no women candidates for the
presidency. For that is the issue that my title promises, and that I
now begin to approach.

It is very easy for a citizen in a large nation like this one to wash
her hands of any responsibility for any decision taken by any public
officials. Especially when one deplores a particular decision, one's

inclination is to say that "*they* should not have done that," where *they* are some decision makers, and we, the critics of it, see ourselves as blameless, not because the pressure we brought to bear on the official decision makers failed to change their mind, but simply because we did nothing except observe and deplore. It was not our decision, we think, and so whatever the harm done by it, that was none of our doing. The dirty hands belong always to the politicians, not to those who let them be elected and who passively contribute to the maintenance of the institutions that give them their particular share of power. We may deplore that a particular judge gets appointed for the rest of his life to the Supreme Court, when many people think him proven unfit, and wonder about the fitness of those who have the power to appoint. There will be ephemeral outbursts of indignation, a flurry of witty cartoons and popular jokes, but few of us tend to feel that "*we* have done something dubious, something our children and grandchildren may curse us for." We think: "*They* did something dubious." We share responsibility by dividing it in such a way that we can always pass the buck to the politicians for the really important decisions that affect many people's lives for many decades. Responsibility is conveniently passed along to those with a taste for the exercise of power, those willing or keen to take public office. The ordinary citizen can tell herself that her share of responsibility is the very modest one of casting an informed and thoughtful vote in the election of representatives, and perhaps writing an occasional letter to a congresswoman, or even going to the lengths of participating in some peaceful protest march. Beyond that, the responsibility rests with elected legislators, with the President and his appointed assistant executives, and with appointees to the Supreme Court. The Fourth Estate, the press, may be seen as having the special public responsibility of keeping others well informed, and of supplying a range of opinions in the commentary it provides. Each person's public responsibility, even that of the President and of the Supreme Court justices, will be circumscribed. That indeed is what Kant took to be the hallmark of republicanism, that there be clear separation of powers. "*Republicanism* is that political principle whereby the executive power (the government) is separated from the legislative power."[16] Kant, a few paragraphs before, had said that "A *republican constitution* is founded upon three principles: firstly, the principle of *freedom* for all members of a society (as men); secondly, the principle of the *dependence* of everyone upon a single common legislation (as subjects); and thirdly, the principle of legal *equality* for everyone (as citizens)." Lest we be misled, we should quickly note that the equality in question is "perfectly consistent with the utmost inequality of the mass in the degree of its possessions"[17] and with the need of wives to obey husbands, and that qualifications for active citizenship include "of course, being an adult male."[18] It seemed to Kant a matter of course that women should be merely passive citizens, since he saw no real chance that they (we) might become economically independent, so in a position to have and express a will of our own, and so be fit to vote, let alone to stand for office. "All women," he writes, "and in general, anyone whose preservation in existence (his being fed and protected) depends not on his management of his own business but on arrangements made by another (except the state) . . . lack civil personality and their existence is, as it were, only inherence."[19] (One might think that professors also could be seen to share this nonsubstantiality, depending as they do for their livelihood on some college to hire them, so allowing themselves to be mere underlings, or *Handlanger*. Kant says that private tutors fall into this category, but not schoolteachers, so presumably professors in state universities count as "independent" in Kant's sense, but those in private universities may be in a dubious position, their existence mere inherence.)

We should note that Tocqueville's views on the proper position of women are no improvement on Kant's. He writes, "I have been frequently surprised, and almost frightened, at the singular address and happy boldness with which young women in America contrive to manage their thoughts and their language . . . amid the independence of early youth, an American woman is always mistress of herself."[20] Not for them the "virginal bloom" and "innocent and ingenuous grace" of young Frenchwomen of the period, which Tocqueville clearly preferred, as promising more "affectionate wives and agreeable companions to man" than did the typical young American woman, with her "masculine strength of understanding and a manly energy," her "confidence in her own strength of character," and "the free vigour of her will." But how was such understanding and free will exercised? In renouncing her independence in the bonds of matrimony. Here Tocqueville waxes near rhapsodic.

Americans, he writes, "admit that as Nature has appointed such wide differences between the physical and the moral constitution of man and woman, her manifest design was to give a distinct employment to their various faculties ... The Americans have applied to the sexes the great principle of political economy which governs the manufactures of our age, by carefully dividing the duties of man from those of woman, in order that the great work of society be the better carried on. In no country has such constant care been taken as in America to trace two clearly distinct lines of action for the two sexes ..."[21] He praises American women for attaching "a sort of pride to the voluntary surrender of their own will," and making it their boast "to bend themselves to the yoke, not to shake it off."[22] In a peroration to his chapter on this enlightened American understanding of the relation of the sexes, he writes, "As for myself, I do not hesitate to avow that, although the women of the United States are confined within the narrow circle of domestic life, and their situation is in some respects one of extreme dependence, I have nowhere seen women occupying a loftier position; and if I were asked ... to what the singular prosperity and growing strength of that [American] people ought mainly to be attributed, I should reply—to the superiority of their women."[23] This lofty superior position of voluntary female bondage was of course one not destined to last, but there are still plenty of Tocquevillians who deplore the less "efficient" current division of labor that the emancipation of women has brought. What Tocqueville called "the clamor for the rights of women" is still seen to tend to bring what he termed a "trampling on her holiest duties."[24] For this redrawing of the lines of male and female responsibility within the family and within society, women have been most responsible. Their "clamor" may have been inadvertently aided and abetted by the demand for their labor in factories during the First World War, as well as patronized by a few male writers such as John Stuart Mill (who in his introduction to Reeve's translation of Tocqueville chooses not to comment on this glorification of women's lofty destiny of domestic servitude, perhaps because he was not in very great disagreement with it). Responsibility for the redrawing of male and female social roles soon became a shared one, since it took men to pass the Nineteenth Amendment, giving women the vote and the right to stand for office. And the responsibility for the non-nomination of any woman for President and for the male club atmosphere of Senate committees such as the Judiciary Committee that the nation saw in memorable televised action in the Clarence Thomas hearings is also a shared one, shared by both female and male descendants of those superior self-sacrificial women whom Tocqueville praised and their enlightened menfolk. These men, like Kant, claimed one version of autonomy for themselves, and showed their respect for women by their confident expectation that they would take pride in voluntarily renouncing any aspirations to autonomy, in order to become more satisfactory helpmeets to men.

Kant writes that the inequality existing between substantial propertied males, with the right to vote, and the rest of their more "passive" and dependent fellow citizens, who lack civil personality, is "in no way opposed to their freedom and equality *as men* [*als Menschen*], who together make up a people," and that the laws enacted by the active members of the state "must not be contrary to the natural laws of freedom and of the equality of everyone in the people corresponding to this freedom, namely that anyone can work his way up from this passive condition to an active one."[25] But Mary Gregor may not have mistranslated in rendering *Menschen* as "men,"[26] since Kant elsewhere (in the *Anthropology*) makes it quite clear that he does not expect women to "work their way up" to civil personality.[27] Individual private tutors may advance to becoming schoolteachers, male professors in private universities to positions in state universities, but women seemed to Kant naturally doomed to be under the control and protection of men.[28] Nor is the inequality between active citizen and ruler seen as incompatible with the autonomy of each active citizen. Kant takes care to "prevent the republican constitution from being confused with the democratic one," and sees direct democracy as "necessarily a despotism," in that "it establishes an executive power through which all the citizens may make decisions about (and indeed against) the single individual without his consent ... this means that the general will is in contradiction with itself, and thus also with freedom."[29] Only by representative government can this contradiction be avoided, and even then, Kant writes, "the smaller the number of ruling persons in a state, and the greater their powers of representation, the more the constitution will approximate to its republican potentiality."[30] So Frederick the Great of Prussia might be taken to represent and serve his people. As ruler, he was separate from the body of active citizens

257

who theoretically constituted the legislature and had theoretically made a social contract giving their ruler his authority, retaining for themselves no shred of any right of rebellion against perceived abuses of such power. "The reason a people has a duty to put up with even what is held to be an unbearable abuse of supreme authority is that its resistance to the highest legislation can never be regarded as other than contrary to law ... For a people to be authorized to resist, there would have to be a public law permitting it to resist, that is, the highest legislation would have to contain a provision that it is not the highest and that makes the people, as subject, by one and the same judgment sovereign over him to whom it is subject. This is self-contradictory ..."[31] This argument of Kant's depends on the assumption that the supreme legislative authority is not the people but some sovereign power who theoretically unifies and acts for the people, that is, for the active citizens among them. "The legislative authority can belong only to the united will of the people."[32] But this union into one will is interpreted to mean general tacit consent to some de facto sovereign, and "a people should not *inquire* with any practical aim in view into the origin of the supreme authority to which it is subject."[33] The claim that there would be incoherence in a supreme law that contained a provision making it subject to some other will repeats, in a logicized version, the earlier claim of Hume's, in his essay "Of Passive Obedience," that no viable constitution can contain the explicit permission to overthrow it. But Hume, unlike Kant, distinguishes the legally recognized entitlement to rebel (which would be a self-destructive measure for any constitution to contain) from the *moral* liberty to resist tyrants. Since morality for him is not seen as a set of laws, he is not under the same pressure that Kant seems to be under to fit positive law neatly into a so-called moral law. He can coherently say that there can be no recognized right to rebel, but there are conditions in which it is not wrong to rebel. It is best not to try to spell those conditions out too precisely, Hume says, because that would give the impression that we *were* issuing a conditional right to rebel. In any case the conditions cannot be so precisely determined in a generalized context-neutral manner.[34] Kant's apparent endorsement of not merely a legal but a moral prohibition of rebellion depends upon the status of the rebelling people as *subjects*, not as sovereign. Their legislative role has been entrusted to a unifier of their wills, to their sovereign ruler, whom they are now obliged to obey. This seems to reduce the actual meaning of autonomy, even for those with civil personality, to something far short of giving to themselves the laws they are expected to obey. They are to obey the powers that be, and to give to the old claim that "all authority is from God" this sense: "the presently existing legislative authority ought to be obeyed, whatever its origin."[35] If supreme authorities are perceived to be abusing their power, imposing unjust taxes, or going to war against the interest of their subjects, subjects can organize to present their complaints, but not resist.[36]

This may seem an odd version of republicanism, and of the moral ideals behind it, to be taken as the model for a representative democratic republic such as this one, which began in a revolution. The notion of equality seems to be degraded by Kant into equality before a law enacted by some de facto sovereign legislative body, and some de facto ruler, to whose authority some mythical consent has been given by a mythical vote of all the propertied males, whose property and male privileges (including disciplining their wives) are taken to be protected by this law. Autonomy is degraded from law-making power into the right to complain against laws seen to be unjust. It is particularly degraded for servants and women, who are required to submit not just to the law and the magistrate but also to other human masters. But even for those deemed to have civil personality it seems an empty sham, if there is no guarantee of a voice in the actual election of lawmakers, let alone of a voice in determining the content of the laws. Can this be a variant of the republican ideal which inspired the Founding Fathers of this nation? Well, clearly they had no worries about the possible claims to autonomy of slaves or of women. So what exactly was and is that ideal?

Gordon Wood, in an article entitled "Classical Republicanism and the American Revolution," quotes from a letter written by John Adams in 1807, saying that he has never understood what republicanism is, and thinks no man ever has or will. He concluded that republicanism "may signify any thing, every thing, or nothing."[37] Wood himself finds that the Roman republican ideals of Cicero, Virgil, Sallust, and Tacitus had a great appeal for eighteenth-century social philosophers, including Hume, Montaigne, and Jefferson. The appeal lay both in the republican alternative to absolute monarchy, the preference for what Hume called "mixed" constitutions, and also in the civic humanist ideals of individual character, emphasizing as they did those of public service, sociability, and the ambition to civilize any remaining "barbarians." Wood quotes from Addison's play *Cato:*

> The Roman soul is bent on Higher views:
> To civilize the rude unpolish'd world,
> And lay it under the restraint of laws;
> To make Man mild, and sociable to Man;
> To cultivate the wild licentious savage—
> With wisdom, discipline, and the liberal arts;
> Th' embellishments of life: virtues like these
> Make human nature shine, reform the soul,
> And break our fierce barbarians into men.

This civic humanist ideal of civilized gentlemen spreading gentility and the rule of their law to licentious savages, whom they felt free to displace and dominate in their civilizing colonial ventures, is seen by Wood to come soon into conflict with the less aristocratic and rather rougher ideals of an increasingly egalitarian frontier and commercial society, of an increasingly "entrepreneurial-minded and bumptious American people," whose tie to one another was to be seen by Tocqueville not as classical virtue but as "Interest," and an interlocking of private and of public interest. Yet the republican ideal did not vanish, and has not vanished.

We get an interesting variant of it in Ronald Dworkin's concept of the "personification" and the "integrity" of a political community. It is of particular interest for my purposes here because Dworkin links these ideas to a concept of the collective responsibility of such a community. Taking the case of corporate responsibility as an example, he argues that we can and do hold corporations responsible for, say, defective products, even in cases where no individual can be blamed for failing in his or her special responsibilities within the corporation. We treat the corporation or other community as a moral entity, even while allowing that "the community has no independent metaphysical existence, that it is itself a creature of the practices of thought and language in which it figures."[38] This "deep personification" affects the practices of thought and language, in particular of responsibility-allocating language, that will be used. Even in bids for exoneration from responsibility for such scandals as

260

Watergate, Dworkin notes that the bumper stickers that appeared read not, "Don't blame me; I voted against Nixon," but "Don't blame me, I'm from Massachusetts," where the innocence claimed was not that of a powerless voter but of a proud member of a relatively innocent alternative and smaller community. We sometimes spontaneously take on a share in the collective responsibility of a group we belong to, even a very large and not very unified group. One rather ghastly example of this is given by Kant. Writing about appropriate forms of punishment for crimes such as murder and treason, he endorses the death penalty, but not the drawing, quartering, and exposing of the criminal's corpse, because, Kant writes, "that could make the humanity in the person suffering it into something abominable."[39] (Not, notice, the humanity of those who do such things, but of those to whom they may be done—it is public decency that is seen to be offended by them.) In a similar vein Kant notes, in the *Lectures on Ethics,* that women who were found guilty of poisoning their husbands were in England burned at the stake, rather than hanged and exposed on a gibbet, as both a more decent and an appropriately fearsome public death for those guilty of "insidious, underhand conduct . . . far viler than violence." The English punishment is apparently endorsed by Kant, "for if such conduct spread, no man would be safe from his wife."[40] (Kant seems to assume that all wives will have a nonmoral motive for such a master-destroying act, and indeed by his account of the rights of husbands they surely do. How convenient that the *Jus Talionis* supplies an appropriately fearsome penalty which at the same time does not offend too much against public decency. The veil of flames is to protect the public from unseemly visions of female depravity.) Kant takes it that we may identify, qua human beings, with the publicly shamed and dishonored criminal, and he also sees the people to have at least a residual responsibility to see to it that murderers are duly executed, so we may also identify with the executioner's deed and share responsibility for it.[41] These will be cases of the sort that Dworkin cites, of our reacting as involved members of some group, even when our direct responsibility (for the crime or for its punishment) may be most minimal.

Dworkin applies his idea of deep personification, and of group integrity, to political association, to co-citizenship. He writes, "Once we accept that our officials act in the name of a community of which we are all members, bearing a responsibility we therefore share, then this reinforces and sustains the character of collective guilt, our sense that we must feel shame as well as outrage when they act unjustly."[42] Part of the appeal of the personification idea to him is that it helps us to make sense of the weight given, in legal decision making, to very general principles such as "equal protection," enshrined in the Constitution. We do not simply change our laws to fit them to current perceptions of morality or justice; we strive to show that the changes are licensed or demanded by something already in our legal tradition. We strive for an "integrity" that is cross-generational. So changes on matters such as slavery and the rights of women are seen as changes demanded by something in the spirit of the laws we already had, however strained it may be to make that claim. Communities have principles, ideals of justice, that may, at a given time, be only imperfectly encoded in their laws and constitution. The procedure for amendment of the U.S. Constitution itself implicitly allows for this contrast between the content of the law and the principles expressed in that content. Dworkin sees commitment to integrity as a political virtue to rule out arbitrary differences of treatment and to safeguard us from legislation motivated only by political compromise. And he sees a particular version of political community to cohere best with the recognition of integrity as a political virtue. This is what he calls the "model of principle," which understands people to be "members of a genuine political community only when they accept that their fates are linked in the following strong way: they accept that they are governed by common principles, not just by rules hammered out in political compromise."[43] Politics then becomes "a theater of debate about which principles the community should adopt as a system,"[44] while also recognizing that each member's rights and duties "arise from the historical fact that his community has adopted that scheme, which is then special to it, not the assumption that he would have chosen it were the choice entirely his. In short, each accepts political integrity as a distinct political ideal . . ."[45] The choice has been made, by the Founding Fathers, and integrity demands that current citizens respect their choice, and fit their own reforms into the rhetoric inherited from their tradition.

The founders were "fathers," and Dworkin apparently has no time for currently fashionable he/she's in his text. It is a male citizen whose version of the ideal of integrity he gives, and one of the cases he uses to show how the ideal of integrity works is that of a father's authority over daughters in such matters as marriage. Since Dworkin wants to treat a political community as an association, then the structure of other nonvoluntary or not fully voluntary associations like the family is of natural interest to him. Taking the actual historical fact of a culture that believes "in good faith" that equality of concern for men and women requires "paternalistic protection for women in all aspects of family life," Dworkin supposes that a proper appreciation of the responsibilities of family membership would lead even someone who regards such paternalism as unjust to hold that "a daughter who marries against her father's wishes in this version of the story has something to regret. She owes him at least an accounting, and perhaps an apology . . ."[46]

This would seem to leave female citizens of this nation with a tremendous amount of apologizing to be done to the paternalistic culture whose laws and legislature[47] they are slowly changing. Integrity as an identification with the faith of our fathers may be a lot easier for white men than for blacks and women, the way Dworkin presents it. For there is no denying the sexism and racism[48] present in this tradition, just as there is no denying the sexism in Kant's much admired version of autonomy, which turns out on closer inspection to be a monopoly of a few representative propertied males. Those who are latecomers to civil personality, to the right to liberty and political participation, will tend to see the discontinuity more than the continuity in amendments like the Fifteenth and Nineteenth.

Still, even passive citizenship had its responsibilities, and those of us who accept Dworkin's plea for use of the concept of cross-generational shared responsibility, and who are women, will take some responsibility for the long toleration of our own domination and relegation to the category of passive subjects. Adult daughters who trusted fathers to look after their interests, wives who trusted husbands to vote for them or to represent them in legislative assemblies, bear the responsibility for their foolish entrustings, just as much as the trusted are accountable for their abuses of their trust. We allocate individual responsibility by our trusting and our acceptance of trust, but the responsibility for the allocation rests on both trusters and trusted,[49] as well as on those distrustful lookers-on who deplore the way discretionary powers are being distributed to individuals and to agencies, yet do nothing to stop it or to try to reform the system. We share the responsibility for the way we allow responsibility to be individually divvied up, and so we cannot escape some of the blame when that individual responsibility is badly exercised.

Divvying up responsibility—"you see to the luggage while I pay the cab driver"—is one way to share tasks that we both want done, and normally such forward-looking division of responsibility will be accompanied by a similar allocation of backward-looking responsibility.[50] So if something goes wrong—I let myself be cheated by not counting the change the cab driver gives me, you abandon one piece of luggage because your bad back makes carrying all of it at once too painful for you, and that piece disappears—we may each take the blame for our separate failures to get our separate agreed tasks done competently. But if we both knew about your bad back and my tendency to be over-trusting as a receiver of change, then should we divvy up the blame in this way? Who is responsible for the bad task allocation? Both of us, equally? Or I more, because I was proposer, you a mere accepter of my proposal? In as far as financial loss is involved, we will have to come to some agreement about how it is to be shared, and it is certainly not obvious that I should accept the mere ten dollar loss on the cab fare, while you fork out several hundred dollars to cover the cost of replacing the missing case and its contents. And if your bad back is injured by the initial attempt to cope with all the luggage, it will surely be unfair to make you bear the larger financial loss as well as the pain—not because you were the mere accepter of a plan that I suggested, but rather because we were in this together, both at fault for acting on a bad voluntarily entered-into cooperative scheme.

The intended point of this example is to illustrate that there is always a question not just of responsibility for discharging one's accepted task in an acceptable manner but of accepting the task in the first place, of going along with the scheme that allotted one this particular task. In the example I gave there was no coercion to complicate the matter: where the task allocator possesses significant threat advantage over the other parties, so that their agreement to the proposed division of labor is not a free agreement, then of course the proposer of the plan bears a special responsibility, especially when his proposal includes provisions to see to it that he keeps the upper hand. But even then, the other parties bear some responsibility

264

for going along with the bad cooperative scheme. Women who let men keep the role of initiator and decision maker, despite their proven abuse of the powers which that role allocation gives them, are not merely victims of the oppressive scheme but co-conspirators, even when their agreement to their own role of meek helpmeet is not entirely unforced. (If the women are forced, of course, then they are purely victims.) Just as, if you knew of my unreliability as handler of the purse, you could and should have risked my anger by stepping in to say "No, better if I do the paying and you take the luggage," so women might have been better advised to risk the ire of the master sex by disputing their right to rule. As I, if I knew of your bad back, should not have proposed that you carry the luggage, so men, if they believed that women were indeed more "ductile" than men, should for that very reason not have encouraged them to take on roles that carried the risk of disempowerment, roles that might have long-term ill-effects on their moral spines. The responsibility for the continuation of schemes of cooperation that progressively disable some of the cooperators and progressively concentrate coercive power in the hands and voices of others is almost always shared, and is never easy to divide out without remainder into individual portions. Nor, where past evils are concerned, is there any particular point in trying to allocate individual blame, unless what we are doing is trying to recompense living victims of a bad scheme by taking from the living victimizers. When our main goal is to change the cooperative scheme for the better, we may adopt affirmative action measures toward those who as a class were disabled by the old bad scheme, and we may even engage in some temporary "reverse discrimination" in order to get the scheme effectively changed. But we should see such measures as attempts to end dangerous concentrations of power, attempts to empower those who were disempowered by the old scheme, not as attempts to do individual justice, to give to each what that one deserves. If we, oppressors and oppressed, accept a joint responsibility for the bad old scheme, then we need not look at the disempowerment of the old masters as their "penalty," nor at the new advantages of the formerly disadvantaged class as something that each one of them "deserves," as compensation for earlier mistreatment. For individual persons in that class may have avoided suffering the usual disadvantages—some women were not oppressed, some men were not oppressors.

If we insist on clinging to the idea that moral responsibility must divide without remainder into the bit that is mine and not yours and the other bits that belong exclusively to other specific individuals, then not only will we limit the sorts of shared action we engage in, but we will drastically limit our ability to reform our inherited schemes of cooperation for the better. We will bog down in endless disputes about just who should get what portion of the blame for past evils, about just who deserves what compensatory advantages now. Kant in the *Metaphysics of Morals* writes that ownership is a concept correlative with that of a noumenal self—a property right is *possessio noumenon.*[51] Kant is speaking here of rights to external things, and he believes that such things, particularly land, were originally possessed in common *(communio fundi originaria),* private ownership being consequent upon a general will to allow individual claims by occupation. What Kant believes with respect to which tasks are a given person's own tasks, and whether originally there was a common task, from which private tasks were divided out by general agreement, is less clear. Rawls, who invokes the idea of a common fund of human talents,[52] may be adapting the Kantian concept of common fund of at least some crucial components of human life, human work, and human responsibility. (Did Kant believe that there was a common fund of reason, from which your reason and mine derive? Can a Kantian take a social view of reason? Did Kant believe that the respect-worthy humanity in each person is a derivate of some species-being that commands respect? The answer is not clear.) But it is hard to see how essentially *individual* responsibility for action can be geared to essentially *collective* rights to goods, and to essentially shared responsibility for the "general will" that divvies up the individual tasks and goods which particular persons get as their individual allotments. If the noumenal self is an individualist, he will insist on dividing up what was common, blurring the traces of the act of division, and disowning responsibility for this crucial action as well as for maintaining what it brought about.

The Kantian form of individualism that has been and is still being appropriated in the American tradition has two fatal and connected flaws. It has no account of really shared responsibility, but only for pooled or passed-along individual autonomy and responsibility. Its version of the way the realm of ends legislates for itself, far from providing the basis for a democratic society, in fact degenerates into lawgiving by some elite, accompanied by willing subjection of the rest. And when we look in Kant's writings and in most of the tradition that honors him to see just how this legislating elite is to be constituted, we find there the fairly undisguised "integrity" of a patriarchal and sexist tradition. If we are to avoid the deficiencies of the mind and the perversity of the heart which this Kantian tradition incorporates, then it is time that we stopped paying deferential lip service to Immanuel Kant or, indeed, to any other preachers of the piety that consists in reverence for the faith of our patriarchal fathers.[53] If we do turn to continental Europe for our social theorists, we should turn not just to the Prussian who glorified individualism but to the Frenchman who criticized it and to those who rejected the sexism of which both of them were guilty. We must mine our multifarious traditions for worthier versions of equality, of mutual respect, and of how responsibility is to be shared than the versions that we find in Kant. If we cannot find them in any of our inherited traditions, we should be willing to be called revolutionaries. In the American tradition, that surely is not a dishonorable label.

thirteen

MORALISM AND CRUELTY: REFLECTIONS ON HUME AND KANT

We know what Kantians should think about Hume's version of morality, since Kant more or less told us that. But what Humeans should think about Kant's version is more open to free inquiry. David Wiggins[1] has suggested that Humeans could and should take over a naturalized version of the categorical imperative, covering behavior that expresses natural as well as artificial virtues. My view is that it is not so easy to detach Kantian obligations from their metaphysical and quasi-theological foundations or from their political and practical implications, as Kant himself perceived them. I shall in this essay look not primarily at what a Humean would say about the differences between what Hume and Kant took to be the content of an enlightened morality (for example, at their differing attitudes toward pride, and pleasures of the flesh) but at what is being relied upon to pressure people into conformity to the morality in question, at what the two philosophers advocate in the way of responses to what is perceived to fall short of the moral standards which they advocate. For the Humean, and I think also for the Kantian, what has to bear its own survey is not just the normative morality which has been endorsed, but its foundations or "principles," as Hume calls them, and also the whole practice of inculcating and to some measure enforcing the morality in question. I shall focus on the question of the humaneness or cruelty of the whole morality, and this is a Humean focus. The Kantian may not care so much about our findings here, since she, if she is true to the master, regards masturbation and suicide as the very worst things a person can do,[2] whereas it was cruelty that Hume regarded as the worst vice.[3] (Both Judith Shklar[4] and Richard Rorty[5] have reaffirmed this Humean moral judgment.) I shall look at the relative cruelty of Hume's and Kant's versions of morality and its sanctions. I leave it to the Kantians to balance my obviously Humean bias by a return inquiry into the relatively self-abusive or suicidal nature of the two versions of morality. I shall also leave aside the very tricky question of just what should count as cruelty. Spinoza seems to have defined it as doing evil to those one loves, that is, to those whom one perceives to have done one good, and this is such a disturbing definition that some translators take it that what he must have meant was doing evil to those loved by those of us who are applying the label "cruelty."[6] I take torture of humans or animals to be paradigm cases of cruelty, so I would not want as restrictive a definition as Spinoza's, however we translate it, but just how close to torture the pain inflicted in cruel treatment has to be to count as "cruel" is impossible to get agreement on. Nor is there agreement about how to relate psychic hurt to physical agony.

Alexis de Tocqueville, discussing impeachment for misconduct by American public officials, first contrasted the "mildness" of this response to wrongdoing with European tribunals' assumed or traditional rights to inflict a more violent penalty, such as execution. He noted that the very severity of the European penalty inhibited such tribunals from acting against officials except in extreme cases. Then he corrected himself, saying that the milder American sentence, easier to pronounce since it left the wrongdoer "uninjured in life and limb," was nevertheless "fatally severe to the majority of those upon whom it is inflicted ... ordinary offenders will dread it as a condemnation that destroys their position in the world, casts a blight upon their honour, and condemns them to a shameful inactivity."[7] I, like Tocqueville, will contrast apparently severer responses to perceived vice and wrongdoing with milder Humean alternatives, then correct myself to wonder if the apparently milder alternative is not also "fatally severe," especially given how easy it is to administer, and then I shall correct my correction. My focus will not be on response to vice in public officials, but to vice in ordinary people, and of course my contrast will not be between European severe measures and at first sight milder American measures, but between severe Kantian responses and apparently milder Humean responses.

Allan Gibbard[8] has given new life to the old distinction between a guilt morality and a shame morality, and up to a point I think we can see Kant's as a guilt morality, Hume's as a shame morality. Kant explicitly likens negative moral judgment to a finding of "guilty" in a law court,[9] although his words for what the guilty person then feels are noncommittal between shame and guilt.[10] Gibbard sees the feeling of guilt to be a way of anticipating, and so placating, others' anger at our faults, and he sees anger to be a reaction we are stuck with. "Anger, it seems, will be with us whatever we decide."[11] The best that an enlightened morality can do is to redirect it, to try to make it conform to reflective norms for anger. And anger, with guilt-feelings "meshed" to it, is "tied to the voluntary, and to motivations at the time of action. They are costly, but they work discriminately where motivation makes a difference; thus they can be cost-effective."[12] This of course is not a very Kantian way to look at the appropriateness of feelings of guilt, since the cost-effectiveness which is appealed to here is not efficacy in making people what Kant would regard as morally better, deserving of happiness, but simply efficacy in fostering "peace and cooperation."[13] Anger is to be used to limit itself, to cut down on the occasions when it makes sense to be angry. Hume at the end of the *Treatise* writes that a sympathy-based morality will be superior to other versions of morality in that "not only virtue must be approv'd of, but also the sense of virtue: And not only that sense, but also the principles, from whence it is deriv'd. So that nothing is presented on any side, but what is laudable and good."[14] By "principles" here is meant sources, what Hume had earlier in the paragraph called "rise and origin." Extensive sympathy is, he claims, a "noble source." But if the disapprobation of vice which flows from that source is a form of anger or anticipated anger at injury to ourselves or those with whom we have sympathy, then morality itself may look less great and good. Hume had earlier written that "where these angry passions rise up to cruelty, they form the most detested of all vices." He had just allowed that angry passions are not always vicious, indeed that "the want of them, on some occasions, may even be a proof of weakness and imbecillity."[15] To the extent that anger is a part of Humean morality, it will indeed introduce a "disagreeable" element into what he had hoped would be thoroughly "great and good," but it need not make that morality internally incoherent, if moral "greatness" requires proper pride, and that rules out complacency at injury.

In Hume's version of morality, some moralized version of anger at injury will be expressed through the procedures of law enforcement. Magistrates are invented to provide "the *execution* and *decision* of justice,"[16] and some occasional shows of magisterial wrath may be needed to prevent any appearance of "weakness and imbecillity," which would be quite fatal flaws in a magistrate. Hume believed that revenge was an instinctive human passion, so that "there is a certain indulgence due to human nature in this respect."[17] Gibbard is echoing Hume when he writes that anger will be with us whatever we decide. "Anger and hatred are passions inherent in our very frame and constitution," Hume writes.[18] The best we can do is try to prevent them "rising up" to cruelty, and to "bestow our applauses" on those whose anger appears "only in a low degree," enough to show proper spirit, but not enough to evoke sympathy with the victims of their anger, let alone to make sympathetic bystanders come to hate them for their very hatred and anger. Hume at this point appeals to hatred as a control on hatred.[19] Angry cruelty will provoke, in those who feel pity for its miserable victims, "a stronger hatred than we are sensible of on any other occasion."[20] Hume may speak for a minority within the party of humankind in this finding. His own detestation of cruelty, including cruel punishment by magistrates or other masters, is amply evidenced in his writings.

Both in the *History of England* and in his essay "Of the Immortality of the Soul"[21] he shows an almost obsessive interest in the nasty details of the forms of punishment human punishers have thought up and acted out, perhaps because these human phenomena are not well accounted for by his version of human nature. The Romans, he tells us, punished confessed parricides by putting them in a sack along with an ape, a dog, and a serpent, and throwing them in the Tiber, but humane judges such as Augustus would encourage the accused not to confess, or to retract earlier confessions, so as to get merely a death sentence, not the especially cruel one designed for self-admitted parricides. (Augustus would in the final interrogation of a convicted parricide ask, *"You surely did not kill your father?"* gently putting a saving lie into the accused's mouth for him, and

271

Hume says, "this lenity suits our natural ideas of *RIGHT*." It suits his ideas, perhaps, but not everyone's, by any means. By his ideas of right, it cannot conceivably be right of any God to inflict "eternal punishment for the temporary offences of so frail a creature as man."[22]) He tells us in the *History* of the brutal revenge exacted by church officials (Archbishop Odo's men) on the newly crowned Queen Elgiva, when they "burned her face with a red hot iron, in order to destroy that fatal beauty, which had seduced Edwy," the young king who had dared to defy the canon law prohibitions by marrying his second cousin. She was exiled to Ireland, and on her later attempt to return to her husband in England was seized again by the odious Odo and his men, and "the most cruel death was requisite to satiate their vengeance. She was hamstringed; and expired a few days after at Glocester in the most acute torments." Hume goes on to comment that "the English, blinded with superstition, instead of being shocked with this inhumanity, exclaimed that the misfortunes of Edwy and his consort were a just judgment for their dissolute contempt of the ecclesiastical statutes."[23]

By some versions of the *Jus Talionis,* Elgiva's initial punishment, the disfiguring of her face, would count as appropriate, a fitting of punishment to crime. Kant, who believes that courts of justice should administer the *Jus Talionis,* returning like for like as far as this is possible and seemly, endorses the public humiliation of the convicted humiliator, the killing of convicted murderers, the castration of rapists and pederasts, and the total exclusion from human society of those found guilty of bestiality. In the last three cases of "unnatural crimes," the ideal of penal "reciprocity" cannot be carried out, since to rape the rapist and so on would themselves be "punishable crimes against humanity," so human magistrates have, with Kant's approval, fallen back on a different sort of appropriateness of penalty, and have appointed not just official killers of killers but official castrators and deporters[24] (and perhaps wielders of red-hot irons for those who use their beauty to seduce others into incest). His moral approval of these adjuncts to just human judges is expressed with near-biblical eloquence: "The principle of punishment is a categorical imperative, and woe to him who crawls through the serpentine windings [*Schlangenwindungen*] of the doctrine of happiness in order to discover something that releases the criminal from punishment or even reduces its amount!"[25] The rightness of killing killers is as clear to him as, for Hume, was the rightness of intense hatred of cruel angry hatred. "Even if a civil society were to be dissolved by the consent of all its members (e.g., if a people inhabiting an island decided to separate and disperse throughout the world), the last murderer remaining in prison would first have to be executed, so that each has done to him what his deeds deserve and blood guilt does not cling to the people for not having insisted upon this punishment."[26] Although Kant is perfectly clear that only God and the magistrate have the right to fix what punishment is appropriate and to punish, nevertheless "the people" will have "blood guilt" if murderers are not executed. One wonders about the moral quality of mind and heart of the moral philosopher who is so sure of who deserves death, castration, and ostracism, and so sure that rational social contracts will provide jobs for executioners, castrators, and deporters. Or should we (would we) mitigate the blame by wondering how a spokesman for the voice of reason could so uncritically take over the time-honored customs of his own society, and the Germanic concept of *Blutschuld*, equating them with deliverances of reason? Kant did this not merely with punitive customs but also with other customs, such as the subordination of women, and his morally decent contemporary defenders have their work cut out separating what they see to be his correct from his incorrect applications of his own supreme moral imperative. (Might it be that he was deluded about most or all the applications he gives of the categorical imperative? But then why suppose that he would have accepted it, if it were not seen to be in reflective equilibrium with approved Pietist customs?)

In "Of the Immortality of the Soul" Hume writes: "Were one to go round the world with an intention of giving a good supper to the righteous and a sound drubbing to the wicked, he would frequently be embarrassed in his choice, and would find, that the merits of most men and women scarcely amount to the value of either."[27] This gives us a pretty good indication of the very limited extent of Hume's own disposition to follow up what he calls "blame" by punishment and praise by reward. In this passage Hume is imagining some overall assessment of persons, some human analogue to the final judgment and sentencing that some believers in the immortality of the soul profess to expect—a judgment in which all a person's traits, actions, inactions, fantasies, and daydreams are taken into account, the good and the bad aspects weighed against each other, and a summary judgment reached as to whether a given person counts among the sheep or the goats. Neither ordinary criticism of an individual's character nor human punishment is of this summary pass-fail sort, but is given fault by fault, crime by detected crime. But hurtful criticism hurts the whole person, not just the faulty aspect of the person, and similarly the whole punished person suffers because of some one action, displaying some limited number of the agent's character traits. We cannot localize the target of the punitive response, restricting the hurt to the criminal traits of the agent, and leaving the rest unscathed. We hurt the whole person. Hume in the *Treatise* wrote some much criticized sentences about the need to believe that a "temporary and perishing" criminal action flows from something "durable and constant" in the person, something still there "infecting the whole character," in order for the person to be the proper object of punishment. But, unless there is unity in the vices,[28] even lasting bad traits need not "infect the whole character," and in punishing the habitual thief we may thereby be inflicting suffering on someone who is also a loving parent. Those who are taken to have the right to punish put the virtues of the accused into the scales of justice only if they provide evidence that the accused could not have done the crime (character witnesses), or provide some excuse for the admitted crime—if, say, the thief was stealing to feed his children, so that the virtue of parental devotion had "infected the whole character," including the thieving tendencies, which themselves contaminate the parental devotion. But this mutual adaptation need not be the way in which virtues and vices coexist in one person, and Hume's imaginary separation out of the wicked, deserving a drubbing, from the righteous, deserving a good supper, is not based on consideration only of internally "infectious" character traits, but on all of them. We can read his *Treatise* remarks about the propriety of directing punishment only at the surviving culprit as a recognition of the intrinsic difficulty of making punishment fair. The "object" of our punishment will always be a "whole character," whereas what we intend to hit out at is one or a few bad character traits. We always affect more than there is good reason to affect. We typically hurt and injure the criminal's virtues when we strike at her vices. Punishment is one thing that typically does "infect the whole character," not to mention its effects on the punished person's dependents.

274

Some horrendous forms of human punishment, decreed by versions of the *Lex Talionis,* can be charitably explained as vain attempts to localize the hurt inflicted on the criminal. Chopping off the thief's thieving hand leaves the rest of him theoretically intact. Castrating the pederast and the rapist in the same way might be seen to restrict the injury to the offending member. In all these cases, of course, the whole person is in fact hurt and injured, the injury being a maiming. With offending parts of the body, this hypothetical isolation of one "guilty" part from other less involved parts is theoretically possible, but when the focus of our blame is not the outer action but the inner character trait, the separation out of the real culprit, so that it can become the main focus of the punitive act, is much more difficult. Even the keenest of punishers will have difficulty persuading themselves that they have succeeded in focusing only on *mens rea,* when for example they punish attempted murder less severely than successful murder.[29]

With very good reason, then, does Hume emphasize that moral disapprobation is not and should not be seen as a preliminary step on the road to deserved punishment. For finding any morally acceptable punishments is not so easy, nor is it easy to find forms of punishment that really can be seen to have an eye to future good, and so in keeping with Hobbes's seventh law of nature, a law which the Kantian in any case seems to reject. Kant's is an overtly moralistic morality, holding us to account for all failures in which our faulty will has played a role, encouraging us to anticipate a just judgment by an all-seeing God who endorses the *Jus Talionis* and properly responds to our radical evil with eternal damnation,[30] unless his divine right of pardon is mercifully exercised. Human conscience is to be a stand-in for the just divine judge, but not for the merciful pardoner, so forgiving ourselves is not encouraged. We are to demand moral perfection of ourselves, as God demands it of us. We are to be punctilious about leaving it to magistrates to punish people for breaches of their perfect obligations, and leaving it to others to demand, each of herself, her own perfection. We are to show some concern for the happiness of our fellows, but only as far as the moral law allows room for that concern. Punishment will be left to God and the magistrate, but we will have understanding for each other's self-accusatory consciences, and no sympathy for any self-pardoning proclivities. The Kantian conscience accuses, recognizes that punishment is deserved, but leaves it to God or the magistrate to inflict it. Monkish self-laceration is definitely out, for the Kantian as much as for the Humean, and the right to whip others is for the Kantian to be a jealously guarded monopoly. The response to guilt which is appropriate for the individual is repentance and reform, and in *Religion within the Limits of Reason Alone* Kant seems to merge the divine just punishment with what is involved in the individual's sincere repentance and attempts at reformation. "The coming forth from the corrupted into the good disposition is, in itself (as 'the death of the old man,' 'the crucifying of the flesh'), a sacrifice and an entrance upon a long train of life's ills."[31] Thus "the infliction of punishment can, consistently with divine wisdom, take place ... *during* the change of heart itself."[32] Damnation and salvation are to go on simultaneously in one life, in this world, here and now.

This odd Pauline strain in Kant, in the *Religion,* is found also in his equally strange attempt, in section 53 of the *Doctrine of Virtue,* on "Ethical Gymnastic," to combine discipline with obligatory joy. This self-discipline is to be a self-transformation program, a slaying of monsters within, a coping with radical evil. Its aim, Kant says, is to get oneself in a position to do one's duty cheerfully, without feeling it to be against the grain. We are to practice subduing our sinful natural impulses or temptations to adopt wrongful maxims, so that, when they "threaten morality," we will be able successfully to control them, and to do so without painful effort, gloom, and sullenness. Good cheer seems to be a meta-duty to the Kantian—it is the duty to do our other duties with cheerfulness and without any resentful sense of sacrifice. "[W]hat is not done with pleasure but merely as compulsory service has no inner worth for one who attends to his duty in this way."[33] This is the ultimate in deontology—a string of commands, of which the last reads, "Enjoy obeying the above commands." A real-life example of this sort of ethical gymnastic is to be found in the public code of Singapore, where to the many injunctions issued by the authorities to the people and proclaimed in large letters on billboards throughout the city ("Don't spit," "No gum-chewing," etc.) was recently added: "Have some spontaneous fun!"[34] One Kantian moral imperative apparently tells the moral subject to rejoice, to have fun doing her duty, to be *"wacker und fröhlich."* This could be seen as deontology's bad conscience, its backhanded concession to a more Epicurean ethics. But it is not at all clear that this extra duty not to let duty appear unattractive to one, this duty to have a joyful heart, to achieve a resurrection after one's self-crucifixion, really makes Kantian morality more joyful. Duty's voice does not become less stern just because one of the commands it issues is "Obey these commands joyfully," "Turn your Good Friday into an Easter Sunday." Nietzsche's comment in the *Genealogy of Morals* (one of the milder of his comments on what he called that "catastrophic spider," Kant) seems fair enough: that a bad smell of sado-masochism, the reek of blood and torture, lingers on the categorical imperative.[35]

There is an interesting qualification that Kant makes on the rightness of the official killing of killers, one that shows the close link he seemed to see between the voice of reason when it enunciates and applies the categorical imperative and the mores of his own Prussian society. He is not sure that intentional killings done to defend the killer's "honor" really do deserve the death penalty. The cases he discusses are killings by military men engaged in duels, and killings by women of their illegitimate newborn infants. I should think that Kant's current defenders and admirers must find the latter discussion particularly difficult to recast in a sympathetic way. Kant's reason for advocating leniency toward those unmarried mothers found guilty of infanticide is not a humane concern for the mothers' situation, faced as they were with social disgrace, but rather the legalistic point that the victim of the killing in such cases is not a person whom the law need protect. "A child that comes into the world apart from marriage is born outside the law (for the law is marriage) and therefore outside the protection of the law. It has, as it were, stolen [*eingeschlichen*] into the commonwealth (like contraband merchandise), so that the commonwealth can ignore its existence (since it rightly [*billig*] should not have come to exist in this way), and can therefore also ignore its annihilation."[36] Any killing of a human being deserves death, but in this case the appropriate avenger is God, not the human magistrate, since the magistrate's job is restricted to protecting people who have been born under a valid license. At this point in his moral deliberations, Kant seems to forget his earlier edict that "a man . . . can never be put among the objects of rights to things [*Sachenrecht*]."[37] Unlicensed children are now likened to contraband goods. They are to be treated as innocent outlaws, denied any protection of law. (I emphasize that Kant is speaking here not of aborted fetuses but of illegitimate children of any age, although the mother's presumed motive for the killing, concealing her shame, will normally operate only for newborns.)

This is a pretty shocking and cruel bit of Kantian moral reasoning, cruel in its apparent disregard of the fate of innocent victims. It might at first sight charitably be taken to show a humane concern for the cruelty of the operation of a public shame morality on the disgraced mothers, a sentiment more like Lorca's in *The House of Bernarda Alba*. But only at first sight. Of the "honor of womanhood," soiled by extramarital sex, and of military honor, defended in duels, Kant writes, "both [are] indeed true honor which is incumbent as duty on each in each of these two classes of people."[38] What he finds "barbaric" in eighteenth-century Prussia is not the public's attitude to illegitimacy but the misfit between ideals of honor and actual behavior. Women's sexual drive sometimes proves stronger than the moral incentive of honor, and so there is a failure of the institutions regulating sex and reproduction to do their job adequately. Here we might recall Hume's words: "All human creatures, especially of the female sex, are apt to over-look remote motives in favor of any present temptation: The temptation is here the strongest imaginable: Its approaches are insensible and seducing ..."[39] and so on, as Hume explains the conspicuously artificial duty of female chastity. As Hume presents the matter, the "barbaric" element lies more in the artificial restraint, the punishment of "bad fame" and "a peculiar degree of shame," imposed not only by interested husbands and guardians of family virtues but also by "batchelors, however debauch'd."[40]

Hume in the passages on chastity I have just quoted is clearly invoking shame, not guilt, as the enforcer of the demands of the version of conventional morality that he is here considering. And shame, or "bad fame," comes into play here, he suggests, precisely because of the lax standards of evidence the world is content with, in imposing "bad fame." It is "inflicted by the world upon surmizes, and conjectures, and proofs, that wou'd never be receiv'd in any court of judicature."[41] Courts cannot give men the security they crave concerning the chastity of their wives, and so of the paternity of their children, because legal proof is "difficult to meet with in this subject." So instead of the threat of a finding of legal guilt, on adequate evidence, those who have "an interest in the chastity of women" resort to the threat of bad fame, where the standards of evidence are conveniently loose. Normally, with the "artificial" vices, magistrates and courts, with their appropriately strict standards of evidence, will be what determines the display of a vice, so chastity is exceptional among the Humean artificial virtues in the informality of its enforcement.

Gibbard also has something interesting to say about shame, a reactive attitude often contrasted with guilt. He takes shame to have a looser tie to the voluntary, and so to others' anger at our voluntary actions. It is a reaction that is meshed not with others' anger but with their disdain or derision, and so it might be felt at a great range of facts about oneself, from parentage and schooling, shabby clothing, deformed feet, and lower-class accents to ignominious failures of all sorts, be they social gaffes, intellectual mis-moves, or displays of cowardice and other vices of character. Teenagers might feel shame for their virginity, along with guilt for their lying denials of it. Kant speaks in the *Lectures on Ethics* on the possibility of feeling shame for one's piety, when in "wholly wicked and wholly defiant company."[42] What people feel shame for will depend on what they expect others to sneer or laugh at or treat as grounds for excluding them from some charmed circle of initiates. Shame is a very potent passion, sometimes driving its victims to suicide, sometimes to amazing self-transformations. As Gibbard writes, "To cope with disdain . . . we need either to withdraw or to display our powers."[43] To display them, we first must have them, and perhaps acquire them, and so, when shame motivates, it may motivate some self-empowerment, "a program of redemption."[44]

Shame, as Gibbard understands it, can extend to all the faults that might lead others to despise us or to exclude us. It can include stupidity as much as pettiness, flabby muscles as much as cowardice. Its sanctions seem even more threatening than those of the Kantian guilt-for-bad-choice morality, since it can extend what we are to suffer for, and to attempt to change for the better, from the will, even the fairly omnipresent Kantian will, to those aspects of ourselves which Kant contrasts with will—our physique, our innate appetites, and our native intelligence. Is this not an even more threatening version of the sort of sanction faced by faulty persons? And, to come to Hume, does not his list of vices include many that Kant would not treat as falling within the scope of the will—stupidity, inarticulateness, lack of wit? (He does not include bodily deformities.) Who would not opt for Kant's version of the moral world, if the alternative is a social world with some version of a shame morality, where each faulty person faces this threat: somehow get rid of your character fault, or rid us of your faulty presence, or stay and put up with our disdain, mockery, and avoidance. But as we have seen, at places in his writings such as the discussion of the penalty for infanticide by unmarried women, Kant seems to merge in his version of morality the harsher features that Gibbard finds typical of guilt and of shame. The accusing voice of Kantian conscience will always focus not only on voluntary actions but on maxims and motives, and on any disabilities that better earlier choices might have lessened: "However evil a man has been up to the very moment of an impending free act (so that evil has actually become custom or second nature) it was not only his duty to have been better [in the past], it is *now* still his duty to better himself. To do so must be within his power, and if he does not do so, he is susceptible of, and subjected to, imputability in the very moment of that action, just as much as though, endowed with a predisposition to good (which is inseparable from freedom), he had stepped out of a state of innocence into evil. Hence we cannot inquire into the temporal origin of this deed, but solely into its rational origin . . ."[45] The *scope* of Kantian guilt is almost as wide as the notoriously wide scope of Humean disapprobation. Among psychological traits, only innate intellectual disabilities escape it, whereas Hume lets them in. "Who did ever say, except by way of irony, that such a one was a man of great virtue, but an egregious blockhead?"[46] The Kantian conscience will not accuse itself of blockheadedness or lack of wit, unless they have been self-induced, but its scope is otherwise pretty wide, and, as we have seen, he seems to assume that societal concepts of "honor" will reinforce what private conscience requires of us.

Are crippling guilt and effacing shame and their mixtures the only options, as far as response to one's moral failings goes? If so, then Nietzsche is surely right, that morality is not just a peculiar but an intrinsically cruel, indeed a sado-masochistic institution. And if Hume's version of moral disapprobation is tantamount to shaming, with accusing left for law courts, whose magistrates' authority gets endorsement by general moral approbation, then the Humean shame morality may look even worse than the Kantian guilt morality, for now it looks unfair, as well as cruel, very likely to shame its victims on shoddy evidence, on mere "surmizes and conjectures." (It regularly judges inner quality on the basis of "external signs,"[47] so seems to have to employ some conjecture in most of its workings.) Before looking to see if it is guilty of greater-than-Kantian cruelty, I first want to give a bit more evidence that Hume does equate moral disapprobation more with what Gibbard calls disdain and derision than with any analogue of a verdict of guilty in some court, be it inner conscience, divine judgment, or informal jury of one's peers. Although Hume's use of the words "blame" and "judgment" for the deliverances of the moral sentiment might seem to suggest a Kantian law-court model for moral assessment, his detailed accounts of that sentiment effectively cancel that suggestion. When he is trying to persuade us to accept some of the more controversial items on his list of moral virtues and vices, he appeals to what we would be gratified or "mortified" to have others discern in us, to what "renders a man either an object of esteem and affection, or of hatred and contempt; every habit or sentiment or faculty, which, if ascribed to any person ... may enter into any panegyric or satire of his character and manners."[48] "Contempt" is a word used very often in the second *Enquiry* for our spontaneous attitude to a person displaying vices. The relevant words for moral evaluation, for Hume, are "*honourable* and *shameful, lovely* and *odious, noble* and *despicable.*"[49] The untrustworthy person is "contemptible, no less than odious ...,"[50] for he neglects his own interest as well as that of others. The fool must expect "disgust" from everyone except his doting parents.[51] "Aversion and disgust" are directed at those of "melancholy, dejected, sullen, anxious temper."[52] Those who, by their loquacity, deprive others of their turn to talk, must expect to be regarded "with a very evil eye."[53] "A gloomy, hairbrained enthusiast ... will scarcely ever be admitted ... into intimacy and society, except by those who are as delirious and dismal as himself."[54] Awareness of our own folly will "mortify," and memory of past "stupidity or ill manners" will bring "a secret sting or compunction."[55] "[C]owardice, meanness, levity, anxiety, impatience, folly, and many other qualities of the mind, might appear ridiculous and deformed, contemptible and odious, though independent of the will."[56] Hume is not denying that there are different reactions to different vices, horror for some, indignation and hatred for others, contempt or derision for yet others, but the range of reactive terms he uses definitely falls more into what Gibbard treats as the disdain and shame family than the anger and guilt family, which is appropriate since the vices Hume lists include many that are judged to be "independent of the will." The picture we get is of morality as public scorn and faultfinding as well as "applause" and "panegyrics." Hume elsewhere refers to the Roman custom of making elderly bachelors who had not contributed their bit to the supply and rearing of new citizens parade naked through the streets, to be jeered at by their more useful fellow citizens. Moral evaluation, Hume-style, may seem a bit like this, a public baring of an individual's failures, a whole series of scarlet letters to be worn by almost everyone, so that others may deride us, shun us, disdain us. But merely to draw this implication is to show it to be incoherent. We cannot *all* be shunned, and even if we can all be occasionally derided, this must be merely occasional. Unless just a few of us display any Humean vices in a high degree, then we simply cannot make avoidance our normal response to perceived vice in others.

In his essay "Of Some Remarkable Customs," Hume looks at practices of ostracism as employed in ancient Athenian democracy, and his interest in that can be seen to be appropriate for a moralist whose preferred method of moral criticism seems to be disdain, derision, and withdrawal rather than imitation law enforcement. What he emphasizes there is that this response, of banishment from Athens, on the face of it a very cruel one, was reserved for those who had proposed a law for enactment by the people, and who by their persuasive powers had got them to pass it, but that law, once in operation, proved generally hateful so that the voters came to regret their support for it. Ostracism was a check on demagoguery, one esteemed by Aeschines to be obviously essential to the subsistence of any direct democracy. Hume calls it a "remarkable" custom. Remarking it is supposed to show us that "all general maxims in politics ought to be established with great caution." For my purposes now, what is worth remarking is that the general maxim that this case should make us cautious about is presumably one disapproving of such a cruel and unusual penalty for influential politicians who are judged by hindsight to have made unwise public initiatives, however well-meaning they may have been. Hume clearly worried about the cruelty, and the wisdom, of any form of ostracism, and was interested in tried ways of keeping a very restricted form of it.

Is the Humean alternative to puritan moralism any less cruel to those found wanting by its critical standards than is Kantian moralism? Might it not be better for the vicious to be left to crucify their own sinful flesh, or be harshly but justly punished by God and the magistrate's administration of *Jus Talionis,* than to be continually at the mercy of the Humean's disdain, ridicule, or disgust? *Is the Humean morality, which boasts of its nonmoralistic avoidance of "useless austerities and rigours, suffering and self denial" and promises that "nothing appears but gentleness, humanity, beneficience, affability; nay even, at proper intervals, play, frolic and gaiety,"*[57] really so gentle if it condones derision, scorn, disdain, and avoidance of those who do not measure up to its standards? Is it not cruel to the dour, to those lacking in the virtue of wit, to those whose dejected melancholy might blight our gaiety unless we avoid them? Not every stupefied understanding, hard heart, obscured fancy, or sour temper[58] is due to avoidable monkish habits of life, and it may seem that the play and frolic of the Humean pleasure-valuing morality is as cruel to those whose temperament is found unattractive as it may seem also to be to the unfortunate poor, whose "dirty furniture, coarse or ragged cloaths, nauseous meat and distasteful liquor"[59] may present such "disagreeable images" that we try to avoid them. The cost of a nonmoralistic Humean epicurean morality, it may seem, is even higher than that of Kantian moral law enforcement.

There are two avenues of escape the Humean can try from this criticism of excessive cruelty to those with the Humean vices, to those who are stupid, boring, graceless, unobservant, inexpressive, deaf to poetry, clumsy, unimaginative, cold, unresponsive, sour, gloomy, and "hairbrained." For the Humean must take this criticism very seriously, if she is to continue to claim that cruelty is the most detestable vice. One escape route is the excuse of fatalism. Just as anger will always be with us, so will disdain, scorn, and derision. The best we may be able to do is to redirect their aim so that the occasions for them will be minimized. There is not much point in simply deploring them, labeling them as vices (as for example Spinoza does—he rules out both the Kantian's call to repentance and the Humean's derision and even self-directed irony, in what may be the toughest, most impossibly perfectionist ethical standards yet suggested). If we are the animals who laugh just as truly as we are the animals who propose laws to ourselves, then we will likely go on laughing at some of our fellows, and our laughter, like our legislation and our law enforcement, will sometimes degenerate into cruelty, to others and to ourselves.

That first escape does not get the Humean very far. She turns out to have as good an excuse for her cruel methods of moral criticism as the Kantian has for harsh condemnation and punishment. But since cruelty is not the worst vice for the Kantian, as it is for the Humean, the Humean must try to do better than this. Can she? Well, she can surely criticize cruel laughter, even when the laughter may not be within the laugher's immediate control. She can criticize a sexist and a racist sense of humor, and equally she can criticize the excessively derisive, scornful, disdainful personality. Since she leaves it to "divines" and philosophers who are disguised divines, obsessed with punitive sanctions, to make fine distinctions between the voluntary and the involuntary,[60] it does not matter to her whether the sexist could have helped his sexist sense of humor, nor whether the sarcastic person, including the sarcastic moral critic, can help her sarcasm. Most of us who enjoy occasional sarcasm as much as we do occasional "frolic and gaiety" probably could, if we tried, learn to inhibit our sarcastic tongues, and a proper task of Humean moral thinking will be to ask when such inhibition would be best. We have shown ourselves capable of stopping parading the useless bachelors, and we can surely alter other displays of our evil eye, if and when we see good reason to do so. The control on derision and other hurtfully critical responses to our fellows may, if Hume is right, have to come slowly, from redesign of educational and social customs, not by individual self-transformation schemes. Hume did not put much faith in self-improvement regimens. Even if one is blessed with the strength of will needed to carry them through (or perhaps has acquired it by some prior bit of moral gymnastics, enforced in childhood or voluntarily embarked on later), he believes that it is "almost impossible for the mind to change its character in any considerable article, or cure itself of a passionate or splenetic temper, when they are natural to it."[61] He may here be overgeneralizing from the failure of his own self-improvement attempts during his delinquent youth, when he was neglecting his law studies. He reported in his famous "letter to a physician" that, smitten with the beauty of the representations of virtue that he found in Cicero, Seneca, and Plutarch, "I undertook the improvement of my Temper and Will, along with my Reason and Understanding. I was continually fortifying myself with Reflections against Death, & Poverty & Shame & Pain & all the other Calamities of Life." And what did he achieve? He temporarily ruined his health, and got "scurvy spots" on his fingers. The moral ascetic "served to little Purpose, than to waste the Spirits." When, later, he writes in the *Treatise* of that "infirmity of human nature" that shows in our lack of firmness of purpose, in our difficulty in keeping our eye on the greater good when that is remote, his words seem almost an autobiographical report of his own experiences as a nineteen-year-old: "I may have recourse to study and reflexion within myself; to the advice of friends; to frequent meditation, and repeated resolution: And having experienc'd how ineffectual all these are, I may embrace with pleasure any other expedient."[62] The expedient advocated there is to "change our circumstances,"[63] as indeed the young Hume did shortly after his letter to the physician—he took a job in a business in Bristol, where at least his scurvy spots, if not his moral flaws, went into remission. Hume does believe that there can be a remedy for at least some of our troublesome infirmities of character, but that remedy does not lie in individual moral asceticism and gymnastics. It may take a change of scene and occupation, and often it takes social organization and the redesign of institutions.

Hume himself is obviously willing to employ ridicule for his purposes as a moral reformer, and indeed a morality that values "play, frolic, and gaiety" will certainly have to be careful about its strictures against laughter. Laughter is part of the *goal* of the Humean morality, and this may be in the end its deepest difference from the Kantian. Not obligatory rejoicing, not fun as a duty or as dutiful recreation, but genuine joy, Spinoza's *hilaritas,* with solemnity and obligation tolerated only as a sometimes needed means to the removal of obstacles to human happiness—this is what Hume offers us as the goal of his alternative to a puritan morality. Still, cruel laughter, exclusionary laughter, will not serve the goals of Hume's "party of humankind," even when its members are united against puritan vice and disorder, and so against excessive solemnity and pompous stands on dignity. So derisive laughter will need to be restrained, to make it cost-effective, and so will all other hurtful expressions of criticism of character. The best way to restrain ridicule may be to ridicule the unrestrained ridiculer, to turn the hurtful laughter against the hurtful laugher. Of course this will work only if she is not too much more thick-skinned than her victims—just as impeachment does not very much hurt the really shameless who, after a short retirement, bounce back into public life as ex-presidents, pontificating as before—so the ridiculed ridiculer may be invulnerable to the sort of treatment that she metes out hurtfully to others. No version of morality will work unless we keep ourselves more or less equally vulnerable to the same sorts of wounds. There is no morality that could work between, say, thin-skinned humans and carapaced cockroaches, even if we could effectively communicate. Shared rationality is, *pace* Kant, not enough—we need also to care about each other's disapprobation, and so be vulnerable to the typical form the expression of that disapprobation is likely to take. With human beings, it takes the form of incipiently cruel laughter, incipiently cruel isolation, and incipiently cruel humiliation as well as solemn condemnation and angry infliction of physical pain.

Worries about derision, social ostracism, and any hurtful informal pointing out of individual faults are, for the Humean moralist, most appropriate, as appropriate as concern about cruel official punishment. We have seen that Hume did worry about ostracism, as well as about torture. His own practice, as a moral theorist and moralist, was certainly not to avoid a derisive tone of voice. Nor is he content to turn ridicule only on the ridiculers—it is typically preachers, not ridiculers, whom he makes fun of. Usually his target is not some vulnerable individual, but general personality types or else individuals who are safely dead. He did write one brief essay criticizing a contemporary politician, Walpole, but withdrew that essay when Walpole retired as prime minister. Politicians, presumably, are special cases, who in a sense offer their characters up for public assessment. In his *History of England* Hume regularly analyzes the character of the kings, archbishops, and chancellors whose deeds and achievements he has chronicled. Paragraphs on "death and character" punctuate the history, and in his autobiography it may be significant that he analyzes his own character only when he has declared his own life to be over, and has moved into the past tense. If the deliberate pointing out of faults of character is restricted to the times when character is still being formed (childhood), to law courts, to politics, and to obituaries and histories, then moral judgment, Humean style, can avoid unnecessary and pointless as well as purely vindictive hurtfulness. Not that we will not usually know and be mortified to know what faults of character others discern in us—that is unavoidable, if we develop shared standards of character assessment and are incapable of completely inhibiting our more spontaneous expressions of pleasure and displeasure, amusement and sorrow, in each other's character traits. Even the blind eye that most of us turn on our own faults will not altogether protect us from seeing our own likenesses of character to some of those whose character we ourselves find unwelcome and disagreeable, and so some self-dislike, and perhaps self-derision, will be a normal consequence of normal powers of self-survey and of moral discernment. And some of us may prefer criticisms to be put to us, face to face, than to have them spoken behind our back, in places and times when we cannot answer back or return the ridicule.

Hume's version of moral approbation and disapprobation, like Shaftesbury's and Hutcheson's, makes them into special reflective pleasure and displeasure taken in characteristics of human persons. They are very like the disinterested pleasure in beauty and displeasure in ugliness that Kant discusses in the *Third Critique*, when these are taken not just in nature and art but also in human characters. The relevant disinterest does not prevent some link with motivation, the sort of weak link that there is between appreciation of nature and fine art and willingness to help conserve nature and to support the arts, for example, to contribute to the design and support of social institutions that will encourage the preservation of natural beauty and the production of great art. Pleasure in beautiful human character and displeasure in ugly human character may lead to all sorts of action, but they need not lead to deliberate expression of displeasure to each person in whom fault is found. We are no more compelled to make our displeasure known to the faulty person than we must tell the bad poet that we judge his poetry to be bad. (If he submits it to a poetry competition, that is another matter.) Even our spontaneous displays of displeasure (frowns, sneers, derisive laughter) can fairly easily be inhibited, if we see good reason to inhibit them. That they inflict gratuitous and pointless hurt on their targets will, for the Humean, be good enough reason to "throw a veil of love of man over their faults not merely by softening but also by keeping these judgments to ourselves" (as Kant put it).[64] That our expressed criticisms are on good evidence judged to influence the person for the better, so that the hurt is not judged to be pointless, or that their victim's response might influence the critics for the better, so that moral dialogue is advanced, will be reason to allow disapprobation its natural expression. But the good Humean will need reliable empirical evidence that good can be expected to come from any hurt that is inflicted, and she will show "delicacy" of sentiment in judging when anger was and will be the better response to others' faults, when sorrow, and when laughter. The deliberate, contrived, and calculated hurting of the faulty person, in order to reform him, will be left to magistrates and other licensed coercers. The good Humean will want to keep a careful check on how such persons (parents, schoolteachers, judges, police, prison guards) are exercising this grave responsibility. Morality must be solemn when it risks angry cruelty, as it does in its endorsement of society's self-protective coercive activities. A morality would certainly be cruel that did not try to protect people from rapists, bullies, and murderers, so some risk of cruelty to criminals must be taken. (The O.E.D. entry on "cruelty" cites a statement by Sir Henry Blount in *Voyages in the Levant,* that "the want of crueltie upon delinquents causes much more oppression of the Innocent.")

The Humean looks for the social fault behind the individual fault; she takes the responsibility for evil to be shared, never localizable in individual criminals, however essential it may rightly be deemed to be to take forceful protective measures against them. So the Humean moralist will be in favor of the articulation of shared standards of character assessment, and of application of them to particular persons only when the hurt involved in this application can reasonably be expected to do some compensatory good. In general, the disdain for and derision of bad characters will be restricted to character types. Hume's morality of character criticism can be seen as in the tradition of Theophrastus' *Characters.*[65] The point of portraying and jeering at bad character types, at the boor, the surly, the buffoon, the hairbrained enthusiast, is like the point of developing critical standards in appreciation of literature. We do not expect the instant conversion of the boors and buffoons as a result of our portrayal, indeed we may even try to shield the boors and buffoons from realizing that they personally are implicitly criticized by our enunciation of moral standards, since that could amount to the infliction of gratuitous hurt and cruelty. But we will expect social planners, educational theorists, and child psychologists to have an eye on these standards for human character when they redesign our cooperative practices and the sort of sense of humor we develop in each other, and we will ourselves have an eye on such standards as we criticize legislation and as we select legislators.

Humean morality gets expressed in the optative, not the imperative, mood, but that need not doom it to ineffectiveness. Where Kant's version of morality comes in stern imperatives, demanding direct obedience, with any graces of character or room for laughter left as a crown for successful moral endeavor, Hume's comes as a list of welcome characteristics, with enforced commands carefully limited to where they are needed and known to be effective in controlling "incommodious" passions or in protecting others from their fallout. For Kant, Hercules is to be joined by the Graces and Muses only after he has slain the monsters.[66] For Hume, the Graces are to employ Hercules only where he is needed. They are to lead him, not he them. The Humean will also remember Spinoza's judgment[67] that those who know how to castigate vices rather than teach virtues are burdensome both to themselves and to others.

Many are skeptical of the very idea of a morality with a light touch, employing laughter more than hectoring commands. I am, however, encouraged to learn that the president of NOW, Patricia Ireland, plans to use laughter as a means of moral pressure. "What do pompous men hate more than being laughed at?" the *New York Times Magazine* reports her as asking.[68] Hume tries to describe what such a nonpompous morality could be like. In his life he managed pretty well to live by the standards he had endorsed, and he even managed to keep up his wit, humor, and gentle self-irony while he was dying. (He did at one point get angry with Rousseau, but the provocation on that occasion was very great.) He certainly employed derision, and employed it brilliantly, against the forces that he perceived to present the greatest obstacles to a gentle, nondomineering morality. (He did this most spectacularly in his *Natural History of Religion.*) He also at times gave eloquent expression to moral horror and disgust at inhumane punitive practices and at the recorded treatment of slaves in ancient Rome (in "Of the Populousness of Ancient Nations"). But it was not part of his moral campaign to attack living individuals in an unnecessarily hurtful manner, and nor could it be if he was to remain true both to his belief that human persons are as much part of the causal order of nature as is anything else whose behavior we can fairly confidently predict and explain, and also to his reflective judgment that angry cruelty is the worst vice. His writings, including his extensive comments on actual human practices as recorded in the annals that he turned to as historian, are a good place to start for those of us who want to explore and develop the very idea of a gentle yet spirited morality, an idea that has strong forces working against it in a culture like ours which produces so many people who find Kant's description of our moral phenomenology so obviously correct. The Humean asks the Kantian moralist and moral psychologist what Milton asks in *Comus:* "Why should you be so cruel to yourself?" In return the Kantian can reasonably request of her Humean critic what Shakespeare's Henry V requested of Kate: "Mock me mercifully."[69] It may reasonably be thought that I have mocked the Kantian position a bit too unmercifully. The Kantian is not permitted by her own version of morality to do much mocking back, but other Humeans may generously step in to do the job of *retorsio iocosa* for them. For the true Humean must somehow learn to mock gently.

POSTSCRIPT

After I presented a version of this essay at the University of Southern California to an audience comprised primarily of faculty and graduate students, a tense male undergraduate, clutching a copy of Kant's *Groundwork of the Metaphysics of Morals,* approached me as the group was breaking up and said, "How can you attack the philosopher who wrote this book? It has shown me who I am." I replied that there were indeed inspiring moral ideals of equality and freedom to be found in Kant, but that it might be easier for men than for women to be helped to self-definition by a reading of the full corpus of Kant's works. Still, this upset young man had a point, that one should give credit to the positive moral power of a text as well as deploring its deficiencies. Barbara Herman, on the same occasion, asked me why I chose to read the deplorable bits, gently charging me with muckraking. She herself has done wonders with what one might have thought were fairly deplorable bits in Kant about the nature of sexual attraction and of marriage,[70] finding insights there which reflective women could accept, so there may be less dismissive ways of reading the mucky bits to which I have drawn attention. I do not see how the serious reader of Kant can ignore the offensive texts, nor avoid the task of considering what their relation is to the more general foundations and principles of his moral theory. His defenders will say they are unfortunate misapplications of his principles. (Herman has to take this line about Kant's condemnation of all "unnatural" sexual practices.) I see them as data that we should use to check our readings of the more general principles which he enunciated. Controversy on this point is bound to continue.

One offensive Hume text which I should attend to is his famous racist footnote, conspicuously undiscussed in this essay or in other essays of mine which praise Hume. If as a social philosopher Hume was as enlightened as I have made him out, how could he, in the essay "Of National Characters," write what he did about blacks, or, more generally, about races with darker skins than his own rosy North European skin? What exactly did he write? "I am apt to suspect the negroes to be naturally inferior to the whites. There scarcely ever was a civilized nation of that complexion, nor even any individual eminent either in action or speculation. No ingenious manufacture amongst them, no arts, no sciences . . ." This long note goes on to claim that no Negro slave in Europe has "discovered any symptoms of ingenuity"—the point presumably being that even when among more "civilized" people, black slaves had not to Hume's knowledge shown eminence in civilized activities. This note is appended to the discussion in the text of the effects of climate on national character. Hume had cautiously written, "there is some reason to think, that all the nations, which live beyond the polar circles or between the tropics, are inferior to the rest of the species, and are incapable of all the higher attainments of the human mind."[71] But he warns against quick generalizations here, and himself tends to favor not the physical cause of climate but the moral cause of habit of life, influenced as it usually is by climate. In the polar regions people live in too much misery for the arts to flourish; in the tropics they live in indolence, because nature too easily supplies their necessities. It is to this rejection of a direct appeal to physical causes to explain variation in accomplishment that Hume adds his footnote, admitting to a "suspicion" of the natural inferiority of "negroes" (presumably African blacks). Hume the empiricist speaks here, and so his reasons include the record of individual blacks living not in the indolence-encouraging and promiscuity-tempting tropics but in Europe, or under European masters in Jamaica. (The term "complexion" in Hume's note need not refer to skin color or to any physical feature but rather to the complex of characteristics, especially character traits, typically displayed by Negroes.[72])

We can fault Hume's anthropological knowledge, and also wonder that he did not consider the fact of slavery to be itself a sufficient explanation of the failure of any black slaves to distinguish themselves in such arts, science, or manufacture as were open to them after they had been enslaved and forcibly transported from their native cultures. But we should also give credit to his tentativeness in making any generalization, his respect for such empirical evidence as he had, and his refusal to see any such "natural inferiority," should it be thought to exist, to justify the institution of slavery.

In his essay "Of the Populousness of Ancient Nations," Hume gives eloquent expression to his "disgust" at "the remains which are found of domestic slavery, in the American colonies, and among some European nations . . . the little humanity, commonly observed in persons, accustomed, from their infancy, to exercise so great an authority over their fellow creatures, and to trample on human nature were sufficient alone to disgust us with that unbounded dominion."[73] His main topic there is slavery in ancient Rome, the cruel details of which arouse "horror" and even a rare misanthropic Humean reflection. After referring to the inhuman sports to which slaves were condemned, he writes: "One's humanity is apt to renew the barbarous wish of Caligula, that the people had but one neck: A man could almost be pleased, by a single blow, to put an end to such a race of monsters."[74] Could one find more strongly expressed condemnation of slaveowners? There may, however, be a touch of guilt by association on Hume's part, since the shipping firm for which he briefly worked in Bristol was importing sugar from the West Indies, and probably calling in at West African ports to fill its ships with slaves for the westward journey. It would be pleasing to think that Hume's quarrels with his employers, leading to his dismissal, had to do with his presumption in criticizing more than just his employers' style of English composition. But that is pure speculation.

Hume certainly did believe that women were inferior to men in some fields (athletic prowess, for one), and he "suspected" some inferiority in African dark-skinned people, as well as in Eskimos. But that any such empirically verified natural inferiority in some areas would justify social inferiority is not a thesis that he even wastes much time dismissing. It might be seen as implicitly considered in the *Enquiry* section on justice, where his main concern is with the rights of women. The power to make resentment of slavery effectively felt would be possessed by the Indian and black as much as the white women with whom dominant males hoped to "propagate their kind," and so the case which Hume makes there for the rights of women can be extended, via darker-skinned women, to all those human beings who are threatened by would-be "lordly masters." Hume's opposition to slavery, and to any institution that encourages tyranny, is firm and explicit. "The reciprocal duties of gentleness and humanity"[75] are extended to all members of the "party of humankind."

fourteen

ETHICS
IN MANY
DIFFERENT VOICES

What difference do the increasing numbers of women philosophers
make to the way ethics gets thought about in philosophy seminars,
at philosophy conferences, in the philosophy books and the articles
now being published? They are making many differences. The new
voices that are joining the debate are interestingly various. We
should no more expect agreement in views, in method, and in style
among women who write on ethics, of course, than we expect to find
agreement among male moral philosophers. There are as big and
important disagreements between, say, Judith Jarvis Thomson and
Catharine MacKinnon, or Mary Daly and Simone Weil, as there are
between Aquinas and Hobbes, or Hume and Kant. Some women
moral philosophers dislike being perceived as *women* philosophers,
while others glory in being so perceived; some call themselves "feminist," some refuse that label, and some of us welcome it when others
apply it, while having felt no need to proclaim it for ourselves.

It is dangerous to make suggestions about what difference
women are making to the ethics getting done in philosophy departments, since any generalization will be disputed by some women.
Male observers down the centuries have seen women as a quarrel-
some lot, given to mutual hair pulling and jealous spite as well as to
maternal solicitude and gentle soothing of the hurt feelings of others.
We have shown ourselves capable of pandering to male fantasies as
well as of having our own alternative fantasies. In philosophy semi-

nars, as in the boudoir, some will prove protective of fragile male egos, others will fulfill the worst male nightmares of the castrating woman by putting some teeth into their philosophical grip on male moral theories. Some try gentleness where the style of debate has been aggressive cut and slash. Others try new modes of slashing, and yet others alternate their styles in disconcerting ways, or simply display that postmenopausal rise in assertiveness which should be no surprise, but often does disconcert those who suffer assaults from feisty old women who had been meeker and more diplomatic when younger. Some women focus on women's issues, such as abortion, others avoid those and prefer to rethink the issues that concern men as closely as they do women, issues such as environmental protection, health care, civil disobedience. Some do theory, some engage in antitheory campaigns. Whatever else we are doing, we are helping to diversify the philosophical scene.

Those who undoubtedly altered the moral philosophy agenda include some women whose academic home base was not philosophy but literature, law, politics, theology. (The revolt of the nuns is a significant and still reverberating social event.) Mary Daly from theology, Catharine MacKinnon from law, Adrienne Rich from literature, Hannah Arendt, Judith Shklar, and Carole Pateman from political science have voiced challenges that moral philosophers today can scarcely ignore. Women who were or are not academics—such as Virginia Woolf, Rebecca West, Doris Lessing, Nadine Gordimer, and Alice Walker—are altering our sense of the moral issues, as are former academics such as Iris Murdoch. When we look beyond writing in English, at least to Europe (and I am not knowledgeable enough to look to Asia, South and Central America, or Africa), there is of course the voice of Simone de Beauvoir to be taken into account. *The Second Sex*[1] continues to provoke both men and women, and certainly provokes many feminists. Other women writing in French, such as Hélène Cixous, Luce Irigaray, and Julia Kristeva, are also increasingly impinging on our Anglo-American consciousness.

There are a few English-speaking and English-writing women philosophers whose writings have had great impact of a less agenda-altering sort on the Anglo-American philosophical profession. Judith Jarvis Thomson's article on abortion must be among the most frequently cited twentieth-century English-language publications in ethics. But, like most influential articles, it did not exactly change the agenda—rather it carried a certain style of thinking about this issue, one already popular among men who wrote about it, to its logical conclusion. Some regard it as a *reductio ad absurdum* of that approach, but there is no evidence that it was intended that way, and considerable evidence that it was not. Philippa Foot's work in ethics is very influential, especially among those favoring the "virtues" approach to ethics, but of course this is a very old approach, one favored by those notorious spokesmen for patriarchal values, Aristotle and Aquinas. (No feminist with any sense of etymology is likely to select the word "virtue" for whatever sort of moral excellence she is endorsing, but we have not settled on a better word.) Susan Wolf's "Moral Saints" has become a classic, but there were earlier papers by men, such as Michael Stocker's "The Schizophrenia of Modern Moral Philosophy," which had started the train of thought that Wolf developed so memorably.

There are very many self-styled feminist philosophers, exhibiting a great variety of approaches and opinions. Sandra Bartky, Seyla Benhabib, Claudia Card, Marilyn Friedman, Marilyn Frye, Virginia Held, Alison Jaggar, Maria Lugones, Linda Nicholson, Nel Noddings, Martha Nussbaum, Susan Moller Okin, Sara Ruddick, Elizabeth Spelman, Iris Young, and hearteningly many others are doing ethics in a self-consciously feminist manner. These feminists do not all welcome the idea that the different voice with which they speak on ethical issues is one which puts more emphasis on "care" than on "justice." Some feminist critics of influential theories of justice, such as John Rawls's theory, fault it for its less than adequately acknowledged assumption that someone or ones are caring for the young who are expected to develop a sense of justice in a loving home, ready to go out into the world to maintain just public institutions or to reform unjust ones; others, such as Susan Moller Okin, locate the fault not so much in the accepted parasitism of the virtue of justice on maternal or at least parental love and care as in the lack of attention to the justice of the family as an institution. Some are continuing the fight for justice for women; others are seeing a need for more than justice. These different feminist lines of thought are best seen as complementary and mutually supportive rather than as mutually opposed. But there are some real disagreements among self-styled feminists when it comes to the details of what would count as justice within the family, and who should be socialized to be willing to take care of whom. The influence of traditional patriarchal religions is not automatically canceled by the rise of a feminist consciousness, and so we should expect all degrees of radicalism among those who call themselves feminists, all degrees of determination to distance ourselves from the old oppressors, ranging from lesbian separatism, through resolute spinsterhood, and a rethinking and reform of the roles and priority of careers of wife and husband within a heterosexual marriage, to a willingness to continue as before to "love, honor, and obey" a male lord and master, as long as the service is voluntary, and as long as there is no male conspiracy to restrict all women to the role of devoted wife and mother. There are all sorts of feminists, of all sorts of political persuasion.

A question which bears looking into is that of just when in their careers our more radical self-styled feminist moral philosophers began so styling themselves, when they began to make feminist philosophy their area of specialization. I have here listed the women who made it to some security in the academic system, and I would not like to bet much on the chances of success of more than one or two of all the many bold young women philosophers who are trying to get tenure by their explicitly feminist written work. For they are engaged in exposing the sexist bias of our society, our academic establishment, and so of most of those who will decide their own academic fate. These women are bold; they may be rash. How many tenured women philosophers who write in provocatively feminist ways wrote this way, or wrote mainly this way, before they had tenure? Maybe I stand out as conspicuously cowardly, but I certainly did not. It was not until I had a secure base that I published anything about the position of women. As far as public statements went, I in effect ignored that issue until it was relatively safe for me to speak about it. I admire the courage of my younger colleagues, but such courage will not topple a patriarchal academic establishment that can so easily evict them from its halls. It can easily do so, as long as the senior faculty who are making the tenure decisions can tell themselves, with perfect correctness, that they cannot judge the merits of this sort of philosophy (especially when it is cooperative), and that there is no one whose views they already respect who can judge it and who also judges the candidate's work to be of the quality required for tenure. While such a situation prevails, it will remain professionally suicidal for untenured women philosophers to specialize in feminist philosophy, and perhaps dangerous for them even to pursue their feminist interests openly. Unless some tenured philosophers make it their business to become knowledgeable about feminist philosophy, it will be a no-win situation for younger feminist philosophers.

We should, perhaps, expect different developmental patterns in the writing careers of men and women philosophers, expecting many women to get into their writing stride as men of the same age are losing steam. But can we allow for relative testosterone levels in our tenure decisions? Will enough women professionally survive their high estrogen years, will they be able to squeeze out enough articles while they are menstruating, gestating, and lactating? Some undoubtedly will, but some may be lost to the profession by the prejudice which foists on all people expectations of high intellectual productivity in youth, expectations which make better sense for men than for women. For various reasons, women may delay publication longer than men of the same age. At present we demand quantity as well as quality. If we put the emphasis mainly on quality, women would not be disadvantaged, but it could still be that the philosophical prime of their lives may be as proportionally later than men's as is their prime for sexual pleasure. These thoughts raise ethical issues about our collective management of the profession of academic philosophy and academic ethics, ones that the women who do make it over the tenure hurdle should be addressing. One way to address it would be to press for the provision of special incentives to older women to enter, or reenter, the profession. Other ways, involving not just pregnancy and parental leave but different expectations as to *when* women will get into full philosophical stride (tenure decisions delayed at the candidates' request until age 50?), would be bound to raise reasonable complaints of exploitation of the untenured and of unfairness to men. Still, we need to come up with some new measures. One possibility, perhaps the best solution, would be to make all tenure decisions rest on evaluation only of what the candidate selects as, say, her or his four best articles.

One way that women are certainly changing the profession of ethics is by presenting the professions, including the profession of academic philosophy and ethics, with some acute problems of professional ethics. We are enlarging the subject matter for problem-oriented ethics. It is also clear that there is a lot more attention being paid to the old topic of pornography, and that sexual harassment is joining rape on the normal agenda for applied ethics. Women's voices on those topics are obviously essential for informed debate. Yet they were just as essential for the debate on abortion, which for long enough proceeded contentedly without it, at both Supreme Court and philosophical levels. Even when women did join the philosophical debate, the ones whose voices were listened to most respectfully, on both sides, were those whose views chimed in best with men's way of reasoning on this topic. So we had good Catholic women arguing against abortion and good liberal women arguing for it, each lot saying just what their respective male teachers and lovers would want them to say. We are only recently getting the views of the independent-minded women philosophers who are mothers, the views of single mothers, of lesbians, and of others who are both experience-informed enough about pregnancy and its early termination and liberated enough from male indoctrination to have the best credentials for deliberation on this matter. The philosophical debate on abortion is really just beginning to get going, as it at last gets taken over by those who know what they are talking about.

As to what more general difference has been made by the different way that Anglo-American women philosophers have approached topics in ethics, before and after tenure decisions, there are probably at least as many different answers as the different women whose voices have been heard, and as many as the phases of their articulate philosophical lives. One fairly pervasive difference that I perceive is a greater realism, a reluctance to do "ideal" ethical theory, an insistence on looking for a version of ethics that applies to us now, in the conditions we actually find ourselves in, oppressed or beginning to be liberated, few or increasingly many in the tenured ranks, on the hospital rounds, on the advisory boards, and on the policy-setting councils. We find this real-world emphasis in relatively theoretical writings, such as Virginia Held's *Rights and Goods*,[2] in Cora Diamond's essays on the "realistic spirit" in philosophy,[3] and in the writings of the many women who are choosing to do "applied ethics."

Along with this realism goes a greater emphasis than before on what we could call the ethics of timing. In *The Realm of Rights*[4] Thomson has an interesting discussion of when an invitation lapses,

299

how long the right given in an accepted invitation can be taken to last. Is it fanciful to see it as typically a woman's preoccupation to care about timing and timeliness, indeed to be very interested in ways of dividing up and managing time? Women, because of the rhythm of their biological lives, have had to make themselves think about the precise timing of what they do and what they promise, and relate that appropriately to the timing of what their bodies do. They have to think about ways of undoing what was regrettably done, and of fixing the future so that regrets may be minimized.

I shall now turn to one woman philosopher whose thoughts about our attitudes to time present and time past had considerable impact on me—indeed reading her book, *The Human Condition*,[5] divides my philosophical past into its purely analytic early period and its more eclectic later period. I refer of course to Hannah Arendt. There was a woman who really knew what she was talking about when she spoke of resistance or nonresistance to evil regimes, when she spoke about civil disobedience or about forgiveness. In *The Human Condition* she chooses two human actions as the quintessentially human ones: forgiving a past wrong (unfixing the fixed past), and promising a future benefit (fixing the unfixed future). Concern with past evils and future avoidance of evils is a common human concern, and it would be absurd to suggest that male moralists had not thought about forgiveness or about ways of securing the future. But it took Arendt to couple contract, that favorite moral device of the secular male theorists, with forgiveness, which had been more or less left to the theologians. Arendt writes, "The two faculties belong together in so far as one of them, forgiving, serves to undo the deeds of the past, whose 'sins' hang like Damocles' sword over every new generation; and the other, binding oneself through promises, serves to set up in the ocean of uncertainty, which the future is by definition, islands of security without which not even continuity, let alone durability of any kind, would be possible in the relationships between men" (p. 237). She means "between human agents," of course, not "between *men*," but part of what makes *The Human Condition* the interesting work that it is, is the odd mix of Arendt's originality and her deference to the ideas and the terminology of her teacher and lover, Heidegger,[6] of her teacher and friend, Jaspers, and of the sexist tradition of Hegel and Marx which she is transcending. Her book is about the active life, about various conditions of laboring, working, and acting together, about escape from "the darkness of each man's lonely heart" (ibid.). There is little explicit discussion of women's hearts, or women's work, except in the early chapter "The Public and Private Realm," where (pp. 47–48, n. 38; pp. 72–73) it is noted that women's relegation to the private realm went with the belief that their task was "to with their bodies minister to the needs of life" (Aristotle, *Politics*, 1254b25). Arendt refers to "the odd notion of a division of labor between the sexes, which is even considered by some writers to be the most original one. It presumes as its single subject man-kind, the human species, which has divided its labors among men and women" (p. 48, n. 38). Odd indeed, to take women to be a subdivision of mankind, laboring for it, in or out of the home. But Arendt, after this subversive note, continues to speak of "man" and "men," as those whose powers of action she is analyzing. Their redemptive action possibilities are located, however, in the combined miracles of forgiveness and promise, which come together in what Arendt terms "natality." "The miracle that saves the world, the realm of human affairs, from its normal, 'natural' ruin is ultimately the fact of natality, in which the faculty of action is ontologically rooted ... 'A child has been born unto us'" (p. 247). Appropriating Nietzsche's Zarathustra as much as the New Testament's Jesus of Nazareth, Isak Dinesen as much as Dante, Arendt plunders the Western cultural tradition to get a version of human agency *(praxis)* in relation to human work *(poesis)* and human labor, a version that makes women's labor in childbirth the bringer of redemption, in the birth of a new person whose life story will be a fresh one, a bringer of hope. Action, Arendt believes (with Dante) discloses the agent, and is intended to do so. Individual agents' lives are "enacted stories," unique narratives, produced by action "with or without intention as naturally as fabrication produces tangible things" (p. 184).[7] Arendt's self-disclosure in writing *The Human Condition* can be seen as an act of forgiveness to a tradition which had endorsed and enforced that odd notion that women's labor is for men. It is also a fulfilled promise of better thinking, an act of faith in the possibility of better conditions for women's action and of less tragic narratives with women as heroines.

As far as I am aware, Arendt never called herself a feminist, and probably would not have wanted to be so called. From her youth in

Germany she had opposed the separation of women's issues from more encompassing political concerns. (In 1931 she reviewed Alice Ruhle-Gerstel's *Das Frauen-problem der Gegenwart*.[8]) Her biographer, Elisabeth Young-Bruehl, writes that she urged younger women to independence, "but always, always with a qualification: for women, her maxim was *Vive la petite différence*."[9] In an interview which she gave at the time of her Christian Gauss Lectures at Princeton in 1953, she said, "I am not disturbed at all about being a woman professor . . . , because I am quite used to being a woman,"[10] a rather splendid statement. She did not want to be seen as an "exception woman," any more than as an "exception Jew," but of course in 1953 the press were not in error in seeing it as exceptional for a woman to be a professor at Princeton. During a discussion of "women's liberation" by the editorial board of the *American Scholar* in 1972, Arendt is reported to have written a note to Hiram Haydn, commenting, "The real question to ask is, what will we lose if we win?"[11] She clearly valued what she feared we might lose, and was not only used to being a woman but gloried in it, even in conditions of inequality where a married woman's options seemed to be as Ruhle-Gerstel saw them—becoming either housekeepers, princesses, or demonesses.[12] It now seems to me time for those of us who do call ourselves feminists to draw freely on whatever philosophical resources nourish our enterprises, to be feminist in a large and generously appropriative sense, not a narrow sectarian one. Now that we are winning we can afford to disagree about what loss our win entailed, and whether it must be permanent.

Arendt's work certainly nourished my philosophical soul. She led me to re-read Hegel, to read Heidegger, and certainly to re-conceive what "action-theory" might become. Among other twentieth-century books in that genre, hers cries out with the voice of a prophet. The term "action-theory" itself invites reflection, but few of its analytic practitioners reflect, as Arendt does, on the exact links between theory and action, on how various sorts of thinking can transform action, on how thinking and theorizing are themselves actions that are as self-disclosing as any other. As the current rage for "applied ethics" in the health professions, in business, in engineering and in scientific research can be expected to revivify ethical theory, so attention to these various sorts of professional action would revivify our moribund analytical action theory, a field where things are still more or less where they were when I opted out twenty years ago—at best a matter of cooperative house painting, at worst one of solitary agents vainly willing to move their missing limbs. Arendt-type action, such as civil disobedience, emigration, proclamation, let alone pardoning and forgiving wrongs, has yet to make it into the discussions of the self-styled action theorists. (Even those who do ethics and social philosophy as well as action theory can choose, in their action-theoretical guise, to discuss house-cleaning, not voting or political protest. Anscombe had "bringing down the regime" in her analysis, but her followers have tended to stick with the pumping.)

"For everything there is a season, and a time for every matter under heaven," but since Solomon's time not much has been said about the ethics of good timing. Nor is it easy to say anything general and more helpful than Solomon's pronouncements. Although Arendt's discussion of the twin miracle workers, forgiving and promising, forces our attention on the relation between our backward-looking surveys of action and efforts at wiping of our copybooks and our forward-looking agreements and solemn signings, she does not in *The Human Condition* discuss the question of how agents decide when is the time to give their word or to forgive broken words and other wrongs.[13] But in her more political works we do get more such attention,[14] and it is a natural follow-up to an account of action which put such emphasis on these two cycle-breaking acts, forgiving and promising, without which "we would be doomed to swing forever in the ever-recurring cycle of becoming" (p. 246). Forgiving is of definite past offenses or debts, which are taken to have been as it were recorded in some doomsday book, complete with date and details. Their remission is also a definite dated act, as it were a crossing-out in the record book, signed and dated. A promise similarly is an act that fixes some aspect or aspects of a limited future, a time future to the time of the promise. Often we promise to do something by a certain day or hour, and even when we promise mutual devotion "till death do us part," death does end the period that was fixed by the promise. Without calendars, there could be no promising of our normal sort, and where clocks are rare or rarely used, promises are interpreted more flexibly. In New Zealand we have the phrase "Maori time," which means Pakeha (European) time, give or take an hour or so. ("We are to meet at noon, Maori

303

time.") Without any rough measures of time, the "pro" element in promising would become simply a future tense marker, and promises would be indistinguishable from totally vague hopes or predictions. "We will overcome" is not a promise, precisely because of its lack of temporal precision.

With forgiving, the need for time specifications is not so obvious, given the religious near-monopoly on that concept and the promiscuous scope of Christian forgiveness. It is typically *all* one's sins, as an undifferentiated bunch, that get forgiven by divine pardoners (although there is that mysterious unforgivable sin, against the Holy Spirit, that has to be sifted out, so maybe some sin-by-sin count does actually have to go on). Human forgivers are selective— typically they forgive particular specifiable doings or omissions. To announce, "I forgive you for any wrongs you have done me, and forgive you in advance for any you may do me," is to debase the moral currency, just as senseless an act as to say, "I promise you that you could count on me, for all our past, and can count on me, in whatever way you wish, in the future." Promises must be for the future, and must be selective as to what aspect of that future they purport to fix. Forgiveness must be of the past, and of selected wrongs within it. The selection is the hard bit. Arendt writes, "the moment that promises lose their character as isolated islands of certainty in an ocean of uncertainty, that is, when this faculty is misused to cover the whole ground of the future and to map out a path secured in all directions, they lose their binding power and the whole enterprise becomes self-defeating" (p. 244). Many of us who have inveighed against contractarianism in ethics have merely repeated Arendt's point, at greater length and with less eloquence.

It may reasonably be objected[15] that my claim that promises typically mention dates or time periods ignores promises of the form "I will never do x again"—the sort of commitment given by those trying to turn away from bad habits, from excessive drinking, smoking, drug taking, or by those entering monasteries. Such promises or vows do seem to be for an open-ended future, and could be made by members of a precalendar culture. Vows of allegiance to superiors, vows of abstinence of various sorts, divide time simply into the prevow and the postvow periods. But "vow," not "promise," is the right word for these acts. They are typically made to some higher-than-human power, to God or one's country. Vows are indeed taken and sometimes honored. It was not vows that Arendt chose to focus on but promises, which "depend on plurality, on the presence and acting of others, for no one . . . can feel bound by a promise made only to himself" (p. 237). It is an important fact about the human person that she can be multiple, play many roles, and play roles before her other personae, but Arendt is surely right that promises lose their grip once the promisee is oneself, one's conscience, or the divine spokesperson within. Our ability to talk to ourselves can be a redemptive power,[16] but the speech acts we can perform to ourselves do seem of a limited variety, compared with the ways in which we can speak to others. We can tell ourselves stories, ask and answer questions, propose courses of action then criticize and reject them, encourage, flatter, mock and denigrate ourselves. But promising to ourselves, like lying to ourselves, seems ruled out, except for those who are seen to suffer from multiple personality disorders or who alter their status within the time between the promise and its expected performance.[17]

The biblical notion of a covenant between God and Israel, which might reasonably be taken to serve the identity-establishing function for a whole people rather well, was a very special sort of commitment, both in the open-ended time which it covered and in the sort of parties it involved—a divine being and the father of a people. Arendt's discussion of the covenant made by Abraham with God is distinctly ironical. "Abraham, the man from Ur, whose whole story, as the Bible tells it, shows such a passionate drive toward making covenants that it is as though he departed from his country for no other reason than to try out the power of mutual promise in the wilderness of the world, until eventually God himself agreed to make a Covenant with him" (pp. 243–244). Such a "covenant" with God, until it acquires human witnesses and public recognition,[18] is no different, on Abraham's part, from cases of "promising enacted in solitude or isolation," and so "without reality . . . no more than a role played before one's self" (p. 237). The covenant as described in Genesis 17 is an "everlasting" one, binding not just Abraham but his seed ("Thy seed after thee in their generations"). Ordinary promises are neither everlasting nor taken to bind the promisor's seed. (Hume relies heavily on this fact in his arguments against a social contract theory of political obligation.) A covenant of the sort that the nation of Israel took itself to have with its God can indeed serve to confer a distinctive identity both on nationals of that nation and on the God in question ("the God of Israel"), but "promise" is the wrong term for the sort of identity-establishing tie for a whole people which the biblical covenant instituted.

Arendt claims that our identity over time is confirmed by those others who recognize the one who fulfills a promise as the same person who gave it, and that this confirmation of identity is needed, if we are not to "be condemned to wander helplessly and without direction in the darkness of each man's lonely heart" (p. 237). This is a strong claim. One might think that a recorded lifetime resolve would be the simplest way to give direction to the aimless wanderer, providing at least as good an identity-marker as that conferred by a series of promises to different people to do differing things by a series of deadlines. (I often have felt torn into pieces by the different promises I have given.) Arendt's "promise" may need overtones of an ongoing "covenant" to do the job that she gives it, that is, to structure a life over a long period.

In a television interview in 1964 she told how, when as a child in Königsberg she encountered anti-Semitism in her playmates and schoolmates, her mother instructed her to defend herself, and if a schoolteacher made anti-Semitic remarks, "to stand up immediately, to leave the class, go home."[19] This policy of standing up and leaving anti-Semitic company seems to have been followed by Arendt throughout her life. She and her mother left Nazi Germany in 1933 (over the Erzegebirge Mountains, into Czechoslovakia), and she eventually made her "home" with other emigrants from Europe in New York. Her last years in Germany were spent working on her study of Rahel Varnhagen (born as Rahel Levin in 1771). She sub-titled this book "The Life of a Jewess" and referred to Rahel as "my closest friend, although she has been dead for some one hundred years."[20] She also wrote a newspaper article entitled "The Jewish Question," and publicly criticized those who (like Adorno and Hei-degger) were cooperating with the Nazis. She certainly "stood up" before "walking out" of the country that had become "nicht für meiner Mutters Tochter."[21] Such clear self-identification involved neither covenants nor promises, simply a consistent line of action and proclamation. (Her "Mutt," as she calls her mother in her letters to Jaspers, seems to have been a splendidly devoted and loyal mother. When both mother and daughter were arrested by the Nazis in 1933 and interrogated separately, Martha Arendt was asked what her daughter Hannah had been doing in her regular visits to the Prussian National Library, where she had in fact been researching anti-Semitic literature for the German Zionist Organization. The mother replied that she did not know, but she knew that, whatever it was, it was right for her daughter to do it, and she herself would have done the same. The Nazis released her after one day, having the sense to realize that she was interrogation-proof.[22])

Do we really need witnesses and records to give us reassurance of who we are? Do we need receipts to reassure us that we are the same persons as the ones who entered into the sale as a buyer? Do we need some "well done, good and faithful servant," to be sure that we are the same ones who entered into that service? Arendt, when she makes her claim about the role of promises, is writing about the active life, the life of labor, work and action, about the bringing into existence of the means of subsistence, of artifacts, of narratives or commitments, of meaningful lives such as her own. If our service is mere labor, which another laborer or a relay team of laborers could have done as well as one and the same person, then there may be no signature, as it were, left on the outcome of our labor, on the field that is ploughed or the house that is cleaned. But if we have made something or built something—a pot, say, or a church—then we may leave our signature on the base of the pot, or our face carved into the door lintel. Even if we do not, the work may exhibit our distinctive personal style and so not be just what any other potter or architect (or team of them) could as easily have come up with. Our work is not fungible, in the way that our labor is. But the work of our hands and minds, like our labor, is alienable and can have a price put on it. What Arendt calls our actions, by contrast, are inalienable. Their distinctive style, if indeed they have that, results not in any saleable product but in a unique life story, a succession of words and deeds bounded by birth and death, a sequence of commitments and refusals to commit oneself, of forgivings and refusals to forgive, and of words and deeds in reaction to others' actions, and to their deaths and births. For women, that life story may include the births that they commit themselves to or refuse to commit themselves to, that is, to childbirths or abortions. Like any other outcome of human action (in Arendt's rich sense), the child who is born because of the mother's decision to carry to term will be unique, with its own life

307

story and distinctive character, not merely a continuation of that of any parental agent. Action typically results in new possibilities for action, but not so typically in new actors. Only when nations, religions, or other collective agents are intentionally brought into being do we get any other human action that is at all like intentionally giving birth to a new human person.

Yet as Arendt emphasized when discussing the traditional place of women in the private sphere, giving birth is often not free action, but coerced "labor" for others. As long as there is no individual control and no individual choice, then labor and childbirth are for the species' survival, not for any laborer's or labor-owner's survival or satisfaction. As long as the initiative, the control, and the choice rests with men rather than with women, then the labor and birth will be less than the mother's action. Arendt gives a central role to the idea of natality, and she views it as having a closer connection with action than with the idea of labor, or with the work that must "provide and preserve the world for . . . the constant influx of newcomers who are born into the world as strangers" (p. 9). This is because "the new beginning inherent in birth can make itself felt in the world only because the newcomer possesses the capacity of beginning something anew, that is, of acting" (ibid.). Of course, as she later notes when discussing Marx's concept of labor power (p. 88), the newcomer can also be seen merely as a replacement of labor power, rather than as one capable of acting. If the child is consigned to factory labor or (if she is a female) simply to reproducing her mother's unchosen procreative labor, then nothing new will have been begun, merely the old cycle continued. Birth will be paired with unchosen death, as correlative happenings that preserve a sort of species status quo not only at the biological level but also at the socioeconomic level. Births sustain a more or less steady labor force for the creation and procreation of saleable goods and labor. Yet despite these all too often actualized possibilities for birth, it still retains its power to symbolize the new start, the hope of new and better directions. Hence Arendt can write "since action is the political activity par excellence, natality, and not mortality, may be the central category of political, as distinguished from metaphysical, thought" (p. 9). Heidegger had made mortality a central category of metaphysical thought. Arendt is balancing his act by a move that totally transforms it.[23] Natality for us today is a fairly central topic of political debate, if not so central a category of metaphysical[24] or political theory. The Hegelian "truth" of Arendt's political thought may be found not in contemporary political theory so much as in the debate over *Roe v. Wade* and in the confrontations outside abortion clinics.

Arendt's prophetic powers, or should one say her thought initiatives, extend to the metaphysical as well as to the political. The final section of *The Human Condition* is devoted to various reversals in the "modern age" and one of these is the "reversal of the hierarchical order between the *vita contemplativa* and the *vita activa*" (p. 289). She introduces this theme by a discussion of René Descartes' method of doubt and of Copernicus's and Galileo's "alienation" of the earth, their "dislocation" of it, from their imaginary Archimedean point beyond it. She quotes Copernicus's words about "the virile man standing in the sun ... overlooking the planets" and seeing the earth move with them. Descartes' doubt and his thoughts about himself as a thinker, as much as his analytical-geometrical physics, are taken as expressions of this alienation of the familiar world brought about by the new science. Whitehead is quoted as likening the new sciences' beginnings in the discovery of the telescope and in Galileo's use of it to "a babe ... born in a manger,"[25] a great thing happening with little stir. Arendt adds: "Like the birth in a manger, which spelled not the end of antiquity but the beginning of something so unexpectedly and unpredictably new that neither hope nor fear could have anticipated it, these first tentative glances into the universe through an instrument, at once adjusted to human senses and destined to uncover what definitely and forever must lie beyond them, set the stage for an entirely new world ..." (pp. 257–258). The inquiring and imaginative mind too can give birth to inventions and ideas that break cycles and introduce new directions. It is not merely in social philosophy but in physics and metaphysics that the category of natality provides a favorite metaphor for what the innovative thinker aspires to. (David Hume mourned the apparent fate of his *Treatise of Human Nature*,[26] fallen "deadborn from the press.")

In the final part of *The Human Condition*, Arendt treats thinking, including the sort of earth-shifting thinking that Galileo and Descartes did, as activity, properly seen as part of the *vita activa*. (She continued her exploration of thinking in her 1973 Gifford Lectures, published as *The Life of the Mind*.[27]) The Cartesian doubt and exploration of subjectivity, as much as the telescope-using and technology-linked thinking of modern scientists, involved the "removal of the Archimedean point into the mind of man" (p. 285). They involved mental labor, the making of books, and self-revealing or self-concealing action. Although Descartes called his metaphysical masterpiece *Meditations,* which may suggest contemplative stillness, and in the course of the *First Meditation* contrasted his thought with action in order to excuse the dangerousness of his strategy of radical doubt, his own language there was certainly the language of action. In the first paragraph he reports a resolve; he keeps making new resolves, and says he will stick "stubbornly" to them; he complains of how arduous he finds his chosen path; he gives his mind a rest from its tough new sense-distrusting discipline for the duration of his discussion of the piece of wax; he celebrates the near divine freedom of his will in the *Fourth Meditation;* he takes himself to be made in the image of a self-expressive powerful creative God. Although earlier (after hearing of Galileo's fate), he had announced that he would go forth masked, his masks are mere veils, his writings acts of self-expression. His ethics, put forward in the *Passions of the Soul* under the thin mask of a gift of requested advice to the spiritually troubled and mentally sharp Princess Elizabeth of Bohemia, exalt that generosity of mind which, disdaining both jealousy of competitors and fear of human enemies, indulges its own desire for truth and enjoys its love or willing union with the God-or-universe which it is trying better to understand.

A recent interesting philosophical phenomenon in this country is the number of women working on Descartes' writings, including his writings on ethics. Maybe this phenomenon is no more significant than that of the number of women Kant interpreters, but whereas the women Kantians prefer to stay off the topic of Kant's relations with women, women (such as Ann W. MacKenzie,[28] Margaret Atherton,[29] Ruth Mattern,[30] and Eileen O'Neill[31]) who are working on Descartes' thought can turn without defensiveness to those (mostly royal and aristocratic) women who took up his ideas and carried them further, who engaged with him in his strenuous pseudo-meditative labor, work, and action.[32] Perhaps Descartes appeals to women[33] not just because of the refreshing disdain of deontology in his ethics and the engaging directness and apparent simplicity of his metaphysical moves but also for his very doubleness—he is both solitary meditator and impassioned correspondent, both self-protective mask wearer and reckless intellectual exhibitionist. His books ended on the Index, but he led the church an entertaining dance for years before the full irony of his dedication of the *Meditations* became apparent to the professors of theology to whom they were offered.

As Naomi Scheman sees Ludwig Wittgenstein as a philosopher of the cultural margin[34] who, precisely for that reason, has a special appeal to rebellious women, so one can see René Descartes as an inspiring rebel. He tried ways of subverting his culture from within, wearing the masks of orthodoxy while busy replacing the foundations and rebuilding the edifice of belief. His quite astonishing attempt, or pretended attempt, to persuade the church that he had an intellectually superior account of how, in the Eucharist, bread could become flesh and wine blood is, for its sheer effrontery, one of the high points of European intellectual and cultural history, a moment of supreme intellectual intoxication and divinely willful *joie de vivre*. When a century later Hume offers the believers in religious miracles the thought that they have a continuing confirmation of the occurrence of miracles in their own ability to sustain belief in the miracles on which their religious faith is grounded,[35] when he ends his *Dialogues on Natural Religion* with Philo's switch to humble pietism, we get echoes of this philosophical playfulness, this daring dance on the edge of cultural abysses which may be typical of our greatest thinkers.[36]

In his *Discourse on the Method*[37] Descartes told us how he resolved to avoid making promises, which would have bound him to others and restricted his freedom, but how he had made and intended to keep this and other resolves. To get out of any forests he might seem lost in, he would walk as best he could in a straight line, pursuing his research strategy wherever it took him. It took him far, and he did, until near the end, avoid commitments to other people. He did not marry his daughter's mother, and he preferred to live as a resident alien in the relatively tolerant Netherlands to living as a presumptively loyal citizen in France. He showed devoted concern for the Princess Elizabeth of Bohemia and was a faithful correspondent to her, but all without any formal promises. His commitment to serve Queen Christina of Sweden did restrict his freedom, turning him from his straight scientific and philosophical path back toward the musical interests with which he had begun. His ties to her proved to be lethal, so he may have been wiser in his initial stubborn resolves than in his later capitulations to sociability and personal commitment. At any rate his life serves as a challenge to Arendt's thesis that, without promises to others, and without others' recognition of our later promise-fulfilling selves as identical with the earlier promise-making selves, we would lose ourselves. In the privacy of his study Descartes made resolves, including the resolve not to give promises, and then he published his resolves in the vernacular to the reading public. He did not seem to lose himself in the darkness of his doubtlessly lonely heart, and his actions of self-revelation (and also of sometimes judicious, sometimes playful self-concealment) are a standing challenge to those of us who live less dangerously. They are also a salutary challenge to those of us who criticize modern variants of individualism, since he is both an unparalleled individualist and the philosopher who celebrated love as the central ethical fact; both a despiser of tradition and the founder of a new tradition; both the solitary thinker and the energetic correspondent and dedicated friend.

I have in these ruminations exhibited two undeniable facts about women who write about ethics—that they often see fit to discuss the writings of nonfeminists and of men, and that they are usually interested in more than ethics. For ethics refuses to stay neatly in the bounds of, say, the personal as contrasted with the political, or the practical as contrasted with the theoretical. Moral psychology spills over into metaphysics, as moral commitment does into political action. Descartes' philosophy of mind is scarcely separable from his ethics. In *The Human Condition* Arendt merges philosophy of action, ethics, politics, and history of science, and this was one reason why I found her so stimulating, and why I chose to focus here on that book of hers. And a striking feature of that book is the way that she takes up and transforms the ideas of male thinkers from Aristotle to Marx, from Augustine[38] to Heidegger. Feminists could well take up and emend her ideas.[39] We women whose voices are joining those of others in contemporary ethics will often choose to try to transfigure old ideas, to divest them of their antifeminist or excessively masculinist aspects, to indulge in a bit of philosophical transvestism, as well as to try out androgyny, and to invent new styles. Ethics is a polyphonic art form, in which the echoes of the old voices contribute to the quality of the sound of all the new voices.

fifteen

A NATURALIST VIEW
OF PERSONS

According to John Knox, in his First Blast of the Trumpet against the monstrous regiment of women, it is "repugnant to nature," as well as "contumely to God, and the subversion of good order," to promote a woman to any position of superiority in any realm. We in the Eastern Division of the American Philosophical Association have not often subverted the patriarchal order that John Knox so passionately defended. Our first woman president was elected surprisingly early—in 1918 Mary Whiton Calkins gave the eighteenth presidential address at Harvard,[1] and her title was "A Personalistic Conception of Nature." I chose my title with hers in mind. After Mary Calkins, Grace de Laguna was the next woman president, in 1941, and Katharine Gilbert was president in 1946. So in the first half of our ninety-year existence, we elected three woman presidents. In the second half of our existence there have been only two, Alice Ambrose Lazerowitz in 1975, and now me.

Mary Calkins took it that a personalist view of nature was one that emphasized the *interdependence* of different natural things, all to some degree like ourselves, and I take a naturalist view of persons similarly to emphasize the interdependence of persons.[2] Persons are born to earlier persons, and learn the arts of personhood from other persons. These arts include the self-consciousness that follows from mutual recognition, along with the sort of representation that speech makes possible. Mary Calkins noted that the *first* persons we recognize as such are those who greet us, call to us, answer our calls. Our personhood is responsive, called into full expression by other persons who treat us as one of them. There may *be* persons who lack the ability to communicate with other persons, as Mary Calkins believed, but our own easiest and most natural understanding of persons is of communicative persons. As Amelie Rorty has reminded us,[3] the theatrical roots of the word "person," literally the mask through which a speaking voice emerges, make expressive voice the first essential of persons.

The tradition in which Mary Calkins spoke, in her presidential address, was the idealist one. Royce, and before him, Berkeley, were the philosophers whose themes she took up. Our own recent discussions of personhood owe more to Locke than to Berkeley or Royce. Locke makes our answerability on Judgment Day the central fact about our personhood. On that "Great Day," he writes, "no one shall be made to answer for what he knows nothing of; but shall receive his doom, his Conscience accusing or excusing him." Response to accusations is the form of responsiveness that Locke emphasizes as essential to personhood, and the ability to excuse oneself by saying "I don't recollect doing that" becomes a key ability that persons must possess.

Our modern discussions of personal identity have put more weight on Lockean individual memory than on social role and answerability. We have taken the individualist emphasis from Locke, and treated persons as moral atoms. In the Kantian tradition, where a person's moral answerability is emphasized, this individualism remains central. The atoms have to have an eye on the molecules they are obliged to join, but it is in terms of ideal and imaginary, not actual, communities that they define their duties. Individual and not collective responsibility is taken to define personhood, and the separateness and autonomy of persons becomes a treasured doctrine.

Now of course you and I are separate persons, each with a voice of her own and a will of her own. Does that fact distinguish us from cats or gorillas or dolphins? A current television advertisement for a roach killer has someone say, "Their sort deserve to die." We do not bother with individual responsibility in our forensic dealings with roaches and their sins. It is their *sort* we punish and make war on. But then, when we make any kind of war, we are very ready to switch from individual to collective responsibility. It always becomes "their sort" who deserve to die, whenever our fighting blood is up on behalf of us against them, Christians against Muslims, capitalists against Communists, humans against roaches. And when it comes to questions of reparation, we are willing ourselves to accept some collective responsibility. We are adept at quick switches from individual to collective responsibility, not just when our reason is deranged by battle cries, but in the calmer aftermath of wars, and in such cool theological hours as those in which the doctrine of original sin was conceived. Our philosophical focus *ought* to be as much on collective as on individual responsibility, when we seek to understand ourselves as persons. We should be as concerned with *our* responsibility for, for example, the despoiling of the planet, and with *my* responsibility as a resident of a country more responsible than most for the greenhouse effect, as with my sole responsibility for not taking my recyclable garbage to the neighborhood recycling plant. Included in the full inquiry into what we do and have done to us, as distinct from what I alone do and have done to me, will be those frequent cases where I act or am acted upon as one of a certain class, of which I am taken to serve as an informal representative. My own nomination and election to the office of president, for example, is not, I believe, due to any single-handed achievements or individual services of mine, and is almost certainly not independent of the fact that I am a woman. Any of a fair-sized group of other women philosophers of or near my philosophical generation and with a similar sort of record could easily have stood here today.[4]

Locke's discussion of personal identity launched our modern discussions of answerability, of personhood as a moral concept, and of the identity of continuants. For all his dismissal of the older notion that each of us is a unique immortal soul, created by and answerable to a father-god, Locke keeps much of the theological framework in place while transforming us from immortal souls into responsible and possibly transmigrating persons with anticipated futures and remembered pasts.[5] The last judgment sets his frame of discussion, as it did that of the theologians. Like them, he looks not only to last but also to first things. For origins also matter, since "one thing cannot have two beginnings of existence."

When, according to Locke, do we find a beginning of a new person? Not, it seems, at the conception or birth of a child to two parent persons, jointly responsible for such a new beginning. In carefully distinguishing the identity of the person both from that of "the Man" and from that of any soul substance enabling a man to do his thinking and other soulful activities, Locke writes that if "same immaterial soul" made "same man," then we would have to allow for the possibility that the same man could be "born of different women and in distant times." It will be not qua man, but rather qua soul or qua person, that Socrates, as in Locke's example, might be born twice, once in Athens and once in Queenborough. Birth is his origin as a man, but not as soul or as person. Qua person, he has no mother or an accidental mother, or perhaps exchangeable ones. (It is interesting how Locke takes it for granted that the meaning of "same woman" and "different women" *is* clearly fixed by biological and genealogical niche, in order to do his thought experiments on what "same man" should be taken to imply. Women, it seems, are to keep their biological places, while male persons plan their biology-transcending time travels.) Locke in these thoughts about thinking persons is in effect agreeing with Descartes, who in the *Third Meditation* declared that his human parents, Madame and Monsieur Descartes senior, "are not in any sense authors of my being, in as far as I am a thinking thing." A naturalist, on the other hand, takes it as obvious that a person is, as Montaigne put it, "marvelously corporeal,"[6] and that a person's ability to think is affected by genetic inheritance from parents and is vitally dependent upon the sort of care received in childhood—for example, in being introduced into a language community. So naturalists see persons as having person-progenitors and person-parents who cared for them. Locke is splendidly aware of the importance of how we are helped to learn to speak, but it is at best unclear whether Lockean persons have person-progenitors or can have person-progeny as distinct from *human* progenitors and human progeny. Do Kantian persons, later, have person-progenitors? At any rate it seems clear that, in this tradition, persons do not need mothers. As a contemporary philosopher puts it, "What is important about us is that we are persons. One's dignity does not depend upon one's parentage, even to the extent of being born of woman, or born at all."[7]

And now we have got to that vital Kantian conceptual link between personhood and *dignity*. To be a person is *not* to be born of woman, nor indeed to be born at all, but to spring forth from some fertile noumenal field of Ares fully formed and upright. Some philosophers who, like Locke and Kant, distinguish our personhood from our living human presence are willing to say quite straightforwardly that infants, who so obviously are lively and do have parents, and whose dignity is not immediately obvious, are not yet persons.[8] "Person" is always a status term; by these philosophers it is reserved for those at least trying out a dignified gait or mien. It is not our ability to tease and play (an ability which infants display better than most adults) but our upright stature, our would-be commanding presence, our pretensions to importance, that are decreed by the founding and sustaining members of the fraternity of persons to be the qualifications for membership. Persons, especially if they are men, matter, and decree who and what matters. "We are beings to whom things matter," they self-importantly proclaim. Aristotle, who of course did fairly straightforwardly profess the belief that persons had accidental mothers but essential fathers,[9] launched a still flourishing tradition of finding moral significance in our upright posture (ours, that is, after infancy, and before the decrepitude of old age).[10] We are the descendants of *homo erectus,* we are told by our wise men, the anthropologists. (Could it be that men have a thing about uprightness?) A recent male writer, who stresses that "to be a person is to exist in a space defined by distinctions of worth,"[11] and who sees us as special in our divine knowledge of "hyper goods" and hyper evils, finds symbolic significance in our peculiar mode of strutting: he writes, "Our dignity is so much woven into our very comportment . . . Our style of movement expresses how we see ourselves as enjoying respect or lacking it, as commanding it or failing to do so."[12] Not our clever and expressive hands, nor our capacity for laughing at strutters, let alone our variations on the raised eyebrow and the shoulder shrug, but our upright heaven-gazing stance and our spectator-conscious respect-demanding walk. Kantian persons cannot boast of being no respecters of persons. They lie under solemn obligation to be just that and, in particular, to be respecters of themselves as persons.

Naturalistically minded philosophers such as David Hume[13] and philosophically inclined naturalists such as Charles Darwin have gently reminded these dignity fetishists and aspirants to uprightness that birds too are two-footed, and can strut and look aloft before they soar aloft, that gorillas can be imposingly self-important. Here is Hume on "the pride of animals": "The very port or gait of a swan, or a turkey, or a peacock, shows the high idea he has entertain'd of himself, and his contempt of all others. This is the more remarkable that the pride is discov'd in the male only."[14] Hume's word "pride" is itself calculated to humble the pretensions of those dignity-preservers who paradoxically had declared pride to be a sin. For in the theological tradition one had to believe oneself to be one of a special breed, who, in Descartes' words at the end of the Fifth Part of his *Discourse on the Method,* have "more to fear and hope for than flies and ants" or, for that matter, than apes or dolphins. We must believe ourselves special precisely in the prospect of coming before a divine judgment seat, where each will answer for her deeds and misdeeds. We are the chosen ones, chosen, in virtue of our group membership in humankind, precisely for *individual* responsibility. *Our* kind deserve to be judged and sentenced one by one. Mass extermination is for lesser breeds. But our cosmic privilege is supposed to make us quake as much as it makes us swagger. We are to bow our proud stiff necks, and bend our upright carriage into a kneeling suppliant's pose. To be a person is to be one of the chosen people, chosen for individual guilt, individual conscience.

This theological and Kantian version of what we are is a remarkable and revealing bit of self-portrayal, deserving a place in the best ethnographic museums along with other headdresses, masks, and fetishes. The capacity for self-portrayal is of course itself one of the marks of personhood that the continuers of this theological tradition, as well as the naturalists, have singled out for emphasis. Conscience, self-consciousness, and self-representation appear together, and with them comes reflexivity, so that the self-representers have in truthfulness to represent themselves *as* self-representers, have to paint themselves in the act of painting themselves. We must not merely see ourselves in the mirror but see ourselves looking at ourselves, catch our own self-important self-inspection in the very narcissistic act itself. Nor is this all; we have to catch also our own shame at this very self-preoccupation. We are furtive narcissists, stealing our admiring glances at ourselves from lowered eyes, and sometimes self-flagellating narcissists, willing to pay in self-condemnation for our guilty self-satisfactions.

As Hume wrote of the typical religious manifestation of such unhappy human self-consciousness, these surely are sick men's dreams.[15] Yet they are the dreams that many of us choose to continue, as we nourish the Lockean and Kantian notion that to be a person is to transcend biological nature altogether, to enter into some supernatural realm where we are no longer essentially related to and dependent on others unless we *choose* such relationships, no longer ones born to others, with a place in a sequence of mortal generations, but rather autonomous responsible egos, each separately possessed of the dignity, the "unconditional incomparable worth" of one destined to stand alone before his own conscience, that "representative within us of the divine judgment seat," as Kant puts it.[16]

Kant explicitly likens the "court of conscience" to an ordinary law court, complete with prosecutor, advocate, accused, and judge (no mention of a jury of one's peers). And the game of judging, in all its variants, does indeed take several players. In its core courtroom form, someone must play judge, while others play prosecutor, advocate, and accused. The role of jury-cum-judge, in the theological tradition, has officially been reserved for a patriarchal God, but there has been no shortage of human stand-ins, of men eager to show their godlike ability to draw distinctions of worth, to separate the good persons from the evil persons, the nobler from the less noble sex, and the higher from the lower values. Our self-portrayals, when it comes to acknowledging our capacity for accusing, finding guilty, judging and sentencing, have often been less than fully self-conscious. We have tended to project our capacity for condemnation onto our gods, even more than we have projected other ingredients of our personhood. We make unfavorable judgments, and we act on them, but we also like to soothe ourselves by intoning "not my will, but thine, be done." We evade answerability for passing judgment. We like to think that some superperson both assigns the responsibilities and judges how well they have been discharged, and that we merely pass along these authoritative judgments from on high. But as we all know, it is we collectively who are responsible for allocating and reallocating responsibilities, we who divide the labor and decide if the laborer is or is not worthy of her hire, we who appoint the judges.

It is now an old oft-told tale that our religious propensities show us a lot about ourselves. To see that we see ourselves as made in a divine image, made in the image of a judgmental self-imaging god, is to see something about our special proclivities, both our strengths and our weaknesses. As Xenophanes wisely remarked, if horses had religious inclinations, their god would be a horse.[17] Our God is a jealous, monopoly-claiming, and self-imaging God, and what is undeniable about us who have conceived of such a God is our arrogance, our need to see ourselves as special[18] and as worthy of multiple portraits. This combines with our taste for disguised and distanced self-representation, for puzzle portraits, pictures that need some decoding before they appear as what they really are, self-representations. Our taste for disguised self-representation goes along with a more general taste for disguises and with a fascination with stories about metamorphosis. We each learn to fit a variety of roles and become adept at quick switches of guise and disguise. We each really do come to contain multitudes. Religious ceremonies and all the dressing up that goes with them obviously cater to this taste. But more fundamentally, the very doctrine of a god in human guise itself expresses our fascination with guises and disguises. To be a person, we could say, is to be one apt for impersonation, one to be impersonated and one to impersonate others, or other aspects of oneself.[19]

The alternative to this theological self-mystification is a naturalist view of persons, like Hume's or Darwin's or Freud's, that takes our biological nature seriously, takes it not as a handicap but as the source of strengths as well as weaknesses. In virtue of our long and helpless infancy, persons, who all begin as small persons, are necessarily social beings, who first learn from older persons, by play, by imitation, by correction. The naturalist knows that pride and shame are as often directed at parentage, home, and schooling, or at inherited wealth or inheritable diseases, as at individual strength of will or solitary vice. A naturalist will keep in view the full range of what we claim as our own. She will attend to our capacity for representation (and misrepresentation) of our own origins as well as of everything else of interest to us. She will take account of our taste for pomp (and for jeering at pomp), our delight in guises and disguises.

For a naturalist view of persons, our religious propensities present the greatest challenge. The naturalist must aim to understand them better than the supernaturalist can, just as the opponent of naturalism attempts to explain the tempting appeal of naturalism.[20] Hume, in perfect consistency with his naturalism, took the human phenomenon of religion to be the toughest problem that his philosophy faced, and one that remained "a riddle, an aenigma." A naturalist view of persons should relate religious displays of personhood to its other displays, and Hume in fact did a lot to leave these displays less of an "inexplicable mystery" than they might otherwise have appeared. The "playsome whimsies" of religious ceremonies are not so very different, after all, from our other playsome whimsies, such as graduation ceremonies or, for that matter, presidential addresses.

Our capacity for play is, as Hume, Nietzsche, and others have recognized, an important member of the skills of personhood. Hume took this capacity to be continuous with that found in all the higher animals, and to show itself in our case in our truth-seeking games as much as in backgammon and chess. In most of our games, something counts as winning, as defeating an opponent. Hume writes: "Almost all animals use in play the same member, and nearly the same action, as in fighting; a lion, a tyger, a cat their paws, an ox his horns; a dog his teeth, a horse his heels; yet they carefully avoid harming their companion, even tho' they have nothing to fear from his resentment" (T. 398). Pretend aggression is one of the arts of personhood, and one we share with "almost all animals." What do *we* use, in play and in fighting? Primarily our wits, by which we invent gunpowder and plan strategies, and our persuasive powers, by which we con our competitors into a false sense of security, our enemies into amassing their forces on a different border than the one we will attack. Our special weapon in any struggle for survival is our flexible intelligence, along with our glib tongues and our equally flexible and articulate moral sense. (Descartes, Hume, and Darwin all agree on this.) We are adept at deals, and at double dealing, at promising and at suspecting lying promises, at judging and at denouncing judges. We will expect, then, to find whimsical play-displays of all our intellectual, verbal, and moral skills, especially in their aggressive and aggression-dependent guises. Religions cater to our taste for such dangerous games, and the care taken to avoid harming the players can become vanishingly small as the boundaries between what is play, or rehearsal, and what is for real get blurred. The philosophical naturalist will not expect that we will lose our tastes for dangerous games, for drawing boundaries, crossing them, redrawing them. She will not expect religion as it has commonly been found in the world, or in philosophy, to depart in peace, but she may hope that we can palliate what we cannot cure.

She might indeed hope that philosophers, whose special boast is superior self-consciousness, will become a little more embarrassed than they seem to be when their own games are blatantly imitative of patriarchal aggressive games, in both their religious and their not-so-religious versions. We, and it seems from this address that I have to mean *we,* seem fairly content to make our philosophical discussions war by verbal means. Like religious confrontations, our philosophical engagements often are a not-so-moral equivalent of war. Many of us knowingly try, in moral philosophy, to convert morality into its most warlike equivalent, a superstrategy for winning, and then defend our theories by preemptive attacks on their rivals.[21] And in our more peaceable discussions of personhood we have recently engaged in games of metamorphosis that rival the most playsome whimsies of the religious. Not just Socrates into the mayor of Queenborough, and Heliogabalus into his hog, but contemporary male philosophers into Greta Garbo,[22] and other marvels of transfiguration.[23]

Hume wrote that errors in religion are dangerous, errors in philosophy only ridiculous. It is true that no one is likely to go to war to defend the real presence of Socrates in the mayor of Queenborough, or of Garbo in one or several of us. At worst we become laughing-stocks, and that need not be a dishonorable post.

To a naturalist, a striking feature of these recent neo-Lockean philosophical fantasies is the way they displace, into one person's continuing life history, the sort of tree or vine structure that has traditionally been used to represent a family's history over many generations. Simultaneous with the denial that a person, qua person, need be born at all, need *be* a family member, goes an assimilation of the *structure* of a family's history into a single person's history. Philosophical fantasies of "fusion" and "fission" may owe something to the nuclear power industry, but they owe more to the traditional representation of the way two families join by marriage, in which new branches are started when there are several children of the marriage. Genealogy, it seems, has been internalized: each person becomes his own family tree, complete with multiple continuers. So liberated are these philosophically conceived persons from mere biology that in this fairyland male persons may lose their Y chromosome, new persons may come into being by parthenogenesis from a man-person, and even death gets diluted into mere weakened continuity. Persons, on this version of them, need not be born and need not die. Mary Calkins in her presidential address said that it would take a very sleepy self, in Leibniz's words "a momentary unremembering and unrecognizing" one, to think of itself, like the priest Melchisedec, as "without father, without mother, having neither beginning of days nor end of life."[24] Paradoxically, it is the very will to identify oneself as a lasting remembering self that prompts these generation-forgetting and death-transcending modern whimsies, if not of doing without parents, at least of switching one's own for Garbo's, if not of being immortal, at least of becoming a potentially endless series of successive "selves." It is Locke's memory criterion, generalized into psychological connectedness, that is thought to license these ignorings of actual biological origins, actual pasts there to be recalled, and to encourage these fantasized transfigurations, as persons wander freely across the gene pool, from memory to memory and from gender to gender. For strictly, on Locke's criterion, a person is one who was born only if he remembers being born, was dependent on others only if he remembers that dependency. The autonomous adolescent person, if he has succeeded in forgetting that he was a heteronomous child, can rightly disown that childhood as really his. These fantasies of freedom from our own actual history, actual dependency, actual mortality, actual biological limitations and determinate possibilities, have on the whole been male fantasies, and many women philosophers have found them strange.[25] Susan Wolf sensibly says: "my reasons for being interested in persons never had much to do with my beliefs about their metaphysical composition."[26] Accepting a metaphysical "reduction" of persons into a sequence of conscious experiences or doings need not, she claims, in any way alter our conception of more-central-than-metaphysical aspects of persons as we view them and as we are concerned with them. On a generous construal, we might see these male fantasies as the Y chromosome trying to disown itself. It is unlikely that women, who have been traditionally allocated the care of very dependent young and old persons, will take persons as anything except interdependent persons.[27] It is just as unlikely that women can pretend that new persons come into being in any other way than by being born of women, after a conception for which two persons are jointly responsible, in all cases except those resulting from rape or from the seduction of the nonculpably ignorant. The *facts* of shared responsibility, and of the frequently less than equally shared burdens of responsibility, are not facts about persons that women find it so easy to forget. It is not merely upright stature, nor even opposed thumbs, it is navels too that are essential to such persons as we have any knowledge of. Metaphysics, so far, has had little to say about navels.

Now of course many women philosophers do participate in the neo-Lockean metaphysical thought experiments, just as there are women Kantians, and as there have always been eager women adherents of patriarchal religions. Women's reputation for docility is not entirely unearned, and often it has been our best survival strategy.[28] The schizophrenia of modern philosophy of mind and of the person, its back-handed tribute to our mammalian nature, to our place in a sequence of generations of living, mating, and dying human persons, is our joint responsibility, not just Locke's, or Kant's, or any few persons' doing. What can we now do about it? The term "person" is a status term, and it is *our* term.[29] It is we who have to decide what that status is, and whether we give it to a human fetus, to other animals, to corporations; whether we reserve it for those, like corporations, who really do have nonbiological origins, along with those "honorary corporations" who dream of forgetting any actual biological origins. Sometimes one wishes we could just drop the term, so heavily freighted is it with its theological past and with current controversies. But words are hard to kill. The only realistic strategy is to make do with the old concept, heavily burdened though it is. Like Hume, we can try to rethink, debunk, and *level* all its elitist implications, see our intelligence as one among many forms of "reason in animals," our much vaunted dignity as just a variant of the peacock's pride, or what Jenny Teichman recently demoted to the "rooster factor,"[30] our interesting games just one form of animal play. Mary Calkins's rather extreme proposal was that we personify without restriction, and call "a person" every perceptible part of our own environment, whether living or nonliving. We would then go on to distinguish the communicating from the noncommunicating persons around us. Hers might be one way to defang the concept of person, or at least to let it play harmlessly, if uselessly, in our language. Or we could let it be a purely grammatical category, an attribute of pronouns.

The more refined arts of personhood are learned as the personal pronouns are learned, from the men and women, girls and boys, who are the learners' companions and playmates. We come to recognize ourselves and others in mirrors, to refer to ourselves and to others, we learn to draw, and to draw ourselves drawing, to talk, and to talk about talk, to criticize, and to criticize criticisms, to put on dignified airs and to laugh at those who put on dignified airs. We listen to fairy tales about princes who become frogs, Cinderellas who become princesses. When displeased with our parents, we have fantasies of having been stolen by gypsies from nobler or wealthier or more indulgent parents, of turning out to be members of some other family, of really being princes and princesses. And some of us become philosophers, and transpose all these fairy tales into new versions of transformation, new metaphysical metamorphoses, new denials or distortions of our actual origins. Some of us have invented a special fallacy, the so-called genetic fallacy, to license ourselves to ignore actual origins, or treat them as irrelevant to current capacities and current debts. Some of us even try to effect "total alterations" in philosophy, to turn it from being an offshoot of theology, or a compensation for the loss of theology, into something more naturalistic, more continuous with the rest of our real life. And others of us, resigned to the unlikelihood of total alterations, try at least to develop alternative self-understandings to those proposed by the witting and unwitting continuers of the theological tradition.

We naturalists see persons as intelligent, talkative, playful mammals who have become conscious of ourselves, of our mammalian nature, its possibilities and the constraints it imposes. As we become conscious of our actual origins and history, we become aware of the wide range of capacities that go into our personhood. We can then see our intelligence ("Mistress Clever, the clever whore," as Luther called it) in relation to the intelligence of other smart animals, our communicative and expressive powers in relationship to theirs, our linguistic powers in the context of our other powers of expression and representation, and so on for all our multiple arts of personhood. We will be aware in particular that cooperation, sometimes cooperation against the grain, has been the saving strength of our mammalian species, and so we will realize that for a fuller understanding of ourselves as persons we must continue to cooperate, not only with like- and unlike-minded philosophers, but with those in other disciplines who study human persons in their natural context. Our natural habitat, as persons, is among other persons. Our personhood shows in the way we are responsive to one other, responsive to earlier and later generations, responsive to the presence of other groups of persons, groups with differing histories and interestingly different self-understandings. Self-understanding is a shared taste, and cultivating it calls for our full capacities for mutual response.

1. WHAT DO WOMEN WANT IN A MORAL THEORY?

1. Carol Gilligan, *In a Different Voice: Psychological Theory and Women's Development* (Cambridge, Mass.: Harvard University Press, 1982).
2. Ian Hacking, "Winner Take Less," a review of *The Evolution of Cooperation* by Robert Axelrod, *New York Review of Books,* vol. 31, June 28, 1984.
3. Carol Gilligan, "The Conquistador and the Dark Continent: Reflections on the Psychology of Love," *Daedalus,* 113 (Summer 1984): 75–95.
4. "Caring about Caring," a response to Harry Frankfurt's "What We Care About," both in "Matters of the Mind," *Synthese,* 53 (November 1982): 257–290. My paper is also included in my *Postures of the Mind: Essays on Mind and Morals* (Minneapolis, Minn.: University of Minnesota Press, 1985).
5. I defend this claim about trust in Essay 6.
6. Susan Moller Okin, *Justice, Gender, and the Family* (New York: Basic Books, 1989), esp. chap. 3.

2. THE NEED FOR MORE THAN JUSTICE

1. John Rawls, *A Theory of Justice* (Cambridge, Mass.: Belknap Press of Harvard University Press, 1971).
2. Alasdair MacIntyre, *After Virtue* (Notre Dame, Ind.: Notre Dame University Press, 1980).
3. Michael Stocker, "The Schizophrenia of Modern Ethical Theories," *Journal of Philosophy,* 73 (1976): 453–466; and "Agent and Other: Against Ethical Universalism," *Australasian Journal of Philosophy,* 54 (December 1976): 206–220.

4. Lawrence Blum, *Friendship, Altruism, and Morality* (London: Routledge & Kegan Paul, 1980).

5. Michael Slote, *Goods and Virtues* (Oxford: Clarendon Press, 1983).

6. Laurence Thomas, "Love and Morality," in *Sociobiology and Epistemology,* ed. James Fetzer (Dordrecht and Boston: D. Reidel, 1985); "Justice, Happiness, and Self-Knowledge," *Canadian Journal of Philosophy,* 16 (March 1986): 63–82; "Beliefs and the Motivation to Be Just," *American Philosophical Quarterly,* 22 (1985): 347–352; and *Living Morally: A Psychology of Moral Character* (Philadelphia, Penn.: Temple University Press, 1989).

7. Claudia Card, "On Mercy," *Philosophical Review,* 81 (1972): 182–207; and *Choices and Values* (New York, N.Y.: Columbia University Press, 1994), and *Character and Moral Luck* (Philadelphia, Penn.: Temple University Press, expected 1995).

8. Alison Jaggar, *Feminist Politics and Human Nature* (London: Rowman & Allenheld, 1983).

9. Susan Wolf, "Moral Saints," *Journal of Philosophy,* 79 (August 1982): 419–439.

10. Carol Gilligan, *In a Different Voice: Psychological Theory and Women's Development* (Cambridge, Mass.: Harvard University Press, 1982). Hereafter cited as *D.V.* For a helpful survey article, see Owen Flanagan and Kathryn Jackson, "Justice, Care, and Gender: The Kohlberg-Gilligan Debate Revisited," *Ethics,* 97 (April 1987): 622–637.

11. Nancy Chodorow, *The Reproduction of Mothering* (Berkeley, Calif.: University of California Press, 1978).

12. Carol Gilligan, "The Conquistador and the Dark Continent: Reflections on the Psychology of Love," *Daedalus,* 113 (Summer 1984): 75–95; and "The Origins of Morality in Early Childhood Relationships," in *Mapping the Moral Domain,* ed. C. Gilligan, J. Ward, and J. Taylor (Cambridge, Mass.: Harvard University Press, 1988), pp. 111–137.

13. Lawrence Kohlberg, *Essays in Moral Development,* 2 vols. (New York: Harper & Row, 1981, 1984).

14. Bernard Williams, *Ethics and the Limits of Philosophy* (New York: Cambridge University Press, 1985).

15. Philippa Foot, *Virtues and Vices* (Berkeley, Calif.: University of California Press, 1978).

16. I have written about the significance of her findings for moral philosophy in Essays 1, 4, and 6.

17. Immanuel Kant, *The Metaphysics of Morals,* trans. Mary Gregor (New York: Cambridge University Press, 1991), sec. 46.

18. Laurence Thomas, "Sexism and Racism: Some Conceptual Differences," *Ethics,* 90 (1980): 239–250; reprinted in *Sexist Language: A Modern Philosophical Analysis,* ed. Mary Vetterling-Braggin (Totowa, N.J.: Littlefield Adams, 1981).

19. See articles listed in note 6.

3. UNSAFE LOVES

This is a revised version of a talk given at a conference on love organized by John O'Connor and held at William Patterson College in February 1988. I have been helped by the discussion on that occasion, by perceptive criticisms from Lynne Tirrell, and by editorial suggestions from Robert Solomon and Kathleen Higgins.

1. Epigraph: David Hume, "Of Polygamy and Divorces," in *Essays: Moral, Political and Literary,* ed. Eugene F. Miller (Indianapolis, Ind.: Liberty Classics, 1985), p. 185.
2. Robert Brown, *Analyzing Love* (New York: Cambridge University Press, 1987), p. 126.
3. Ibid., pp. 126–127.
4. Jerome Shaffer, "An Assessment of Emotion," *American Philosophical Quarterly,* 20 (April 1983): 171.
5. Immanuel Kant, *The Metaphysics of Morals,* trans. Mary Gregor (New York: Cambridge University Press, 1991), pt. 2, sec. 24, p. 244.
6. Ibid., sec. 23.
7. Immanuel Kant, *Lectures on Ethics,* trans. L. Infield (New York: Harper & Row, 1963), p. 207.
8. Ibid.; p. 208.
9. Ibid., p. 206.
10. Ibid.
11. René Descartes, *Passions of the Soul,* in *The Philosophical Writings of Descartes,* vol. 1, trans. J. Cottingham, R. Stoothoff, and D. Murdoch (New York: Cambridge University Press, 1988), arts. 79, 80, p. 356.
12. Ibid., art. 147, p. 381.
13. Ibid., art. 90, p. 360.
14. I am drawing a sharp contrast between theological and naturalistic views, but they can be combined in one philosopher. St. Augustine is a good case of a thinker who takes our natural condition seriously enough, but goes on to superimpose a supernatural framework on it, in a platonistic way working up from childhood experience of love between mother and child, through love of comrades, the experience of sexual love and what he in the *Confessions* calls "the madness of raging lust," to transcend all these in eventual love of God.
15. David Hume, *A Treatise of Human Nature,* ed. L. A. Selby-Bigge and P. H. Nidditch (Oxford: Clarendon Press, 1978), p. 353.
16. Ibid.
17. See ibid., p. 581. "A man, that lies at a distance from us, may, in a little time, become a familiar acquaintance."
18. Ibid., p. 363.
19. Ibid.
20. Ibid., p. 322.
21. David Hume, "A Dialogue," in *Enquiries,* ed. L. A. Selby-Bigge and P. H. Nidditch (Oxford: Clarendon Press, 1975). Hume discusses

homosexual love as Plato knew it, and treats it much more sympathetically than he elsewhere (for example, in "Of Polygamy and Divorces")
treats some forms of heterosexual love, such as that of a sultan for his
harem.

22. See Hume, *Treatise,* "Of Chastity and Modesty" and "Of Polygamy
and Divorces."

23. Ibid., pp. 308–309.

24. Hirself = her- or himself.

25. William Shakespeare, *Shakespeare's Sonnets* (New Haven, Conn.: Yale
University Press, 1977), Sonnet 62.

26. I discuss this feature of love in "What Emotions Are About," in *Philosophical Perspectives,* 4: *Action Theory and Philosophy of Mind,* ed.
James E. Tomberlin (Atascadero, Calif.: Ridgeview Publishing Co.,
1990), pp. 1–29.

27. Hume, *Treatise,* p. 329.

28. Shakespeare, *Sonnets,* Sonnet 49.

29. A similar view is taken also by Robert C. Roberts, in an article which
came to my attention after I had written this essay. He writes: "the
responses characteristic of such attachment are too various and
conflicting for it to be an emotion. They can be joy when the beloved is
flourishing, indignation when she is insulted, gratitude when she is
benefited, fear when she is threatened, hope when her prospects are
good, grief when she dies, and much more. Love in this sense is not an
emotion, but a disposition to a range of emotions." "What an Emotion
Is: A Sketch," *Philosophical Review,* 97 (April 1988): 203.

30. Richard Wollheim, *The Thread of Life* (Cambridge, Mass.: Harvard
University Press, 1984), p. 279, see also p. 212.

31. Thomas Hobbes, *Leviathan* (New York: Everyman's Library, 1973),
chap. 10. "To have friends, is power: for they are strengths united."

32. Hume, *Treatise,* p. 497.

4. HUME, THE WOMEN'S MORAL THEORIST?

1. David Hume, *A Treatise of Human Nature,* ed. L. A. Selby-Bigge and
P. H. Nidditch (Oxford: Clarendon Press, 1978), p. 348. References in
the text will be given as *T.* Other works by Hume referred to in the text
are *Enquiries,* ed. L. A. Selby-Bigge and P. H. Nidditch (Oxford:
Clarendon Press, 1975), to be given as *E;* and *Essays: Moral, Political
and Literary,* ed. Eugene F. Miller (Indianapolis, Ind.: Liberty Classics,
1985), to be given as *Es.* I also refer to *History of England,* any edition.

2. The three essays referred to in this section were published by Hume in the
first edition of *Essays Moral and Political* (1741–42), but were removed
by him in subsequent editions. They can be found in David Hume,
Essays: Moral, Political and Literary, ed. Eugene F. Miller (Indianapolis,
Ind.: Liberty Classics, 1985) in the appendix "Essays Withdrawn and
Unpublished."

3. Lawrence Kohlberg, *The Philosophy of Moral Development* (San Francisco, Calif.: Harper & Row, 1981), p. 12. See also Kohlberg, *Collected Papers on Moral Development and Moral Education* (Cambridge, Mass.: Harvard University, Moral Education Research Foundation, 1971).
4. See Introduction to Eva Kittay and Diana Meyers, eds., *Women and Moral Theory* (Lanham, Md.: Rowman & Littlefield, 1987). I discuss Kohlberg's theory in Essay 2, pp. 21–22.
5. Carol Gilligan, *In a Different Voice: Psychological Theory and Women's Development* (Cambridge, Mass.: Harvard University Press, 1982), pp. 25 ff. Future references to this work will be given in the text as *D.V.*
6. Robert Rosenthal, J. A. Hall, M. R. DiMatteo, P. L. Rogers, and D. Archer, *Sensitivity to Nonverbal Communication: The PONS Test* (Baltimore, Md.: Johns Hopkins University Press, 1979). See also Judith A. Hall, *Non-Verbal Sex Differences* (Baltimore, Md.: Johns Hopkins University Press, 1984). Immanuel Kant, *The Metaphysical Elements of Justice,* trans. John Ladd (Indianapolis, Ind.: Bobbs-Merrill, 1965).
7. Carol Gilligan, "Moral Orientation and Moral Development," in *Women and Moral Theory,* ed. Kittay and Meyers, pp. 19–33.
8. "Natural Virtues, Natural Vices," *Social Philosophy & Policy,* 8, Ethics, Politics, and Human Nature (Autumn 1990): 24–34.

5. HUME, THE REFLECTIVE WOMEN'S EPISTEMOLOGIST?

1. See Lorraine Code, *Epistemic Responsibility* (Hanover, N.H.: University Press of New England, 1987); and *What Can She Know? Feminist Theory and the Construction of Knowledge* (Ithaca, N.Y.: Cornell University Press, 1991).
2. David Hume, *A Treatise of Human Nature,* ed. L. A. Selby-Bigge and P. H. Nidditch (Oxford: Clarendon Press, 1978), p. 662. References to this work will be given in the text as *T.* Other works by Hume referred to in the text are *Enquiries,* ed. L. A. Selby-Bigge and P. H. Nidditch (Oxford: Clarendon Press, 1975), to be given as *E.; Essays: Moral, Political and Literary,* ed. Eugene F. Miller (Indianapolis, Ind.: Liberty Classics, 1985), to be given as *Es.*
3. I have written about this in "Hume on Women's Complexion," in *The Science of Man in the Scottish Enlightenment,* ed. Peter Jones (Edinburgh: Edinburgh University Press, 1990), and alluded briefly to it in "Hume's Account of Social Artifices—Its Origins and Originality," *Ethics,* 98 (July 1988): 757–778.
4. In *A Progress of Sentiments: Reflections on Hume's* Treatise (Cambridge, Mass.: Harvard University Press, 1991), esp. chaps. 4 and 12.
5. See Christine Korsgaard, "Normativity as Reflexivity," talk given to the sixteenth meeting of the Hume Society, Lancaster, England, 1989.
6. See Ruth Mattern, "Moral Science and the Concept of Persons in Locke," *Philosophical Review,* 89 (January 1980): 24–45.
7. Or we could say Aristotelian, or proto-Hegelian, or proto-Brandomian.

See Robert Brandom, "Freedom and Constraint by Norms," *American Philosophical Quarterly*, 14 (April 1977): 187–196.

8. "Reply to Korsgaard," sixteenth meeting of the Hume Society, Lancaster, England, 1989.

9. Passages that suggest this interpretation are the formulation of the categorical imperative given in the *Groundwork* thus: "Handle nach Maximen, die sich selbst zugleich as allgemeine Naturgesetze zum Gegenstande haben können." There are similar formulations in the second *Critique*.

10. See Hume, "Idea of a Perfect Commonwealth," in *Es*. Although a minimum income is the qualification for voting, only freeholders can stand for election.

11. See Lorraine Code, *What Can She Know?* chap. 7, for a discussion of the need to listen to how aggrieved social groups actually present their situation, in order to be capable of properly informed sympathy with them. There she takes issue with the belief "that epistemologists need only to understand propositional, observationally derived knowledge, and all the rest will follow" (p. 269).

12. Calling someone a virtual woman will be an insult in the mouth of a patriarch, a compliment in more enlightened contexts.

13. I am consciously presenting an unsympathetic reading of Kant's views, in the knowledge that others will present more sympathetic readings, and in the confidence that their views will balance mine, so that justice can be done.

14. Hume, "Idea of a Perfect Commonwealth," pp. 512–529.

15. See "Of the Rise and Progress of the Arts and Sciences," "Of Polygamy and Divorces," "Of Refinement in the Arts," "Of Some Remarkable Customs," "Of Moral Prejudices," "Of Suicide."

16. Robert Brandom, *Making It Explicit* (Cambridge, Mass.: Harvard University Press, forthcoming).

17. Code, *Epistemic Responsibility,* and *What Can She Know?*

18. The need for "security," before curiosity or the love of truth can flourish, and the need for a climate of trust to give modern scientists security are explored by John Hardwig in "The Role of Trust in Knowledge," *Journal of Philosophy,* 88 (December 1991): 693–708.

19. In his *History of England,* Hume develops this theme, especially when he describes the civilizing effect of the rediscovery, in 1130, of Justinian's *Pandects.* "It is easy to see what advantages Europe must have reaped by its inheriting at once from the ancients, so complete an art, which was also so necessary for giving security to all other arts" (chap. 23).

20. This passage should give pause to those who want to dub Hume a conservative in politics.

21. A significant recent exception to this generalization is John W. Danford, in *David Hume and the Problem of Reason* (New Haven, Conn.: Yale University Press, 1990), esp. chap. 7. See also his essay "Hume's His-

tory and the Parameter of Economic Development," in *Liberty in Hume's History of England,* ed. Nicholas Capaldi and Donald W. Livingston (Dordrecht: Kluwer Academic Publishers, 1990).

22. This passage, originally in "Of the Rise and Progress of the Arts and Sciences," was omitted from later editions.
23. I develop this claim in *A Progress of Sentiments,* chap. 12.

6. TRUST AND ANTITRUST

I owe the second half of this essay's title to the salutary reaction of Alexander Nehamas to an earlier and more sanguine version, read at Chapel Hill Colloquium in October 1984. I also owe many important points which I have tried to incorporate in this revised version to John Cooper, who commented helpfully on the paper on that occasion, to numerous constructive critics at later presentations of versions of it at CUNY Graduate Center, Brooklyn College, Columbia University, the University of Pennsylvania, and to readers. I received such a flood of helpful and enthusiastic advice that it became clear that, although few philosophers have written directly on this topic, very many have been thinking about it. It is only by ruthlessly putting finis to my potentially endless revisions and researches into hitherto unfamiliar legal, sociological, psychological, and economic literature that any essay emerged from my responses to these gratifying and generous responses.

1. Epigraph: Sissela Bok, *Lying* (New York: Pantheon Books, 1978), p. 31n. Bok is one of the few philosophers to have addressed the ethics of trust fairly directly. The title of the chapter from which this quotation comes is "Truthfulness, Deceit and Trust."
2. Plato, *Laws* 4.705a. I owe this reference to John Cooper, who found my charge that Plato and Aristotle had neglected the topic of trust ungenerous, given how much they fairly clearly took for granted about its value and importance. (But taking for granted is a form of neglect.)
3. Besides Bok and Locke, whom I refer to, those who have said something about it include N. Hartmann, *Ethik* (Berlin: W. de Gruyter, 1962), p. 468 ff.; Virginia Held, *Rights and Goods* (New York: Free Press, 1984), esp. chap. 5, "The Grounds for Social Trust"; D. O. Thomas, "The Duty to Trust," *Aristotelian Society Proceedings,* 79 (1978–79): 89–101. It is invoked in passing by Aurel Kolnai in "Forgiveness," in *Ethics, Value, and Reality,* ed. Bernard Williams and David Wiggins (Indianapolis: Hackett Publishing Co., 1978): "Trust in the world, unless it is vitiated by harebrained optimism and dangerous irresponsibility, may be looked upon, not to be sure as the starting-point and the very basis, but perhaps as the epitome and culmination of morality" (p. 223); and by John R. S. Wilson in "In One Another's Power," *Ethics,* 88 (1978): 303.
4. A reader for *Ethics* suggested that, when one trusts one's child to mail an important letter for one at the mailbox on the corner, no discre-

tionary powers are given, although one is trusting him with the safe, speedy transfer of the letter to the box. But life is full of surprises—in Washington on Inauguration Day mailboxes were sealed closed as a security precaution, and in some parts of Manhattan mailboxes are regularly sealed after dark. One trusts the child to do the sensible thing if such an unforeseen problem should arise—to bring the letter back, not leave it on the ledge of the sealed mailbox or go too far afield to find another.

5. This point I take from the fascinating sociological analysis of trust given by Niklas Luhmann in *Trust and Power* (New York: Wiley, 1979), which I discovered while revising this essay. In many ways my analysis agrees with his, inasfar as I understand the implications of his account of it as "reduction of complexity," in particular of complex future contingencies. He makes much of the difference between absence of trust and distrust, and he distinguishes trust from what it presupposes, a mere "familiarity," or taking for granted. I have blurred these distinctions. He treats personal trust as a risky investment and looks at mechanisms for initiating and maintaining trust. Tact is said to play an important role in both. It enables trust-offering overtures to be rejected without hostility ensuing, and it enables those who make false moves in their attempts to maintain trust to recover their position without too much loss of face. "A social climate . . . institutionalizes tact, and knows enough escape routes for self-presentation in difficult situations" (p. 84). It is important, I think, to see that tact is a virtue which needs to be added to delicacy of discrimination in recognizing *what* one is trusted with, good judgment as to whom to trust with what, and a willingness to admit and forgive fault as all functional virtues needed in those who would sustain trust.

6. See David Hume, *A Treatise of Human Nature,* ed. L. A. Selby-Bigge and P. H. Nidditch (Oxford: Clarendon Press, 1978), p. 497.

7. Luhmann, *Trust and Power,* p. 8, n. 1. It is interesting to note that, unlike Luhmann and myself, Bernard Barber begins his sociological treatment of trust in *The Logic and Limits of Trust* (New Brunswick, N.J.: Rutgers University Press, 1983) not by remarking on the neglect of the topic but, rather, by saying, "Today nearly everyone seems to be talking about 'trust'" (p. 1). He lists "moral philosophers" along with "presidential candidates, political columnists, pollsters, social critics and the man in the street" as among those talking so much about it but cites only two moral philosophers, Bok and Rawls (who by his own account is *not* always talking about it). Between Luhmann's work on trust, first published in Germany in 1973, and Barber's, sociologists had ten years to get talk and publication about trust going, but it has not yet spread to most of the moral philosophers I have read.

8. Hume, *Treatise,* p. 521.

9. My thoughts about the role of the words "Trust me!" are influenced by T. M. Scanlon, "Promises and Practices," *Philosophy & Public Affairs,*

19 (Summer 1990): 199–226. Indeed Scanlon's talk on this topic to the University of Pittsburgh philosophy department in April 1984 was what, along with Hume's few remarks about it, started me thinking about trust in and out of voluntary exchanges.

10. Luhmann says, "It is not possible to demand the trust of others; trust can only be offered and accepted" (*Trust and Power,* p. 43). I am here claiming something stronger, namely, that one cannot offer it or accept it by an act of will—that one cannot demand it of oneself or others until some trust-securing social artifice invents something like promise that *can* be offered and accepted at will.

11. Hume, *Treatise,* p. 522.

12. Ibid., p. 521.

13. I have discussed and defended Hume's account in "Promises, Promises, Promises," in my *Postures of the Mind: Essays on Mind and Morals* (Minneapolis, Minn.: University of Minnesota Press, 1985), pp. 174–206.

14. Hume, *Treatise,* p. 541.

15. Ibid., p. 522.

16. For Hume's thought, see ibid., p. 521.

17. Friedrich Nietzsche, *Beyond Good and Evil,* trans. Walter Kaufmann in *Basic Writings of Nietzsche* (New York: Modern Library, 1968), pt. 7, sec. 238, p. 357.

18. I defend them a little more in Essay 1.

19. Carol Gilligan, *In a Different Voice: Psychological Theory and Women's Development* (Cambridge, Mass.: Harvard University Press, 1982).

20. Norbert Hornstein has drawn my attention to an unpublished paper by the economist Peter Murrell, "Commitment and Cooperation: A Theory of Contract Applied to Franchising." Murrell emphasizes the nonstandard nature of franchise contracts, in that they typically are vague about what is expected of the franchisee. The consequent infrequency of contract termination by the franchisor is linked by him to the long duration of the contracts and to the advantage, to the more powerful proprietor of the trademark, of keeping the trust of the less powerful scattered franchisees and maintaining quality control by means other than punitive contract terminations. This, I persuade myself, is a case where the exception proves the rule, where the nonstandardness of such inexplicit and trusting contracts points up the explicitness and minimal trustingness of standard contracts.

21. Hume, *Treatise,* p. 544.

22. Objections of this sort were raised by a reader for *Ethics.*

23. Hume placed on the title page of his *Treatise of Human Nature* these words of Tacitus: "Rara temporum felicitas, ubi sentire, quae velis, and quae sentias, dicere licet" (Rare the happy times when we can think what we like and say what we think).

24. Luhmann, *Trust and Power,* p. 69.

7. TRUST AND ITS VULNERABILITIES

This essay and Essay 8 were given as the Tanner Lectures at Princeton University in March 1991, under the titles "The Pathologies of Trust" and "Appropriate Trust." Their revision was greatly helped by the prepared comments of Francine du Plessix Gray, Geoffrey Hawthorn, Thomas M. Scanlon, Jr., and David Shipler on that occasion, by suggestions from the audience, by later discussion with Princeton faculty and students, and by subsequent correspondence with Sarah Buss, Pamela Foa, Richard Moran, and Thomas Scanlon. The revisions were made at the Rockefeller Study Center, Bellagio, Italy, and I am very grateful for the opportunity to enjoy the beauty, peace, and good company to be found there. The peace was also instructive for my study of trust, since our idyllic headland was protected, during most of my stay there, by an armed guard. Italian soldiers with machine guns patrolled the grounds and guarded the entrances against perceived terrorist threats. So our easy mutual trust within our sanctuary had as its exterior face an apparent distrust for all outsiders. I am pleased to report that by the time I left, the perceived danger, and with it the guard, had gone.

1. Epigraph: Sir Thomas Wyatt, *Poems,* ed. K. Muir (London: Routledge & Kegan Paul, 1949), p. 28 (28th poem in the Egerton M.S. 2711).
2. *The Correspondence of John Locke,* ed. E. S. de Beer (Oxford: Clarendon Press, 1976), I, 123 (letter 81).
3. Geoffrey Hawthorn quotes these words of Elizabeth to Parliament in 1596 in his essay "Three Ironies of Trust," in *Trust: Making and Breaking Cooperative Relations,* ed. Diego Gambetta (New York: Basil Blackwell, 1988), p. 115.
4. According to Niklas Luhmann, trust always involves some assessment and acceptance of risk, so that to call trust risky becomes pleonastic. See his essay "Familiarity, Confidence, Trust: Problems and Alternatives," in Gambetta, ed., *Trust,* p. 100.
5. Here and in what follows I develop the analysis of trust given in Essay 6.
6. T. M. Scanlon, "Promises and Practices," *Philosophy & Public Affairs,* 19 (Summer 1990): 199–226.
7. "*Principle F:* If (1) A voluntarily and intentionally leads B to expect that A will do x (unless B consents to A's not doing x); (2) A knows that B wants to be assured of this; (3) A acts with the aim of providing this assurance, and has good reason to believe that he or she has done so; (4) B knows that A has the beliefs and intentions just described; (5) A intends for B to know this, and knows that B does know it; and (6) B knows that A has this knowledge and intent; then, in the absence of some special justification, A must do x unless B consents to x's not being done." Scanlon, "Promises and Practices," p. 208.
8. John Updike, *Trust Me: Short Stories* (Greenwich, Conn.: Fawcett Pub., 1965), p. 3.

9. See my "Trusting Ex-Intimates," in *Person to Person*, ed. George Graham and Hugh Lafollette (Philadelphia, Pa.: Temple University Press, 1989), pp. 269–281, for some peculiarities of trust between intimates and its breakdown.

10. David Hume, *A Treatise of Human Nature*, ed. L. A. Selby-Bigge and P. H. Nidditch (Oxford: Clarendon Press, 1975), p. 521.

11. Francis Bacon, *Remains* (London: Robert Chiswell, 1679), p. 70.

12. Saul Bellow, *More Die of Heartbreak* (New York: Dell Books, 1987), pp. 47–48.

13. Hume, *Treatise*, p. 377.

14. David Hume, *Enquiries*, ed. L. A. Selby-Bigge and P. H. Nidditch (Oxford: Clarendon Press, 1978), p. 261.

15. I argue that rights are a way of avoiding having to beg or be begged from in Essay 11.

16. Hume, *Enquiries*, p. 261.

17. Hugo Grotius, *The Rights of War and Peace*, trans. A. C. Campbell (Westport, Conn.: Hyperion Press, 1979), bk. 3, chap. 25, sec. 4.

18. I discuss the special problems that arise when insulted or especially aggrieved peoples and nations resort to terrorism in Essay 10.

19. I may appear to have a bit of a hang-up about the fidelity of mail carriers (see Essay 6, p. 104, and "Trusting Ex-Intimates," p. 278), but in fact the international mail service, along with the International Red Cross, is one of the few stable cooperative schemes that function across national boundaries, even in wartime, so faithful mail carriers and trustworthy ambulance drivers are quite proper moral paradigms.

20. Bacon, *Remains*, p. 63.

21. Quintus Cicero, *Com. Pet.* 39–40.

8. SUSTAINING TRUST

1. That volume (*Trust: Making and Breaking Cooperative Relations*, ed. Diego Gambetta, New York: Basil Blackwell, 1988), the outcome of a series of seminars at King's College, Cambridge, begins with Bernard Williams's essay "Trust Considered: Formal Structures and Social Reality," and the other contributors, mostly social scientists, refer back to it frequently.

2. My study of trust, begun in "Good Men's Women: Hume on Chastity and Trust," *Hume Studies*, 5 (April 1979): 1–19, continued in Essay 6 and in "Trusting Ex-Intimates" (see note 9 of Essay 7), was pursued further while I was a fellow at the Wissenschaftskolleg zu Berlin in 1988–89. There I gave a lecture on trust and had helpful discussions following it. I was also privileged to discuss the topic with Dieter Claessens, author of *Familie und Wertsystem* (Berlin: Duncker & Humbolt, 1979), and *Instinkt, Psyche, Geltung: zu Legitimation menschlichen Verhaltuis* (Koln: Westdeutscher Verlag, 1970).

3. Williams, "Trust Considered," pp. 12–13.

4. Ibid., p. 13.

5. Geoffrey Hawthorn, "Three Ironies of Trust," in *Trust,* ed. Gambetta, p. 113.

6. I have discussed the sorts of reason why deceit might on occasion be acceptable in "Why Honesty Is a Hard Virtue," in *Identity, Character, and Morality: Essays in Moral Psychology,* ed. O. Flanagan and A. Rorty (Cambridge, Mass.: MIT Press, 1990), pp. 259–282.

7. Hawthorn, "Three Ironies," p. 115.

8. It could be that, in our culture, it is men who typically see mature morality as reflective *altruistic* constraints on more spontaneously egoistic motivation, whereas women see it as reflective more *egoistic* constraints on the altruistic caring motivation they have been trained from childhood to feel and display.

9. David Hume, *A Treatise of Human Nature,* ed. L. A. Selby-Bigge and P. H. Nidditch (Oxford: Clarendon Press, 1975), p. 522.

10. P. S. Atiyah, *Promises, Morals, and the Law* (Oxford: Clarendon Press, 1981), passim.

11. Thomas Scanlon, in "Promises and Practices," *Philosophy & Public Affairs,* 19 (Summer 1990): 199–226, tells a story about an attempt to get an agreement for the return of a boomerang in exchange for the return of a spear. His example is more apt for his purpose than he may have realized.

12. Hume, *Treatise,* p. 525.

13. Hawthorn, "Three Ironies," p. 112.

14. Richard A. Epstein, "The Varieties of Self-Interest," *Social Philosophy and Policy,* 8 (Autumn 1990): 102–120.

15. Judith Jarvis Thomson's example of "trespass" in *The Realm of Rights* (Cambridge, Mass.: Harvard University Press, 1990) is a kiss on the bent bare neck of an attractive fellow library user, a total stranger. Would caressing his hair have been as good an example? (Do we grant our hairdressers liberties with our person?)

16. Robert Nozick, *Anarchy, State, and Utopia* (New York: Basic Books, 1974), p. 57.

17. Allan Gibbard, *Wise Choices, Apt Feelings: A Theory of Normative Judgment* (Cambridge, Mass.: Harvard University Press, 1990), pp. 69–70.

18. For some time I took it that infant trust is displayed in willingness to be held close, and to accept food from others (see Essay 6, p. 107). But sociologists and psychologists more plausibly take infant trust to be displayed by willingness to let the parents *out* of sight, trusting that they will return. See E. H. Erikson, *Childhood and Society* (New York: Norton, 1950), and Claessens, *Familie und Wertsystem,* pp. 109–110.

19. I toyed with but rejected the idea that the special vulnerability of closeness comes with a special kind of *being known,* warts, body odors, and

all, so that absolute trust would be willingness both to be vulnerably known by the trusted and to be vulnerably ignorant about the trusted. But the torturer's power need not require special personal knowledge of the victim, so I reject that attempted unification.

20. Williams, "Trust Considered," p. 9.

21. *De Officiis*, III, 70.

22. News item, CBS Evening News, November 29, 1990.

23. *De Officiis*, I, 26.

24. Hugo Grotius, *Rights of War and Peace*, bk. 3, chap. 20, sec. 11.

25. Patrick Bateson, "The Biological Evolution of Trust and Cooperation," in *Trust*, ed. Gambetta, p. 19.

26. In Essay 6, I proposed a test for appropriate trust, that the trust relationship be able to withstand mutual knowledge of each party's motives for trusting and/or trustworthy behavior. Not only was this "test," as I recognized then, unusable, but it also supposed a degree of understanding of human motives that we do not have. Of course *mysterious* motives might still be reassuring to the trust partner, or disillusioning, but it now seems to me that my erstwhile "test" for trust did take self-understanding too much on trust.

27. Williams, "Trust Considered," p. 9. The term "reality condition" is used by Hawthorn, not Williams, but is taken from Williams's title "Formal Structures and Social Reality."

28. David Hume, *Enquiries*, ed. L. A. Selby-Bigge and P. H. Nidditch (Oxford: Clarendon Press, 1978), p. 270.

29. See Essay 7, pp. 133–134, and note 6 to that essay.

30. Hume, *Treatise of Human Nature*, p. 603, lists fidelity among the "natural" virtues, that is, ones not consisting in obedience to the rules of a social artifice or practice.

31. I discuss the details of Hume's account in chapter 10 of *A Progress of Sentiments: Reflections on Hume's* Treatise (Cambridge, Mass.: Harvard University Press, 1991), and discuss the Humean virtue of truth in chapter 12, and also in "Why Honesty Is a Hard Virtue."

32. T. M. Scanlon, "Contractualism and Utilitarianism," in *Utilitarianism and Beyond*, ed. Amartya Sen and Bernard Williams (New York: Cambridge University Press, 1982), pp. 103–128.

33. Ibid., p. 110.

34. Alternatively we could call them "Tongans." My "Friends" have only their name in common with Quakers, members of the Society of Friends, who will not take oaths, but will give promises and assurances. Real Tongans, supposedly, once did manage without solemn assurance-giving. See Fred Korn and S. R. Decktor Korn, "Where People Don't Promise," *Ethics*, 93 (April 1983): 445–450.

35. See note 7 in Essay 7.

36. I am grateful to Scanlon for actually making this reply.

37. See Immanuel Kant, *Lectures on Ethics*, trans. Louis Infield (New York: Harper & Row, 1963), p. 228, for Kant's reported reference to lying as

breaking our pact with fellow speakers.

38. As my sympathetic treatment in *A Progress of Sentiments* of what I take to be a reflexivity test employed by Hume in epistemology and ethics makes clear, I should be the last person to deny the normative relevance of reflexivity tests. They can be relevant, however, without being sufficient.

39. J. L. Austin, *How to Do Things with Words,* William James Lectures (New York: Oxford University Press, 1962), esp. lectures 2, 4 (pp. 12–24, 39–52).

40. See Austin, *How to Do Things with Words;* Paul Grice, *Studies in the Way of Words* (Cambridge, Mass.: Harvard University Press, 1989); Stanley Cavell, *Must We Mean What We Say?* (New York: Scribner, 1969; Cambridge: Cambridge University Press, 1976).

41. John Locke, *Some Thoughts Concerning Education* (Menston: Scholar Press, 1970), sec. 143.

42. Intentional eye contact, interestingly, itself exhibits that self and mutual reference of intentions that Grice finds essential to meaningful speech.

43. I have given them some notice in "Getting in Touch with Our Own Feelings," *Topoi,* 6 (September 1987): 89–97; and "Why Honesty Is a Hard Virtue."

44. This is true also of trust as a commodity, something that makes our living more commodious (and that we have reason to try to produce, get by barter, or even buy and sell, as when the purchaser of a business buys its "goodwill"). See Partha Dasgupta, "Trust as a Commodity," in *Trust,* ed. Gambetta, pp. 49–72.

45. Hirschman says of trust (among other "moral resources"), "These are resources whose supply may well increase rather than decrease through use; . . . these resources do not remain intact if they stay unused; like the ability to speak a foreign language or to play the piano, these moral resources are likely to become depleted and to atrophy if *not* used." A. O. Hirschman, "Against Parsimony: Three Easy Ways of Complicating Some Categories of Economic Discourse," *American Economic Review Proceedings,* 74 (1984): 88–96, quoted by Dasgupta in *Trust,* ed. Gambetta, p. 56.

46. For a vindication of the rationality of offering assurances, and getting others to accept them, see David Gauthier, "Assure and Threaten," forthcoming in *Ethics.*

47. There I also say that it is because Scanlon's account is so close to what I think is the right account that I engage so passionately with it. As I say in note 9 of Essay 6, it was a version of this paper of Scanlon's that got me started in thinking about trust, so I am very much indebted to him. The odd but typical form of gratitude which philosophers display is to argue with those whose views have influenced them.

48. In "Promises, Promises, Promises," in *Postures of the Mind: Essays on Mind and Morals* (Minneapolis, Minn.: University of Minnesota Press, 1985).

9. TRUSTING PEOPLE

A version of this paper formed the Bugbee Lecture, given at the University of Montana, Missoula, October 9, 1991. The epigraph and first two paragraphs were not included in the version published in *Philosophical Perspectives*.

1. John Locke, *An Essay Concerning Human Understanding,* ed. P. H. Nidditch (Oxford: Clarendon Press, 1975), bk. 1, chap. 4, sec. 24.
2. Josiah Royce, "The Philosophy of Loyalty," especially lecture 3, "Loyalty to Loyalty," in *The Basic Writings of Josiah Royce,* ed. John J. McDermott (Chicago, Ill.: University of Chicago Press, 1969), II, 855–1014.
3. Diego Gambetta, ed., *Trust: Making and Breaking Cooperative Relations* (New York: Basil Blackwell, 1988).
4. J. Elster and K. Moene, eds., *Alternatives to Capitalism* (New York: Cambridge University Press, 1988), introduction.
5. Here they agree with most analysts of economic transactions. Kenneth Arrow, in "Gifts and Exchanges," *Philosophy & Public Affairs,* 4 (Summer 1972): 357, writes, "Virtually every commercial transaction has within itself an element of trust, certainly any transaction conducted over a period of time."
6. Gambetta, ed., *Trust,* p. 234.
7. Ibid., p. 217.
8. Ibid., p. 218.
9. In Essay 6, I define it as accepted vulnerability to another person's power over something one cares about, in the confidence that such power will not be used to harm what is entrusted.
10. In Essays 7 and 8.
11. John Updike, *Trust Me: Short Stories* (Greenwich, Conn.: Fawcett Pub., 1965).
12. David Hume, *A Treatise of Human Nature,* ed. L. A. Selby-Bigge and P. H. Nidditch (Oxford: Clarendon Press, 1978), p. 521.
13. A. S. Byatt, "Art Work," *New Yorker,* May 20, 1992, p. 42.
14. Immanuel Kant, *Lectures on Ethics,* trans. Louis Infield (New York: Harper & Row, 1963), pp. 204–205.
15. Immanuel Kant, *The Metaphysics of Morals,* trans. Mary Gregor (New York: Cambridge University Press, 1991), pt. 2, *The Doctrine of Virtue,* sec. 32.
16. Ibid., sec. 31.
17. My Protestant upbringing gave me, as a child, such a distrust and terror of "priests in their gowns making their rounds" that when I was about ten, and sent by the headmaster of my school to take some message to the nearby parochial Catholic school, it took real courage for me to control my fears enough to walk into that school and hand over the note. I remember it as my first test of courage. So ashamed of this attitude was I later, as a young woman, that I eagerly welcomed an oppor-

tunity I was offered to become acquainted with a young priest who shared my literary interests. The acquaintance ended fairly abruptly when he proposed that my current accommodation problem, in a city where rents were high and apartments scarce, be solved by his providing me with a comfortable place, since his responsibilities gave him some control over housing owned by the church, in return for his having rights of visitation and sexual favors. When I inquired how such a proposal sat with his religious and moral conscience, he cheerfully assured me that he would not dream of making such a proposal to one of his own flock, but lapsed Protestant women were a different matter. So my initial irrational distrust of priests in their gowns was replaced by a more rational distrust.

18. I discuss this in "Trust and Distrust of Moral Philosophers," in *The Applied Ethics Reader,* ed. Earl Winkler and Jerrold Coombs (Cambridge, Mass.: Blackwell Publishers, 1993), pp. 131–142.

19. After my anecdotal Tanner Lectures on trust (Essays 7 and 8), several women members of the audience, mostly younger women, expressed appreciation of my willingness to break the traditional reticence on these matters of personal experience.

20. A respected older mentor, after an anecdotal talk of mine about trust, said, "This may all be great fun, but is it real professional work?"

21. Diego Gambetta, "Can We Trust Trust?" in Gambetta, ed., *Trust,* p. 217, note 6, cites Woody Allen's insight, in *Hannah and Her Sisters,* that "Why the Holocaust?" is the wrong question—what we should ask, rather, is why it does not happen more often.

22. See Niklas Luhmann, "Familiarity, Confidence, Trust: Problems and Alternatives" in Gambetta, ed., *Trust,* pp. 84–107.

23. Ibid., p. 97, distinguishes trust from confidence, requiring some sort of risk assessment to be present in the case of trust.

24. I discuss this, in the case of trust in intimates, in "Trusting Ex-Intimates," in *Person to Person,* ed. H. Lafollette and G. Graham (Philadelphia, Pa.: Temple University Press, 1989), pp. 269–281.

25. Francis Bacon, *Remains* (London: Robert Chiswell, 1679), p. 70.

26. Albert Hirschman, "Against Parsimony: Three Easy Ways of Complicating Some Categories of Economic Discourse," *American Economic Review Proceedings,* 74 (1984): 88–96.

27. See Thomas Schelling, *Micromotives and Macrobehavior* (New York: Norton, 1978), for a study of such self-fulfilling beliefs about how others will behave.

28. Distinguished opponents of divorce, such as David Hume in his essay "Of Polygamy and Divorces," rest much of their case on the duty of parents to put the good of their children before their own preferences, but the empirical assumption that young children are more harmed by the breakup of their parents' marriage than by sustained mutual hostility in marriage seems very dubious. Significantly, after making his case for no-exit marriages, Hume kept clear of matrimony.

29. Luhmann, "Familiarity, Confidence, Trust."
30. Ibid., p. 103.
31. I develop this claim that distrust is properly directed at those who try to prevent their inferiors from advancing in Essays 7 and 8.

10. VIOLENT DEMONSTRATIONS

I have been helped in revising this essay by comments made by many persons during the discussion at the Bowling Green State University Conference on Violence, Terrorism, and Justice, and from critical comments from Kurt Baier, Wulf Schiefenhövel, Christian Vogel, and anonymous readers for Cambridge University Press. By no means have all their criticisms been met in this revision. The topic is one that I find of daunting difficulty, and I expect to continue revising my views about it.

1. Doris Lessing, *The Good Terrorist* (London: Grafton Books, 1986), p. 146.
2. See *Q.Q., Report from the Center for Philosophy and Public Policy,* 7 (Fall 1987).
3. Here I adopt the useful terminology used by Terry Moore in "The Nature and Evaluation of Terrorism" (Ph.D. diss., University of Pittsburgh, 1987).
4. For a discussion of terrorism by powerful states, see Noam Chomsky, *The Culture of Terrorism* (Boston, Mass.: South End Press, 1988).
5. Essay 6, p. 98.
6. Michael Walzer, *Just and Unjust Wars* (New York: Basic Books, 1977), p. 197.
7. See Thomas Schelling, "What Purpose Can International Terrorism Serve?" in *Violence, Terrorism and Justice,* ed. R. G. Frey and Christopher W. Morris (New York: Cambridge University Press, 1991), pp. 18–32.
8. If the deaths of the PanAm passengers in the plane that was destroyed over Lockerbie, Scotland, in December 1988 were seen by the perpetrators as revenge for the deaths of the Iranians in the airbus mistakenly downed earlier by U.S. forces in the Persian Gulf, then this act of "terrorism" would be more like a punitive strike than is the typical terrorist act, as I have construed it. A kind of crude justice, one airbus full of innocents for another, would then have been involved.
9. Walzer, *Just and Unjust Wars,* p. 204.
10. Hugo Grotius, *The Rights of War and Peace,* trans. A. C. Campbell (Westport, Conn.: Hyperion Press, 1979), bk. 3, chap. 20, sec. 2.
11. Aristotle, *Nicomachean Ethics,* trans. M. Ostwald (Indianapolis, Ind.: Bobbs-Merrill, 1962), bk. 2, chap. 6, 1107a, 9–14.
12. David Hume, *A Treatise of Human Nature,* ed. L. A. Selby-Bigge and P. H. Nidditch (Oxford: Clarendon Press, 1978), pp. 487, 491.
13. Ibid., p. 376.

14. Ibid., pp. 410–411.
15. Ibid., p. 526.
16. Ibid., p. 538.

11. CLAIMS, RIGHTS, RESPONSIBILITIES

This essay is a revised version of a talk given at the University of Pennsylvania in March 1987, during a Bicentennial conference on human nature organized by Charles Kahn. I have been helped by the discussion on that occasion and by comments by my colleague Robert Brandom.

1. David Hume, *History of England, from the Invasion of Julius Caesar to the Revolution in 1688,* 6 vols. (Indianapolis, Ind.: Liberty Classics, 1985). The first quotation is from the second appendix, the others from the end of chapter 23.
2. For an account of Ann Lee and the Shaker faith she founded, see Edward D. Andrews, *The People Called Shakers: A Search for the Perfect Society* (New York: Oxford University Press, 1953), and Henri Desrochem, *The American Shakers: From Neo-Christianity to Presocialism* (Paris: Editions de Minuit, 1955), trans. and ed. John K. Savacool (Amherst, Mass.: University of Massachusetts Press, 1971).
3. "Person" is a status term, for Pufendorf and the dominant tradition, as much a will-imposed "moral entity," or artifice, as "sovereign" or "slave."
4. My source is the *New York Times,* "Week in Review," December 21, 1986.
5. Stanley Benn and Richard Peters, *The Principles of Political Thought* (New York: Free Press, 1965), earlier published as *Social Principles and the Democratic State* (London: Allen and Unwin, 1959), in chapter 2 of that work (on which I cut my social philosophical teeth), link respect for persons with the attitude shown by Socrates when he reasoned with a slave. "For what has a man's social position to do with the truth or falsity of what he says? . . . If we are prepared seriously to attend to what another person has to say, whatever his personal or social attributes, we must have at least a minimal respect for him as the source of an argument." They attribute the germs of this idea to Karl Popper, who had developed it in seminars. It obviously has a strong family resemblance to the theses defended more recently by Jürgen Habermas.
6. John Locke, *Some Thoughts Concerning Education* (Menston: Scholar Press, 1970), sec. 83.
7. Ibid., sec. 196.
8. Ibid., sec. 185.
9. Ibid., sec. 145.
10. Ibid.
11. Ibid.

12. Thomas Hobbes, *Leviathan* (New York: Everyman's Library, 1973), chap. 4.
13. Ibid., chap. 4.
14. Ibid., chap. 3.
15. Ibid., chap. 5.
16. Ibid., chap. 4.
17. Ibid., chap. 6.
18. Ibid., chap. 4. Hobbes here adds a significant qualification "unlesse it be one whom wee are obliged to govern; and then it is not to grieve, but to correct and amend."
19. Richard Tuck, *Natural Rights Theories: Their Origin and Development* (New York: Cambridge University Press, 1979).
20. Ronald Dworkin, *Taking Rights Seriously* (Cambridge, Mass.: Harvard University Press, 1978).
21. J. L. Mackie, "Can There Be a Rights-Based Theory?" in *Theories of Rights,* ed. J. Waldron (New York: Oxford University Press, 1984), pp. 168–181.
22. Joseph Raz, "Rights-Based Moralities," in *Theories of Rights,* ed. Waldron, pp. 182–200.
23. Joel Feinberg, "The Nature and Value of Rights," *Journal of Value Inquiry,* 4 (Winter 1970): 243–257.
24. See Tuck, *Natural Rights Theories,* p. 8.
25. Quoted ibid., p. 40.
26. See ibid., pp. 54 ff.
27. Hugo Grotius, *The Rights of War and Peace,* trans. A. C. Campbell (Westport, Conn.: Hyperion Press, 1979), bk. 1, chap. 1, sec. 4.
28. I have discussed this in "Rights of Past and Future Persons," in *Responsibility to Future Generations,* ed. E. Partridge (Buffalo, N.Y.: Prometheus Books, 1981), pp. 171–183. Republished, in part, in James P. Sterba, ed., *Morality in Practice* (Belmont, Calif.: Wadsworth Publishing Co., 1985).
29. I have discussed this in "For the Sake of Future Generations," in *Earthbound,* ed. Tom Regan (New York: Random House, 1984), pp. 214–246.

12. HOW CAN INDIVIDUALISTS SHARE RESPONSIBILITY?

This essay derives from a talk given at Yale University in April 1992. I have benefited from the critical comments prepared for that occasion by David Schmidtz and also from comments by other members of the Yale audience. My colleagues Nicholas Rescher and Stephen Engstrom also offered helpful criticisms.

1. Immanuel Kant, *The Metaphysics of Morals,* trans. Mary Gregor (New York: Cambridge University Press, 1991), p. 265 (app. to pt. 2, *The Doctrine of Virtue,* sec. 48).

2. But wise Kantian friends will retain some reserve with one another, "lest humanity be outraged. Even to our best friend we must not reveal ourselves, in our natural state as we know it ourselves. To do so would be loathsome." Lecture on Friendship in *Lectures on Ethics,* trans. Louis Infield (New York: Harper & Row, 1963), p. 206.

3. Kant, *Metaphysics of Morals,* pt. 1, *Doctrine of Right,* p. 265.

4. Ibid., p. 62.

5. See ibid., General Remark following sec. 49, pp. 129–133.

6. René Descartes, *Principles of Philosophy* (Boston, Mass.: Reidel; Hingham, Mass.: distributed by Kluwer Boston, 1983), pt. 3, sec. 52.

7. Alexis de Tocqueville, *Democracy in America,* trans. Henry Reeve, in two volumes with a critical appraisal of each volume by John Stuart Mill (New York: Schocken Books, 1967), vol. 2, chap. 2, p. 118.

8. Ibid.

9. Ibid.

10. Ibid., chap. 5, p. 132.

11. Ibid., p. 133.

12. Gordon S. Wood, *The Radicalism of the American Revolution* (New York: Alfred A. Knopf, 1992).

13. Even those who have fairly fundamental disagreements with Kant, such as David Gauthier, seem to feel obliged to offer "subversive reinterpretations" and to appropriate the Kantian terminology, as if to give a borrowed authority to their own views. See "The Unity of Reason: A Subversive Reinterpretation of Kant," in David Gauthier, *Moral Dealing* (Ithaca, N.Y.: Cornell University Press, 1990), pp. 110–126.

14. Tocqueville does, of course, discuss at length the advantages and disadvantages of a union or federation of republics, and marvels at the "surprising facility" of the plain American citizen in distinguishing the jurisdictions of state and federal law. See *Democracy in America,* vol. 1, chap. 8, quotation at p. 185.

15. Immanuel Kant, *Perpetual Peace,* in *Kant's Political Writings,* trans. H. B. Nisbet, ed. Hans Reiss (New York: Cambridge University Press, 1970).

16. Kant, *Perpetual Peace,* p. 101.

17. Ibid., p. 75.

18. Ibid., p. 78.

19. Kant, *Metaphysics of Morals,* pt. 1, sec. 46.

20. Tocqueville, *Democracy in America,* vol. 2, chap. 9, p. 238.

21. Ibid., chap. 12, p. 252.

22. Ibid., p. 253.

23. Ibid., p. 255.

24. Ibid., p. 253.

25. Kant, *Metaphysics of Morals,* pt. 1, sec. 46.

26. See Mary Gregor's remark on the translation of that term in her "Note on the Text," p. xii, in *The Metaphysics of Morals.*

27. In *What Is Enlightenment* (1784) Kant might charitably be read as including the "fair sex" in the class of those who might take "the step to

maturity," but the *Anthropology* and the *Metaphysics of Morals* do not take this possibility seriously. For a different and more charitable reading of the passages I have been citing, see Christine Korsgaard, "Creating the Realm of Ends: Reciprocity and Responsibility in Personal Relations," in *Philosophical Perspectives, 6: Ethics,* ed. James Tomberlin (Atascadero, Calif.: Ridgeview Publishing Co., 1992).

28. "Only if placed in positions of authority over others should we point out to them their defects. Thus a husband is entitled to teach and correct his wife . . ." Kant, *Lectures on Ethics,* trans. Louis Infield (New York: Harper & Row, 1963), p. 232.

29. Kant, *Perpetual Peace,* pp. 100–101.

30. Ibid., p. 101.

31. Kant, *Metaphysics of Morals,* p. 131.

32. Ibid., pt. 1, *Doctrine of Right,* sec. 46, p. 125.

33. Ibid., p. 129.

34. See Richard H. Dees, "Hume and the Contexts of Politics," *Journal of the History of Philosophy,* 30:2 (April 1992): 219–242, for a helpful discussion of Hume's position.

35. Kant, *Metaphysics of Morals,* p. 130.

36. For a different more liberal reading of Kant, see Christine Korsgaard, "Taking the Law into Our Own Hands: Kant on the Right to Revolution," manuscript.

37. Quoted by Gordon S. Wood, in "Classical Republicanism and the American Revolution," *Chicago-Kent Law Review,* 66 (1990): 14.

38. Ronald Dworkin, *Law's Empire* (Cambridge, Mass.: Belknap Press of Harvard University Press, 1986), p. 171.

39. Kant, *Metaphysics of Morals,* pt. 2, sec. 39, p. 255.

40. Kant, *Lectures on Ethics,* p. 232.

41. See Kant, *Metaphysics of Morals,* pt. 1, General Remark following sec. 49, p. 142.

42. Dworkin, *Law's Empire,* p. 175.

43. Ibid., p. 211.

44. Ibid.

45. Ibid.

46. Ibid., p. 205.

47. I am thinking of the activity of political organizations such as EMILY ("Early Money Is Like Yeast") and WISH ("Women In Senate and House").

48. For documentation see, for example, Andrew Hacker, *Two Nations: Black and White, Separate, Hostile, Unequal* (New York: Scribner, 1992).

49. I have explored the ethics of trust and distrust in Essays 6, 7, 8, and 9.

50. See Kurt Baier, "Moral and Legal Responsibility," in *Medical Innovation and Bad Outcomes: Legal, Social, and Ethical Responses,* ed. Mark Siegler, Stephen Toulmin, Frank E. Zimring, and Kenneth F. Schaffner (Ann Arbor, Mich.: Health Administration Press, 1987), pp. 101–130,

for a discussion of forward-looking, or "task" responsibility, to backward-looking responsibility.

51. Kant, *Metaphysics of Morals,* pt. 1, sec. 5.

52. See John Rawls, *A Theory of Justice* (Cambridge, Mass.: Belknap Press of Harvard University Press, 1971), pp. 100 ff.

53. I do not of course want to deny that many who saw and see themselves as Kantians or neo-Kantians have had a welcome liberalizing influence on political and social developments. The idea of equal respect for all persons continues to be a liberating and inspiring one.

13. MORALISM AND CRUELTY

This essay has been prepared with an ear for the anticipated response of Stephen Engstrom, Barbara Herman, Christine Korsgaard, and Alisa Carse, all respected admirers of Kant, as well as for Allan Gibbard and other friends of Hume, and for Stephen Darwall, respected arbitrator between Hume and Kant.

1. At a talk at the University of Michigan, March 27, 1992, and in "Categorical Requirements: Kant and Hume on the Idea of Duty," *Monist,* 74 (January 1991): 83–106.

2. See Immanuel Kant, "Duties to Oneself," in *Lectures on Ethics,* trans. Louis Infield (New York: Harper & Row, 1963), esp. p. 124. See also *The Metaphysics of Morals,* trans. Mary Gregor (New York: Cambridge University Press, 1991), pt. 2, Doctrine of Virtue, sec. 7.

3. Of course both moralists agree in regarding cruelty as *a* vice, and in regarding other vices as also of importance. (Kant, in *Religion within the Limits of Reason Alone* [New York: Harper Torchbooks, 1960], p. 28, mentions the cruel "murder-dramas enacted in Tofua New Zealand" as indicators of our radical evil, doubtless there referring to slaughter of, rather than slaughter by, Europeans.)

4. Judith N. Shklar, *Ordinary Vices* (Cambridge, Mass.: Belknap Press of the Harvard University Press, 1984), chap. 1, "Putting Cruelty First."

5. Richard Rorty, *Contingency, Irony, and Solidarity* (New York: Cambridge University Press, 1989), p. xv, and passim.

6. "Crudelitas, seu Saevitia, est Cupiditas, qua aliquis concitatur ad malum inferendum ei, quem amamus, vel cujus nos miseret." *Ethics,* pt. 3, def. 38, in the definitions of the affects, following prop. 59. See Edwin Curley's note on his translation, in *Collected Works of Spinoza* (Princeton, N.J.: Princeton University Press, 1988), note 53, p. 540. See also pt. 3, prop. 41, scholium.

7. Alexis de Tocqueville, *Democracy in America,* trans. Henry Reeve, in two volumes with a critical appraisal of each volume by John Stuart Mill (New York: Schocken Books, 1967), vol. 1, chap. 7, pp. 115–116.

8. Allan Gibbard, *Wise Choices, Apt Feelings* (Cambridge, Mass.: Harvard University Press, 1990), pp. 297–298.

9. See Kant, *Metaphysics of Morals,* pt. 2, Doctrine of Virtue, sec. 13, pp. 233–235.

10. *"Schuld"* is a status-term for Kant, as indeed is "guilt" in its original sense in English.

11. Gibbard, *Wise Choices, Apt Feelings,* p. 298.

12. Ibid., p. 299.

13. Ibid., p. 299. Contrast Kant's fourth thesis, in *Idea for a Universal History,* that we should thank nature for the incompatibility and antagonism that produces discord, since without those, our excellent capacities might have lain dormant, in an Arcadian peace where men would be as docile and as silly as the sheep they tended. Perpetual peace is for Kant a regulative moral ideal, but only if it is achieved by the triumph of discord-forged rational capacities.

14. David Hume, *A Treatise of Human Nature,* ed. L. A. Selby-Bigge and P. H. Nidditch (Oxford: Clarendon Press, 1978), p. 619.

15. Ibid., p. 605.

16. Ibid., p. 538.

17. Ibid., p. 605.

18. Ibid.

19. Compare Shaftesbury: "By means of this reflected sense, there arises another kind of affection towards those very affections themselves, which have been already felt, and are now become the subject of a new liking or dislike." *Characteristicks,* in *British Moralists,* ed. D. D. Raphael (Oxford: Clarendon Press, 1969), I, p. 172.

20. Hume, *Treatise,* p. 606.

21. Paul Russell, in "Hume on Responsibility and Punishment," *Canadian Journal of Philosophy,* 20 (December 1990): 539–564, draws attention to the importance of this essay for grasping Hume's views on punishment.

22. David Hume, *Essays: Moral, Political and Literary,* ed. Eugene F. Miller (Indianapolis, Ind.: Liberty Classics, 1985), pp. 594–595. Contrast Kant: "It would seem to follow [from radical evil in human dispositions], then, that because of this infinite guilt all men must look forward to *endless punishment* and exclusion from the kingdom of God." *Religion within the Limits of Reason Alone,* p. 66. This apparent conclusion is indeed avoided by Kant, but only by faith in God's pardon to the truly repentant. Divine *justice* would, he believes, dictate endless punishment.

23. David Hume, *History of England, from the Invasion of Julius Caesar to the Revolution in 1688,* 6 vols. (Indianapolis, Ind.: Liberty Classics, 1983), I, chap. 2, pp. 95–96.

24. See Kant, *Metaphysics of Morals,* pt. 1, the "Doctrine of Right" discussion of the right to punish, following section 49, pp. 140–145 and 168–169.

25. Ibid., p. 141. I have not followed Gregor's translation here. She has "windings of eudaimonism."

26. Ibid., p. 142.

27. David Hume, *Essays: Moral, Political and Literary,* ed. Eugene F. Miller (Indianapolis, Ind.: Liberty Classics, 1985), pp. 594–595.

28. In discussion of a version of this paper read at Harvard, Robert Nozick suggested that, to get around this difficulty, we might see the different character traits of a person as sharing responsibility for each other's workings.

29. See David Lewis, "The Punishment that Leaves Something to Chance," *Philosophy & Public Affairs,* 18 (Winter 1989): 53–67.

30. Kant, *Religion,* p. 67.

31. Ibid., p. 68.

32. Ibid., p. 67.

33. Kant, *Metaphysics of Morals,* p. 273.

34. Stan Slesser, "A Reporter at Large (Singapore)," *The New Yorker,* January 13, 1992.

35. Friedrich Nietzsche, *The Birth of Tragedy and The Genealogy of Morals* (Garden City, N.Y.: Doubleday, 1956).

36. Kant, *Metaphysics of Morals,* pp. 144–145.

37. Ibid., pp. 140–141.

38. Ibid., p. 144.

39. Hume, *Treatise,* p. 571.

40. Ibid., p. 572.

41. Ibid., p. 571.

42. Kant, *Lectures on Ethics,* p. 114. This passage suggests that the occurrence of shame is not, for Kant, a reliable indicator that one really has some moral failing.

43. Gibbard, *Wise Choices, Apt Feelings,* p. 139.

44. Ibid., p. 298.

45. Kant, *Religion,* p. 36.

46. David Hume, *Enquiry Concerning the Principles of Morals,* ed. J. Schneewind (Indianapolis, Ind.: Hackett Publishing Co.), pp. 99–100.

47. Hume, *Treatise,* p. 477.

48. Hume, *Enquiry Concerning the Principles of Morals,* p. 16.

49. Ibid., p. 39.

50. Ibid., p. 54.

51. Ibid., p. 55.

52. Ibid., p. 62.

53. Ibid., p. 69.

54. Ibid., p. 74.

55. Ibid., p. 100.

56. Ibid., p. 105.

57. Ibid., p. 79.

58. See ibid., p. 74.

59. Ibid., p. 60.

60. Ibid., p. 105.

61. Hume, *Treatise,* p. 608.

62. Ibid., p. 536.

63. Ibid., p. 537.
64. Kant, *Metaphysics of Morals,* sec. 43.
65. Theophrastus, *Characters,* trans. J. M. Edmonds (London: W. Heinemann; New York: G. P. Putnam's Sons, 1929). For a reading of Hume as a follower of Theophrastus, see Annette Baier, *A Progress of Sentiments: Reflections on Hume's* Treatise (Cambridge, Mass.: Harvard University Press, 1991), chap. 9.
66. See note on Schiller to Book I of Kant, *Religion,* p. 18.
67. Spinoza, *Ethics,* pt. 4, app. 13 and 25, in *Collected Works of Spinoza,* trans. Edwin Curley (Princeton, N.J.: Princeton University Press, 1988).
68. Jane Gross, "Does She Speak for Today's Women?" *New York Times Magazine,* March 1, 1992, quotation at p. 18.
69. William Shakespeare, *Henry V* (New Haven, Conn.: Yale University Press, 1955), v, ii, 216.
70. See Barbara Herman, "Could It Be Worth Thinking about Kant on Sex and Marriage?" in *A Mind of One's Own: Feminist Essays on Reason and Objectivity,* ed. Louise M. Antony and Charlotte Witt (Denver, Colo.: Westview Press, 1993), pp. 49–67.
71. Hume, *Essays,* p. 207.
72. See my "Hume on Women's Complexion," in *The Science of Man in the Scottish Enlightenment,* ed. Peter Jones (Edinburgh: Edinburgh University Press, 1990), pp. 33–53.
73. Hume, *Essays,* pp. 383–384.
74. Ibid., p. 386, n. 16.
75. Ibid., p. 384.

14. ETHICS IN MANY DIFFERENT VOICES

1. Simone de Beauvoir, *The Second Sex* (New York: Vintage Books, 1974, 1952; Bantam Books, 1961).
2. Virginia Held, *Rights and Goods: Justifying Social Action* (New York: Free Press; London: Collier Macmillan, 1984).
3. Cora Diamond, *The Realistic Spirit: Wittgenstein, Philosophy, and the Mind* (Cambridge, Mass.: MIT Press, 1991).
4. Judith Jarvis Thomson, *The Realm of Rights* (Cambridge, Mass.: Harvard University Press, 1990), esp. chap. 14. For an earlier discussion of the ethics of timing by Thomson, see her "The Time of a Killing," *Journal of Philosophy,* 68 (1971): 115–132.
5. Hannah Arendt, *The Human Condition* (Chicago, Ill.: University of Chicago Press, 1958). Page references in the text, unless otherwise indicated, are to this work.
6. She went at age nineteen to Marburg, studied philosophy, became Heidegger's lover, then at the end of one year, transferred to Freiburg to study with Husserl, then to Heidelberg. She wrote *Die Schatten* as a sort of record of her relationship with Heidegger, which continued intermittently during her student years.

7. See Seyla Benhabib, "Hannah Arendt and the Redemptive Power of Narrative," *Social Research*, 57 (Spring 1990), for an exploration of Arendt's emphasis on narrative, not just in *The Human Condition* but also in other works, especially *The Life of the Mind* (New York: Harcourt Brace Jovanovich, 1978).

8. Alice Ruhle-Gerstel, *Das Frauen-problem der Gegenwart*, reviewed by Hannah Arendt, *Die Gesellschaft* 10 (1932): 177–179.

9. Elisabeth Young-Bruehl, *Hannah Arendt: For Love of the World* (New Haven, Conn.: Yale University Press, 1982) p. 238.

10. Ibid., p. 273.

11. Ibid., p. 513, n. 54.

12. Ibid., p. 96.

13. Did she forgive Heidegger when she met him again after the war? And for what exactly? In her letter to Jaspers shortly before that meeting she sounds very condemnatory of his "dishonesty." After their meeting in Freiburg in 1950, she described Heidegger's demeanor to a friend as like a "begossener Pudel" (Young-Bruehl, *Arendt*, pp. 246, 514, n. 81). His tail was between his legs not for his Nazi activities, which had led to the break in their relationship in about 1930 (ibid., p. 69), but for wrongs against her personally, presumably at least the secrecy which he had imposed on their affair. At any rate the form his penitence took was to make, to his wife Elfriede Heidegger-Petri, a belated declaration of the fact that Arendt had been the passion of his life and the inspiration of his work. This news was not well received (ibid., pp. 247, 514, n. 83). Jaspers's ironic words are apt: "poor Heidegger." Arendt had written to Jaspers, in the letter discussing Heidegger's habitual dishonesty (and his "quite awful babbling lectures on Nietzsche"), that what Jaspers saw as Heidegger's "impurity" she would call "a lack of character ... At the same time, he lives in depths and with a passionateness that one can't easily forget." *Hannah Arendt and Karl Jaspers Correspondence*, ed. Lotte Kohler and Hans Saner (New York: Harcourt Brace Jovanovich, 1992), p. 142, letter 93, Hannah Arendt to Karl Jaspers, September 29, 1949. She did not forget him. Did she forgive him his cold reaction to her gift of *Vita Activa* (her German version of *The Human Condition*)? He had not acknowledged the gift, and when Arendt was in Freiburg in 1960, he not only ignored her presence but pressured his disciple Eugen Fink to refuse an invitation to a reception given in her honor. *Correspondence*, p. 447, letter 293, Hannah Arendt to Karl and Gertrud Jaspers, August 6, 1961. Her explanation to Jaspers of Heidegger's change of attitude to her, while it is generous in assuming some blame herself, is not notable for any forgiving note: "[L]ast winter I sent him one of my books, the *Vita Activa*, for the first time. I know that he finds it intolerable that my name appears in public, that I write books, etc. All my life I've pulled the wool over his eyes, so to speak, always acted as if none of that existed and as if I couldn't count to three, unless it was in the interpretation of his own works. Then he was always very pleased when it turned out that I

could count to three and sometimes even to four. Then I suddenly felt that this deception was becoming just too boring, and so I got a rap on the nose." *Correspondence*, p. 457, letter 297, Hannah Arendt to Gertrud and Karl Jaspers, November 1, 1961. Jaspers replied that Heidegger must have been long aware that she had become a famous author, and that "the only thing that is new is that he received a book directly from you—and then such a reaction!" *Correspondence*, pp. 459–460, letter 298, Karl Jaspers to Hannah Arendt, November 6, 1961.

14. For a very comprehensive and helpful study of Arendt as a political philosopher, see Margaret Canovan, *Hannah Arendt: A Reinterpretation of Her Political Thought* (New York: Cambridge University Press, 1992).

15. Walter Sinnott-Armstrong, in conversation, made this objection.

16. I have only recently come to realize that part of what I like so much about New York City is the number of people a pedestrian encounters there who are unabashedly talking aloud to themselves.

17. An interesting case occurs when a promise is made by a person in some special capacity, say, as provost, to a group, say, a department of which the now ex-provost becomes chair. Then her successor in the provost's chair could break that promise, to herself as departmental representative, so the promise that one person made is broken to that very person, in another role. Thanks to Paul Benacerraf for alerting me to this real possibility.

18. Spinoza, in chapters 8 and 12 of his *Theological Political Treatise*, discusses the renewals of the covenant made by Moses and Joshua, and implicitly raises questions about the criteria of identity for such a covenant, which apparently was interrupted by periods of idolatry and desecration of the ark of the covenant, an ark eventually lost track of. With mock innocence he writes, "I find it strange that Scripture tells us nothing of what became of the Ark of the Covenant." *Tractatus Theologico-Politicus*, trans. Samuel Shirley and E. J. Brill (Leiden: Københaven, 1989).

19. Young-Bruehl, *Arendt*, pp. 11–12.

20. Ibid., p. 56.

21. Ibid., p. xv.

22. Ibid., p. 106.

23. That, perhaps, was what he found unforgivable, once he got to read his former student-mistress's book, when in 1960 she forced it on him.

24. See Essay 15.

25. Alfred North Whitehead, *Science and the Modern World* (New York: Macmillan, 1960), p. 12, quoted by Arendt in *The Human Condition* at p. 257.

26. David Hume, *A Treatise of Human Nature*, ed. L. A. Selby-Bigge and P. H. Nidditch (Oxford: Clarendon Press, 1978).

27. Hannah Arendt, *The Life of the Mind* (New York: Harcourt Brace Jovanovich, 1978).

28. Ann W. MacKenzie, "Descartes on Life and Sense," *Canadian Journal of Philosophy,* 19 (1989): 163–192.

29. Margaret Atherton, "Cartesian Reason and Gendered Reason," in *A Mind of One's Own,* ed. Louise B. Anthony and Charlotte Witt (Boulder, Colo.: Westview Press, 1992), pp. 19–34.

30. Ruth Mattern, "Descartes' Correspondence with Elizabeth: Concerning the Union and Distinction of Mind and Body," in *Descartes: Critical Interpretative Essays,* ed. Michael Hacker (Baltimore, Md.: Johns Hopkins University Press, 1978).

31. Eileen O'Neill, "Mind and Mechanism: An Examination of Some Mind-Body Problems in Descartes' Philosophy" (Ph.D. diss., Princeton University, 1983), and "Mind-Body Interaction and Metaphysical Consistency: A Defense of Descartes," *Journal of the History of Philosophy,* 25 (1987): 227–245.

32. See Erica Harth, *Cartesian Women: Versions and Subversions of Rational Discourse in the Old Regime* (Ithaca, N.Y.: Cornell University Press, 1992).

33. Naomi Scheman, in "Though This Be Method Yet There Is Madness in It: Paranoia and Liberal Epistemology" (in Anthony and Witt, eds., *A Mind of One's Own,* pp. 145–170), allows that Descartes has had appeal for feminist women, despite his emphasis on the supposed need for control of the passions by a somewhat dictatorial reason. See p. 167, n. 15.

34. Naomi Scheman, "Closets, Margins, and Forms of Life," in *Companion on Wittgenstein,* ed. Hans Sluga and David Stern (New York: Cambridge University Press, forthcoming).

35. This Humean move repeats one which Cicero makes in *De Natura Deorum,* where Balbus suggests that the most providential thing of all is the human propensity to believe in providence.

36. Some read Kant as equally daring in his *Religion within the Limits of Reason Alone,* trans. Louis Infield (New York: Harper Torchbooks, 1963). I am grateful to Onora O'Neill for her suggestion that this work, especially given Kant's reference at p. 123 to the Bible as "das Buch, was einmal da ist" ("that book which happens to be there"), should be read as a conscious continuation of the sort of biblical interpretation which Spinoza gave in his *Theological Political Treatise,* an interpretation which offered the pious a way of accepting much of what their Holy Scriptures contained while at the same time effectively undermining any claim which might be made for the foundational nature of religious doctrines for moral or other knowledge.

37. René Descartes, *Discourse on the Method of Rightly Conducting One's Reason and Seeking Truth in the Sciences,* ed. C. Adam and P. Tannery (Paris: Vrin CNRS, 1964–1976), VI, 24–25; *The Philosophical Writings of Descartes,* trans. John Cottingham, Robert Stoothoff, and Dugald Murdoch (New York: Cambridge University Press, 1985), I, 123.

38. Arendt's doctoral dissertation was on Augustine's views about love. It was published in Germany in 1929: *Der Liebesbegriffe bei Augustin: Versuch*

einer Philosophischen Interpretation (Berlin: Springer-Verlag, 1929). It was translated into English in 1966 by E. B. Ashton, entitled "Love and Saint Augustine: An Essay in Philosophical Translation" (manuscript).

39. Seyla Benhabib seems to be doing just this. See her "Judgment and the Moral Foundations of Politics in Arendt's Thought," *Political Theory* 16 (Feb. 1988): 29–51; "Hannah Arendt and the Redemptive Power of Narrative," *Social Research* 57 (Spring 1990): 167–196; and "The Reluctant Modernism of Hannah Arendt" (manuscript).

15. A NATURALIST VIEW OF PERSONS

This essay was originally delivered as a presidential address before the Eighty-Seventh Annual Eastern Division Meeting of the American Philosophical Association in Boston, Mass., December 29, 1990.

1. It is ironic that this was where she spoke as president. In 1895 she had been refused a Ph.D. by Harvard, despite a special petition signed by Hugo Munsterberg (who had earlier petitioned in vain for her to be allowed to become an official doctoral candidate), Josiah Royce, G. H. Palmer, William James, George Santayana, and Paul H. Harris, testifying in glowing terms to her performance at an "informal and unofficial examination" they had given her, after she had (unofficially) satisfied other requirements. "The Harvard Corporation is not prepared to give any Harvard degree to any woman, no matter how exceptional the circumstances." In 1902, when Radcliffe College was permitted to grant women degrees, she was begged to accept a Ph.D. retrospectively conferred. Splendidly proud woman that she was, she refused. My information comes from Bruce Kuklick, *The Rise of American Philosophy* (New Haven: Yale University Press, 1977), app. 4, and Otto Strunk, "The Self-Psychology of Mary Whiton Calkins," *Journal of the History of the Behavioral Sciences*, 8 (1972): 196–203.

2. Mary Calkins, a psychologist as well as a philosopher, wrote in 1930, in her last year of life: "With each year of life, with each book read, with each observation I initiate or confirm, I am more deeply convinced that psychology should be conceived as the science of the self or person, as related to its environment, physical and social." C. Murchison, *A History of Psychology in Autobiography* (Worcester, Mass., 1930), vol. 1, pp. 41–42, quoted by Edna Heidbreder in "Mary Whiton Calkins: A Discussion," *Journal of the History of the Behavioral Sciences*, 8 (1972): 56–68.

3. A. Rorty, "A Literary Postscript," in idem, ed., *The Identities of Persons* (Berkeley: University of California Press, 1976), p. 309.

4. I take the recognition to be of all of us older women who have been participating in the philosophical dialectic in our own ways, sometimes in ways that introduce distinctive voices into that conversation. However intersubstitutable we may be, and may be willing to be, for some

people, on some platforms (and I *have*, in fact, several times been confused, on my way to or from platforms, with another woman philosopher of my generation), we each of course have a voice of our own, and I speak in merely my own voice in what I say here today, in response to a recognition that I do not take to be of me individually (a recognition that takes the interesting form of being allowed to speak without the usual expectation of instant rebuttal by commentator or audience). No one else is answerable with me for what I say, and it is doubtless the worse for that. It is, however, the better for some helpful suggestions from Jennifer Whiting.

5. I am indebted to Martha Bolton's paper "Locke on Identity: Simple and Compounded Things," read to the Pacific Division of the American Philosophical Association, March 1989, for awareness of the seventeenth-century theological debates about what the soul did while awaiting the resurrection of the dead, debates that led to Locke's interest in our identity as souls, persons, living human beings. The paper is forthcoming in a volume on identity and individuation in the early modern period.

6. Michel de Montaigne, *Essays* III, viii. Charles Taylor quotes this in *Sources of the Self* (Cambridge, Mass.: Harvard University Press, 1990), p. 181.

7. Daniel Dennett, "Conditions of Personhood," in A. Rorty, ed., *Identities of Persons,* p. 176.

8. Ibid.

9. Aristotle, *On the Generation of Animals,* books 1–3. Perhaps it would be fairer to say that Aristotle believes that *male* persons have essential fathers and accidental mothers. The interpretation of his claims about the form-giving role of the father in procreation is a vexed matter. It is discussed by Cynthia Freeland in "Aristotle on Bodies, Matter and Potentiality," in Allan Gotthelf and James Lennox, eds., *Philosophical Issues in Aristotle's Biology* (Cambridge and New York: Cambridge University Press, 1987), and by John Cooper in "Metaphysics in Aristotle's Embryology," *Proceedings of the Cambridge Philological Society,* no. 214 (1988): 14–41. Cooper explains how, despite Aristotle's unwavering conviction that only what Cooper felicitously calls "honest-to-god semen" (p. 16) can determine the essential form of the offspring, they nevertheless sometimes inherit traits from the mother and her ancestors. It is a failure of the father's active formative semen to impose his own or his ancestors' male form (a failure due to insufficient heat, Aristotle hypothesizes) on the inert female fluid that leads to its giving up, as it were, and imposing the opposite (female) form, indeed the specific version of it that the mother (and her fluid) exhibit (*Generation of Animals,* 768a24–6). This makes the mother not quite accidental, since *who* she is may select what particular sort of female (second-best) offspring the semen forms. Aristotle has, one would think, some difficulty in accounting for any male offspring's inheritance of (nonsexual) form

356

from the mother, but Cooper believes not merely that he has the seeds of an explanation of the empirically undeniable facts of the inheritance of traits by offspring of both sexes from parents of both sexes, by his thesis that the male seminal fluid contains, in potentiality, all the movements of the seminal fluid of any female with whom the male might copulate, and so can impose any of a vast array of forms of offspring, but also that "there is nothing outlandish or extravagant here at all, once Aristotle's idea is fully and properly understood" (p. 22). There is no limit, it seems, to the female forms that honest-to-god semen can impose, once it despairs of imposing its own godlike form.

10. Aristotle, *Parts of Animals,* 653a, 658a, and *On Youth and Old Age,* 468, *History of Animals,* 494. I am grateful to John Cooper for instruction in this Aristotelian lore.

11. Charles Taylor, Introduction to *Philosophy and the Human Sciences: Philosophical Papers,* vol. 2 (Cambridge: Cambridge University Press, 1985).

12. Taylor, *Sources of the Self,* p. 15.

13. Allan Gibbard, who is a refreshingly naturalistically minded philosopher, observes that we adopt a dignified manner as attempted deterrent against the importunings not merely of human beggars but also of stray dogs. *Wise Choices, Apt Feelings* (Cambridge, Mass.: Harvard University Press, 1990), p. 267.

14. David Hume, *A Treatise of Human Nature,* ed. L. A. Selby-Bigge and P. H. Nidditch (Oxford: Clarendon Press, 1978), p. 326. References to this work will be given in the text as *T.*

15. David Hume, *Natural History of Religion* (Stanford: Stanford University Press, 1957), final section.

16. Immanuel Kant, *Lectures on Ethics* (New York: Harper & Row, 1963), lecture on conscience.

17. Mary Midgeley, in *Beast and Man: The Roots of Human Nature* (Ithaca, N.Y.: Cornell University Press, 1978), p. 160, wisely adds that any species capable of raising the question of who is on the "top" of an evolutionary ladder will naturally put itself there.

18. Nietzsche observes that even this claim, that we are distinctive in our vanity, is itself a piece of vanity. He writes, "perhaps the ant in the forest imagines it as the goal and objective of the forest" (*Human, All Too Human,* part II, section 14, "Man, the comedian of the world").

19. The doctrine of the Trinity, too, expresses our fascination with puzzle cases of reidentification.

20. See Taylor, *Philosophy and the Human Sciences: Philosophical Papers,* vol. 2, p. 6.

21. Virginia Warren, in "Feminist Directions in Medical Ethics," *Hypatia,* 4 (Summer 1989): 73–87, p. 86, note 5, refers to this style of moral philosophy as "The Gladiator Theory of Truth."

22. Derek Parfit, *Reasons and Persons* (Oxford: Oxford University Press, 1984), p. 237.

357

23. There are, however, some neo-Lockeans who are restrained by biological realism. See in particular David Wiggins, *Sameness and Substance* (Cambridge, Mass.: Harvard University Press, 1980), chap. 6, and "Locke, Butler, and the Stream of Consciousness: And Men as Natural Kind," in A. Rorty, ed., *Identities of Persons,* pp. 139–174.
24. *Philosophical Review,* vol. 28, p. 131.
25. Mary Warnock, in *Memory* (London: Faber and Faber, 1987), has a refreshingly brisk way with puzzles about who would be who after a brain switch: "We may indeed ourselves be muddled about who we are, and what our pasts have been. But the nurses and doctors will not be muddled. We shall have our operating theatre labels round our wrists, and that will be that" (p. 71).
26. Susan Wolf, "Self Interest and Interest in Selves," *Ethics,* 96 (July 1986): 705.
27. Carol Rovane, in "Branching Self-Consciousness," *Philosophical Review* (July 1990): 355–396, argues that for persons whose life history includes branching to have the sort of forward-looking self-consciousness that we find essential to personhood, they must be supposed to have advance knowledge of the real possibility of branching, just as *we* have "highly reliable knowledge that persons do not branch" (p. 376). Only then could their intention formation have anything approximating the coherence that ours can have, given our reliable knowledge of the constraints within which we shape our lives. This reliable knowledge that agents must have, of whether or not persons in their world *do* branch, is empirical. Rovane writes that *our* confidence that in our world persons do not branch is based on such facts as that "no one else in the world remembers our past experiences in the way we do" (pp. 376–377). Rovane does not stress this, but such highly reliable empirical knowledge surely must be interpersonal. We depend on other persons for it. Branching persons would similarly depend upon the brain-duplicating persons and their patients for the knowledge *they* would need in order to plan for their futures, to see their lives as able to amount to some sort of whole. So both actual nonbranching persons and fantasized branching persons depend upon other persons in their world for what Rovane regards as minimally coherent self-consciousness.
28. I myself meekly did the philosophy that men had initially instructed me to do, and rewarded me for doing, until I safely had tenure. Subversion under the cover of apparent docility is also a fairly popular female tactic, one that I tried out occasionally.
29. "We connive with our language to make it, and us, seem special." Donald Davidson, "Rational Animals," in *Actions and Events,* ed. Ernest LePore and Brian McLaughlin (New York: Basil Blackwell, 1985), p. 473.
30. Jenny Teichman, "Review of Alasdair MacIntyre, *Three Versions of Moral Enquiry,*" *New York Times Book Review,* August 12, 1990, p. 14. This review elicited the predictable protest of a male reader, in a letter to the editor published September 1.

CREDITS

1. "What Do Women Want in a Moral Theory?" *Noûs*, 19 (March 1985): 53–63. Reprinted by permission of Blackwell Publishers, Cambridge, Mass., and Oxford.

2. "The Need for More than Justice," *Canadian Journal of Philosophy, Supp. Vol. on Science, Ethics, and Feminism,* edited by Marsha Hanen and Kai Nielsen, vol. 13 (1987): 41–56. Reprinted by permission of the University of Calgary Press, Calgary, Alberta, Canada.

3. "Unsafe Loves," *The Philosophy of (Erotic) Love,* edited by Robert C. Solomon and Kathleen M. Higgins (Lawrence, Kans.: University Press of Kansas, 1991), pp. 433–450. Reprinted by permission of the University Press of Kansas.

4. "Hume, the Women's Moral Theorist?" *Women and Moral Theory,* edited by Eva Kittay and Diana Meyers (Lanham, Md.: Rowman & Littlefield, 1987), pp. 37–55. Reprinted by permission of Rowman & Littlefield Publishers.

5. "Hume, the Reflective Women's Epistemologist?" *A Mind of One's Own: Feminist Essays on Reason and Objectivity,* edited by Louise M. Antony and Charlotte Witt (Boulder, Colo.: Westview Press, 1993), pp. 35–48. Reprinted by permission of Westview Press, Boulder, Colorado.

6. "Trust and Antitrust," *Ethics* 96 (January 1986): 231–260. Reprinted in *Feminism and Political Theory,* edited by Cass Sunstein (Chicago: University of Chicago Press, 1990). Reprinted in *Ethics and Personality: Essays in Moral Psychology,* edited by John Deigh (Chicago: University of Chicago Press, 1992). Reprinted by permission of the

7, 8. "Trust and Its Vulnerabilities" and "Sustaining Trust." Originally titled "The Pathologies of Trust" and "Appropriate Trust," delivered at Princeton University as the *Tanner Lectures on Human Values. Tanner Lectures on Human Values,* vol. 13 (Salt Lake City: University of Utah Press, 1992).

9. "Trusting People," *Philosophical Perspectives, 6, Ethics* (1992), edited by James E. Tomberlin (copyright by Ridgeview Publishing Co., Atascadero, Calif.). Reprinted by permission of Ridgeview Publishing Company.

10. "Violent Demonstrations," *Violence, Terrorism, and Justice,* edited by R. G. Frey and Christopher W. Morris (New York: Cambridge Univeristy Press, 1991), pp. 33–58. Reprinted with the permission of Cambridge University Press.

11. "Claims, Rights, Responsibilities," *Prospects for a Common Morality,* edited by G. Outka and J. P. Reeder (Princeton, N.J.: Princeton University Press, 1993), pp. 149–169. Reprinted by permission of Princeton University Press.

12. "How Can Individualists Share Responsibility?" *Political Theory* 21 (May 1993): 228–248. Reprinted by permission of Sage Publications Inc.

13. "Moralism and Cruelty: Reflections on Hume and Kant." *Ethics* 103 (April 1993): 436–457. Reprinted by permission of the University of Chicago Press. ©1993 by The University of Chicago. All rights reserved.

15. "A Naturalist View of Persons," *Proceedings and Addresses of the American Philosophical Association,* 65 (November 1991): 5–17. Reprinted by permission of The American Philosophical Association.

INDEX

Abortion, 6–7, 8, 30, 65–66, 295–296, 299

Accountability, 139, 181, 187

Action theory, 301, 302–303, 307–308, 309, 310

Alienation, 23, 24

Altruism, 143, 152, 154, 165

Anger, 270–271, 279

Animals, 39, 42, 193, 225, 269

Anscombe, Elizabeth, 1, 303

Aquinas, Saint Thomas, 26–27, 55, 97, 231, 296

Arendt, Hannah, 295, 300–303, 304–309, 312; Heidegger and, 338n13

Arendt, Martha, 307

Aristotle, 53, 67, 84, 97, 136, 218, 296, 317

Atherton, Margaret, 310

Atiyah, P. S., 155

Austin, J. L., 77, 133, 168, 174, 175

Authority, 79–80, 81, 84, 90, 91, 235; governmental, 162–165, 166, 183–184, 258–259; trust and, 192–193

Autonomy, 20, 21, 22–23, 31, 62–63, 249, 259, 266; lack of attribution to women, 26, 257, 263; obedience and, 85; trust and, 103

Bacon, Francis, 141, 150, 196–197

Barcan Marcus, Ruth, 1

Bartky, Sandra, 296

Bateson, Patrick, 165, 179

Beauvoir, Simone de, 295

Benevolence, 166–167, 191

Benhabib, Seyla, 296, 341n39

Betrayal of trust, 142, 144–145, 146, 149, 151, 185, 196

Birth, 301, 307–308, 309

Blacks, 18, 21, 26. See also Slavery

Blount, Henry, 288

Blum, Lawrence, 18, 19

Bok, Sissela, 2, 97

Brandom, Bob, 90

Bribery, 163–164

Brown, Robert, 22

Burnett, Ivy Compton, 199

Calkins, Mary, 313–314, 323, 324

Card, Claudia, 1, 18, 296

Care and caring, 11, 25, 296; ethics of, 19, 25, 27, 29; perspective (Gilligan), 19, 20–21, 22, 52, 74; responsibility of, 30, 63, 74; mutual, 63; trust and, 101, 102–103, 138, 139; parental, 109; due care principle, 171

Cartesian philosophy. See Descartes, René

Index

Categorical imperative, 268, 273, 277
Cavell, Stanley, 175
Characters (Theophrastus), 288
Character traits, 60, 74, 83, 291; repeatable, 88; punishment and, 274, 275, 284–285, 286–287; assessment of, 287, 288–289
Children, 12–13, 61, 147; obligations to, 5–8, 9; trust and, 14, 69, 105, 106–109, 110, 120–122, 129, 147, 177, 188–190, 195, 324n18; gender differences, 20; moral development, 20–21, 27–28; love for parents, 40, 41–42; ability to sympathize, 72; child abuse, 158; trust in parents, 195; rights of, 200; punishment of, 215, 216; arts of language and, 233–234, 236; illegitimate, 277–278; divorce and, 328n28
Chodorow, Nancy, 6, 20
Christianity, 26, 31, 211, 227; love for God, 36, 37, 38, 46; test of reflection and, 86
Cicero, 151, 159, 160
Citizenship, 248–249, 255, 263
Cixous, Hélène, 295
Claessens, Dieter, 323n2
Code, Lorraine, 76, 90
Coercion, 4, 13, 14, 96, 203, 288; trust and, 12, 14, 15, 156; in task allotment, 264–265
Collective: rights, 23–29, 246; responsibility, 236, 240, 243, 247
Communication, nonverbal, 68–69, 176, 177
Community, 19, 21, 24, 25, 227; political, 260–262, 263
Comus (Milton), 290
Confessions (Rousseau), 194
Connan, François de, 238
Constitution, U.S., 162–164, 167, 179, 243, 246, 252; amendment procedure, 262
Contract(s), 110, 235, 248, 300, 304; trust and, 97, 109, 111–112, 116, 125, 139–140; morality of, 106, 114; marriage as, 113; male fixation on, 114–120, 300; breach of, 117–118; rights, 166
Control, in trust relationships, 152, 153, 158

Cooperation, 76–77, 92, 97, 106, 114, 152, 237, 242, 264–265. *See also* Contract(s); Trust
Copernicus, 309
Covenants, 305–306
Criticism, 287, 289
Cruelty, 86, 268–269; defined, 269; angry, 270–271, 273, 288, 290; of punishment, 271, 282, 284, 286
Customs and culture, 80–82, 191–192, 200

Daly, Mary, 294, 295
Darwin, Charles, 42–43, 46, 49, 176, 317, 320, 321
Deceit, 179, 324n6
Decision making, 253–254; moral, 65–68, 69, 87; public, 86; by children, 147
Demonstration, 81–82, 203–205, 207–209, 211–212, 214, 221
Deontology, 276–277, 310
Dependency, 106, 115, 255, 256; in trust relationships, 153, 154, 156
Derision/disdain, 281–288
Descartes, René, 249–250, 309–312, 316, 318, 321; on love, 36, 38–39, 41, 42, 43, 46; on ethics, 310–311
Descent of Man, The (Darwin), 42
Dialogues on Natural Religion (Hume), 311
Diamond, Cora, 1–2, 299
Dignity, 316–317
Disagreement, 232–233, 236
Discourse on Method (Descartes), 311
Discretion, 101–102, 103, 104–105, 118
Disease, 47, 48, 49, 75
Disempowerment, 176, 177–178, 179, 196, 197, 198
Distrust, 15–16, 35, 97, 105, 107, 110, 111, 120, 129, 131, 185, 199; suspicion as, 141, 187; betrayal and, 142, 145; power and, 146; sustained, 149; micro and macro motivations for, 153; costs of, 185–186; right to, 244
Divorce, 137, 199, 200, 328n28
Doctrine of Virtue (Kant), 276
Dominance (oppression), 225, 227, 256
Double negatives, 174, 175

Double standards, 146–147
Durkheim, Emile, 154
Duties, 231, 237, 256, 280. *See also*
    Obligation; Responsibility
Dworkin, Ronald, 237, 260–262, 263

Egoism, 152–158, 165, 250–251
Egotism, 251
Elites, 112–113, 154–155, 236, 250,
    267
Elizabeth, Princess of Bohemia, 310, 311
Elster, Jon, 185
Emergence of Norms, The (Ullmann
    Margalit), 2
Emotions, 28, 30, 31, 65; of love,
    33–34, 35, 37, 42, 43, 46, 47
Empiricism, 77, 83, 84
Ennius, 160, 164, 178
*Enquiry Concerning Human Under-
    standing, An* (Hume), 76, 80, 89, 90,
    92, 221, 281, 293
*Enquiry Concerning the Principles of
    Morals, An* (Hume), 51, 92
Envy, 219
Epicharmus, 151
Epistemology, 76, 82
Epstein, Richard, 156
Equality and inequality: in interpersonal
    relationships, 28–29, 31, 60–61, 62,
    196; power and, 28; social, 30, 52; for
    women, 79, 114; in trust relation-
    ships, 119–120, 160–161, 192, 197
Essays: Moral, Political, and Literary
    (Hume), 52, 64, 73, 90–91, 92, 93,
    94
Ethics: feminist, 294–296, 298–299,
    312; applied, 302–303
Exclusion, 221–222
Experience: of interconnection, 63, 89;
    instructive, 77, 78, 81; reason and, 80,
    81
Exploitation, 71; of women, 16, 115,
    131, 155; ideal of care and, 25; of
    workers, 131; in trust relationships,
    131, 146
Expressibility test, 105, 106, 123, 124,
    125
Expression, 68, 77; freedom of, 228
*Expressions of Emotion in Man and
    Animals, The* (Darwin), 42

Family, 296–297
Fear, 153, 159
Feinberg, Joel, 237
Feminist philosophy, 294–298
Ferguson, Adam, 30
Fetishism, 232
Feuerbach, Ludwig, 37
Fidelity: in trust relationships, 134, 135,
    167, 169–173, 175, 181; to promises,
    159, 168, 181
Foot, Philippa, 1, 21, 296
Forgiveness, 44, 103, 154, 300, 301,
    303, 304, 307
Foucault, Michel, 90
Freedom, 14–15, 91, 255; in theories of
    justice, 19, 61; of choice, 28, 29–30;
    of thought, 91–92; sexual, 199
Freud, Sigmund, 4, 37, 46, 49, 320
Friedman, Marilyn, 296
Friendship, 35–36, 38, 40, 156, 190;
    trust and, 97, 168, 170, 190; asexual,
    154; lies in, 154–155
Frye, Marilyn, 2, 296

Galileo, 309, 310
Gambetta, Diego, 152, 165, 184, 187
Game-theoretic approach to morality, 2
Genealogy of Morals (Nietzsche), 277
Generations, human, 42, 46, 47–48, 49, 127
Gibbard, Allan, 157, 270, 271, 279,
    280, 281
Gifts, 190–191
Gilligan, Carol, 1, 2, 11, 17, 30, 64–65,
    67; influence on philosophers, 18–19;
    care perspective, 19, 20–21, 22, 52,
    74; justice perspective, 19, 20–21, 26,
    52; moral maturity and development
    theory, 22, 24, 28, 30, 52, 53, 54, 62,
    63, 65, 72, 115; interconnection
    among people, 24, 25; on autonomy,
    31; on gender differences, 31–32
Good, concept of, 74–75. *See also*
    Virtue(s)
Goods, 240–241, 242, 246, 249
Good Terrorist, The (Lessing), 204
Goodwill, 98–100, 106, 107, 118, 125,
    132, 197
Gordimer, Nadine, 295
Government, 162–165, 166, 183–184,
    223, 231

Gratitude, 63, 102, 109, 190–191
Gregor, Mary, 257
Grice, Paul, 175
Grotius, Hugo, 148, 161, 169, 173, 217, 238; on rights, 231, 239–240
Groundwork of the Metaphysics of Morals (Kant), 253
Groups, 237, 246, 249
Guilt, 85, 270, 273, 275, 279, 280, 281

Habermas, Jürgen, 330n5
Hacking, Ian, 2
Hall, Judith, 68
Hand kissing, 197–198
Handshakes and greetings, 176, 177–178, 179, 195, 197–198
Harvard University, 313, 355n1
Hawthorn, Geoffrey, 154, 155, 156
Hegel, G. W. F., 24, 27, 31, 53, 90, 106, 114, 300, 302, 309
Heidegger, Martin, 300, 302, 308; Arendt and, 338n13
Held, Virginia, 2, 296, 299
Herman, Barbara, 290–291
Heterosexuality, 38
Hirschman, Albert, 176, 197
History of England (Hume), 64, 73, 76, 92, 271, 272, 286
Hobbes, Thomas, 28, 43, 97, 100, 107, 114, 153, 294; theory of trust, 107, 119, 145, 173; on laws of nature, 169, 217–219, 275; on violence, 218, 219; on rights, 231, 234–235; on reason and speech, 234–236
Homosexuality, 315n21
Human Condition, The (Arendt), 300, 301, 303, 309, 312
Hume, David, 30, 77–79, 87, 90, 179, 194, 226, 294, 311, 317–318, 320, 321, 322, 324; theory of justice, 11, 63, 69, 148, 220–221, 271, 272; on contractual obligation, 13, 61, 63, 109, 116, 140; on human love, 39–41, 42, 43, 45–46, 49, 54, 57, 70, 71–72; on women, 51–53, 62, 72–73, 79, 86, 93, 114, 278, 293; moral theory, 52–58, 60, 61–62, 66, 67, 70–72, 166–167, 194–195, 221, 222, 268, 270, 283, 285; comparison with Kant,

53, 54–55, 61, 285; ethics, 54–55, 76; on reason, 56, 94; on virtue, 58–60, 63, 64, 71, 74–75, 88–89; on interpersonal relations, 60–62, 69, 119; concept of self, 69–70, 71, 72; concept of "reflexion," 72, 81, 86, 131; epistemology, 76, 77, 78, 80, 81, 82, 89, 90, 91–93; skepticism, 79–80; on moral judgment, 88; on trust, promising, and fidelity, 104, 111–112, 118, 147, 155, 156, 167–168; on motives, 166, 219; on friendship, 190; on violence, 219–220; on government, 258, 259; on cruelty, 268–269, 271, 282–283, 284; on principles, 268, 270; on shame, 270, 281–282; on punishment, 271–272, 273–274, 275; on chastity, 278–279; on vice, 279, 282; on human nature, 284–285; racism of, 291–292, 293; on divorce, 328n28
Humiliation. *See* Shame/humiliation
Huxley, T. H., 42

Ibsen, Henrik, 199
In a Different Voice (Gilligan), 1, 4, 17, 18–19, 21; moral theory in, 53, 65
Independence, 73. *See also* Autonomy
Individualism, 24, 25, 85, 237, 241, 247, 314; vs. isolationism, 247–249, 249; defined, 250; responsibility and, 266
Infant trust. *See* Children: trust and
Instinct, 81, 83
Integrity, 262–263
Interconnection, 23–24, 25, 63, 93
Interdependence, 46, 49, 148, 201
Interests, 244–246
Ireland, Patricia, 289
Irigaray, Luce, 295

Jaggar, Alison, 2, 18, 296
Jaspers, Karl, 338n13
Jefferson, Thomas, 252, 259
Judgment, 151, 152, 160, 319
Jus Talionis, 272, 275, 283
Justice, 7, 55, 57–58, 97, 296; freedom and, 19, 61; perspective, 19, 20–21, 26, 52; as social value, 19, 61; violence and, 221–222; divine, 335n22. *See also* Law

Kant, Immanuel, 21, 39, 114, 119, 294, 314, 316–317, 318, 319, 324; theory of autonomy, 22, 26; moral theory, 28, 53, 55, 56, 65, 85, 182, 249, 268, 275, 281, 283, 288, 291; theory of rational control, 30, 31; on love, 34–35, 36, 38, 39, 40–41, 45, 47; theory of knowledge, 53; comparison with Hume, 53, 54–55, 61, 285; ethics, 53, 54–55, 61; theory of justice, 55, 57, 261; theory of reason, 56, 72; on reflection, 86; on moral decision making, 87, 88; on friendship, 190; on rights, 231, 232; on social virtues, 247–248; concept of realm of ends, 248–249, 266–267; republicanism, 253, 254, 257, 258, 259; on women, 255, 257, 261, 273, 310; on task allotment, 266; on cruelty, 269, 281, 284; on guilt, 270, 279, 280; on punishment, 272–273, 275–276, 277–278, 284
Killing/murder, 203; by terrorists, 206, 207–209, 211, 214; moral attitudes toward, 209, 218; religious, 210–211
Knox, John, 313
Kohlberg, Lawrence, 21–23, 53; theory of moral development, 54, 55, 64, 65, 72
Korsgaard, Christine, 82
Kristeva, Julia, 295

Language, 224, 231, 232, 233–234, 237, 243, 245, 260
Laughter, 45, 284, 285–286, 288, 289
Law, 237–238, 258–259, 262, 281; natural, 27; divine, 83–84; moral, 85, 97, 258; of nature, 89, 169, 220–221; of nations, 148; constitutional, 162–164, 165; rights and, 231; basic, 236; collective, 240; punishment under, 269, 271; enforcement of, 282, 283
Laws (Plato), 97
Lectures on Ethics (Kant), 35, 261, 279
Lee, Ann, 226–227
Leibniz, Gottfried, 82, 323
Lessing, Doris, 204, 295
Life of the Mind (Arendt), 309
Locke, John, 82–84, 119, 175, 314, 315–316, 317, 319, 323, 324; on

trust, 130, 183–184, 197; on language, 233–234, 246
Logic, 56, 81
Love, 12, 33, 36, 38, 45–46, 49; ethics of, 4, 12; in female moral theories, 4, 10, 11–12; parental, 6, 12, 37, 41; emotions of, 33–34, 35, 37, 42, 43, 46, 47; mutual, 34, 36, 39, 47; risks of, 34, 40, 43–44, 47, 48–49, 50; of God, 36–37, 38, 46; of a superior, 37, 38, 39; sexual, 38, 42, 46–47; generative, 42, 46, 47–48, 49; as attachment, 46; justice and, 57; as common good, 108; trust and, 153
Lovibond, Sabina, 1
Loyalty, 12, 184
Lugones, Maria, 296
Luhmann, Niklas, 129, 149, 200, 201
Lying, 325n37

MacIntyre, Alasdair, 2, 17, 18, 21, 31, 53
MacKenzie, Ann W., 310
Mackie, J. L., 237
MacKinnon, Catharine, 294, 295
Manipulation, 173, 174, 178–179
Marriage, 73, 131, 198–200, 263, 277–278, 282, 291; predictability and, 136; dissolution or divorce, 137, 199, 200, 328n28; fidelity in, 168; as contract, 248
Marx, Karl/Marxism, 20, 24, 53, 90, 300, 308
Maternal instinct, 7, 29. See also Mother(s)
Mattern, Ruth, 310
Meditations (Descartes), 310, 311
Memory, 68, 82, 83
Metaphysical Elements of Justice, The (Kant), 52
Metaphysics of Morals, The (Kant), 190, 248, 266
Midgeley, Mary, 2
Mill, John Stuart, 53, 91, 114, 256
Milton, John, 290
Mistrust, 185–186, 196–197
Moene, Karl, 185
Montague, Elizabeth, 79
Montaigne, Michel, 259
Moral development, 2, 22–23, 52, 64–69, 71

Moral judgment, 83–84
Morality, 61, 65, 96–97, 173–174, 241
Moral theory (general discussion), 2–3,
    10–11, 26, 194, 237; liberal, 3, 7–8,
    9, 11, 25, 26, 28–29, 31, 113
Moral theory, female, 1–2, 7, 52–54, 63,
    115–116, 294–295; ethics of love, 4,
    10, 11–12; care perspective, 19–20,
    22, 52, 74; justice perspective, 19,
    20–21, 26, 52; construction of, 24,
    52; egoistic, 324n8
Moral theory, male, 1, 2, 16–17, 52–54,
    63, 115–116, 295; ethics of obliga-
    tion, 4–5, 10; altruistic, 324n8. *See
    also* Patriarchy
Morgenbesser, Sydney, 174–175
Mother(s), 7, 20, 29, 31; -child love, 39,
    42–43, 46; infant trust in, 106–107
Motives, 152, 160–161, 164–165, 176,
    280; altruistic, 152–156, 158, 167;
    micro- and macro-, 153, 154, 155,
    158–159; gender differences in, 324n8
Murdoch, Iris, 1, 295
Murrell, Peter, 321n20

Narcissism, 84
Natality, 308–309
Naturalist view of persons, 313, 316,
    317–318, 320–321, 322, 325–326
Nicholson, Linda, 296
Nietzsche, Friedrich, 112, 113, 115,
    153, 162, 213, 280, 321
Noddings, Nel, 296
Norms, 81, 86, 87, 91, 114, 174–176
Nozick, Robert, 157, 249
Nussbaum, Martha, 296

Obedience, 85, 159
Obligation, 12, 14, 61, 63, 191, 237,
    238–239; ethics of, 4–6; to children,
    5–8, 9, 60–61; appropriate trust
    and, 10–11, 13; of care, 30, 109; to
    women, 113; law-imposed, 231; basic,
    232; collective, 238, 240–241; cross-
    generational, 240. *See also* Contract(s)
Okin, Susan Moller, 17, 296
O'Neill, Eileen, 310
On Liberty (Mill), 91
Ostracism, 282–283, 286
O'Sullivan, John, 205

Parent(s), 21, 27, 30, 177, 223; obliga-
    tion to children, 5–8, 9; love of, 6, 12,
    37, 39, 41, 42–43, 57–58, 60, 61,
    296; responsibility of, 10, 109–110;
    authority of, 21, 178; -child relation-
    ship, 28, 69; influence on children,
    74–75; trust between, 120–122, 129;
    transmission of trust attitudes to chil-
    dren, 135, 140, 189–190; care for
    children, 156, 178, 296; violence by,
    215, 216
Passions of the Soul (Descartes), 310
Pateman, Carole, 295
Patriarchy, 26–27, 50, 58, 76, 87, 199;
    violence and, 209, 211; religion of,
    227, 296, 297. *See also* Moral theory,
    male
Peacemaking, 217–218, 219, 222
Persons, 229, 231, 313–326
Piaget, Jean, 21, 22, 53
Plato, 35, 36, 97, 125, 236
Politics (Plato), 97
Popper, Carl, 330n5
Power: discretionary, 101–106,
    121–123, 137–138, 180; in relation-
    ships of trust, 105, 106, 107,
    119–120, 126, 146–148, 180; equality
    of, 116, 119; monopoly of, 160–161,
    202; political, 161–162, 164–165,
    167; cultural variations in, 198; vs.
    rights, 226, 228, 230–231, 232;
    abuse of, 258
Prejudice, 88, 229
Pride, 41, 42, 71, 74, 318, 320
Progress of Sentiments, A (Baier),
    326n38
Promise(s), 4, 13, 111–112, 117, 118,
    119, 182, 300, 303–307, 312; fidelity
    and, 134; altruism and, 153; keeping,
    153, 154, 155–156
Property/property rights, 55, 57, 87,
    111, 113, 166, 168, 199, 232, 266
Protest, 243, 244
Punishment, 163–164, 220; right
    to administer, 13–14, 274; severity
    of, 269–270; cruel, 271, 282,
    284, 286; appropriate, 272–273,
    274, 282; capital, 272, 273, 275,
    277; divine, 272, 275, 283; forms of,
    275, 276

Racism, 31, 229, 263, 284, 291–293

Radicalism of the American Revolution, The (Wood), 252

Rape, 143, 146, 209

Rationalism, 30–31, 80

Rawls, John, 2, 21, 53, 65, 119, 250, 253, 266; on justice, 6, 18, 19, 24–25, 296

Raz, Joseph, 237

Realm of Rights, The (Thomson), 299–300

Reason, 30, 42, 56–57, 94; morality and, 55, 56; gender differences in, 64; experience and, 80, 81; deductive, 81, 82

Rebellion, 214, 258–259

Reciprocity, 34, 37, 38, 45, 191, 197

Reflection, 64, 65, 66, 72, 83, 131; test of, 81–82, 86, 174; reason and, 82; pleasure and, 83; moral judgment and, 84, 85–96 .

Relationships of trust, 119, 120–124, 136, 137, 141–142, 149, 191; power in, 105, 106, 107, 119–120, 126, 146–148, 180; equality and, 119–120, 131, 147–148; expressibility test, 123, 124; moral test, 123–129; as contract, 125–126; network of, 126–127, 149–150, 160, 163, 164, 175; between enemies, 127–128; false pretenses and, 132–133; letdowns in, 133, 134–136, 140, 144, 145, 149, 150, 153, 179, 184; culture and, 157, 198; absence and distance and, 157–158; age and, 189–190

Religion, 320–322; morality and, 24, 31; love and, 36–37, 46, 48, 49–50; monastic virtues, 58–59; trust in God, 97, 106, 107, 108, 119, 187, 192, 193; patriarchal, 227, 296, 297; power of the church, 232; power of God, 259; punishment by God, 272, 275, 283; covenants with God, 305–306; divine justice, 335n22

Religion within the Limits of Reason Alone (Kant), 276

Reproduction, 73, 227

Reproduction of Mothering, The (Chodorow), 20

Republic (Plato), 97

Resentment, 218, 220, 221, 222

Respect, 22, 34–35, 36, 38, 41, 119, 317–319

Responsibility: 225, 237, 238, 239, 244–246; gender-based, 9–10, 256; parental, 10, 109–110; of care, 30, 63, 74; shared, 76, 243, 262, 263–266, 288; collective, 236, 240, 243, 260–261, 315; cross-generational, 240–241, 254, 263; individual vs. collective, 247, 253, 264, 266, 314–315, 318, 323–324

Rich, Adrienne, 295

Ridicule, 282, 285, 286

Rights, 25–26, 28, 227–228, 244, 245; universal, 160–161, 224–230, 243, 244; contractual, 166; to govern, 166; protection of, 221, 231; begging for, 225, 246, 323n15; disputes about, 225–237, 246; role-related, 225; implicit denial of, 226, 228; special, 227; claim to, 229, 236, 237, 242; language of, 231, 232, 237, 244, 245, 246; basic, 232, 236, 241, 242; parasitism of, 237, 241–242; individual vs. group, 238–239, 240, 243; allocation of, 240–241; defined, 240; welfare and, 243, 245, 246; interests and, 244–246. *See also* Property/property rights

Rights and Goods (Held), 299

Risk: of trusting, 15, 100, 104, 118, 131, 150–151, 154, 157, 196, 200–202, 207; of loving, 34, 40, 43–44, 47, 48–49, 50

Roberts, Robert C., 316n29

Roe v. Wade, 309

Rorty, Amelie, 314

Rorty, Richard, 269

Rosenthal, Robert, 68

Rousseau, Jean Jacques, 61, 63, 72, 85, 88, 119, 194, 289

Ruddick, Sara, 296

Ruhle-Gerstel, Alice, 302

Rules, 55–56, 58, 64, 87, 116, 137, 138, 169, 192; for trusting, 139, 151, 152, 160, 162, 165; for promise keeping, 155

Scanlon, Thomas, 133, 140, 144, 145, 168, 175–176; fidelity principle, 134,

135, 167, 169–170, 171–173, 175, 181–182
Schelling, Thomas, 207
Scheman, Naomi, 311
Second Sex, The (Beauvoir), 295
Security, 15, 118, 170, 184
Self: -trust, 12, 15, 179; -interest, 14, 15, 55, 57–58, 62, 63, 64, 68–71, 166; -love, 45, 71–72, 167; -control, 57; -definition, 72; -will, 84, 85; invasion of, 157; -disempowerment, 178; -defense, 244, 245; -discipline, 276; -consciousness, 313, 318–319, 322, 325; -representation, 319–320
Selfishness, 65, 68, 71
Sex, 6, 7, 73, 291; love and, 38, 42, 46–47; freedom of, 146, 228; rights of, 227
Sex/gender bias, 9–10, 31–32, 51–52, 64, 65, 230, 324n8; double standard, 146–147, 200
Sexism, 31, 131, 145, 229, 267, 284, 300; in Hume, 51–52, 53, 62, 72–73; of societal roles, 255–257, 263
Shaffer, Jerome, 34, 36
Shame/humiliation, 35, 270, 278, 280–281, 286
Shklar, Judith, 269, 295
Sidgwick, Henry, 119
Sincerity conditions, 174–175
Skepticism, 79–80
Slavery, 226, 228, 239, 240, 259, 289, 291–293; laws, 262
Slote, Michael, 18
Society: social institutions, 18, 19, 70–71; social practices, 134, 167, 171, 172, 176, 178, 180, 182; social roles, 165, 166, 200, 224, 256–257; social structures, 185, 201, 232; customs, 200; trust in, 201
Socrates, 101, 236, 330n5
Speech, 179, 224; norms of, 174–176, 182; right of, 224, 232–233, 234, 242–244, 245, 246; conflict and, 233, 235–236; forms of, 235
Spelman, Elizabeth, 296
Spinoza, Baruch, 38, 39, 249, 269, 283, 289, 339n18, 340n36
Stoker, Michael, 2, 18, 19, 296
Suicide, 269

Suspicion, 141
Sympathy, 34, 38, 43–45, 54–55, 62, 69, 72, 270, 271; self-interest and, 56, 57, 69–71, 72; corrected, 64; development of, 68; informed, 87

Tanner Lectures (Baier), 181
Taylor, Gabriele, 1
Taylor, Harriet, 114
Teichman, Jenny, 1, 324
Terrorism and terrorists, 159, 203–204, 213, 214, 220, 223, 323n18; motivation for, 205–207, 215–217, 218; killing by, 206, 207–208, 211; revolutionary, 206; methods, 215; response to, 216, 217; justice and, 221
Theology. *See* Religion
Theophrastus, 288
Third Critique (Kant), 287
Third parties, 176–177, 178
Thomas, Laurence, 18, 19, 31
Thomson, Judith Jarvis, 294, 295, 299–300
Time/timing, 300, 303–304, 305–306
Tocqueville, Alexis de, 229, 250, 251, 252, 253, 255–256, 257, 269
Torture, 246, 269
Treatise of Human Nature, A (Hume), 39, 42, 59, 64, 69, 76, 77, 78, 270, 285, 309; social epistemology in, 89, 92; on criminal action, 274
Trust, 57, 63, 95–99, 118, 126, 131, 158, 185; appropriate, 10–11, 12, 15, 16, 180–181; conditions for, 11–12, 13–14, 15–17, 99, 202; in self, 12, 15, 179; for infliction of penalties, 13–14, 163–164; children and, 14, 69, 105, 106–110, 120–122, 129, 147, 177, 188–189, 324n18; risk of, 15, 100, 104, 118, 131, 150–151, 154, 157, 196; vulnerability of, 35, 99–100, 104–107, 109, 118, 132, 133–134, 142, 146, 148, 152, 157–158, 162, 177, 197; forms of, 96, 100–103, 105, 107, 111, 119, 125, 184, 185; morality of, 96–97, 111, 115, 126; in God, 97, 106, 107, 108, 119, 187, 192, 193; care and, 101, 102–103, 138; discretionary, 101–102, 103, 104–105, 121–123, 132, 136, 149,

150, 163, 180, 187; abuse of, 103–104, 105, 123, 146, 196; selective, 107, 188; contractual, 109, 111–112, 116, 125; mutual, 109, 127, 128, 140, 156, 162, 176, 179, 180, 195, 196, 198, 202; voluntary abilities and, 110–114; women and, 113, 115, 194, 263–264; in governments, 116, 162–164; equal/unequal, 119–120; moral test for, 120–129; defined, 128, 185, 186; false, 132–135, 160, 189; false expectations of, 133–134, 140, 141, 149; principles of, 133–134, 140–141, 144, 168–173; impersonal, 137, 139; institutional, 137–139, 145, 160, 181, 184, 192–193, 200–201; checks and tests of, 139–140, 141, 145, 149, 163, 187, 325n26; public, 154, 155, 163; withdrawal of, 155, 164, 165, 167; in appearances, 159, 174; societal, 165, 201; assurance of, 166, 167, 168–172, 173–174, 176, 177–178, 182, 184; in people, 184, 185–186; sustained, 184–185, 187–188; in trust, 185, 186–187; due, 188; cultural factors, 191–192, 200; judgment of, 193–194, 195. *See also* Betrayal of trust; Relationships of trust
Trust: Making and Breaking Cooperative Relations (Williams), 152, 154
Tuck, Richard, 237, 239
Tyranny, 93, 97, 244, 249, 258–259

Ullmann Margalit, Edna, 2
Understanding, 77, 82, 89
Updike, John, 135, 140, 189

Values, 93, 166
Varnhagen, Rahel, 306
Violence, 203, 204, 219, 220, 222–223; of war, 8, 9; of demonstrations, 203–204, 205, 207, 208–209, 211–212; terrorist, 203–204, 205, 216, 221; moral attitudes toward, 209, 223; domestic and sexual, 209, 211; just, 213; against women, 213; right to, 222, 244
Virtue(s), 8, 13–14, 88–89, 92, 97, 220, 222–223; of parental love, 6, 57–58, 60, 61; theory of, 14, 60–62, 63, 74–75; moral, 57–58, 60, 168; mar-

tial/political, 58–59, 73, 262; monastic, 58–59; social, 92, 247; trust and, 188; public, 252
Voluntary associations, 251–252, 263
Voting rights, 229, 255, 256, 257
Vows, 304–305
Vulnerability, 35, 157–158; of trusting, 99, 100, 104–107, 118, 132, 133–134, 142, 146, 152, 157, 177; mutual, 109, 148, 162, 197

Walker, Alice, 295
Walzer, Michael, 206, 207, 216
War, 48, 49, 58–59, 98, 147, 161, 165, 209–210, 213, 217–218
Weil, Simone, 294
West, Rebecca, 295
Whitehead, Alfred North, 309
Wiggins, David, 268
Williams, Bernard, 21, 152–153, 154, 155, 158, 159, 166
Wittgenstein, Ludwig, 179, 311
Wolf, Susan, 1, 18, 296, 323
Wollheim, Richard, 46, 49
Wollstonecraft, Mary, 26, 226
Women: exploitation of, 16, 115, 131, 155; rights of, 18, 21, 226–228, 255, 256, 262, 293; ethic of care and, 20, 22, 25; autonomy and, 26, 259; non-verbal communication and, 68–69; position in society of, 93, 255, 256–257; trust and, 113, 115, 142–146, 194, 263–264; marriage and, 198–199, 227, 229, 255–256; male violence against, 213; oppression of, 227, 256, 265, 273; emancipation of, 256; punishment of, 261; responsibility of, 263; chastity of, 278–279; philosophers, 294–298, 312; and the individuation of persons, 316; and the origin of persons, 323 *See also* Mothers; Moral theory, female
Wood, Gordon S., 252, 259, 260
Woolf, Virginia, 295

Xenophanes, 320

Young, Iris, 296
Young-Bruehl, Elisabeth, 302